ZONPOWER

and

Profound

Honesty

Dare to Get it All?

Take this Real-Life Journey

from

Earth's Anticivilization

to the

Civilization of the Universe

A3C
PROFOUND HONESTY

guarantees

Limitless Prosperity

and an

Exciting Romantic Life

1st Printing, October 1996
2nd Printing, November 1996
Printings after 2nd
5 7 9 10 8 6

ISBN # 911752-78-1
Library of Congress # 96-069932

Copyright © 1996
Zon Association
Las Vegas, Nevada

b

ZONPOWER

RICHES
from a
New World

Fully Integrated Honesty: Those three words deliver prosperity and excitement. Indeed, those three words will deliver a new civilization to mankind — a civilization of endless riches. Yet, without new information, those three words carry little meaning. Today, however, for the first time, a manuscript comes from another world to deliver this information — powerful new information that evokes different views of life and reality. With those new views, a person outcompetes everyone stuck in today's irrational civilization[1].

For 2300 years, everyone on Earth has been hoodwinked into accepting mystically distorted, force-oriented views of life and reality. Consequently, once one captures the all-powerful views delivered by *Profound Honesty*, he or she will find little acceptance in today's anticivilization. But, so what! That non acceptance by today's boring Establishment is what "quantum leaps" a person over competition — over everyone else into a new-color dynamic that controls both the present and the future.

Profound Honesty is composed of New-World Music — four Concertos and two Songs that build into a Symphony. Through the opening Concertos, one discovers the ground upon which to stand. That ground is an omnipotent foundation called Neo-Tech Objectivism. Next, through a brace of Songs, one discovers how that foundation joins *Profound Honesty* to the future. Those Songs introduce the New-Color Symphony from which one crescendos into exciting adventures and happiness. And, finally, in the Closing Ceremonies, one rides toward riches from another world.

---

[1]Everyone is born blind into this Earthbound civilization. Thus, like the congenitally blind, everyone becomes so acclimated to this force-controlled, loser anticivilization that none can see the coming business-controlled, winner Civilization of the Universe. ...*Profound Honesty* cures that blindness.

e

Opening Ceremonies
Cyberspace Concertos #1-4

PROFOUND HONESTY
and
Neo-Tech Objectivism

> Limitless Prosperity and Romantic Excitement
> via
> Profound Honesty and Neo-Tech Objectivism

Concerto #1

New-World Music

Only conscious beings can distort reality. Only conscious beings can act dishonestly and unjustly. Yet, all distortions, dishonesties, and injustices are temporary — illusionary — not part of reality. ...Conscious beings can assert honesty and justice to control their existence within the laws of nature. In that way, conscious beings can control their future. Thus, they can enter a new world of limitless prosperity and romantic excitement.

The Pre Cyberspace World

Before cyberspace, before the Internet, reality often asserted itself slowly — often after years, sometimes only after centuries or millennia. Yet, no matter how dishonest or unjust an individual or a society, reality ultimately prevails. For example, decades after their deaths, the reality of the great values produced by Francis Bacon, Johann Sebastian Bach, Joseph Smith, Herman Melville, and Vincent van Gogh finally came forth. And, today, honesty and justice are revealing scorned businesspeople like Jay

i

Gould, John D. Rockefeller, Leona Helmsley, and Michael Milken as life-giving benefactors to conscious life. Also, eventually, honesty and justice will reveal Homeric icons like Alexander the Great, Napoleon, Lincoln, and Woodrow Wilson as life-destroying malefactors to conscious life.

Throughout history, dishonesties and injustices have caused deep, widespread distortions of reality. Those distortions arise from one fundamental source: people who choose to live by forcefully or fraudulently draining values from others. Such people do not live naturally — they do not live by producing values for others. They live as unnatural human organisms — as parasitical humanoids.

Many such humanoids glean affluent, respectable, even famous livings by expertly disguising their criminal parasitisms. They live as rulers, politicians, academics, journalists, religious leaders. Such people often manipulate envy from the populace by dishonestly ripping facts out of context in order to drain the real benefactors of society — the competitive job-and-value producers. The direct victims are those precious risk-taking businesspeople who deliver the values and jobs necessary for conscious life to survive and prosper. The indirect victims are all conscious beings living on Earth today.

At every level of activity and visibility, criminal parasites drain the heroic value producers of this world under the facade of altruism — force-and-fraud backed altruism. Such criminal altruism is the underlying deception of this unnatural civilization. For that reason, Earth beings live in an upside-down civilization — an anticivilization — in which uncompetitive, value-destroying parasites control competitive, value-producing heroes.

A New World

Today, a new world — a cyberspace information world — is bringing a new paradigm to planet Earth. Is this rising new paradigm for better or worse? Consider the single most harmful irrationality of Earth's anticivilization: the apathetic acceptance of criminal parasites draining the life and well-being from everyone. ...Will this new cyberspace paradigm empower or emasculate those who purposely harm society?

Usenet: A Paradise or Graveyard for Parasites?

In today's anticivilization, the Internet Newsgroup system called Usenet is a world of ironies in which all values, honesty, and justice can be wantonly attacked and seemingly destroyed by shrunken spirits ranging from ersatz philosophers to certain tax-supported academics and criminal-minded nihilists. On Usenet, do-nothing shrunken spirits can seemingly smother any and every great value or accomplishment. Dishonesty seemingly reigns. Nonentities seem to be able to unjustly destroy anything and everything with out-of-context attacks, mendacious innuendos, and fabricated scenarios.

Yet, within that paradoxical picture lies the promise of a new world. A world of fully integrated honesty in which justice asserts itself. For, in the cyberspace world, all dishonesties and injustices become entrapped and then extinguished by reality.

Cyberspace: The Dishonesty Trap

Cyberspace forms self-exposure traps that will eventually eliminate purposeful destructions from this planet. Through such traps, all dishonesties move toward extinction. Every dishonesty and injustice launched in cyberspace by malevolent value destroyers is permanently recorded and retrievable through Internet search engines. Likewise, every example of honesty, justice, and value production is also permanently recorded and retrievable. How does Usenet combine with the World Wide Web to trap and eventually vanish purposely destructive people? Consider the following:

On Usenet Newsgroups, all varieties of dishonest people, do-nothing idlers, destructive parasites, even criminal psychopaths can delude themselves with feelings of false self-worth and unearned power. Swarms of negative loudmouths seem to out-shout everyone else. Their barrages of achieve-nothing negativities can seemingly trash any laudable effort, positive achievement, or value-producing hero. By contrast, genuine heroes seldom raise their voices. Moreover, they are too busy producing values to defend themselves against attention-seeking nonentities.

In cyberspace, the most insignificant nonentities seem to have free reign to hack apart any positive achievement or value. But the opposite is the fact. For example, achieve-everything Bill Gates has many achieve-nothing flamers dishonestly attacking him on Usenet. Yet, Bill Gates continues to soar — soaring toward becoming perhaps the greatest value-and-job producer in history. Simultaneously, his attention-seeking flamers are self-exposing their nonentity natures while publicly shrinking their souls toward nothingness.

Half-Life of Usenet

Justice comes to cyberspace as value destroyers shrink toward nothingness and value producers expand toward limitlessness. ...How exactly does that dynamic work in cyberspace?

That dynamic works through the half-life decay (like radioactive half-life decay) of items posted on Usenet Newsgroups — a half-life perhaps as short as a few hours. How does that half-life of Usenet interact with the doubling-life (increasing value delivery) of the World Wide Web? Long-term doubling lives occur for Web sites on which competitive values are constantly building and being delivered to increasingly wider audiences. By contrast, to counter their decaying messages on Usenet, value destroyers must spew more-and-more dishonesties to sustain their illusions of credibility and self-importance. Yet, while their attacks are relentlessly decaying, their dishonesties and malevolences are building in archives that are always available through search engines.

Likewise, integrations of reality are also accumulating and being archived. Thus, whenever needed, those dishonest attacks can be gathered and simultaneously compared to fully integrated honesty on the World Wide Web or in printed literature. ...Such juxtaposition of dishonesty versus honesty makes reality obvious and justice certain.

When nihilistic attacks or ego-boosting smears are gathered and then viewed as a whole, the evil leaps forth, smacking every observer foursquare, eternally trapping unjust attackers in their own disintegrated dishonesties. Consider what happens when disintegrated dishonesty is publicly contrasted to integrated honesty — contrasted point-by-point from every angle. Such vivid contrasts accelerate the public understanding and use of radically new, life-enhancing values. Previously, such values may have taken decades or centuries to gain public acceptance and beneficial use in everyone's life.

Neo-Tech, meaning fully integrated honesty, will publicly advance through the Usenet dynamic via a book titled *Flame-War Justice*. In that book, fully integrated honesty is unjustly, dishonestly attacked from every conceivable angle. Those attacks are then contrasted to widely integrated, fully contextual responses. From such contrasts, the value of even the most radical aspects of fully integrated honesty will become not only publicly clear but publicly acceptable in shorter time frames than possible in the pre cyberspace world.

The Doubling-Life of Web Sites

The above process of accelerating Neo-Tech Objectivism globally through cyberspace dynamics is catalyzed by widening networks of hyperlinked World Wide Web sites. Fully integrated honesty in the form of hyperlinked Web sites plays off the accumulating Usenet archive and search-engine dynamics. Those Neo-Tech dynamics will be constructed and integrated on the Internet

v

in late 1997 through an interactive Java/ActiveX dynamic called "Ask Zon".

Neo-Tech Objectivism in cyberspace has already cracked the ersatz "leadership" that has stagnated the worldwide advance of Objectivism. What is Objectivism? It is the philosophy of Ayn Rand and Leonard Peikoff. It is the philosophy for benefiting conscious beings. Objectivism is based on the primacy of existence and integrated reason — the new-world philosophy of limitless prosperity and romantic excitement.

Objectivism is the philosophy upon which Neo-Tech/ Zonpower rests. In turn, Neo-Tech/Zonpower is the tool for advancing the primacy of existence around the world. That advance will eliminate irrationality and dishonesty from conscious beings. ...Neo-Tech/Zonpower is the most effective, practical expression of Objectivism, life-enhancing business, and romantic excitement.

Additionally, that Neo-Tech dynamic is breaking the bubbles of irrationality polluting all philosophies, including breaking intolerances toward "different people" and "different believers". Breaking those stagnant intolerances toward people — toward potential customers — will allow an open, honest form of no-compromise Objectivism to advance — Apostle-Paul, reach-everyone style — into realms of limitless prosperity and exciting romance.

Cyberspace Heaven

The non cyberspace world today has grown for 3000 years from roots of criminal-minded Homeric "heroes", irrational Platonic mysticisms, and fraudulent Augustinian[1] religions — all fed by intentional value destruction, demagoguery, and envy backed by force and fraud. In this criminally manipulated civilization, the duped public is promised life, prosperity, and

---

[1]As a youth, St. Augustine stole other people's property not for need but for kicks. As the Bishop of Hippo, he stole other people's souls not for salvation but for power.

justice in some after-death, imaginary heaven or in some "heroic" remembrance. Indeed, in this anticivilization, everyone has to sacrifice his or her life in order to reach that unreal celestial "reward".

By contrast, today's new cyberspace world will bring conscious beings exciting lives with undreamed prosperity in a real heaven right here on Earth. In that Earthly heaven, fully integrated honesty and justice will mean oblivion for Homeric heroes and all other criminal parasites. Eradication of those humanoids means limitless growth for every competitive human being on this planet.

The Civilization of the Universe

In the upside-down civilization of the pre cyberspace world, fraud and war are glorified as noble and heroic: Platonistic noble-lie frauds and Homeric macho-hero wars have been historically hyped as ways to bring people to greater heights: political, parasitical heights — *not* competitive, productive heights. Such irrationality eventually brings spiritual and physical death to everyone. By contrast, in the rational Civilization of the Universe, competitive value production, not force and fraud, is what lifts people toward eternal life and happiness.

In cyberspace, harmful parasitical minds remain behind in the closed-circle anticivilization. By contrast, competitive business minds move ahead into the open-ended Civilization of the Universe.

Discovering New-World Music

Specific metaphors and general metaphors can be the most powerful and sometimes the only means of communicating certain ideas and emotions. Much of classic prose as well as most poems and songs are metaphorical. In fact, general metaphors such as Ayn Rand's novel *Atlas Shrugged* are often the only effective way to introduce radical ideas that are alien to this anticivilization.

While Neo-Tech/Zonpower literature is broadly metaphorical, even right-brain lyrical at times, the literature is not right-brain enough to reach the emotional heart and soul of everyone in this anticivilization. When people emotionally feel the shrunken spirit of this anticivilization, they will actively care about eliminating the unjust harms inflicted upon innocent value producers by intentional value destroyers. Through such active caring for the value producers, all professional value destroyers and their parasitical political leaders will eventually vanish along with their tools of force and fraud.

Until Neo-Tech, no one was willing to consistently stand up and do something about the injustices and purposeful destruction of values that perpetuate this anticivilization. Who really cared about the injustices inflicted by the professional value destroyers upon the competitive value producers? Who really tried to protect and cherish those upon whom the well-being of conscious life depends? Until Neo-Tech, no one consistently stood up to protect unjustly aggrieved value producers from destructive parasites — sub rosa parasites ranging from force-backed politicians and dishonest academics to criminal-minded nihilists and ersatz philosophers.

Yet, no amount of left-brain Neo-Tech literature can deliver the emotional realizations of the sins and virtues woven throughout this bizarrely unnatural anticivilization. Spectacularly new, right-brain metaphorical lyrics are required. ...As an artistic analogy, right-brain impressionists Claude Monet and Vincent van Gogh discovered entirely new ways to emotionally communicate the reality of nature through impressionist art. From another perspective, the abstract art of Pablo Picasso versus the romantic art of Eugéne Delacroix are examples of untouchably different modes for fixed left-brain communication of abstract ideas versus emotional right-brain communication of romantic ideals. Also, consider Mozart's intelligence-boosting piano Concerto #21 and Beethoven's piano/orchestra-dueling Piano Concerto #5. ...The rising Zon literature harnesses the artistic right brain — the exciting romantic brain.

Indeed, weaving a lyrical, right-brain narrative throughout cyberspace is necessary to emotionally communicate the natural Civilization of the Universe currently known to no one on Earth, but necessary to everyone...versus the unnatural anticivilization currently known to everyone on Earth, but necessary to no one.

The rising Zonpower literature has become increasingly metaphorical, even lyrical in parts. Still, further movement toward the right-brain metaphor must evolve over the next few years in order to deliver across all populations a radically new thinking paradigm. A new generation of literature, art, and music will rise from history's longest narrative poem or song comprising up to three-hundred-thousand lines woven through conscious minds. That new-world music will capture the epic journey from Earth's anticivilization to the Civilization of the Universe. ...Those lyrics, which reflect the emotional basis of the Civilization of the Universe, will replace the Homeric poems, which reflect the emotional basis of this anticivilization.

That narrative journey will be titled "Quantum Crossings". It will draw hostility and scorn as it is released in unfinished segments during the years before its completion. Hostility from all quarters is expected. For, acceptance would signal that the Neo-Tech/Zon literature is evolving too slowly — to conservatively — and would fail to accomplish its goal of curing irrationality before everyone is killed by that disease.

Strength grows from resistance. Neo-Tech/Zon must flush out "enemies" and push the limits of scorn and hostility in this anticivilization. Only from actively confronting this irrational anticivilization will come an Objectivist civilization — the Civilization of the Universe for us and our children.

Wanted: Commercial Objectivists

Harnessed into a competitive business tool, Objectivism can bring never-ending gains in prosperity and happiness to everyone on Earth. With fully integrated honesty, people can heal themselves of anticivilization corruptions. In that process, a Neo-Tech business world will need the services of self-healed people with wide-scope knowledge of Objectivism. To be commercially competitive, however, Objectivists must understand the hard-to-achieve profit dynamics inherent in business. Such businesses advance civilization by aggressively delivering competitive values and jobs to maximum people — a risky, difficult, heroic task.

One derives values from Objectivism by applying its principles to the benevolently tolerant dynamics of business. Does that mean compromising the principles of Objectivism? Absolutely not. To the contrary, competitive success is achieved by developing and delivering the open-ended values of *no-compromise* Objectivism to anyone and everyone worldwide.

For a no-compromise Objectivist professional to become commercially profitable, that person cannot stand on a pedestal, offering only boring, uncompetitive preaching. Instead, he or she must get into the muddy-risky trenches of a nitty-gritty profit battle to demonstrate through hard work the exciting, step-by-step profits available from no-compromise Objectivism.

Discovering Eternal Prosperity

Neo-Tech Objectivism evolves in cyberspace through confrontation with "enemies" and their hostilities. Additionally, such confrontations provide much of the material for the forthcoming, eye-opening book titled *Flame-War Justice*. That book comprehensively chronicles real-life examples of irrational attacks on the good — dishonest attacks from every angle on newly developing values that benefit everyone. Such a chronicling both in print and across cyberspace will lift the barricades of ignorance and malevolence to bring new knowledge — an eternal knowledge that arises when injustice succumbs to justice, when dishonesty succumbs to honesty, when ignorance succumbs to knowledge.

Thus, comes the limitless prosperity reflected from the Civilization of the Universe. In the Civilization of the Universe, businesspeople become supreme artists — universal composers of heavenly melodies. By contrast, criminal-minded politicians, war makers, and nihilists often march to clanging, nationalistic Wagnerians. Indeed, Wagner is the cocaine of music, making those who get hooked feel ten-feet tall — making destructive parasites feel invincibly powerful.[1]

In counterbalance, businesspeople work through melodiously sensuous, individualistic Debussyans. They deliver the La Mers and Clare de Lunes to this world. They create the seas of value on Earth. They deliver the beams of natural light into night darkness — light reflected from the other side — from the eternally bright Civilization of the Universe.

---

[1]This identification is *not* a criticism of Richard Wagner's great music, which is a supreme example of human creativity, art, and beauty — music that anyone can greatly enjoy.

Concerto #2

Profound Honesty
brings
Limitless Prosperity

In the 1950s, a group called Quadri-I Research[1] discovered that a small minority of persons thought in whole pictures rather than in segments that subsequently built into whole thoughts. Quadri-I also found that each such person generated nearly the same picture for any given thought or idea. Those pictures were similar because they formed immediately — uncorrupted by biases or agendas. Thus, those pictures were more accurate — more in accord with reality. Arbitrary information and errors had no time to enter the thought process. Such corruptions simply dissipated when the whole picture flashed into consciousness.[2]

In the early 1980s, Neo-Tech literature identified that thinking process as Neothink. ...Neothinking is a whole-picture-thinking process that brings riches and excitement to conscious beings as described in the publications, *Neo-Tech Business Control* by Mark Hamilton and *Neo-Tech Global Business Control* by Eric Savage.

Today, most adults think by an opposite process. They begin their thought processes with discrete percepts, concepts, ideas, emotions. From those segments rise the larger segments or thoughts used to make decisions, take actions, and experience emotions. The problem is that those segments can be manipulated and distorted to fit almost any illusion or dishonesty promoted by this anticivilization. Such distortions yield life-diminishing decisions and actions. ...That method of thinking builds profound dishonesties, often well hidden, that block a person's capacity to gain wide-scope understandings and valuable new knowledge.

---

[1]Reference: Larry McNaughton, Tampa, Florida, 1996.

[2]That picture-language thinking has no connection to today's mystical, new-age fads of imaging or visualizing — pictures built from delusions or wishful thinking.

The Neothink Mind

The Neothink mind thinks simultaneously with both the left brain (full integrations) and the right brain (without boundaries). The Neothink mind thinks in a picture language, which means thinking in integrated, no-boundary images — the ultimate, most sensuous, most powerful form of metaphorical thinking. That mind, in turn, breaks those images into small, powerful segments. Such a breakdown from whole pictures into separate parts provides sources of new knowledge for advancing conscious life toward limitless prosperity and romantic happiness. ...Everyone had a Neothink mind as a young child. And, today, any adult can recapture that young, wide-open mind through fully integrated honesty.

Free of preconceived notions, young children think by an uncorrupted picture process. But, they lose that invaluable picture-language thinking as they are driven by their parents and teachers into the profoundly dishonest, narrow-scope anticivilization. ...By building small distortions into larger distortions, most adults unknowingly think dishonestly about the widest, most important aspects of life. They distort their thoughts by adjusting them to the rationalizations and agendas needed to feel acceptable in this anticivilization. Such a bottom-to-top process becomes a reality-distorting language that cripples the conscious mind.

By contrast, the rare top-to-bottom process retains the honest visual-language mind of childhood. That visual language lets one integrate wide-scope pictures and emotions that cannot be expressed in spoken language or even thought about by people with spoken-language minds. Thus, when encountering ultra-powerful, radical-breakthrough values, most people either ridicule those values or their eyes glaze over as their minds sleep. Such spoken-language minds are blind to the new knowledge, emotions, and values that evolve from visual-language minds.

Right brained, often dyslexic left-handed, even mirror-writer artists and scientists as da Vinci, van Gogh, Cézanne, Monet,

xiii

Newton, and Einstein functioned through picture-language thinking. Einstein could visualize the entire cosmos in a single thought. Then, in one sweep, his mind broke that thought down to submicroscopic particles. In that way, he converted his thoughts into many segments of shockingly new, accurate information that delivered the theories of Special Relativity and Quantum Energy. Only over time did his peers and later others grasp what evolved from Einstein's wide-scope pictures of reality. Even today, aspects of his work are just now being grasped.

Einstein, van Gogh, and Cézanne discovered entirely new aspects of reality from their picture thinking. Years passed, even decades, before society discovered the values flowing from their unusual thinking. Indeed, each canvas of van Gogh and Cézanne today commands many millions of dollars. And, today, Einstein's discoveries are the foundations for all natural sciences. Yet, their wide-scope benefits were initially ridiculed, ignored, or considered boring. ...When society finally awoke to their tremendous values, insightful exploiters parlayed those values into fortune and fame.

Many new, wide-scope values flow from today's Neo-Tech/ Zonpower literature. Most people today, however, are blind to the powerful, practical values of Neo-Tech. But, that blindness will end. ...Consider the discoveries flowing from the following six Neo-Tech pictures:

Neo-Tech Picture 1: The discovery of two opposite, conscious-created civilizations: Our current, unnatural anticivilization versus the natural Civilization of the Universe.

Neo-Tech Picture 2: The discovery that the dynamic for conscious death versus conscious life is criminal parasitism versus competitive business. The anticivilization dynamic propagates through criminal value destruction. The Civilization of the Universe propagates through competitive value production.

Neo-Tech Picture 3: The discovery of mankind's shrunken spirit

xiv

— the dishonesties, criminalities, and irrationalities that diminish the spirit of *every* citizen living in this anticivilization. Failure to see the unnecessity of that shrunken spirit is what perpetuates this unnatural anticivilization. ...Failure to reject such spiritual and physical diminishments ultimately brings impotence and death to conscious beings.

Neo-Tech Picture 4: The discovery that the future for everyone on Earth *is* the Civilization of the Universe — an Objectivist civilization free of dishonesty, irrationality, criminality, disease, aging, and death itself.

Neo-Tech Picture 5: The discovery that value-and-job producers of this world are caught in history's highest-stake poker game. That game is run by professional value destroyers — by hidden killers and neocheating looters who propagate this anticivilization through guns, envy, and parasitism. The stakes are the life and death of every conscious being living on Earth.

Neo-Tech Picture 6: The discovery that profound honesty will nonviolently vanish those professional value destroyers, criminal neocheaters, and their anticivilization. ...Chapters 16 and 35 of *Zonpower from Cyberspace* provide an understanding of the white-hat honesties that eradicate professional value destroyers and their black-hat neocheating.

Profound Honesty delivers Limitless Prosperity

The time frame to bridge the gap for solid, public understandings of the above six discoveries would probably extend beyond the lifetime of every person living on planet Earth today. Thus, the task of Neo-Tech Publishing Company is to collapse that indefinitely long time span into the next few years. Such time-span shrinkage can be accomplished by delivering to everyone the practical, wide-scope values pouring from the Neo-Tech/Zonpower discoveries. The benefits from those values will be unleashed through a series of unusual publications titled

Quantum Crossings. As those publications accrue during the next five years, they will vanish the criminal parasites and black-hat neocheaters to end their 2200-year-old poker game of bilking every conscious being out of prosperity, happiness, and life itself.

Those today who have no access to or understanding of Neo-Tech and Zonpower need not worry. The coming *Quantum Crossings* will build the top-to-bottom pictures to let everyone prosper from the profound honesties of Neo-Tech/Zonpower woven around the world.

Making Everyone a Value

On Usenet in early 1996, a "jobless ex-postal worker living off government checks" anonymously posted hundreds of embittered, envious attacks on successful value-and-job producers and competitive business. He also declared across the Internet his desires for limitless, promiscuous sex. Then, between blizzards of uncontrolled Tourette-like sexual profanities, he publicly posted his intentions to murder U.S. army officers and nuke an American city filled with innocent citizens and children. According to legal counsel, that post constituted a domestic-terrorist threat of murder publicly made over the Internet — a serious crime. For that criminal act, he could face both state and federal felony charges upon revealing his identity.[1]

Later in 1996, that envy-embittered, "ex-postal employee" carrying a virtual-reality AK-47 reappeared on the Internet to emphasize his passion for mass murder as shown in his post quoted below:

>In article <4jgqpc$p6r@utopia.hacktic.nl>,
    nobody@flame.alias.net
>(Anonymous) wrote:
>>I would destroy the entire universe rather than live as a
    slave.
>>And you can quote me on that.
  <snip>
>>Ah - so I have nihilistic "tendencies" now.
>>Nihilism is the belief in NOTHING.
>>I believe in all sorts of things very strongly.
>>I might be a terrifyingly immoral egoist from the point of
    view of
>>communitarian and altruist moral codes, but I'm no nihilist.
>>I am something MUCH, MUCH WORSE!

---

[1]In reality, probably the biggest danger from such a person is blowing out his own brains over his compulsive hatred of life and envy of success — just as Goethe's hateful envy-monger "Young Werther" blew his brains out for the exact same reason. ...Becoming a value producer through Neo-Tech cures such hatred and envy.

How could such a person be a value to Neo-Tech? Herein lies the justice dynamics of cyberspace: That person was transformed into a Neo-Tech servant. Indeed, a controlled servant indentured by integrated honesty that brought forth two public revelations: (1) the deep dishonesties of self-proclaimed Objectivist "leaders" and (2) the deep-rooted destructiveness that dwells in everyone invested in this anticivilization. Consider the following paragraphs:

Neo-Tech Objectivism Rises from Flames

Dr. Leonard Peikoff is a genuine philosophical leader. He is courageously leading a philosophical Reformation toward Ayn Rand's Objectivism — a Reformation away from destructive, primacy-of-consciousness (i.e.: subjective-authority led) philosophies to a productive, primacy-of-existence (i.e.: objective-reality led) philosophy. ...Dr. Peikoff is to philosophy what the 16th-century Martin Luther was to religion.

Yet, in April 1995, Leonard Peikoff, while making valid points about illegal private armies, made an irrational, potentially murderous error by "condemning" innocent militia self-defenders to the initiatory force of a corrupt government. Martin Luther in the early 16th century made the same murderous error by condemning innocent peasant self-defenders to the initiatory force of a corrupt government. Luther's moral error triggered the brutal government slaughter of many innocent peasants. ...Dogmatist John Calvin followed Luther in purifying the religious Reformation by directly committing premeditated murder: On gaining access to the initiatory force of government, he had "evil" heretics burned alive at the stake.

Today, Objectivist dogmatists follow Peikoff in purifying the philosophical Reformation. If they gained the physical-force power of government, what would those "Calvinist" dogmatists do to "evil" heretics like militia members, libertarians, and Neo-Tech Objectivists?

Indeed, this is the anticivilization. In advancing one's

anticivilization investments, each becomes malicious, even murderous — directly or indirectly. Thus, certain Objectivist "leaders" eagerly embraced as their ally that embittered nihilist described above who, chained to an Internet keyboard by Neo-Tech, proclaimed his passion to commit mass murder and have promiscuous sex with everyone possible.

Why did those Objectivists publicly, dishonestly abandon principle to embrace such an entity as their protector and ally? Solely because he uncontrollably libeled and physically threatened their competition — their perceived "enemy" — the Neo-Tech Objectivists. He recklessly endangered the lives of innocent value producers with defaming libel and malignant innuendo that no Objectivist would dare display. Thus, such a person became their sanctioned anti Neo-Tech mouthpiece. ...Objectivist honesty? Objectivist principles? What better demonstration of people supporting their irrational investments in this bizarre anticivilization at any self-destructive cost or hypocritical dishonesty. At some point, however, each will have to look at his or her picture and discover a Dorian Gray — the visual results of one's pact with destructive irrationality.

Consider, for example, a dishonest Objectivist "leader" who cheered on that nihilist servant and fed him libelous information to expand his attacks toward her enemy — fully integrated honesty. Therein lies her investment in this anticivilization. Still, in the broadest sense, that Objectivist "leader" is no better or worse than anyone irrationally investing in this anticivilization — no better or worse than that jobless nihilist.

Indeed, any person ultimately promotes criminally murderous behaviors whenever he or she promotes irrationality — whenever that person upholds dishonesty to protect his or her anticivilization investments. ...Yet, even she can, as can any Objectivist, self-heal the wounds of dishonesty to become a growing value in an Objectivist world — in the Civilization of the Universe.

Through fully integrated honesty, people can open their eyes to the irrationalities practiced by every investor in this anticivilization, ranging from murderous psychopaths, to dishonest academics, even to outstanding Objectivist value producers, *including* Neo-Tech Objectivists and risk-taking business heroes. ...The pervasive diseases of irrationality and dishonesty beget criminality and destructiveness, directly or indirectly, by force or by sanction, in every conscious being on Earth. Without fully integrated honesty, *everyone* will ultimately kill directly or indirectly to preserve his or her anticivilization investment, ego, or livelihood.

But, the mental illnesses, irrationalities, and dishonesties of this anticivilization will shrivel and vanish in cyberspace driven by fully integrated honesty. Indeed, the profound honesty of Neo-Tech is taking over Objectivism, healing it, and propagating it worldwide — propagating it through competitive business.

Among the most moving testimonials for *The Neo-Tech Discovery* are those that reveal its extraordinary effectiveness in curing mental illnesses — psychoses, neuroses, alcoholism, obesity, mysticism, drug abuse, depression, criminalities. Consider that after several months immersion into the integrated honesty of Neo-Tech, the profane government-dependent nihilist described above was transformed by a Neo-Tech editor[1] into a propagator of Neo-Tech ideas on the Internet. ...A similar transformation could occur with criminal-minded President Clinton as explained on page 5 of the Golden-Helmet "Victory" Overture at the end of this manuscript.

---

[1]Drew "Kaiser" Ellis, an editor of Neo-Tech Publishing Company, developed the string-controlled KOAH/ACSE machine to study the dishonesty disease in public cyberspace.

Neo-Tech Empowers Objectivists

From August 21, 1995 to June 19, 1996, the profound honesty of Neo-Tech flowed through cyberspace. Through the Internet Newsgroup alt.philosophy.objectivism (apo), that flow of honesty liberated "official" Objectivists from their closed circles of stagnation as summarized below:

1. Broke their thirty-year-old dogmatic structure and exposed their pseudo-intellectualism. Such do-nothing, closed-circle intellectualisms will disappear with the publication of a book titled *Flame-War Justice*.
2. Deflated their illusions of philosophical "authority", which for thirty years harmfully retarded the wide-scale advance of Objectivism.
3. Compelled "official" Objectivists into accepting as allies their previous worst enemies such as Libertarians, Kelley-type Objectivists, and other "evil" heretics. Those "official" Objectivists became comrades with their previous enemies in trying to defeat their new, worse-than-worst enemy: the evilissimo Neo-Tech. For, through its honesty templates, Neo-Tech publicly revealed the dishonesties, hypocrisies, and impotence of "official" Objectivists.
4. Contrasted the backward-looking, intellectualizing-mode of "official" Objectivists to the forward-looking, business-mode of Neo-Tech Objectivists.
5. Caused Objectivist "officials" to create a tightly monitored newsgroup humanities.philosophy.objectivism (hpo). Their entire purpose for creating hpo was to explicitly censor and prevent fully integrated honesty — Neo-Tech — from breaking false authority. But, ironically, hiding from Neo-Tech in their cloistered hpo newsgroup, those same "officials" are now demystifing and liberating themselves.

For, they are compelled to deal rationally with their new allies — their previous worst enemies. Thus, through Neo-Tech, stunted Objectivist "leaders" are growing again, empowering themselves. They are learning to communicate more maturely, more effectively — with less flaming, less name calling, less emotionalism...less stagnating dogmatism.[1]

6. Drove cyberspace Objectivism into a stronger position for worldwide growth.

Liberating Objectivists for future growth was the goal of Neo-Tech Publishing. Moreover, achieving that goal never involved compromising Objectivism. For, Ayn Rand's and Leonard Peikoff's Objectivism is a universal philosophy of exquisite consistency.

---

[1]Neo-Tech associates hold no hostile attitudes toward anyone posting on Usenet. While they will counterpunch with fully integrated templates when dishonestly attacked, they never initiate attacks, flames, insults, or profanities toward anyone. Yet, very important, the attacks on Neo-Tech provide the material to evolve commercial products needed for delivering an Objectivist civilization — the Civilization of the Universe — to everyone on Earth.

The profound honesty and resulting values of Neo-Tech Objectivism are rejected by today's Establishment. Yet, that Establishment rejection is what keeps Neo-Tech pushing into ever deeper areas of non acceptance. Such non acceptance will culminate in Quantum Crossings — the one-way bridges into the Civilization of the Universe.

Neo-Tech does not benefit by acceptance from *any* quarter in this anticivilization. Thus, as each new level of Neo-Tech begins gaining acceptance, Neo-Tech Publishing must push beyond the pale — into ever more "outlandish" realms of objective reality and knowledge. Indeed, profound honesty is used to constantly move beyond acceptance in this anticivilization — beyond acceptance even by Neo-Tech supporters and associates. That wide-scope, long-range progress must continue until the dishonest, irrational, murderous anticivilization has vanished from Earth — until we all live with eternal prosperity and romantic excitement in an ever growing honest, rational, benevolent Objectivist civilization.

By reading the book version of *Profound Honesty,* one can easily, contextually grasp Neo-Tech and Zonpower. Indeed, those who carefully read *Profound Honesty* will be joyfully awakened as they jump beyond competition in this anticivilization. ...Eventually, everyone will be happily jolted out of this anticivilization by the compelling simplicity of Neo-Tech/Zonpower.

One, Two, Three...Prosperity
Song 1

The Journey
from
Earth's Anticivilization
to the
Civilization of the Universe

---

think999@ix.netcom.com
"We are dealing with something powerful here.
The most powerful ideas in the Universe.
We are dealing with Neo-Tech in Cyberspace."

The Mozarts, Byrons, Shelleys, Keatses, Raphaels, Büchners, Bizets, and Schuberts are not the only ones who die too young. We all die too young. So little of our potential is ever realized. After youth, survivors unnaturally age, grow old, and die. None come close to the full-scope happiness and prosperity possible to conscious life. None find the spiritual answers tragically sought by Tolstoy. Some live bound within Baudelaire's visions of man-made cities...others within Frost's visions of snowy country nights. Yet, what was Emily Dickenson saying in her poems of nature, consciousness, and death? How can we live our natural lives — lives without limits, yet within the limits of nature? The answer is Neo-Tech. For, Neo-Tech will bring a profoundly honest civilization within cyberspace to create the Civilization of the Universe on planet Earth.

INTRODUCTION

The profound honesty of Neo-Tech is taking over a philosophy called Objectivism and implementing it through worldwide business dynamics. What is Objectivism? And, why implement it worldwide?

Objectivism is a philosophy rooted in Aristotle,

1

discovered by Ayn Rand, nailed down by Dr. Leonard Peikoff, and now being dispersed globally through Neo-Tech. The goal is to rapidly bring an Objectivist civilization to planet Earth. For, an Objectivist civilization will bring every conscious person wide-open prosperity. How will every person gain such prosperity through a philosophy? What powers and riches are derived from implementing Objectivism worldwide? ...*Profound Honesty* answers those questions.

To be of universal value, mankind's one valid philosophy — Objectivism — must be liberated from its stagnant leaders and academic authorities. Objectivism must be injected into the action-mode dynamics of competitive value production. That liberation of Objectivist philosophy is outlined in Song 2.

The liberation of Objectivism will deliver prosperity to every honest person through the three epiphanies:
ONE, TWO, THREE...PROSPERITY

Three Epiphanies from Three Facts
Conscious beings will gain eternal prosperity through three epiphanies arising from three facts:

Fact 1: The Civilization of the Universe and an anticivilization are antithetical domains of honesty and dishonesty — the either/or domains in which all conscious beings dwell throughout time and space.

Fact 2: Conscious beings on Earth unknowingly live in an anticivilization built upon (a) Homer's criminal-minded heroes, (b) Plato's noble-lie dishonesties, and (c) Augustine's death-demanding mysticisms.

Fact 3: Fully integrated honesty (Neo-Tech) and wide-scope integrations (Neothink) dissolve the anticivilization dynamics of value destruction, aging, and death. ...In its place appears the Objectivist-civilization dynamics of value production, youth, and prosperity.

Three Epiphanies

Until liberated by epiphanies rising from those three facts, we remain as blind mice trapped in the bizarre maze of an irrational civilization. Indeed, trapped in Earth's domain of illusions, we remain unaware of our stunted spirits and shrunken visions. Moreover, we knowingly or unknowingly cling to the life-losing investments and commitments that uphold this anticivilization. As such, whenever the circumstances arise, each of us will commit injustices and harm innocent others by voice or deed. ...Thus, after youth, we all shrink toward death, then to dust.

But, on opening our minds and actions to fully integrated honesty, we gain the wide-scope integrations needed to vanish this mystically twisted anticivilization. In its place will rise an Objectivist civilization — the rational Civilization of the Universe. In that natural realm of universal honesty, everyone thrives with abiding happiness and limitless vision. In that illusion-free empyrean, even the most aggressive competitor never acts unjustly or inflicts harm upon others. ...Thus, after youth, honest people grow beyond the stars toward eternal prosperity.

EPIPHANY ONE

Liberating Philosophy

Philosophy. Who understands philosophy? Who really cares about philosophy? Very few. For, it is a highly technical subject reserved mainly for professional philosophers dwelling in academic realms. Yet, everyone lives by a philosophy — subconsciously, implicitly. Only one philosophy is based on the total, wide-scope well-being of conscious life — the philosophy of Objectivism.

The Civilization of the Universe depends on Objectivist philosophy. Thus, Epiphany One involves liberating stagnant Objectivism from its anticivilization dogmatizers.

3

Objectivism is the philosophy of rational, conscious life — of fully integrated honesty. Yet, no one on planet Earth has consistently lived by the philosophy of Objectivism — not even its originator and developer, Ayn Rand and Leonard Peikoff. Even though Rand and Peikoff could discover, develop, and intellectually deal with Objectivism, they nor anyone else can live by it any more than can Hillary Clinton, the Pope, or O. J. Simpson. For, the modus operandi of everyone in this anticivilization rests upon a foundation of dishonesty and criminality.

Epiphany One sweeps a floodlight beneath the rickety structure of criminal dishonesty that supports all anticivilization investments and commitments. Once permanently spotlighted in one's mind, that person can finally identify the destruction-driven irrationalities and criminalities of this anticivilization.

Eureka! I have found the light to identify and isolate the anticivilization. I can now banish it from my life, bit by bit, piece by piece.

EPIPHANY TWO

Neo-Tech Stimulants

Epiphany Two makes the crystal-clear identification that the anticivilization and the Civilization of the Universe are two inescapable facts. Through Neo-Tech arises a new, wide-scope vision. Within that vision lie the stimulants needed to vanish each perpetrator of that anticivilization.

Eureka! I have found the stimulants to identify and isolate each anticivilization perpetrator. I can now banish them from my life, one by one.

EPIPHANY THREE

Vanishing the Anticivilization

Epiphany Three reveals a specific tool: The wide-scope accounting tool called the Golden Helmet as detailed in the

Appendix of this manuscript. That tool provides a protocol for vanishing the archetype institution of wide-scope destruction in today's anticivilization — the United States Internal Revenue Service (IRS). Moreover, that concrete example serves as a model for vanishing other destructive, anticivilization institutions and bureaucracies.

Through that Golden-Helmet protocol, the unnecessary acceptance of destructive institutions is first recognized, then undermined, and finally vanished. Indeed, that change from intimidated acceptance to unequivocal rejection will vanish the destructive institutions of this anticivilization to bring forth the Civilization of the Universe.

Eureka! I have found the tool to identify and isolate each destructive institution of this anticivilization. I can now banish them from my life, one after the other.

Epiphany One, Two, Three...here comes eternal prosperity.

ETERNAL PROSPERITY

The Neo-Tech Discovery

Neo-Tech is the action mode that cures the disease causing this anticivilization. That disease is dishonesty. In turn, dishonesty comprises irrationality and mysticism. ...The *Neo-Tech Discovery* published by Neo-Tech Worldwide is a separate telephone-book size book — an 800-page document that identifies and isolates the information matrix for ending the irrationalities and mysticisms of this anticivilization.

Zonpower Rules Cyberspace

Zonpower is the first document written on Earth from the perspective of an Objectivist civilization. *Zonpower* gazes deep into the radically different Objectivist realm — into the Civilization of the Universe realm. Through *Zonpower*, that

5

Objectivist civilization is already rising on planet Earth. Each bit and piece of that new-color Objectivist civilization forever replaces bit by bit, piece by piece, this 2300-year-old dishonest anticivilization.

The Key

The key to jumping the abyss from today's anticivilization into tomorrow's Objectivist civilization is discovered in Epiphany Two. That discovery is the vivid recognition of the dishonest anticivilization that dominates planet Earth versus the honest Civilization of the Universe that reigns throughout existence. ...Those two opposite civilizations represent the two fundamental choices faced by conscious beings: dishonesty versus honesty — death versus life.

Indeed, death or life *is* the fundamental choice of conscious beings. Moreover, no conscious being on Earth can escape aging and death until he or she identifies, understands, then acts upon fully integrated honesty. Anything less condemns one to a shrinking life leading to death and dust. ...To survive and prosper eternally one must first see everything in concrete terms of an anticivilization versus an Objectivist civilization.

One of many specific steps already being taken in that direction through Neo-Tech — fully integrated honesty — is described below:

Scarlet Lettering Baleful Philosophers

The importance of Objectivism to everyone's future is captured in a single fact: Objectivism *is* the philosophy of the Civilization of the Universe.

A forthcoming book titled *Flame-War Justice* will demonstrate how anyone can identify and then scarlet letter those who are blocking Objectivism from sweeping planet Earth. That scarlet lettering will vanish their baleful influence.

Flame-War Justice will bury the stagnation of Objectivism caused by ersatz Objectivists and their closed-circle "leaders".

From May 1995 to April 1996, a furious flame war was waged in cyberspace by the Objectivist dogmatists against the closest ally of Objectivism — Neo-Tech. Why did the self-appointed "guardians" of Objectivism attack the action-mode producers of Neo-Tech? Because Neo-Tech is tearing Objectivism away from their elitist

---

6

"leaders" and propelling it forward, into the hands of the honest, non intellectual, working class — beyond the control of dogmatists and elitists.

In a pyrotechnic display of dishonesty, those self-aggrandizing dogmatists made their last stand against Neo-Tech — their last stand for shrinking Objectivism into a cloister of dark-age scholastics. ...At this historic juncture of exploding technology and apocalyptic threats to mankind's survival, such shrinking of Objectivism would mark mankind's greatest disaster. But, instead, Neo-Tech, the wide-open, worldwide facilitator of Objectivism will safely carry everyone into the next millennium, eventually delivering eternal prosperity to all.

Neo-Tech never initiates attacks on Objectivists or their ideas. Moreover, it has never attacked a single tenet of Objectivism. Indeed, Neo-Tech has always supported, without compromise, the tenets of Objectivism. ...Certainly, Neo-Tech parries and counterpunches dishonest attacks by baleful Objectivists and their nihilist allies. Neo-Tech, moreover, profitably uses those attacks and responses in its published literature.

Yes, some aggressive Neo-Tech self-leaders made learning errors on Usenet. But, they openly admitted those errors once realized...and then corrected them. Also, the editors of Neo-Tech literature have appreciatively acknowledged and corrected errors in their publications whenever pointed out. For, Neo-Tech is wide-open — void of defensiveness — always correcting, improving, forever growing. ...Neo-Tech is the new direction Objectivism must now travel.

Objectivism for the Proletariat

Because the working classes do not intellectualize philosophy, elitist Objectivists dismiss them as the great "unwashed". Fully integrated honesty, however, is drying up those uncompetitive, elitist Objectivists. But, no one needs to fear diminishment of Objectivism. To the contrary, Neo-Tech is taking over elitist-crippled Objectivism to heal it and spread its practical values among "non-intellectual" working people. Neo-Tech is weaving the practical benefits of Objectivism among the honest working classes. Indeed, fully integrated honesty — Neo-Tech — will bring an Objectivist civilization to everyone via those working classes. ...One, two, three, here comes eternal prosperity.

The "Philosopher" Zoo
Objectivists Caged in Cyberspace

From July 1995 to June 1996, Neo-Tech Publishing Company (NTP) posted documents on three Usenet newsgroups in cyberspace for two purposes:

Song 1: One, Two, Three...Prosperity

1. The first purpose was to expose ersatz philosophers and cultist Objectivists who dishonestly used Usenet — specifically the newsgroup: alt.philosophy.objectivism (apo) — to promote their own false importance through mixtures of dishonest arguments and name-calling attacks against anyone who questioned their dogmas. Neo-Tech exposed their fakeries through templates of integrated facts. As a result, those cultists were driven to create a closed newsgroup — humanities.philosophy.objectivism (hpo) — designed to ban explicitly any mention of Neo-Tech and to censor any dynamic of fully integrated honesty.

Into their self-created newsgroup the cultists fled, locking the door behind. ...They had herded themselves into a caged zoo for public viewing.

Those Objectivists found they were not alone in their no-escape zoo. Unwittingly, they had locked themselves in with a warrior band of ferocious Libertarians flanked by savvy Kelley-freed Objectivists. Those warriors are now tearing to pieces the hypocritical spoutings of every flowing-robe Randian cultist. Indeed, today, those desperate cultists are arguing more shrilly, senselessly, and frequently than ever from their sealed cage. But, now, they have been publicly discredited and are unable to further retard the advance of Objectivism. As a result, propelled by integrated honesty, orgasmically exciting Neo-Tech/Objectivism is spreading throughout the World Wide Web, advancing beyond the closed circles of stagnant Ayn-Rand disciples.

Neo-Tech, as anything else, does not advance through time-wasting, do-nothing arguments on philosophical newsgroups. It advances through dynamic cyberspace communications reaching all classes of people in all nations. With 15,000 daily visits[1], the lively Neo-Tech web site introduces far more new people to Objectivist/Libertarian ideas in one day than do all the Objectivist and Libertarian sites combined in a month.[2]

With the worldwide cyber communication of Objectivist/

---

[1]Daily hit statistics are now publicly displayed on the Neo-Tech web site: http://www.neo-tech.com

[2]Neo-Tech Publishing (NTP) and its associates have always recognized and supported the many genuine, value-delivering works of Objectivists and Libertarians. For years, NTP and its associates have been financial contributors to the Ayn Rand Institute (ARI), the Institute for Objectivist Studies (IOS), and many Libertarian organizations. NTP also offered to support Dr. Peikoff's daily radio show with paid spots, but the offer was declined. Rejecting good-paying business sponsors is perhaps one reason the daily show failed commercially and now struggles as a subsidized weekend show. ...While explicitly criticizing their mystical errors and public

(footnote continued on page 9)

Libertarian values free from dogmatic elitists, cyberspace will increasingly become the Civilization of the Universe ruled by the fully integrated honesty of Neo-Tech. The Civilization of the Universe, which is an Objectivist civilization, is now entering planet Earth through Neo-Tech from cyberspace. ...Neo-Tech was made for cyberspace. Cyberspace was made for Neo-Tech.

2. The second purpose of NTP posting on Usenet was to generate commercially publishable material. Some of that commercial material is on the Neo-Tech web site and published in a book titled *Get It All*. Usenet was also used to gather the material for NTP's forthcoming book titled *Flame-War Justice*. Now, those caged Objectivist cultists are carping about NTP's intention to publish their dishonest Usenet posts without their permissions. They huff and snort about copyrights, property rights, and lawsuits. Thus, for the record, NTP states: Any dishonest, out-of-context post used to attack innocent parties has no claim under objective law for copyrights, intellectual rights, or property rights. Such posts will be used without permission at any time in any way, in part or full, by the attackee to (1) answer dishonest attackers, (2) defend against libelous attackers, (3) set the public record straight, and (4) deliver justice to dishonest attackers. Furthermore, NTP would welcome any lawsuit challenging its free use of such public posts and will mount countersuits whenever appropriate and advantageous.

NTP and its associates have always welcomed fair criticisms and honest arguments. They have gratefully learned how to change and effectively benefit from valid criticisms on the Internet. But, pips who dishonestly attack innocent value producers must deal with the poker-ruthless, sandbagging Frank R. Wallace who has a long record of subtle goading and laying back to "suck 'em in". Then, springing the fully integrated honesty of Neo-Tech, Wallace converts such attacks and adversaries into both short-term profits and long-term advantages. And, Dr. Wallace will continue to do so until maximum profits are extracted and full justice is delivered. ...Neo-Tech wins today. Neo-Tech owns tomorrow.

(footnote continued from page 8)

misbehaviors, NTP always recognizes and openly defends the values of many major Objectivist "authorities", including Harry Binswanger, Peter Schwartz, and especially the heavily pip-attacked Leonard Peikoff (even though Dr. Peikoff badly needs a banker's haircut and a Wall-Street business suit to help unleash his greatly under exploited values and power.) ...Today, caged in cyberspace, the old Objectivist preachers and their monotone choirs are being left behind by the lively spread of Neo-Tech. Sadly, their thirty years of productive efforts are now calcifying into endless, do-nothing arguments on Usenet.

Song 1

Person, Author, and Book Index
for the
Addendum, Opening Ceremonies, and Song 1

Liberation in Cyberspace
Song 2
in
Three Stanzas

Liberating

Objectivism

Stanza I

Table of Contents

Outline
for
LIBERATING OBJECTIVISM

Stanza I outlines the takeover of Objectivism by fully integrated honesty — Neo-Tech.

Stanza II reveals the cyberspace tools for vanishing Luddite Objectivists. Illustrates the lesson of tolerance and compassion without compromising philosophical principles or personal integrity.

Stanza III provides a glimpse into the future — into the coming Neo-Tech Objectivist civilization in which all conscious beings live naturally — live with eternal honesty, prosperity, and happiness.

Scng 2

Stanza #1

Song 2

LIBERATING OBJECTIVISM

Stanza I

THE LIBERATION MANIFESTO

Probably every Objectivist at some time has reasoned: "Objectivism is so logical, correct, certain. Its benefits to conscious beings are so obvious. Why isn't Objectivism applied everywhere by everyone? Why don't we have an Objectivist civilization now?" Yet, Objectivism is profitably applied almost nowhere. Why? The reason lies in the leadership of Objectivism — an obstructionist leadership. The deep-rooted failure of that leadership prevents Objectivism from spreading to populations worldwide.

Forward-moving applications of Objectivism into new areas by "outsiders" has always been resisted by a clique of self-appointed leaders and authorities. Because that clique demands "purity" before any new action can be taken, it effectively blocks practical, wide-scope applications of Objectivism in most areas of human life and business. Those ever-tightening circles of purity kept everyone ignorant of the wider-scope visions needed to evolve Objectivism into a civilization for the entire planet. ...Today, however, in cyberspace, business-driven Neo-Tech exposes the harm and dishonesties propagated by those closed-circle Objectivists.

The Liberation Manifesto

Bogus Leaders and Authorities

Demands for philosophical purity perpetuates stagnation while protecting the parasitical positions of Luddite leaders and self-appointed authorities. Deriving power from their dogmas, they must condemn anyone who deviates from their control. Like the leaders of the Catholic church during the dark ages, today's Objectivist "leaders" maintain a grip on their followers by attacking competition and condemning deviants.

Such "leaders" of Objectivism must condemn each deviant without consideration of the values that person has contributed to them, others, and society — values that usually vastly outweigh any impurity peccadillo. They must also dismiss all potential future values from that deviant. ...Those Objectivists demand a dependent, following mode from everyone.

Luddite Objectivists are cult-like Randians who attack new, unauthorized applications of Objectivism. They attack aggressive, independent doers or value producers who apply Objectivism beyond authorized realms. They declare such people immoral heretics. They attack with mantras of name-calling nouns such as wackos and adjectives such as evil. They use ad hominem attacks, out-of-context dishonesties, sweeping non sequiturs, and scenario-spun lies rather than rational arguments. Such people should examine their irrationalities and consider Marie Curie's advice: "Be less curious about people and more curious about ideas".

Those closed circles of purity protect the dogmatists from the demands of growth and evolvement — protect them from having to compete in the free market with applications of Objectivism. Listed below are three specific examples in which the dogmatists use dishonesty to avoid competition:

(1) *Politics* with its irrational, ad hominem attacks on drummed-out Objectivist Libertarians.

(2) *Psychology* with its irrational, ad hominem attacks on drummed-out Objectivist psychologist Nathaniel Branden.

(3) *Philosophy* and other academic areas with their irrational, ad hominem attacks on the many other drummed-out

Song 2

Stanza #1

Song 2

Objectivists ranging from philosopher David Kelley to economist Murray Rothbard.

Ayn Rand's Objectivist philosophy requires no leaders or authorities. Objectivism requires no defense or protection. For, Objectivism is rooted in unassailable reality. Luddite leaders block the universal application of Objectivism. Individual self-leaders on the Internet are now ousting those false leaders. Vanishing the Luddites will let Objectivism flow more freely into business, politics, and everyday life. ...No more manipulating dishonesties and ax-grinding agendas as found in their Rand/Branden, Peikoff/Kelley, and Objectivists/Libertarian type wars[1]. Instead, Objectivism will be profitably applied everywhere through Neo-Tech business dynamics. ...What about the wars with Neo-Tech? What wars? Wars do not exist with Neo-Tech. For, Neo-Tech extinguishes all wars — always to its and everyone else's eventual advantage.

Sooner or later, all Objectivists will realize no conflict exists with Neo-Tech. They will realize that Neo-Tech is the business/application mode of Objectivism. They will realize that Neo-Tech literature pushes the furthest known limits — the most future vision of Objectivist business dynamics in order to apply Objectivism to all areas of conscious life. Moreover, they will discover that the extension of Neo-Tech into Zonpower is actually an array of metaphors integrating the most advanced knowledge of objective reality.

The Zonpower theories and hypotheses are presented as metaphors, not proven facts. Yet, none of the Zonpower theories or hypotheses contradict the laws of nature. Indeed, they all correspond to the laws of physics — the laws of nature. ...Moreover, exotic names such as *Zon*, *Zonpower*, and *Cassandra's Secret* are effective marketing tools for the general population.

---

[1]For specific examples arising from those "wars", see footnote on page 18 at the end of this Stanza I.

Why Neo-Tech Sandbagged the Objectivist "Leaders"

As previously done with selected officials in government along with certain white-collar-hoax businesspeople, Neo-Tech sandbagged various self-proclaimed leaders and false authorities on the Internet as part of the world's biggest poker game. On the Objectivist newsgroup (apo), Neo-Tech sandbagged its flamers along with many ersatz Objectivists. Through that process, Neo-Tech achieved its apo agenda. One part of that agenda was to produce material needed for the forthcoming book, *Flame-War Justice,* to be released in 1997 by Neo-Tech Worldwide.

Was another part of the Neo-Tech agenda to "convert" apo Objectivists into Neo-Tech Objectivists? No. Such an agenda is too narrow and minor. Neo-Tech sandbagged the self-appointed leaders of Objectivism to break their false authorities that impeded the worldwide advance of Objectivism.

Vanishing Bogus "Leaders"

To back up some: What about those self-appointed leaders of Objectivism who continue their delusions of being Randian heroes? They use their dogmatisms to draw attention to themselves. They try to gain authority status by tying Ayn Rand's philosophy into knots of narrow-scope purity while blocking others from competitively advancing Objectivism to the masses worldwide. ...In other words, they keep themselves as big fish in a small pond.

But, Neo-Tech draws those false authorities into self-exposure traps that collapse their harmful positions. For, they are the ones who darken Ayn Rand's name and prevent the wide-spread, profitable use of her great work. Indeed, for thirty years, such people have been major impediments to the natural spread of Objectivism and its practical applications around the world.

Progress toward an Objectivist civilization comes not from do-nothing dogmatists posturing as protective purists. Progress

Song 2

Stanza #1

Song 2

comes from aggressively applying Objectivism in the real world. Genuine progress requires constant hard work — consistent discipline, thought, and control. Only by competitively applying Objectivism will the real problems of impurity be out-competed and eventually disappear. Indeed, the totally principled, no-compromise Objectivism of Rand and Peikoff is the most powerful and ultimately the only effective form of Objectivism. But, Objectivism must be competitively evolved in all areas of productive activities, not kept in ever tightening knots of hypocrisy and stagnation.

Saving Ayn Rand from Aristotle's Tragedy

Consider a parallel example of over 2000 years ago: As with Ayn Rand today, the analogous Aristotelian hangers-on stagnated his philosophy with their self-created dogmatisms. Those self-serving "hero-worshipers" buried the precious opportunity for society to advance toward an Aristotelian civilization. They buried the practical applications of Aristotle's work until the Renaissance 1500 years later. That disastrous stagnation by the Aristotelian dogmatizers eventually allowed the Catholic church to usurp a nicely petrified package of Aristotelian concepts into its official dogma.

In that way, Aristotle's name and work were darkened. His philosophy was viewed out of context, thus, was grossly misunderstood and vigorously maligned when the Renaissance arrived. Civilization-advancing giants such as Francis Bacon, Galileo, Descartes, and Newton were incensed at Aristotle and his philosophy for retarding civilization for two millennia. But, what if they had the opportunity to view Aristotle's work free of its closed-circle packaging by self-appointed "protectors" of the status quo? What if Bacon, Galileo, Descartes, and Newton knew what the dogmatist — the scholastics — had done to Aristotle and his philosophy in order to retain their self-proclaimed authorities?

Those Renaissance giants would have realized that Aristotle

was not the greatest villain against progress but the greatest hero for progress. With that recognition and their use of Aristotle's tremendous values, they would have advanced their own lives and brilliant works even further, especially Descartes. ...The ersatz-philosopher dogmatists, not Aristotle, were the villains who stunted civilization for 2000 years.

Not until the 20th century with the work of Ayn Rand did Aristotle's philosophy rise again to gain its rightful recognition and application as a supreme civilization-advancing value. ...Ayn Rand broke through and evolved Aristotle's great work in a way somewhat analogous to how Einstein broke through and evolved Newton's great work.

Consider also the example of Hippocrates and Galen: Hippocrates with his great civilization-advancing, breakthrough work in establishing the objective practice of medicine. Then, Galen, the physician/surgeon for the Roman gladiators, radically advanced the understanding of human anatomy, physiology, and the effective practice of medicine. The relationship of their work to one another is somewhat analogous to the relationship between Ayn Rand's and Leonard Peikoff's work in discovering and implementing the human-based philosophy of Objectivism.

As happened with Aristotle, the self-appointed authorities of Hippocrates and Galen — tragically with the help of Galen himself — stagnated further major advances for the next 1500 years. ...Not until the 19th century era of Louis Pasteur and Joseph Lister[1] did medicine finally resume its breakthrough advances. But, today, major advances in medicine are again being stagnated by the armed authorities of the FDA and the dishonest machinations of politicians.

---

[1]Pasteur and Lister were masters at taking their radical Zon-like hypotheses and converting them into saving literally hundreds of millions of human lives. In the past few centuries, such value-producing heroes in medicine and business have managed to enhance and save more human lives than the value-destroying bureaucrats and politicians have been able to drain and kill.

(footnote continued on next page)

Song 2: Liberating Objectivism

Will history repeat? Will the spectacular opportunity for advancing civilization through the great work of Ayn Rand and Leonard Peikoff likewise be darkened and stagnated — tragically with the help of Peikoff himself? Will the non competitive "authorities" who dogmatize Objectivism for unearned benefits succeed in burying Objectivism? Will they succeed in preventing business dynamics from unleashing its limitless values to the working populations of today's world?

Will Rand follow Aristotle's fate? Here lies the real danger of the Peikoffian dogmatists: The Catholic Inquisition used a dogmatized Aristotilian philosophy to persecute heretics, including Galileo. That principle, in turn, led to killing countless innocent people. The police-state Peikoffian hierarchy is dogmatizing Rand with its own narrow-scope spin to use government force to persecute militia members, regardless if they are guilty or innocent of objective crimes. Such a principle would eventually lead to the government killing countless innocent people. ...With the fully integrated honesty of Neo-Tech now available, no such disaster is going to occur.

"Save me from the Randians", Ayn Rand once remarked. Neo-Tech is doing that today.

Success through Commercial Dynamics

Consider Ayn Rand's and Leonard Peikoff's work: Objectivism evolved and advanced through commercial dynamics. First were the major publishers rolling out Ayn Rand's books, followed by Warner Brothers through the movie "The Fountainhead". Next came Nathaniel Branden with his own important contributions, including his highly successful NBI corporation that got commercial Objectivism rolling. And,

---

(footnote continued from previous page)
With nuclear and biological weapons available today, that positive ratio of life to death could suddenly, disastrously reverse. Only Objectivism implemented through aggressive Neo-Tech business modes can eliminate that potential disaster.

finally, came Leonard Peikoff with his forward-movement work on Objectivism and its application to new areas with his many commercial products — invaluable books, lectures, courses, tapes. Without those commercial dynamics, Objectivism today would be virtually unknown and unavailable.

Today, unfortunately, the self-serving dogmatists have drawn even Peikoff into their stagnation with his ad hominem, police-state intolerances. They are shrinking Objectivism into ever narrower purities to protect their authoritarian positions. They desperately try to prevent those beyond their influence or control from driving Objectivism forward into new and wider realms.

Today, however, the dynamic of fully integrated honesty — Neo-Tech — is breaking those closed circles of false authorities, freeing Objectivism to advance through competitive business dynamics. Moreover, the Neo-Tech self-exposure traps reveal the unprincipled, dishonest behaviors of Objectivist dogmatists. In seeking allies to fight Neo-Tech, they are now welcoming with open arms their previous "evil" enemies: the Libertarians, IOSers[1], and even scatological nihilists. ...Thus, Neo-Tech has accomplished its first mission: open up Objectivism to all comers and takers, even to its "evil" enemies.

Honesty is the Best Policy

The bottom line: Only honesty counts. So what if one holds different ideas from Objectivism? The fundamental standard of character is honesty. What more can one ask of another's character than honesty? Virtues and values originate not from truth, knowledge, or intelligence, but from those areas to which honesty is applied in identifying reality. Attacking an honest person is a bad policy — a dishonest, destructive policy. The great 19th-century railroad tycoon, Jay Gould, coined in a high-school essay the statement "Honesty is the Best Policy". Contrary to the Establishment's dishonest "Robber-Baron" attacks on Gould, his great business successes arose from a firm policy of honesty. He was poker-game ruthless, but honest: He could

---

[1]IOS: Institute for Objectivist Studies founded by Dr. David Kelley.

Song 2

Stanza #1

Song 2

be absolutely trusted on any handshake business deal. In fact, essentially every long-term, successful businessperson can be trusted. ...Honesty is not only the best policy, it is the only policy for long-term success.

Purity

What good is an "authority" on Objectivism who is dishonest while demanding purity for Objectivism? By contrast, consider the tremendous wide-scope value of the impure Bennett Cerf, the politically liberal but honest Random House publisher of the novel, *Atlas Shrugged*. He and Rand admired one another as they worked together to promote Objectivism to the general population through that novel. Likewise, many other honest businesspeople who have successfully delivered Objectivism to the public were ignorant of or even hostile to fundamental ideas of Objectivism. So what? Let any honest-based action roll out the power of Objectivism, regardless of purity or impurity of anyone's beliefs. For, lying beneath all, always ready to be tapped, is the limitless power of pure, no-compromise Objectivism identified by Rand and solidified by Peikoff.

Indeed, everyone applying Objectivism to whatever degree of dilution, such as impure libertarianism, must eventually come back to the purity of Objectivism for answers, solutions, and increased competitive power — for competitive growth.

Therein lies the tremendous market for those having expert intellectual knowledge of Objectivism: Instead of expert Objectivist dogmatists obstructing advances of Objectivism into new and wider areas, those experts can help guide the application of Objectivism into new areas. But, as with any competitive dynamic, those experts must first understand the competitive marketplace into which they would be offering or selling their expertise.

Business-Oriented Objectivism

Let unrestricted entrepreneurial applications of Objectivism explode everywhere — like the unrestricted entrepreneurial applications propelling the computer/cyberspace boom today. No need to wait for authoritarian purity that, like Godot, will never come. The foundation of Objectivism is rock solid. Current and future errors will self-correct. For, to remain competitive, all business actions will continually return to that rock-solid foundation of Ayn Rand's Objectivism brilliantly nailed down by Leonard Peikoff.

Hang that fake scholastic purity. Focus on net-profit balances. Let business-oriented Objectivism roll freely, everywhere...by everyone. Objectivism will take over the future. Rand and Peikoff have done their work well. Hopefully, Peikoff and other contributors to Objectivism will now break from that circling-wagon syndrome in order to stay competitive and help further advance Objectivism.

Let the power of business-oriented Objectivism roll. The dynamics of wide-open competition and business will drive out the bad — the anticivilization. As the anticivilization fades, an Objectivist civilization will rise. That rising civilization of competitive doers will bring the Civilization of the Universe to planet Earth.

The Business of Neo-Tech

Neo-Tech Worldwide is an ad hoc company designed to put itself out of business upon accomplishing its goal of vanishing this anticivilization so a business-oriented Objectivist civilization can arise. Only then can the Neo-Tech business owners and employees effectively return to their intended business of Bio-Medical Research free of government destructions, especially the FDA — free to pursue its genetic research and human cloning for the elimination of disease, aging, and death.

Today, Neo-Tech Publishing is investing its profits and capital in providing free, universal values on Web sites across cyberspace. The immediate goal is to liberate conscious minds from their closed-circle thinking modes — to release conscious thinking into the widest possible perspectives. Each such

13

conscious mind will then see Earth's civilization from a radically different perspective. Each will realize that all conscious beings on planet Earth suffer and perish from one basic disease — the disease of irrationality from which flows this anticivilization with all its dishonesties, harms, and criminalities.

A Criminal-Based Anticivilization
versus
A Business-Based Objectivist Civilization

Dogmatists seeking false authority have always existed in this anticivilization. In most cases, such dogmatists captured bogus doctrines and then brought out the worst in those doctrines — doctrines ranging from murderous communism and Islam...to violent anti-abortion positions that advocate killing doctors...to government-promoted fat-free (eat-all-you-want carbohydrate) diets that deliver obesity and diabetes to kill health, happiness, and life itself. Objectivism, by contrast, is valid with no harmful aspects to attack. Thus, the Objectivist dogmatists corral powerful "advantages" in having hog-tied a valid, rational doctrine. Nevertheless, such Objectivists are soul mates to those living off murderous doctrines. Not only are they stealing from everyone's present life, they are stealing from everyone's future.

From every perspective, the anticivilization is an inherently diseased, criminal-based civilization. Yet, by breaking through today's closed-circle thinking modes, one discovers a healthy, business-based Objectivist civilization. ...One then discovers the Civilization of the Universe.

Indeed, by recognizing the unnecessity of this irrational anticivilization, one realizes that a fully operating Objectivist civilization can prevail on planet Earth — not after decades or centuries, but now, over the next few years!

The Role of Zonpower

The function of Zonpower is to break people from their stagnant thinking traps. Zonpower frees people to think and act independently, on their own, from the widest possible perspectives — from the most powerful integrations. The thrilling discovery which awaits everyone is that essentially every problem, big and small, can be solved with maximum benefits once the facts are explicitly put into the widest-scope context of Zonpower.

*****

Tradition must always yield to the newly evolving facts of objective reality for conscious life to survive and prosper. But consider the tremendous resistance to fundamental change. Consider Pope Pius IX's closed-circle attack on Charles Darwin and his "outlandish" work on evolution — work that radically changed everyone's fundamental perspective and thinking about human life on planet Earth:

> *[Darwin's system] is a system repudiated by history, by the traditions of people, by exact science, by the observation of facts, and even by reason itself... The corruption of the century, the guile of the depraved, the danger of oversimplification, demand that such dreamings, absurd as they are, be refuted by science, since they wear the mask of science.*

Pope Pius, IX

Such are the popish attacks on Zonpower, especially on its physics, on its view of civilization, on its view of the Universe.

Consider what Galileo said concerning radically changed views about physics, civilization, and the Universe:

> *Facts which at first seem impossible...drop the cloak which has hidden them and they stand forth in naked beauty.*

Galilei Galileo

Indeed, the Civilization of the Universe will arrive as nature's naked beauty through Neo-Tech physics that start with new-world songs and end with a new-color symphony: *Zonpower from*

15

Song 2

Stanza #1

Song 2

Cyberspace. Through that symphony, conscious beings sublimate to eternal prosperity and happiness.

The Harm of Closed-Circle Objectivism
versus
The Value of Wide-Open Objectivism

What does one need in order to reap the benefits of Objectivism? One needs courage, independence, fully integrated honesty combined with the wide-open, business applications of Objectivism. Until this Liberation Manifesto, most Objectivists were afraid of independence — afraid to vanish their leaders and authorities. They were afraid of criticism, of condemnation, of being excommunicated by the high "priests" of Objectivism. ...Thus, they clung to their deadly investments in this anticivilization.

Objectivists become free by independently wielding competitive, action-mode Objectivism. And those who do not free themselves? They will wither and die for some self-proclaimed authority. They will die for their investments in this anticivilization.

Neo-Tech Objectivism offers no icons, leaders, or authorities. Through Neo-Tech Objectivism, each individual lives productively, independently, happily. Indeed, the prize is eternal prosperity and happiness. ...Without fully integrated Objectivism, all crumble to dust. Through fully integrated Objectivism, all rise to the Civilization of the Universe.

Booming Objectivism

Liberating Objectivism will boom the money-making business interests of the Objectivist establishment. Currently, Luddites fear that the liberation of Objectivism will cause a decline in revenues — a decline in (1) support for the scholarly and academic works of Objectivism, (2) attendance at the lucrative Objectivist conferences, and (3) sales of Objectivist-oriented books and tapes. Yet, any diminishment of financial support for the scholarly and business activities of the Objectivist establishment would contradict the goal of Neo-Tech Worldwide.

Neo-Tech Worldwide explicitly recognizes the outstanding values and accomplishments of Objectivist intellectuals, their publications, their conferences, their organizations, and the apo/hpo[1] Usenet newsgroups. Neo-Tech Worldwide along with many of its employees and associates have long admired and supported, both directly and indirectly, the work of Objectivist intellectuals...and will continue to do so.

Brushing aside the above Luddite fear, all Objectivist markets will expand. Objectivism will boom not only financially but in effectiveness and influence. For, the Objectivist establishment has the values and products to market competitively worldwide. They have the most important values for conscious beings on Earth. ...Liberating Objectivism will benefit everyone — more than anyone can imagine.

Neo-Tech/Objectivism

With the publication and distribution of this *Profound Honesty* manuscript, the Neo-Tech/Objectivist writing machine begins inscribing justice into the minds and bodies of people living dishonestly through their investments in this anticivilization.

What is the time frame to complete this inscription process? In Kafka's anticivilization "Penal Colony", his horrendous justice-inscription process took six hours to realize its effects and twelve hours to complete the process. In the real world, a person starts being inscribed on reading *Profound Honesty*. The equivalent time scale to completion for each individual will vary, perhaps from as quick as one-month real time per Kafka hour increasing up to one-year real time per Kafka hour.

Through Profound Honesty, everyone will eventually become inscribed with Neo-Tech/Objectivism. ...Everyone will then experience justice, prosperity, happiness.

---

[1] apo = alt.philosophy.objectivism
hpo = humanities.philosophy.objectivism

Song 2

Stanza #1

Song 2

Song 2: *Liberating Objectivism*

****
(Below is the footnote referred to on page 6)

Consider the specious Objectivist/Libertarian conflict initiated by Ayn Rand. Her own Luddite mode was followed with a vengeance by Leonard Peikoff and his cohorts. Ad hominem evilization of impure Objectivists became standard practice:

Indeed, specific statements and actions by Libertarians contradict at times certain ideas and principles of Objectivism, just as Ayn Rand and Leonard Peikoff contradicted at times the ideas and principles of Objectivism. Yet, the foundations of Libertarianism require the philosophy of Objectivism. Moreover, Libertarianism points the direction toward a practical Objectivist civilization far more principled and uncompromised than any political movement in history. Indeed, Libertarianism would deliver significantly more Objectivist principles in government than America's founding fathers ever envisioned.

Then why do the Luddite Objectivists rightfully praise America's founding fathers while heaping scorn on today's principled Libertarians? Why in 1996 did they heap scorn on the most Objectivist-rooted presidential candidate in history — Harry Browne? ...Indeed, the closer any person or thing comes to actually implementing or advancing Objectivism into new or unsanctioned areas, the more emotionally virulent become the attacks by the Luddite Objectivists. Why? Competition. Competition will knock stagnant Objectivist "leaders" out of their cozy, flowing-robes positions of unearned authority.

Advances of Objectivism beyond its sanctioned, closed-circle domains threaten those dogmatists with extinction. But, why stop with the Luddite Objectivists? The 1996 Libertarian presidential candidate, Harry Browne, clearly offered far more benefits and happiness to all citizens than any politician in American history. By contrast, Bill Clinton is one of the most dishonest, destructive politicians in American history. Yet, hold a political fund-raiser for Harry Browne where perhaps a hundred of the most ardent Libertarian supporters may show up. A sincere, honest Harry Browne delivers a stunningly practical picture of freedom and prosperity through minimal government based mainly on Objectivist principles. Some muted applause is heard and perhaps $4000 in campaign contributions is raised.

Now, in that same area, hold a political fund raiser for Bill Clinton. A crowd of two thousand or more citizens show up. A hypocritical, pervasively dishonest Bill Clinton delivers a silver-tongued, FDR-like speech about irrationally increasing government activities that harm everyone. A cheering, standing ovation is heard and a million dollars in campaign contributions is raised.

How can such ad hoc irrationalities exist in *everyone* — from Randian Objectivists to Libertarian supporters to Clinton liberals? How? Why? Buddy, this is the anticivilization. Everyone has a stake invested in this anticivilization, including the Randian Objectivists and Libertarian supporters alike. A Neo-Tech/Objectivist civilization threatens that stake. *Everyone* in the anticivilization subconsciously fears a totally honest, free-enterprise civilization. No one in the anticivilization, including Objectivists and Libertarians, really want that kind of freedom and responsibility. All want their ad hoc dishonesties and irrationalities to protect their anticivilization investments.

Neo-Tech/Zonpower breaks that self-defeating paradox. How? By using Objectivism, the Neo-Tech/Zonpower dynamic breaks each anticivilization investment encountered, thus, opening the way to an Objectivist civilization — the Civilization of the Universe.

18

Liberating Objectivism

Stanza II

Tools that Win Flame Wars

Time-Saving Templates

cyberspace tools that vanish

Pips, Blowhards, Journalists

and

Nihilists

Any of the Templates listed herein may be copied and reproduced
in part or whole without permission
For latest versions see web site http://www.neo-tech.com/

Flame-War Policy of Neo-Tech Publishing

Most flame wars in cyberspace consist of segments from Usenet posts taken out of context and then attacked — often using ad hominem arguments. ...Flame wars are generally time-consuming, ineffective, and quickly forgotten — a waste of time. Neo-Tech Publishing never initiates flames, only responds in order to protect innocent targets from unjust attacks.

Neo-Tech Publishing has three decades of experience in confronting and squelching unjust attacks on innocent business people by pips — by dishonest academics, establishment journalists, and gun-toting bureaucrats.

The key to benefiting from flames is to design widely integrated, fully honest templates that reduce each flame to an underlying principle based on objective reality. Such templates are permanently valuable and publishable. ...Through their strident complaints, pips themselves demonstrate the effectiveness of such templates. For, those templates reduce them to nonentities — to blatant insignificance.

The Always-Profit Rule

Do not consume irreplaceable time making one-time, quickly forgotten posts and responses. Instead, fashion principled templates anchored in reality to extinguish unjust flames or dishonest attacks. ...Then collect those principled templates for future postings in cyberspace and profitable publications in print. Below are examples of five such templates:

[Notes: 1. These templates are available on FTP sites for free use by anyone on the Internet. See http://www.neo-tech.com for easy copying and pasting of these templates.

2. A most effective response is often achieved by sandwiching a pip attack between, for example, Template #1 and #2 or between Template #1 and #3. Hit with repeated templates, pips shrink into their nothingness. ...In addition to these five templates, an essentially limitless number of powerful templates can be custom constructed by assembling various segments from *Profound Honesty* to squelch pip attacks, in or out of cyberspace.]

List of Templates

Template #1
Who are Pips

Generally pips are dishonest losers who produce few if any *competitive* values for others and society. They seldom if ever exert the hard efforts required to do something really excellent with their lives — something about which they can be proud.

Pips are people who purposely attack values by distorting out-of-context fragments of those values. Using those distortions, pips attack values with false but logical-sounding criticisms. They often conjure up straw men to bash. ...Pips create problems where none exist.

The obsession with and anger over Neo-Tech templates among pips on various Internet newsgroups demonstrate the effectiveness of such templates. Indeed, these templates clearly, precisely identify the dishonesty and malevolence of those people. Thus, such templates should be used whenever appropriate. They are always effective and never lose their punch. More important, they save precious time needed for productive activities.

What Does Pipping Mean? Why Do Losers Pip?

Pipping involves attacking values by isolating out-of-context fragments of the achievements produced by others or their businesses. Pipping means building one's ego by manipulating with words rather than by producing genuine values. Pipping is done to make a loser appear superior to and more moral than the achievements or businesses being attacked.

Pips reject any response that places their distorted fragments back into context. Pips refuse to understand the full context of the values they are attacking. They are not interested in values, honesty, accuracy, answers, explanations, or learning. They are only interested in the level of ego enhancement they can conjure up through spurious attacks on values. Thus, once pipping is detected, further communication or argument is worthless and should cease so no more irreplaceable time is wasted. A principled template such as this becomes an effective response. The attacking pip will then stand alone, recognized as someone seeking unearned importance. Hence, malicious,

21

attack-mode pips will first vanish from cyberspace and then from the world. ...Justice will be served. Everyone will profit.

Throughout history, before cyberspace, civilization-benefiting giants and their work were constantly attacked, always injured, and sometimes destroyed by self-proclaimed "victims" and attack-mode pips.[1] Yet, valid questions and sincere criticisms concerning radically new values will naturally occur. An important example is Objectivist philosophy with its live-action applications of Neo-Tech and Zonpower. Such valuable questions and criticisms deserve patient, respectful responses. But, when ego-pumping pipping is detected, further communication not only wastes irreplaceable time of the respondent, but feeds that pip's ego, allowing him or her to continue draining values created by others. ...Simply template such losers. Let them complain. The templates will eventually vanish them.

Template #2

Giants versus Twerps

Who knows the fierce battle it takes to start from nothing except an idea, and from that idea to build livelihoods, values, jobs, and prosperity for entire populations?

Jay Gould knew, Henry Ford knew, Leona Helmsley knew, Michael Milken knew along with too many other unsung giants. Indeed, each were attacked in a thousand ways by countless twerps, pips, ex-beneficiaries, fired employees, professional value destroyers, government bureaucrats, parasitical elites, ego prosecutors/judges, and demagogic politicians.

Those entrepreneurs knew about fighting day and night, year after year to build job-creating businesses that deliver competitive values to society — values that advance civilization.

---

[1]Business people, honest entrepreneurs, and professional value producers no longer need to stand helpless while being drained by parasitical elites, dishonest journalists, and professional value destroyers. For, those parasites depend on the attacks of "victims" and pips to drain values from heroic value producers. But, now, the value producers can compose and use an endless variety of Neo-Tech templates extracted from *Profound Honesty* to vanish attacking "victims", pips, and professional value destroyers.

Such business people tragically must consume irreplaceable chunks of their precious lives in throwing off envious parasites and do-nothing nonentities who constantly try to drain them and diminish the values they produce for society.

Only those precious few entrepreneurs know the fierce struggle required to competitively succeed where countless others fail. Only they have the toughness to battle nonstop in solving and overcoming the never ending flood of life-or-death survival problems. They seldom or never can "go home" after work to entertainment or diversions. They seldom or never can kick back in the evenings, on weekends, or on vacations. They seldom or never can leave their work or responsibilities. ...Such people do not collect paychecks from others. They create the paychecks that others live on. Such is their responsibility. They work to solve problems that do exist, not to create problems that do not exist.

In a week or even a day, the entrepreneur business builder can face and must solve more survival problems than most people face in a lifetime. Any one of those countless problems can be taken out of context by a malicious value destroyer ranging from a fired ex-employee trying to financially shake down his ex-employer to a nihilistic pip trying to pump up his shrunken self-worth.

What kind of people dishonestly, enviously, maliciously attack the good? What kind of people feel, think, and act in such purposely destructive ways? In Stalin's Soviet Union, Mao's China, and Hitler's Germany, how many millions of value producers met their deaths because of such pips? In America, today, countless envy-shriveled pips stand ready to destroy heroic, competitive value-and-job producers through jail or death as a police state of armed bureaucrats arises — a police state arising today from the self-aggrandizing agendas of criminal-minded politicians and dishonest journalists.

Many pips collect paychecks from tax-funded sources, from tenured-academe positions, from statist-establishment positions,

Song 2

Stanza #2

Song 2

23

or from companies they hate. Indeed, such pips lack the courage, discipline, and effort to profitably build competitive values for themselves, others, and society. Instead, they expose their essence by attacking objective values produced by others while making problems where none exist. Various examples of such pips are provided in the forthcoming book *Flame-War Justice* from Neo-Tech Worldwide.

In any case, such pips and nihilists have no understanding of what it takes to start, build, and run competitive businesses that ultimately provide the livelihoods and well beings for them and everyone else on Earth. And, who else besides such value destroyers has the time or inclination to pip — to ego pump by purposely dragging down successes and values created by others? ...Neo-Tech stands alone in protecting value-and-job producers from intentional value destroyers.

Template #3
Zonpower and Salvador Dali's "Last Supper"

One of the most breathtaking paintings of any age is Salvador Dali's "Last Supper". And, as many Objectivists know, that painting was one of Ayn Rand's favorites. Jesus appears indescribably beautiful, innocent, and benevolent. He appears as the Chairman presiding over a Universe-500 board meeting. Notice even the neatly cropped, modern New York executive haircuts of the Apostles. Dali delivered a radical presentation of Christ never before seen among the thousands of holy paintings by hundreds of master artists over the millennium.

Imagine this crystal-clear painting being cast as a giant, ten-thousand-piece jigsaw puzzle. Now, imagine a dishonest blowhard, journalist, or nihilist — a pip — plucking a piece, any piece, or a handful of pieces, from that painting. Then imagine that pip waving those pieces before a public who had never before seen the whole picture of that masterpiece. Using glib words and dishonest non sequiturs, that pip harangues his audience: In tearing down the great value of Dali and his masterpiece, that pip captures an unearned ego trip.

The pip simply needs to hold up the piece or pieces of the puzzle ripped from the total picture and loudly proclaim: "Look at this Dali-crap! It's valued only by Dali-kooks. This proves that Daliism is new-age cult stuff, pseudo art, a sham", the pip blusters. The attacking pip then swells up with feel-big ego for publicly, effortlessly exposing the Dali "fraud". Through his unjust no-effort attack, the pip feels superior to the lifetime hard efforts produced by Dali.

Those who had never seen Dali's complete painting could not know that the facts were the opposite to the non sequiturs being dishonestly pronounced. How could they know that the exposing "hero" was really a nothingness fraud while the exposed "fraud" was a beautiful gem?

In the same way, pips throughout the establishment constantly tear down Ayn Rand and her work. Likewise, in that same way, pips have often torn down, even killed or destroyed, the most radical yet greatest of civilization-benefiting value producers throughout history — Socrates, Galileo, Michael Milken.

Zonpower found on home page http://www.neo-tech.com/ reflects the most radical value and widest-scope integration in history. Today, the way to know the full power and beauty of Zonpower is to see the entire, fully integrated picture with all its puzzle pieces locked into place. For those not owning this manuscript in a printed book form, that full picture can be achieved by downloading and reading the *entire* web site. But, as opposed to easily reading the printed book, gaining full integrations and understandings from the web-site requires much time and effort.

Because of the vast scope and tight interdependencies of the Zonpower integrations, the printed-book version with all its diagrams, illustrations, and footnotes properly positioned is much easier, quicker, and more convenient to read. The physical book itself lets one see the assembled pieces in an elegant picture of Dali-like beauty. That picture shows who is the heroic value producer and who is the malevolent value destroyer.

Song 2: Liberating Objectivism

Template #4
Objectivist Heroes
(see pages 9-12 of Closing Ceremonies)

Template #5
(Media Template)

Rolling the DICE of Media Pips

Neo-Tech rolls the DICE for the biggest army of professional value destroyers — dishonest journalists. Against Neo-Tech, the dice come up snake eyes for media pips every time.

DICE
Dishonesty, **I**gnorance, **C**owardliness, **E**nvy
The Essence of Journalist/Media Pips

•*Dishonesty* arises in purposely ripping out of context bits and pieces from the values being attacked and then destroying those values through concealed dishonesties, manipulations, distortions, and non sequiturs.

•*Ignorance* arises through intention, carelessness, or laziness in not becoming informed concerning the full facts about the subject of their attacks.

•*Cowardliness* arises in hiding behind deceptive facades and camouflages throughout the media.

•*Envy* arises in malevolently trying to destroy objective values because they *are* objective values — competitive values for others and society that the attackers themselves cannot produce. Only by destroying competitive values produced by others can the envy attackers feel important enough to sustain their livelihoods based on harmful dishonesties.

26

Stanza III

A Glimpse into the Future

An Early Introduction
to

QUANTUM CROSSINGS

(to be constructed on the World Wide Web)

Twelve Quantum Crossings

to the

Civilization of the Universe

The Introduction to Quantum Crossings
is dedicated to
The First Honest Business Leader of Western Civilization:
King Hiero II of Syracuse
In his 54 year reign from 270 BC to 216 BC
his only agenda was peace and progress.
He ruled without armed bureaucrats
He ruled without killing, exiling, or injuring a single citizen
Business not only flourished
but Archimedes, history's greatest inventor, also flourished
In such an atmosphere,
Jesus Christ superstar carpenter
could have built the ancient world's tallest skyscraper
and provided ten-thousand jobs
instead of becoming a self-sacrificing mystic
that cost civilization its free-enterprise economies.
Constantine could have been "The Great" forever
Jay Gould could be alive today
commanding Wall Street with Micheal Milken
Today, here comes Neo-Tech
here comes
Prosperity, Excitement, Romance

Song 2

Song 2

Stanza #3

From
Aeschylus, Sophocles, Epicurus
to the
Businessman-Poet Wallace Stevens
and the
Music of Rush
civilization marches forward
Yet, high above drama, poem, and song
shines
Ayn Rand
elevated from the shadows
by
Branden, Peikoff, Neo-Tech

From teachings and words, civilizations grow
Earth's anticivilization grew
within
Plato's cave for two millennia
Today, crafted dishonesties
in speeches, prose, and journalism
yield
looters, parasites, and killers
hidden by
Homeric heroes, mystical shadows, and noble lies

Behold!
Cyberspace has arrived
Profound Honesty
outcompetes dishonesties
be them
darkly hidden or widely open

Profound Honesty
jumps beyond Earth's anticivilization
into a
Neo-Tech Civilization
into the
Civilization of the Universe

Stanza III
Table of Contents

Introduction

To survive and prosper, the parasitical-elite ruling classes of the anticivilization artfully craft glorious memories of criminal Homeric-hero leaders ranging from Alexander the Great, Julius Caesar and Napoleon Bonaparte to Abraham Lincoln, Woodrow Wilson, and FDR.

More important, to survive, any parasitical ruling class must malign or vanish the memories of history's greatest, competitive value producers. Indeed, criminal-minded leaders have buried the memories of business-minded leaders such as King Hiero II, Jay Gould, and Calvin Coolidge whose prime focus was rationality, peace, and prosperity. And, today, a person like Mark Hamilton or Eric Savage could, as early as 2001AD, become one of those rare business-minded leaders.

Quantum Crossings will vanish the criminal-minded icons and celebrities of this irrational anticivilization while resurrecting the business-minded heroes dwelling in the rational Civilization of the Universe.

Song 2

Stanza #3

Song 2

QUANTUM CROSSINGS

Under construction for the World Wide Web is a primary epic poem. This is the first such epic poem in a thousand years — the first since *Beowulf* in 1000 AD. A primary epic poem not only breaks the eons of conscious silence forever before, but breaks the conscious norm forever after. When nothing is understandable, when nothing is explainable, when communication and understanding break down, only poem and song communicate unity, for better or worse, through everyone's right-hemisphere brain. Neither ignorance nor rationalization from left-hemisphere brains can block that unity. ...No mechanism or defense can prevent primary epics from changing civilizations.

The newly evolving epic, *Quantum Crossings*, will be continuously edited and expanded into thousands of pages. From that epic, the anticivilization will disappear chunk by chunk as the Civilization of the Universe appears jump by jump.

From *Quantum Crossings* will spring the Protocols for the Civilization of the Universe. Those Protocols will turn all major scientific-and-medical research toward health, happiness, and prosperity. How? By unleashing individual competitive business, not gun-point collectivist governments, to eliminate war, crime, mysticism, irrationality, disease, aging, and death.

A Glimpse into the Future

Preliminary Outline
for
Quantum Crossings

THREE FOUNDATIONS
I. Literature Creates Conscious Civilizations
II. Sabotaging the Anticivilization
III. Quantum Crossings to the Civilization of the Universe

TWELVE QUANTUM CROSSINGS
to the
CIVILIZATION OF THE UNIVERSE

Crossing 1: Youth
Crossing 2: Power beyond the Gods
Crossing 3: Power Lost
Crossing 4: Anticivilization Addiction
Crossing 5: Failure and Death
Crossing 6: Quantum Escape
Crossing 7: Life without Mysticism
Crossing 8: Politics without Guns
Crossing 9: Power Regained
Crossing 10: Individual Enterprise Eternal
Crossing 11: Prosperity Forever
Crossing 12: Civilization of the Universe

Song 2

Stanza #3

Song 2

31

Literature Creates Conscious Civilizations

The Odyssey, The Aeneid, The Divine Comedy, The Canterbury Tales, Paradise Lost, The Pilgrim's Progress, Gulliver's Travels, and *Faust* were journeys that created Western civilization. Homer, Plato, Virgil, Dante, Boccaccio, Chaucer, Shakespeare, Bunyan, Swift, Kant[1], Goethe, Balzac, all took journeys that advanced Earth's anticivilization. In the context of this anticivilization, regardless of philosophical errors, those travelers did their work right — exactly right, powerfully right. That fact must be understood to advance beyond this anticivilization.[2]

The lone saboteur was Ayn Rand with her epic *Atlas Shrugged.* Yet, she and her great work were trapped in purgatory — trapped in the unbridgeable gulf between this anticivilization and the Civilization of the Universe.

By contrast, an evolving primary epic called *Quantum Crossings* will reveal a dramatic mind-altering journey for all conscious beings. A journey from this anticivilization into the Civilization of the Universe. In *Quantum Crossings*, the protagonist, Iu, in a life-and-death race for planet Earth, crafts twelve keys to open twelve gates that allow conscious beings to jump across the twelve unbridgeable gulfs leading to the Civilization of the Universe.

[1]Acting without sufficient knowledge and contrary to Objectivism, both Rand and Peikoff subjectively, emotionally attacked Immanuel Kant as "the most evil person who ever lived". When, in fact, Kant was a kind, gentle person who through a lifetime of hard, sincere work produced a key value for mankind: He comprehensively integrated and systematized the philosophy underlying the irrationality dominating this civilization. Thus, Kant's work serves as a valuable servant for advancing Objectivism. By juxtaposing his articulated philosophical system against Objectivism, Earth's anticivilization can finally be understood. Only with that understanding can this criminal-driven civilization be undermined, sabotaged, then finally collapsed and vanished. ...Eternal thanks must be given to Kant, Rand, Peikoff, and fully integrated honesty for the coming Objectivist civilization — for the coming business-driven Civilization of the Universe.

[2]The modern or existential writers of the 20th century such as Proust, Joyce, Sartre, and Beckett do not hold the civilization-determining power of the classicists. Kafka and Camus are two exceptions: Kafka for his "The Law" and his "Writing Machine" (in which the jailer changes places with the prisoner to understand justice) serve to symbolize the metaphysics of this anticivilization; and Camus for his projecting love and happiness as the noble pursuits in this anticivilization. Also, Faulkner captures the soul of dishonest journalists and Letterman-type nihilists. Indeed, their sound and fury mean nothing. Still, Sartre's *Nausea* and Beckett's *Godot* in their Theaters of the Absurd are correct. Even from feminist/lesbian poet Adrienna Rich, we learn and advance. For, this is the anticivilization. And, their work brought forth the understanding needed to sabotage the anticivilization out of existence.

A Glimpse into the Future

Who is Sabotaging this Anticivilization?

Saboteur Supreme
Ayn Rand's anger hid her exquisite victory
Rejected by the intelligentsia, the academe, the media
Ignored by the establishment rulers and big-business leaders
Minimized, ridiculed, ignored by the high, the mighty
Without exception
No establishment elite acknowledges her supreme accomplishment
Not yesterday, not today, never

No establishment figure has ever risen to proclaim
Ayn Rand's Objectivism as civilization's most valuable product
As in Henrik Ibsen's themes of fearing the light
Establishment elites must fear the most brilliant light
The light of fully integrated honesty

Objectivism: the universal philosophy of facts and reason
Based upon the universal needs of conscious beings
Objectivism: eternally benefiting conscious beings
Through fully integrated honesty
Under any conditions, throughout time and space

II
Trapped in literature naiveness
Ranging from Homer and Shakespheare to Blake and Whitman
Ayn Rand lived in her world of narrow-scope accuracies
She lived in her world of blind naiveness
Naive to the wide-scope context of philosophers from Plato to Kant
Naive to the wide-scope power behind the classics of literature
Naive to the anticivilization in which she invested

She never understood why the classics were classics
Or how such classics deliver to the establishment its power
Or why those classics deliver tremendous values that advance civilization

In this anticivilization, mighty authors craft their works correctly
Despite their philosophical errors
The classics control their subjects with an iron grip
For, such crafted words mold all who follow
Even Proust in his life cycle of memories did it right
So did Joyce with his awesome works of nothingness
Along with Sartre's and Beckett's monuments to the Absurd
For, this is the anticivilization
And that is why even the existentialists did their work correctly

In her innocence, Ayn Rand never understood their accomplishments
Thus, she never perceived the establishment's deep secret
The secret of why establishment intellectuals must never accept
Honest value producers, especially giants like Ayn Rand

33

Stanza 2: Liberating Objectivism

In her innocence
She could never belong
Ayn Rand the Saboteur

III
Never belonging made Ayn Rand angry and discouraged
Never belonging made her coworkers frustrated and baffled
Never belonging made her followers shut their minds
None could see beyond this anticivilization

Objectivism will never be proclaimed by establishment elites
Or by anyone whose self-esteem is invested in this anticivilization
Objectivism is never going to be accepted by establishment rulers
So look beyond

IV
But wait! Why look beyond?
Today arises an upward attention sweep
For Ayn Rand and her work
An upward sweep among the establishment
The influence of "Atlas Shrugged" topped only by the Bible
Both read by the Pope today
Victory at last?

No. No victory. No victory ever in this anticivilization
That upward sweep is a fashion surge
A fashion surge captured by the dynamics of profitable business
A fashion surge driven by establishment egos

In the past, *The Fountainhead*, then its movie, and finally *Atlas Shrugged*
Also brought fashion surges from the establishment elites
But, each such surge was emasculated with political correctness
Emasculated with mixes of distortion and equivocation
Emasculated with ridicule or scorn by strutting nihilists

No establishment authority, no establishment powerhouse
No establishment star ever recognized Objectivism as Earth's greatest value
Not then, not now, never
Objectivism threatens the establishment elites

V
Consider those few who break their establishment dependencies
Those who end their investments in this anticivilization
They are the few who can look far, far ahead — toward eternity
They are the few who can see new-color dimensions
In which corrupt establishments and their authorities vanish forever

Consider those free souls who look across the abyss
Into wide-scope reality
Through fully integrated honesty, they hear a symphony
The Symphony of the Universe
They see an approaching civilization
The Civilization of the Universe

34

A Glimpse into the Future

VI

Today, an engine of fully integrated honesty is planted deep
Deep into the veins of this moribund anticivilization
That engine is Neo-Tech
Neo-Tech is fully integrated honesty in action
An engine that injects Objectivism into every act

Neo-Tech opens the gates to quantum crossings
Opens the gates for journeys into wide-scope reality
Into the Civilization of the Universe
Into fully integrated honesty

VII

Allegory reveals the first Quantum Crossing:
Theism is never proclaimed by Hell's elite
Satanism is never hailed by Heaven's elite.
Objectivism is never celebrated by the Anticivilization's elite
Arbitrary, subjectivist philosophies are unknown
In the immortal Civilization of the Universe

Can Hell be Heaven? Can Heaven be Hell?
Can the Anticivilization be the Civilization of the Universe?
Can the Civilization of the Universe be the Anticivilization?
Can A be Z? Or Z be A?
Can death be life? Can life be death?

VIII

Victory is now available for everyone, everywhere, forever.
The gate swings open to the first of twelve crossings
Crossings into wide-scope reality
Crossings into the Civilization of the Universe
Untouched and untouchable by this unreal, mystical anticivilization
Untouched by hecklers, nihilists, and parasitical elites
Untouched by professional value destroyers

The Anticivilization's destination
Means eternal death from nihilistic nothingness
The Civilization of the Universe's destination
Means eternal life from productive prosperity

Ayn Rand saboteur supreme
Her exquisite victory is sublime
Now rising toward the Civilization of the Universe
Nihilists vanish in non competitiveness
Unable to exist in an Objectivist civilization

Stand up
A toast to Ayn Rand
The Saboteur
Fully integrated honesty is here forever

Introduction Topics
for the
Civilization of the Universe

The rigid structures of rhyme and meter change into less rigid structures of meter only then phase into entirely new, conceptual structures of facts and logic that unstoppably enter the right-hemisphere brain via free verse, which in turn will lead to unstoppable left-brain prose — *The Zon Protocols*.

EPICS
Homer's *Iliad* does come first
Delivers life for better or worse
Beowulf points to future fights
Quantum Crossings will end the nights

Epics and poems from far shores
Broke the silence of closed doors
An epic sung to the future now
Will free us from the deadly past

When nothing is explicable,
Nothing is understandable
When communication crumbles,
Epics and poems unite our minds

Traveling beyond time and space
Primary epics fill each place
Free from our neglect or regret
Rising above all friends and foes

Circling high with quiet breath
Singing songs of failure and death
Plato converts workers to slaves
Not even God can break the chains

Virgil and Ovid gripped the past
Using the state to crush life fast
Quantum Crossings bring the future
Far beyond all El Dorados

36

A Glimpse into the Future

YOUTH

Above high God rise youthful might
Soon forgotten in mystic flight
We grow old by dying young
All lost in clouds of God-filled frauds

Binding tight each lively spirit,
Rulers bury the powers of youth
Who will break the grimness of death
To let young spirits rise anew

Rulers on high drain those below
Denying all control of life
Each youth soon trapped in stifling cells
Locked away from growth eternal

Who else will know the hidden truth
Of powers beyond each quick youth
Who else can find the facts right now
To break the grip of gods before

Narrow blackness of rulers past
Or widest light of future bright
The answer lies forever now
In jumping past abyss-like gaps

Quantum Crossings bring keys anew
For love and joy to young and old
The maps of life will show new ways
From which arise eternal wealth

The first step now to break the binds
Finding new keys to open each gate
Vanishing ghosts of past and now
Beyond which lie unbounded life

Song 2: Liberating Objectivism

IU

Iu is we born upon Earth
Life without life, peace without peace
Whence comes progress with no progress
Then comes justice with no justice

Teaching Iu to live for doom
Rulers smother children in bloom
Crushing the minds of all on Earth
Forcing on each, eyes so blind

Compassion blocked by force and guns
Iu's spirit soon succumbs
Leaving facts in prisons dark
Moving blindly from life to death

Yet Iu awoke to new ways
Seeking knowledge beyond the gods
Till lost in altruistic scams
That swap our joy for bleak salvation

Where is growth without stagnation?
Where is bright light without dark gloom?
Where is good life without grim death?
Silence from all, even the gods

Students locked in guarded jails
No way out, tenured teachers preach
Which way out? Iu asks anew
Silence from all, even high God

Years fly by, faster and faster
Iu grows older, younger still
Growing young while growing old
The secret is no secret now

Force brings each code of sacrifice
Till Iu finds the code of life
Rulers on high breathe fire and smoke
Lest Iu frees five-billion slaves

Each upon Earth creates the stars
Who knows those gifts beyond the gods
How soon will Iu rise again
To bring to all eternal life

A Glimpse into the Future

Other Topics to be Posted

before the publication of

Quantum Crossings

Value Producers vs. Value Destroyers
Business vs. Politics
Freedom vs. Addiction
Rationality vs. Irrationality
Reality vs. Mysticism
Health vs. Sickness
Productive Minds vs. Criminal Minds
Objective Law vs. Subjective Law
Honesty vs. Truth
Life vs. Death.

Herein lies the keys to limitless prosperity, power, and romantic love. The keys to the Civilization of the Universe.

CROSSING 1
(under construction)

YOUTH

A newborn cried
Iu awoke
Seventy years or so from then
Iu's eyes should close forever
Like all conscious beings born upon Earth
So says the laws from scriptures supreme
With armed rulers to make those laws seem real
While hiding the laws of physics and nature
Thus, a race against time
A race for death or life

The New-Color Symphony

Zonpower

from

Cyberspace

Globe Designed by Steve Rapella

Neo-Tech Worldwide

Zonpower

lets *you* become

GOD

even without a computer

Relax: Zonpower Rules Cyberspace
You Alone Rule Your Life

Zonpower and cyberspace are made for each other. In cyberspace, the destructive elements of government and the entire parasitical-elite class vanish. Only Zonpower succeeds.

Eventually, through the Internet and beyond, Zonpower will immortalize and deify every conscious *individual* on planet Earth. Through cyberspace, Zonpower empowers the individual by emasculating false authority and vanishing dishonesty. That empowerment comes not from academic philosophizing but from real-life, in-the-trenches business and legal actions. Then shall vanish *government-caused* criminalities and wars.

Blaise Pascal saw only boredom and doom for those who did not believe in God. The fact is: Zonpower removes all boredom and doom from conscious beings.

Additionally, through cyberspace, Zonpower prevents the corruption of youth. Everyone becomes forever young — forever clean, innocent, free. Youth flourishes; corruption vanishes. ...Cyberspace *is* the Civilization of the Universe. There is no God but you.

The New-Color Symphony

Zonpower

New-Color Symphony

Nature is the Will of "God"

Conscious Beings Control Nature
by obeying
Nature
through the
Laws of Physics

Honesty
1. Fairness and straightforwardness in conduct.
2. Adherence to the facts: sincerity.
(Webster's Ninth New Collegiate Dictionary)

Your Route to Riches

Three thousand years ago, our nature-given bicameral minds broke down into chaos. To survive, we invented consciousness, which soon became corrupted with Plato's dishonesties and "noble" lies. Now, today, our Plato-corroded conscious minds are breaking down. To survive, we are finally discovering the all-powerful Neothink mind that functions through wide-scope integrations and fully integrated honesty. Neothink brings Zonpower — the power from the Civilization of the Universe. ...Zonpower provides everyone with riches, romantic excitement, and a god-like mind and body.

Zonpower
A Symphony of Contextual Facts and Metaphors
dedicated to
Henrik Ibsen
and his play
An Enemy of the People
and to
Socrates, Francis Bacon, Voltaire

How can the natural world be preserved
if man dominates?
...Man **is** *the natural world*

ISBN# 911752-72-2
Library of Congress # 95-60719
Copyright © 1995, 1996
by the
Zon Association, Inc.

<u>Cyberspace</u>
Neo-Tech/Zonpower Home Page:
http://www.neo-tech.com/

Zonpower

A Communiqué from the Universe

Orientation

Zon is absent from the entire history of Earth's anticivilization. Yet, Zon embraces all the future. ...Zon answers the *how* and *why* questions of life and existence.

The reader needs only a brief orientation to *Zonpower* rather than an Introduction or Preface as found in most books. This orientation will help the reader capture the Zonpower dynamics that lead to limitless riches, romantic charisma, and nonaging beauty guaranteed by Zon.

Movement I, *The Foundation,* is a nonmathematical presentation of Neo-Tech Physics edited for all readers — from general readers to professional physicists.

After Movement II, *The Problem*, and Movement III, *The Solution*, one captures the Zonpower needed to collect limitless riches, romance, and a god-like mind and body.

New-Color Symphony

"Blessed are the meek: for they shall inherit the Earth"
Matthew 5:4 — 10

Meaning: Blessed are the unassuming value producers not invested in this anticivilization — blessed are those quietly wielding the omnipotent tools of Zon: for they shall inherit the Earth. Condemned are the parasitical elites who live through force-backed criminalities — condemned are those criminally investing in this anticivilization: for they shall vanish from the Earth.

Table of Contents

Table of Contents

Illustrations

Charts and Tables

New Words and Concepts

Zon is a collective word related to the fully integrated honesty of Neo-Tech and comprises (1) the Civilization of the Universe, (2) those operating from its wide-scope perspective, and (3) the power required to control existence — the integrated power to gain limitless wealth and eternal happiness. ...Zon is the mind of God. Zon *is* you!

Zonpower is the power to control (*not* create) existence. Zonpower is derived from applying the fully integrated honesty and wide-scope accountability of Neo-Tech to all conscious actions.

Neo-Tech is a noun or an adjective meaning *fully integrated honesty* based on facts of reality. Neo-Tech creates a collection of *new techniques* and *new technology* that lets one know exactly what is happening and what to do for gaining honest advantages in all situations. Neo-Tech provides the integrations to collapse the illusions, hoaxes, and irrationalities of any harmful individual or institution.

Objectivism is the philosophy for the well-being of conscious beings — the philosophy based on reason — the new-world philosophy of limitless prosperity.

Anticivilization is the irrational civilization gripping planet Earth — an unreal civilization riddled with professional value destroyers causing endless cycles of wars, economic and property destructions, unemployment and poverty, suffering and death. The essence of the anticivilization is dishonesty. ...Through Neo-Tech, the Civilization of the Universe will replace Earth's anticivilization.

Civilization of the Universe is the rational civilization throughout the universe — a civilization filled with value producers providing endless cycles of wealth, happiness, and rejuvenation for everyone. ...Professional value destroyers and parasitical elites are nonexistent in the Civilization of the Universe.

Parasitical Elites are unnatural people who drain everyone. The parasitical-elite class lives by usurping, swindling, and destroying values produced by others. Their survival requires political-agenda laws, armed bureaucracies, ego-"justice" systems, and deceptive neocheating.

Neocheating is the undetected usurpation of values from others: the unsuspicious swindling of money, power, or values through deceptive manipulations of rationalizations, non sequiturs, illusions, and mysticisms. ...All such net harms inflicted on society can now be objectively measured by the wide-scope accounting of Neo-Tech.

Subjective Laws include political-agenda laws conjured up by politicians and bureaucrats to gain self-serving benefits, ego props, and unearned power. Enforcement of political-agenda laws requires the use of force and armed agents against innocent people. ...The only purpose of such laws is to violate individual rights in order to parasitically gain values produced by others.

Objective Laws are not conjured up by politicians or bureaucrats. Instead, like the laws of physics, they arise from the *immutable laws of nature*. Such laws are valid across space and time, benefit everyone, and advance society. Objective laws are based on the moral prohibition of initiatory force, threats of force, and fraud as constituted on page 188. ...The only rational purpose of laws is to protect individual rights.

Ego "Justice" is the use of political-agenda laws to gain parasitical livelihoods and feel false importance. Ego "justice" is the survival tool of many politicians, lawyers, and judges. Ego "justice" is the most pernicious form of neocheating. ...Parasitical elites thrive on subjective laws and ego "justice" to the harm of everyone else and society.

Cassandra's Secret revealed through Zon is the power of the conscious mind to accurately, nonmystically foretell the future. How? Through the mind's power to control its own existence...thus, its own future.

New Words and Concepts

Intelligence is redefined by Neo-Tech as the *range of integrated thinking*. The range, width, or scope of valid integrations is more a function of honesty than of IQ. No matter how high is one's raw IQ, that person can ultimately be outflanked and outperformed by a lower IQ mind that is more honest, allowing wider-scope integrations. In the Civilization of the Universe, wide-scope integrations are what give conscious minds unlimited power. Neo-Tech intelligence supersedes the role of IQ detailed by Richard J. Herrnstein and Charles Murray in their controversial, best-selling book *The Bell Curve* (Simon & Schuster, 1994). Since fully integrated honesty, not IQ, is the key to long-range success and abiding happiness, all races have equal access to the limitless prosperity available from the Civilization of the Universe.

Purpose of Existence and Motive for Controlling Existence: Achieving and expanding happiness is the moral purpose of conscious life.[1] Happiness, therefore, is the ultimate motivator behind conscious-controlled existence. But, to control existence, one must realize that existence itself is *never* derived from thoughts or emotions. Instead, thoughts and emotions, including happiness, are *always* derived from the conscious control of existence. Thus, conscious control of existence is ultimately directed toward creating limitless prosperity, rejuvenated life, and eternal happiness for everyone and society.

---

[1]As identified in Aristotle's *Nicomachean Ethics*, happiness is the highest moral *purpose* of conscious life. ...Life is the moral *standard*. Reason is necessary for human survival. Reason *and* honesty are required to achieve happiness.

[See pages 323-327 for additional word usages]

MOVEMENT I

Neo-Tech Physics

The Foundation

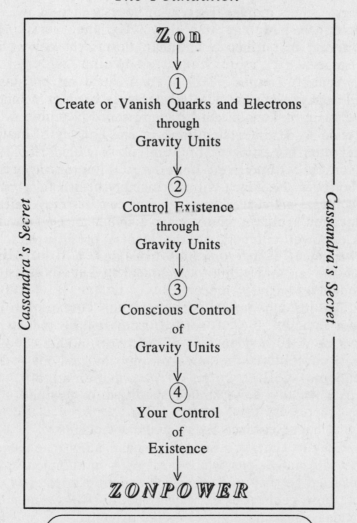

Zon

① Create or Vanish Quarks and Electrons
through
Gravity Units

② Control Existence
through
Gravity Units

③ Conscious Control
of
Gravity Units

④ Your Control
of
Existence

Cassandra's Secret

ZONPOWER

The main body of text for Neo-Tech Physics is simplified for the general, nonscientific reader. Moreover, Neo-Tech physics is but one of several major metaphorical points made in the text. Those interested in knowing the full context in which the physics is presented must carefully read all of the technical footnotes.

The Goal and Purpose of Neo-Tech/Zonpower

The goal of Neo-Tech/Zonpower is to cure the interwoven disease of irrationality and dishonesty.

The purpose of Neo-Tech/Zonpower is to have conscious individuals think about and see everything in a different way — different from the losing way in which everyone on this planet has been chained for the past 3000 years. Indeed, Neo-Tech/Zonpower is a new way of thinking, a new way of seeing everything, a new mode of action that leads to limitless, beneficent power over existence.

Again, "Zonpower" is not a treatise on physics or philosophy. Physics and philosophy are used as metaphors to explain the omnipotent paradigm called Neothink, which is wide-scope, integrated thinking and honesty. The fully integrated honesty part of Neothink is called Neo-Tech. Since fully integrated honesty will increasingly rule cyberspace, Neo-Tech will increasingly banish false biases and illegal authorities from government, business, science, education, politics, philosophy, communication, the arts. ...Zonpower uniquely has no leaders or followers. In cyberspace, every conscious individual will eventually become an individual self-leader living in a value-producing, business mode.

The metaphorical hypotheses in this first section may seem radical. Indeed, some hypotheses are radical and have no direct evidence as of yet. Still, nothing in Neo-Tech contradicts the laws of physics and all radical concepts will eventually be mathematically and experimentally demonstrated, modified, or falsified.

Existence Exists as Gravity Units

Gravity Units are the fundamental units of existence. They are indivisible, windowless units of submicroscopic, quantized geometries from which nothing can enter or exit. Yet, those geometries exist continuously — as a quantum-blended whole through wave-like dynamics and smeared-out resonances. Also, manifestations of certain Gravity Units could form the weakly interacting dark material that accounts for the missing mass in modern cosmological theories. And finally, each Gravity Unit can flux into a universe of gravity, mass, energy, and consciousness.

All wealth arises from conscious-controlled Gravity Units.

Chapter 1

Boundless Prosperity

through

SIGUs and Googolplexes

What are SIGUs and googolplexes? What connection do they have to boundless prosperity? First ask: How do conscious beings meet the energy and communication requirements of an eternally advancing civilization? How does one unleash nature's power to achieve near instant communication throughout the universe? How can one capture the power of universes spanning billions of light years across? How can one unleash the universal power locked in gravity units lurking beneath every subatomic particle? How can one direct the power of Super-Inflation Gravity Units[1] (SIGUs) to eternally expand life and prosperity?

Take a Numbers Ride

Take a ride to the big: The mathematical term googol is the number 1 followed by a hundred zeroes, or 10^{100}, meaning 10 raised to the power of a hundred.[2] How big a number is a googol? Astronomers estimate our universe is 15 billion years old...or 10^{18} seconds old. Over 22 centuries ago, Archimedes calculated that 10^{63} grains of sand would fill the then known universe.

Consider today's known universe contains at least a hundred-billion galaxies each containing an average of a

---

[1] A Super-Inflation Gravity Unit is equivalent to a symmetrical Geometry Unit of the entire universe.

[2] The power of the number 10 means the number of zeros after the number 1. For example, 10 raised to the power of 2 or 10^2 means 100, 10^3 means 1000, 10^{100} means 1 followed by a hundred zeros, $10^{10^{12}}$ means 1 followed by a trillion zeros. Likewise, 10^{-3} is $1/10^3 = .001$. Also, 10^{-43}, for example, is a decimal point followed by 42 zeros then the number 1. ...Human life expectancy is about 2×10^9 seconds. The passing of a light wave takes about 10^{-15} seconds.

hundred-billion stars. Now consider the mind-boggling number of electrons, protons, neutrons, and all other matter-and-energy particles in those stars, planets, dark matter...as well as all additional particles scattered throughout space. That number would equal 10^{86} particles, a number still considerably less than a googol! Now, if our entire universe of about fifteen billion light years across were packed *solid* with subatomic particles with zero space between them, the number of particles would rise to 10^{130}.

But, how large is a googolplex, $10^{10^{100}}$? Just to print the number of zeroes after the number 1 would require enough paper to pack solid our entire universe, fifteen billion light years across.[1] ...And a super googolplex is a googolplex that is raised to an additional 100th power. No scale is available for any conscious mind on Earth to grasp such a number.

Now take a ride to the small: Slice an average-sized pie in half ninety-one times. On the ninety-second slice, you would need to slice the nucleus of an atom in half. How small is the nucleus of an atom? Enlarge a baseball to the size of Earth. One would then see the atoms of that baseball as the size of cherries filling the entire planet. Now, enlarge one of those atoms to the size of the Astrodome. The nucleus would then become visible as the size of a grain of sand.

What about the smallest or shortest unit of time that the human mind can grasp: Planck's time of 10^{-42} of a second — about the time required for light travelling at 186,281 miles per second to traverse the diameter of the smallest subatomic particle of, say, a 2×10^{-33} centimeter

[1]Roger Penrose calculated that to emulate all possible quantum states of the known universe would require $10^{10^{123}}$ bits of information — the maximum capacity for the Universal Computer.

diameter, which is Planck's length. A time less than 10^{-42} of a second measured from the *theoretical* beginning of time in our universe[1] cannot be experimentally simulated or conceptually grasped.

Finally, grasping the smallest and the biggest in terms of eternity requires the axiomatic fact that *existence exists*. Thus, existence has no prior cause and is eternal. Relative to eternity, the smallest unit and the largest unit are equal in occurrence, time, or distance. For example, compare an incredibly fast event that occurs once every 10^{-42} of a second to an incredibly slow event that occurs once every googolplex years. The occurrence of those events are equal in eternity. For, each of those events will occur an "infinite"[2] number of times in eternity.

The smallest units of existence, such as quarks and electrons or the even smaller Gravity Units as explained in Chapters 5 and 7, to the largest expansion of the universe with everything in between and beyond are all a part of eternal existence. Gravity Units, quarks, subatomic particles and energies; protons, neutrons, and electrons; electromagnetism, nuclear forces, and gravity; universes, galaxies, stars, and planets; atoms, molecules, and compounds; gasses, liquids, and solids; air, water, and land; mountains, oceans, and clouds; protoplasm, amoeba, plants, fish, animals, primates, *and conscious beings*...all are part of existence and its natural evolution that has occurred eternally. Indeed, each and every entity of existence has existed forever. Thus, conscious beings as entities of existence have also existed forever throughout the universes as described in Chapter 6 and in Movement III.

---

[1]Contrary to big-bang theories, universes have no natural beginnings or endings as described in later chapters.

[2]Infinity is a mind-created concept, not a part of reality.

Movement I: Neo-Tech Physics

Rapid Communication Across Universes
by using
Super-Inflation Gravity Units Called SIGUs

Reality can never be contradicted. Thus, the laws of nature and physics can never be violated. That means nothing can exceed the speed of light. So, how can near instant communication occur across distances that require light (travelling at 186,281 miles per second) millions or even billions of years to traverse? Even more, how can communication occur between universes from which not even light can escape? Conscious beings and only conscious beings can accomplish such near instant communication. How do they accomplish that communication without violating the laws of nature or physics?

Conscious beings harnessing the Super-Inflation nature of Gravity Units (SIGUs) can produce near instant, gravity-pulse communication not only across an entire universe but possibly between universes — all without violating physical laws, including the speed of light. How? By gravity pulses transmitted through big-bang-type inflations radiating from exploded Gravity Units.

How do gravity pulses communicate faster than the speed of light with nothing exceeding the speed of light? First, realize that the smallest units of existence, Gravity Units, and the largest unit of existence, the full expanding universe, are one and the same: They each contain the same mass and energy potentials. The units are just in different modes throughout time and space. Next, examine the so-called big-bang or hypothetical spacetime birth of our universe from a gravity unit: At 10^{-42} of a second or Planck's time after its birth, the entire universe is 10^{35} times *smaller* than a subatomic proton. Doubling every 10^{-34} seconds or doubling 10^{36} times at 10^{-32} seconds

6

from birth, the universe has grown to 12 centimeters across — about the size of a grapefruit. And then, doubling 10^{50} times by somewhat over 10^{-30} seconds from its hypothetical birth, the universe has exploded to the size of our solar system — all in that tiniest fraction of a second. ...In other words, during that instant in time, the universe has expanded trillions of times faster than the speed of light. Yet, nothing exceeds the speed of light. How can that occur?

The super-fast growth of the universe during its first moment in time can be explained by the Inflation Theory originated by Alan Guth of MIT in 1979. Such inflation involves the brief existence of "repulsive gravity" and the relative positions of spacetime coordinates in accord with Einstein's general relativity. ...That super-fast inflation can also be understood, without complete accuracy, in more simple Newtonian terms: Consider two entities starting at the same point and moving apart near or at the speed of light. At the end of one year, those entities will be about two light years apart. Thus, they will have "communicated" from their respective points A and B at about twice the distance covered by the speed of light without exceeding the speed of light.

Now, consider breaking the geometry or symmetry of a universe-containing Gravity Unit or Geometry Unit, causing a spacetime birth. That occurrence begins the near instant conversion of the smallest unit of existence, the universe-containing Gravity Unit, into the largest unit of existence, the entire expanding universe. Incredibly, that new-born exploding Gravity Unit has the same mass/energy total of an entire universe fifteen billion years old. Consider what occurs in the tiniest fraction of the initial second during a big-bang birth: a near instantaneous unit-after-unit multiplication, perhaps initially with repulsive

7

gravity, into nearly the total number of entities (10^{86}) that will exist in the mature universe billions of years old.[1]

Like the previous, simple example of two entities separating at nearly twice the speed of light, each of the rapidly multiplying, countless entities are also separating at or near the speed of light from all the previous and subsequent formed entities. That process multiplies distances of entity separation by trillions of times the speed of light without any individual entity exceeding the speed of light. In that way, the total range of expansion or "communication" announcing the big-bang birth occurs at trillions of times the speed of light without violating the laws of physics. (See pages 91-92 for another perspective.)

What if conscious beings can control how and when to break the symmetry of Gravity Units? With conscious beings controlling the symmetry breaking of Gravity Units, the efficiencies and power of universe-creating energy and communication multiply. How can that multiplication occur? The most obvious way is by aiming or lasing each spacetime birth in specific directions as energy waves or gravity pulses, rolling out in multidimensional geometries ...rather than allowing the gravity explosion to convert into the "usual" universe-making energy and matter radiating in three geometric directions. ...Also, such communication could possibly flash through hyperspace to other universes.[2]

-----

[1]Each new universe exploded from a single Gravity Unit will then contain its own space-time dimensions filled with its own, new quantized geometries or Gravity Units each of which can in turn form a universe filled with Gravity Units. ...For this, as with certain other hypotheses in Neo-Tech Physics, no direct evidence as of yet exists.

[2]In water, the speed of light slows by about 23% to 142,600 miles/second. Thus, in water very high-energy, charged particles can exceed that slower speed of light to create a light-barrier shock wave producing Cerenkov radiation. Now, throughout existence, no total vacuum can exist in which to measure the ultimate speed of light.

(footnote continued on next page)

Boundless Prosperity

Business: The Power of the Universe

Competitive business is the eternal power of existence. It advances every level of society throughout the universe as described in Mark Hamilton's *Neo-Tech Cosmic Business Control*, 510 pages, Neo-Tech Publishing (1989) and in Eric Savage's *Neo-Tech Global Business Control*, 256 pages, Neo-Tech Worldwide (1992). Business is the natural mode of existence for conscious beings. What is business? Business is the *competitive production* and *voluntary exchange* of values among conscious beings. ...Conscious beings throughout the universe control nature through business.

Knowledge begets knowledge. Thus, knowledge is limitless — limitless power. Harnessing universal energy and communication through business represents one increment of productive achievement along the endless scale of knowledge throughout the Civilization of the Universe. Indeed, conscious beings exert business control over nature. Through the universal virtue of competitive business, advances in value production continue endlessly — beyond the imagination of conscious beings on Earth.

(footnote continued from previous page)

In our universe, the quantum vacuum state or the gravity-unit ether exists at a certain energy level. In a vacuum state at lower-energy levels, light could travel faster than 186,281 miles/second. Does that mean certain particles such as Gravity Units could travel faster than 186,281 miles per second through our universe and not exceed the speed of light travelling through lower energy-level vacuums? Is the Guth's "faster-than-light" big-bang expansion phase simply the speed of light traveling into a lower energy-state vacuum of meta space? Could such particles set up a shock wave that would break or tunnel through the metastable vacuum of this universe into a lower energy state, thus, annihilating at light speed our entire universe as we know it? Or, could lower vacuum states be a conscious-controlled, advanced source of energy and communication? ...What about tachyons? They are hypothetical particles that can never travel *slower* than the speed of light and *increase* in speed as they *lose* energy. Existence of tachyons is entirely speculative and highly unlikely.

9

Movement I: Neo-Tech Physics

Yet, someday, in the eternal Civilization of the Universe, immortal descendents from Earth will routinely function along all levels of unimaginable knowledge and accomplishments.

How can conscious life be immortal — eternal? First, examine the nature of existence: Existence is axiomatic. Existence simply exists — eternally, without prior cause. No alternative is possible. For, existence cannot *not* exist. Thus, as part of existence, the evolution of consciousness is also eternal. Countless conscious societies, therefore, exist throughout the universes with endlessly higher levels of knowledge — with millions or billions of years more advanced societies than ours. Because of such vast and endless differences in knowledge, conscious beings at any specific level of civilization cannot imagine the knowledge or activities of say a thousand years, much less a million or a billion years, more advanced societies.

If communication among conscious beings throughout the universe delivers rational benefits, such communication would develop through competitive-business dynamics. But, probably no net benefits would accrue from communicating with less advanced civilizations. Likewise, communicating with much more highly advanced civilizations would probably yield no net benefits. For, conscious beings in the Civilization of the Universe would not benefit by jumping significantly beyond their own ongoing, step-by-step integrations in developing knowledge and values. Indeed, no matter from what level of knowledge, the *continuity* of experiences and integrations needed to create ever expanding prosperity is the root cause of happiness in any civilization.

Why are net benefits impossible from big-gap jumps into realms beyond current knowledge? For example, conscious beings cannot benefit from "million-year" advanced-knowledge jumps without going through the integrated steps to acquire that knowledge. Indeed, to benefit from advances in knowledge requires meeting the criterion for advancing prosperity. That criterion throughout all universes and all time is fully integrated honesty combined with productive effort. In other words, that criterion *is* Neo-Tech.

On Becoming Zon

Most conscious beings among Earth's anticivilization will encounter the fully integrated honesty of Neo-Tech at least once by the year 2000. That encounter will knock each person down. But, most people will jump right back up. Still enclosed in their mystical bubbles, most will bounce away...never examining what happened, never discovering eternal life and prosperity. Yet, a few will stay to examine Earth-evolved Neo-Tech. They will benefit enormously from applying its fully integrated honesty *within* Earth's anticivilization. ...And, a small number of those people will go beyond Neo-Tech by entering the Civilization of the Universe. As explained in Part III, they will become Zons. For them, the anticivilization will vanish into its nothingness as they experience the power of the universe — the power of Zon.

With the power of Zon, all things throughout the universe can become nonmystical conscious thoughts — *and nonmystical conscious thoughts (T1) can become all things (T2) throughout the universe.* ...As explained in Part III, from the equation T1 equals T2k arises k as the universal constant of Zon. From the constant k flows the power of Zon.[1]

---

[1]The Zon constant k has not yet been determined. But, k would be the fifth and unifying universal constant: unifying the relativistic,

(footnote continued on next page)

Movement I: Neo-Tech Physics

(footnote continued from previous page)
macroscopic universal constants of G (gravity) and c (velocity of light) with the quantum, submicroscopic universal constants of k (Boltzmann) and h (Planck). Perhaps k manifests itself in some sort of unifying ratio with the other four universal constants, such as k: Gc/kh. The Zon constant would relate energy, mass, gravity, and their velocities to the flow of *time* toward decreasing entropy, *not* toward increasing entropy. ...Universal constants, including the quantum cosmological constant, ultimately arise from a deep, compelling symmetry or geometry controlled by conscious beings. *The Zon constant fixes the values of all other constants.*

Except for consciousness, gravity is the weakest yet most pervasive force in nature. Indeed, gravity controls universal motion. But, the fifth force of nature — human consciousness — is the *grand-unifying* force controlling all existence. Conscious force is more subtle to specific measurement and mathematical quantification than gravity. Still, consciousness is the most noticeable force on planet Earth. Moreover, consciousness is the only force that can alter the otherwise predestined courses of the other four forces of nature: gravitational, electromagnetic, weak nuclear, strong nuclear. ...Consciousness is the force that unifies all forces and heals the seeming breaches of nature caused by quantum "uncertainties".

As a law of nature expressed by the Heisenberg Uncertainty Principle, facts asserted as truth are never certain. But, *principles* contextually determined through integrated honesty are always certain. Thus, for example, one can have certainty about the Heisenberg Uncertainty *Principle* without paradox or contradiction: (1) Metaphysically one can be certain that any particle always has an exact position and momentum at any exact time. But, epistemologically one can be certain that exact position and momentum *cannot* be simultaneously measured...at least not directly. (2) Measurements can be validly done in Euclidean/Galilean/Newtonian coordinate systems or in noneuclidean/relativistic/quantum-mechanical systems, depending on the object measured and the accuracy desired. And finally, (3) the indeterminate and probabilistic nature of quantum mechanics does not negate the laws of identity, noncontradiction, or cause and effect. The decay of radioactive atoms, for example, are both indeterminate and probabilistic. But, each decay has an identifiable, noncontradictory cause. ...That means Heracleitus, Plato, and Kant are out; Parmenides, Aristotle, and Rand are in.

As a side note important later: Plato is the father of organized deception through "noble" lies — the father of purposely dishonest government and science. Aristotle not only is the father of logic, science, and biology, but is the father of *rational* metaphysics and epistemology. Plato subjugated conscious life to higher mystical powers. Aristotle exalted conscious life on Earth as the highest value. Portions of Aristotle's ethics and politics, however, remained under Plato's influence, thus, are fallacious. ...Philosophically, Plato and Kant are mankind's villains, Aristotle and Rand are mankind's heroes.

Chapter 2
Your Journey to *Zonpower*

What is Zonpower? To answer that question, you must first take a journey that leads to the center of weirdness. Then, you must go beyond, into the realm of weirder-than-weird. That journey will lead you into the weirdest realm of the entire universe. And that realm is right here on planet Earth in its bizarre, upside-down, anti-power civilization. You must go to that black hole apex in order to go through it and then out into the advanced Civilization of the Universe — the civilization of honesty, prosperity, and happiness.

Journey to the Weirdest Realm

Only from this anticivilization can you discover the realm of weirder-than-weird. Once there, you will find the key to Zonpower. Unlocking the door to all power and prosperity, you will escape the false journey that essentially everyone on Earth is traveling: As one example, consider the false search in today's sciences and religions, especially in astro/quantum/particle physics and the Vatican. That search is for a **Quantum/God Singularity** and the **Big Bang** — the fictional, wished-for birthplace of our forever evolving, plasmatic Universe.

World-class scientists have searched for that single point of creation. Yet, the notion of Singularity contradicts the laws of nature and physics, as do the mystical notions of perpetual motion, cold fusion, low-energy nano-technology, along with various mystical interpretations of chaos and quantum mechanics. Many brilliant scientists

13

are pursuing never ending illusions that demand ever more tax money, such as the twelve-billion-dollar, super collider (SSC)[1] in Texas. Such pursuits can generate ever more intriguing but eventually meaningless science and mathematics.

Singularity is rationalized to occur in an infinite[2] black hole collapsed to an undefinable, single-point entity filled with mathematical stratagems involving infinities. From such a single-point entity or Singularity, certain physicists assert that our universe and all existence was born. In turn, certain religionists enthusiastically point to Singularity as scientific proof of "God". For, the creation of our universe from Singularity would require a "God"

---

[1] The SSC's mission to find the Higgs boson is a valid quest, especially under brilliant Nobelists such as experimentalist Leon Lederman and theorist Murray Gell-Mann...but not under the dishonesties and inefficiencies of tax-funded science.

[2] "Infinite" is a useful mind-created concept that cannot exist in reality. Except for existence itself, which is eternal and has no finites or boundaries, "infinity" violates the law of identity. In accordance with reality, at any point one stops in traveling toward infinity, the entity is defined and finite, never infinite. For example, one's mind knows that a curve can asymptotically approach a straight line forever. Yet, at any point on that curve, all becomes finite and definable about that curve and the straight line.

Now, consider how the notion of a single point can always be approached closer and closer, but can never be reached. For, like the notion of infinity, singularity does not and cannot exist beyond a mind-created notion. As an analogy, think again how a curve can asymptotically approach but never reach that straight line and become a straight line. Nothing in reality can justify a notion that such an ever approaching curve would suddenly contradict its nature — its never-ending course — by arbitrarily and inexplicably jumping over a quantum space to join, straighten out, and become a part of that never reachable straight line.

The laws of identity and noncontradiction always hold in reality. Those laws are eternally fundamental and axiomatic throughout existence. Moreover, existence is not in space or time. Rather, time and space are in existence. The universe is eternal, not infinite.

mystically preexisting in nothingness and creating a universe out of nonreality. ...What an unnecessary, impotent notion.

Why resort to mysticisms, nonrealities, and nothingness to explain the creation of our universe? Why be stuck within such unreal and harmful limitations? Consider the seemingly infinite number of ordinary conscious beings wielding Zonpower throughout the rational civilizations existing among the universes. Most of those conscious beings have the power to create far beyond any imagined creations of a mystical "God". And, unlike the miracles of a made-up "God", conscious-being creations are real — accomplished naturally, within the laws of physics.

Each such conscious being, for example, has the power to create an endless number of universes from an endless number of universe-containing black holes existing at every spacetime point throughout eternity. Even so, most of those conscious beings have technologically and economically advanced so far that they have long ago in their forgotten histories abandoned the creation of universes as an inefficient, primitive activity.

Vanish All "Gods"

With Zonpower, one captures powers far beyond any imagined powers of a "God" conjured up in Earth's anticivilization. Every such "God" is created to demand sacrifice — sacrifice of the productive class to the parasite class. But, with Zonpower, one escapes the "God" trap by entering the Civilization of the Universe.

Blasphemy? No. For, rational Zonpower, not imagined Godpower, is real and good. Zonpower, not wishful thinking, delivers open-ended prosperity and happiness to conscious beings throughout the universe.

15

Individual consciousness throughout the universes *is* the eternal, grand-unifying force of existence.

On planet Earth today, Albert Einstein represents the furthest advance in theoretical science and physics based entirely on a foundation of rationality and reality. Einstein avoided any arbitrary, quantum-mechanical retreats into fashionable nonrealities or Eastern mysticisms. With the recent discovery of Zonpower, Einstein arises anew. For science, physics, quantum mechanics, mathematics, and business can now advance in unison on Einstein's foundation of rationality and reality toward the promised land.

A Journey into the Black Hole

To discover Zonpower, you must first take a journey to the realm of weirder-than-weird.[1] This journey proceeds from Einstein's dual relativity viewpoints — first from the observer's viewpoint and then from the traveler's viewpoint:

THE OBSERVER

Through a special relativity telescope/microscope, you are observing a spaceship hurling toward a universe-containing black hole of such great mass that all matter will collapse seemingly forever.[2] You see the spaceship

---

[1]This metaphorical journey is contextually and descriptively fairly accurate. But out of necessity for nontechnical communication, some descriptions are not *precisely* accurate. Other descriptions await further advances in physics.

[2]Every black hole originates from less than infinite mass and energy. All black holes, therefore, will stop collapsing at some equilibrium point determined by its finite mass/energy: For example, stopping at the Chandrasekhar limit then at the Schwarzschild radius. That equilibrium point of finite size consists of various entities and energies that cannot by definition be a pure point of singularity. Instead, by nature, those entities and energies are simply new, valid, and real sets of physics definable by that particular condition for those entities, masses, energies, and finally gravity at a particular density or geometry.

cross the event horizon to be inescapably captured by the enormous, always increasing gravitational pull of that black hole. That overwhelming gravity continually accelerates the spaceship's plunge toward the center point with ever increasing speeds — speeds always approaching but never reaching the speed of light: 186,281 miles per second.

Observable only through your relativity telescope/microscope, the collapsing, mega-mass black hole itself is now submicroscopic. And that black hole continues to collapse at ever increasing speeds. With fuzzy thinking, you rationalize that the infinitesimally tiny black hole still collapsing ever faster, approaching the speed of light, should in the next instant crunch into one entity at a single-point center. Your fuzzy thinking continues: All entities and forces would then become Singularity — a unified, single-point entity or force describable only in terms of unreal infinities.

Yet, no such thing happens as you continue observing through your relativity telescope/microscope: The spaceship and all surrounding existence keeps hurling toward the center at ever increasing speeds with ever decreasing distances, but without ever reaching the center. How can that be?

By continuing to observe the spaceship, you discover the answer through the laws of physics and Einstein's Special/General Relativity: As any object approaches the speed of light, its mass density increases *toward* infinity and its size shrinks *toward* zero length from the observer's viewpoint. Accelerating toward the speed of light, that spaceship appears to you, the outside observer, to move forward essentially as fast as that same spaceship is shrinking backward. Also, time aboard the spaceship

17

appears to slow toward zero. Thus, as with all the other entities of that black hole, the shrinking spaceship keeps approaching the black-hole center at ever higher velocities, but with ever slowing time, never reaching that center.

At some approaching equilibrium, the collapse will stop accelerating as determined by the laws of physics and the finite mass/energy/gravity geometry of the black-hole center. At that moment, the spaceship and all other surrounding entities of existence captured by the black hole will stop shrinking. All existence will then lock together in a black hole of finite size and specific nature — a nature or physics characteristic to its particular gravity or geometry. Moreover, that or any physics will always be in accord with reality. Thus, such a finite geometry of locked entities can, by definition and nature, never be a single point of mass or energy...or of Singularity. Instead, all that existence will be an energy/entity unit of gravity or geometry...not a single-point.

Without the mind-blocking, dead-end concept called Singularity, a new question and viewpoint arise: What or who could break a black-hole equilibrium of locked-together symmetries, entities, and energies? The answer, as described in later chapters, is that conscious people can break universe-containing black-hole symmetries to create universes and encoded cosmos systems observable today.

THE TRAVELER

Now, let us experience the same journey as a traveler on that spaceship in quest of Singularity. First, you would have to somehow acquire such a spaceship from some advanced civilization. For, if you were capable of building that spaceship, you would also have the knowledge to realize Singularity is a contradiction of reality and cannot exist. Thus, any such quest would be a fool's journey, forever wasting your life. Indeed, when that universe-containing black-hole equilibrium were finally reached, you would be locked together with all entities and energies, entombed apparently forever in that black hole.

Nevertheless, in that spaceship, you are now accelerating toward a seemingly infinite-mass black hole that will collapse almost forever toward its center. Crossing the event horizon, you see the center of the black hole. You fear an imminent crash into that center. But, soon, you realize something entirely different is happening. On looking outside the spaceship, time seems to pass so slowly and then ever slower. To travel the most minute distance seems to take forever. Every tiny incremental approach toward that black-hole center seems to take ever longer as time passes ever slower.

Soon you seem to be standing still with the black-hole center never again appearing to get closer. Yet, the spaceship's instruments show you are traveling at almost the speed of light and continually accelerating toward that center. You realize that you are experiencing not only Einstein's relativity in time and space, you are also experiencing relativity in gravity: Now, even the increases in gravity seem to have stopped. In fact, not even the quantized effects of gravity can escape that universe-mass black hole. ...You seem to be forever frozen in time, space, and gravity.

Finally, you the space traveler realize the ultimate fool's journey of boredom in which you have embarked and are forever trapped. You lose all that conscious life and valid knowledge have to offer. Your fool's journey offers only an endlessly changing physics, energy, and particles that at first seem rapid, interesting, important, and

19

leading to new knowledge for answering questions. But now, your almost infinitely slow journey is leading to nothing new — nothing that can build new knowledge or answer questions in reality. You can only observe endlessly slower changing forms[1] of mass/energy that are forever predictable as a function of existence and its gravitational fields, geometries, and dimensions.

Yet, the moment you awaken from your unreal physics-fiction dream is the moment you recognize what an endless, inescapable fool's journey you have traveled and are now stuck. Then, the door to escape opens. Realizing existence is never born or created, it simply exists eternally, your mind is finally free. Your entire thinking and viewpoint change. You realize existence, *not* consciousness, is primary.[2] You can now gain valid, new knowledge — Zonpower knowledge — that will show you how to escape that meaningless pursuit of a nonexistent grail: the birthplace of existence. You realize existence has no birthplace. You realize conscious beings have always controlled eternal existence through Zonpower.

Indeed, Zonpower brings you into the all-powerful Civilization of the Universe. With Zonpower, you control existence and, thus, can break out of any black hole.[3]

---

[1]Changing from a black hole to a naked black hole from which nothing, not even gravity, can escape...and finally changing into the geometry of a Gravity Unit.

[2]Aristotle is the father of the philosophically correct *primacy-of-existence* concept — a concept fully validated by Rand and Peikoff in the late 20th century. Plato is the father of the philosophically false *primacy-of-consciousness* concept — a concept disastrously advanced by Augustine, Hobbes, Descartes, Hume, Kant, and Hegel. ...Totalitarian-trending governments and their destructive politicians, armed bureaucrats, and parasitical elites require a dishonest, primary-of-consciousness philosophy to advance. *Zonpower in cyberspace vanishes Plato's philosophy, irrational acts, and government evils.*

[3]With conscious beings, rotating black holes can actually become shortcuts through space and time.

20

Chapter 3

Seven Waves
to the
Civilization of the Universe

WAVE ONE

The Journey into a Black-Hole Civilization

* A spaceship travels into a universe-containing black hole: That spaceship can never reach Singularity, all in accord with the laws of nature as expressed by (1) Einstein's general relativity, by (2) *full-context* quantum/particle physics, or by (3) multidimensional superstring or duality string theories.

* Singularity and the big-bang creation of existence is a mystical notion requiring an imagined "God". Thus, the astute Vatican and its Pope, as early as the 1950s, seized out-of-context quantum physics as the long sought-after-link of science to religion "proving" the existence of their mystical "God".

* The fundamental fact of existence is *existence exists*. That means existence is eternal without prior causes. Existence includes the full evolvement of each new universe: from subatomic gravity units, quarks, electrons to the elements and compounds...from land, water, life, conscious beings, buildings, computers to conscious-created civilizations...and finally to conscious-controlled universes — controlled from both above and below. Thus, life and consciousness — like geometry, matter, and energy — have existed throughout eternity. Indeed, conscious beings like us, not an imagined "God", have eternally controlled nature and existence. ...Consciousness within each human being *is* the controlling force of existence.

21

WAVE TWO
Discovering the Civilization of the Universe

* Consider the very few honest philosophers who have lived on Earth: Parmenides, Aristotle, Thomas Aquinas ("variance with reason is evil"), Baruch Spinoza, Adam Smith (economist), John Locke, Ayn Rand, Leonard Peikoff. Consider their struggle against the irrationality of an anticivilization. They all sensed increasing frustration at their inevitable failures because they too were an integrated part of irrationality — of anticivilization. They never knew how to leave or even knew that leaving an anticivilization was possible. They never considered themselves being able to create and then enter the Civilization of the Universe. ...They too were locked in a fool's journey within Earth's black-hole anticivilization.

* Not until mystical, wishful-thinking notions, such as a Quantum/God Singularity, are cut away and discarded can physicists, mathematicians, and astronomers once again move forward in generating major new knowledge. As new-age mysticisms multiply, all fields of knowledge shrink toward darkness. But, as Neo-Tech starts vanishing such mysticisms, those declines in physics, mathematics, astronomy, medicine, law, education, and philosophy will reverse. The resulting forward movement will bring a golden age of knowledge. From that new knowledge and prosperity, we shall learn to live forever with ever increasing wealth and happiness. We shall be in the Civilization of the Universe.

WAVE THREE
Zon Easily Outdoing "God's" Supreme Feat

* A century ago, no religious huckster could even imagine their mystical "God" could create a nuclear-power

reactor or a computer. Yet, conscious beings easily do that today.

* Who would be the winner in any Zon-versus-"God" contest? All conscious beings have the capacity within the laws of nature and physics to outdo the greatest imaginable feat of that mystical "God" — the creation of our universe. Indeed, the creation of universes by conscious-controlled, Guth-type inflations of Gravity Units is elementary child's play long-ago left behind by the more advanced Zons.

* Unchain Jesus[1]: He was a hero of Zon, not "God".

* Cut away and vanish the nothingness trap of mysticism, such as Quantum/God Singularity. Then what happens? An entirely different view, thinking, experiments, and physics unfold:

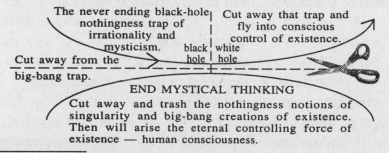

The never ending black-hole nothingness trap of irrationality and mysticism.

Cut away that trap and fly into conscious control of existence.

black hole | white hole

Cut away from the big-bang trap.

END MYSTICAL THINKING

Cut away and trash the nothingness notions of singularity and big-bang creations of existence. Then will arise the eternal controlling force of existence — human consciousness.

---

[1]Not the unreal, dead Jesus of establishment Christianity. Not the chained, captive Jesus manipulated by parasitical "authorities" and vested interests since 400 AD. But, the real, ever-living Israelite Jesus — the free spirit of eternal prosperity and happiness.

The parasitical-elite class with its subjective laws and ego "justice" attacked, jailed, and finally killed Jesus. Why? For his trying to bring the prosperous Civilization of the Universe described in Movement III to the harmful anticivilization described in Movement II. ...The professional value destroyers of the Roman Empire convicted and crucified Jesus solely to protect their ego agendas and harmful livelihoods.

Brief, erratic contacts with the Civilization of the Universe described in Movement III were perhaps experienced by Moses, Confucius, Socrates, Jesus, Bruno, Galileo, Spinoza, Newton, Brigham

(footnote continued on next page)

Movement I: Neo-Tech Physics

* A century ago, any thought of human beings cracking the atom to convert mass into energy was inconceivable. Today, nuclear energy is routine. Likewise, today, any thought of human beings cracking super-dense black holes or Gravity Units (GUs) into new galaxies and universes is inconceivable. Yet, once free of mystical notions such as Singularity and the big-bang creation of spacetime, the cracking of black-hole symmetries will become understood. Then, universe-making energy can be harnessed by conscious beings breaking the symmetry of universe-containing Gravity Units — all consistent with the laws of physics. ...That process, in turn, will spin out the unlimited riches available from the conscious-controlled unleashing of matter and energy from those Gravity Units.

WAVE FOUR
Surpassing Einstein

* A universe-containing Gravity Unit (UGU[1]) is equivalent to all the mass and energy of a universe spun into a submicroscopic geometry of wound-up gravity or antimotion order at zero entropy — the pure, quantized geometry of gravity in which time and space do not exist. Advanced conscious beings create countless universes from such hidden quantized Gravity Units. How? By

---

(footnote continued from previous page)

Young, Einstein. But, today, a consistent, nonstop journey from Earth to the Civilization of the Universe has begun. It began in 1976 with the publication of the *Neo-Tech Reference Encyclopedia*.

The future belongs to fully integrated honesty — to reason, rationality, Neo-Tech, and the Civilization of the Universe.

[1]Universe containing Gravity Units (UGUs) *are* existence, thus, have existed eternally. By contrast, universe-containing black holes (Chapter 2) form whenever an entire universe collapses into a black hole.

breaking symmetries to unwind the endless UGUs into universes of matter and energy...or perhaps into just gravity pulses for communication. Why do conscious beings create universes? To utilize nature's ultimate energy and communication source in advancing their well beings. ...That conversion of UGUs into endless riches and universes by conscious beings is expressed by the equation:

UGU energy/c2$\overset{Eq}{\longleftrightarrow}$UGU mass$\rightarrow\left[\begin{array}{c}\text{broken}\\\text{symmetry}\end{array}\right]\rightarrow$Energy+Mass+Time

    * The UGU state is near pure gravity in an existence field. UGUs are at once *all* energy and *all* mass. The quantized Gravity Unit is the basic unit of existence — the immutable source of all life and riches. Thus, all expanding values and riches rise from that single unit (*not a single point*) — the quantized GU. Additionally, GUs are the energy and communication means among the controlling force of existence — goal-directed conscious life.

    * How does one prove conscious life is the only nongeometrically structured force of nature — the fifth and controlling force of the universe? By discovering anomalies in the universe that are unmistakably obvious as conscious creations — creations that could never be produced or configured by the other four universal forces — the geometrically structured forces of gravity, electromagnetism, weak nuclear forces, and strong nuclear forces. ...Consider one observing a planet in a distant solar system. Did conscious life ever exist there? What if that observer spotted a land-rover vehicle on that planet? That land-rover vehicle would be unmistakable proof of conscious existence. For, no geometric force of nature could produce or configure a land-rover vehicle. Now, extrapolate that example to anomaly configurations in the universe. Are those anomalies a part of a nongeometric, consciously encoded cosmos system? Such anomalies will be resolved only by plugging in the purposeful, unifying force of conscious life into theoretical and mathematical models of our entire universe down to subatomic phenomena. ...Is existence itself encoded by conscious control?

* At every level, from distant quasars to subatomic quarks, from astronomy to quantum physics, certain anomalies will be resolved as purposeful, life-enhancing conscious actions. Within that resolution exists the proof that nongeometrically structured conscious life *is* the fifth and controlling force/dimension of existence.

* The conscious harnessing of Super-Inflation Gravity Units (SIGUs) allows near instant, gravity-pulse communication not only across our entire universe but possibly between universes[1] — all without violating physical laws, including the speed of light. How? By rolling multidimensional geometries into lased gravity pulses transmitted via Guth-type inflations of Gravity Units.[2]

---

[1]Philosophically, only one universe can exist. For existence cannot not exist. No voids of nothingness between universes or anywhere can exist. Thus, interlocking or overlapping gravity units, which must connect everything, must connect all "universes" into one universe.

[2]No single entity or particle can travel faster than the speed of light. But, quantum fluxes can provide "instantaneous" or "superluminal" travel of a particle such as the Bohr-orbit quantum jump of an electron. What happens is a quantum flux produces a physics-permitted, positron-and-electron pair in a vacuum in a different energy level or orbit. The space/energy difference between the two energy levels is the electron-produced wavelength. The positron then annihilates the lower orbit electron leaving the new electron in a different orbit, giving the appearance of an instantaneous jump between orbits when in reality two separate electrons are involved.

Similar rationally explicable phenomena occur with faster-than-light, "big-bang" expansions or quantum fluxes of Gravity Units into universes. ...No mysticism or conscious-created reality exists in physics or reality, from cosmological relativity to quantum mechanics.

26

WAVE FIVE
From Impossible to Succeed to Impossible to Fail

* Civilizations and anticivilizations are conscious-created, just as are land-rover vehicles, airplanes, and television sets. None exist in nature alone. None are created by the other forces of nature without conscious beings.

* The Civilization of the Universe is created by conscious beings objectively integrating reality. But an anticivilization is conjured up by humanoids subjectively disintegrating reality.

* In an anticivilization, endless volumes of philosophy arise in order to rationalize or counter the endless contradictions of reality and rationality. The Civilization of the Universe **is civilization**. *For, civilization is the integration of reason and objective reality*. In such a civilization, philosophy simplifies to a few words and then disappears as self-evident.

* Civilization vanishes any anticivilization on contact — somewhat analogous to matter vanishing antimatter on contact. Both anticivilization and antimatter are anti *by nature*. Therefore, their natures can never be changed. But, they can be annihilated, vanished, or puffed away by actual matter and the actual Civilization of the Universe.

* Throughout the universe, the position of anyone or any civilization on the scale of knowledge makes no difference. Only the process of advancing unimpeded on that never ending scale of knowledge delivers prosperity and happiness to conscious beings.

* The Civilization of the Universe delivers far beyond any mystic's dream of a no-effort paradise. With Zonpower, one can solve life's problems to live eternally in ever expanding knowledge, prosperity, and happiness. For, the Civilization of the Universe is based on rational

efforts integrated with reality — on disciplined thoughts, goal-directed actions, and iron-grip controls — not on lazy rationalizations, wishful thinkings, or sloppy mysticisms.

* In any civilization, the *only* legitimate or beneficial function of government is to **protect** individual property rights. The *only* legitimate use of force is self-defense in protecting those rights. By contrast, criminal-controlled governments of anticivilizations depend on political-agenda laws, ego "justice", initiatory force, threats, coercion, fake compassion, and fraud to survive. They survive by draining value producers and **violating** property rights.

* How can one escape parasitical elites while trapped in their anticivilization? The trap is the attempt to reform their anticivilization, which cannot be done. The key is Zonpower. With Zonpower, one can cut away and vanish the anticivilization. Consider the following: (1) Zonpower is the tool for building unlimited prosperity available to every conscious being, (2) Zonpower is Neo-Tech applied from the Civilization of the Universe, (3) Zon is anyone who is applying Neo-Tech from the Civilization of the Universe.

* In an anticivilization, long-range successes are impossible. In the Civilization of the Universe, long-range failures are impossible.

WAVE SIX
The Source of Eternal Wealth

* Technically, gravitational "forces" do not exist. As Einstein discovered in surpassing Newton, gravity is the relative interaction among the geometries of mass, energy, space, and time.[1] Similarly, universal consciousness as promoted by certain physicists, Eastern religions, and

---

[1]Somewhat analogous to two-dimensional flatlanders feeling the tugs of geometric variances as "gravitational forces" when they traverse for example, a crumpled sheet of paper.

pantheism does not exist. Rather, universal consciousness as the eternal interaction between individual conscious beings and existence is what dominates nature.

* As Einsteinian relativity overtook Newtonian gravity, astronomers and physicists went about empirically proving relativity. Likewise, as the Civilization of the Universe overtakes today's anticivilization, astronomers and physicists will go about empirically proving Zonpower: the control of the universe by conscious beings. ...Einstein's discredited cosmological constant will rise anew from Gravity Units containing the hidden Zon constant that brings eternal wealth and happiness to the universe.

WAVE SEVEN
The Product from Zon — Let There be Light!

* Civilizations are created by conscious beings applying the eternal principles of nature to life. Thus, civilizations can be created by billions of conscious beings or by a single conscious being. Moreover, as a conscious creation, civilizations can be created and expressed in writing — in a document. Once a Civilization of the Universe is created here on Earth, anyone can experience that civilization. And, once one experiences that civilization, he or she captures the power of Zon.

The ancients saw power in the gods among the stars. The golden-age Greeks brought power to man on Earth. Today, Zonpower brings the Civilization of the Universe to Earth. ...Zonpower gives conscious people power over existence.

* On capturing that wealth and power among the Civilization of the Universe, one can never again look back or waste a thought on the boring irrationality of today's anticivilization — today's insane civilization ruled by dishonest parasites who can only drain others and harm society.

29

Movement I: Neo-Tech Physics

* Thus, the first-and-final product from Zon *is* the **Civilization of the Universe**. As explained in Movement III, once one receives that ultimate product, he or she becomes a citizen of the universe. With the resulting Zonpower, that person puffs away the anticivilization to gain eternal wealth, romantic love, and exciting happiness.

Science, Physics, and Mathematics
merge into
Conscious-Controlled Cyberspace

Francis Bacon (1562-1626) the father of the Scientific Method developed inductive reasoning and formulated perhaps the most important maxim of Western thought: "Nature, to be commanded, must be obeyed." To be commanded, nature must first be understood. Thus, "knowledge is power". ...That power resides in conscious-controlled cyberspace.

Galileo Galilei (1564-1642) the father of modern science identified and demonstrated that mathematics was required for the development of physics — its theories and laws. Mathematics as the key to understanding nature was also demonstrated by Johannas Kepler (1571-1630) in his discoveries of algebraic geometries that codified the elliptical orbits and area sweeps of planetary motions.

The Zon Institute is seeking to develop the mathematical descriptions and field formulations of conscious-controlled physics. All universal constants and the laws of physics are formulated through the cyberspace unfurling of Gravity Units. Publishable contributions providing such mathematical descriptions may be submitted to John Flint, The Zon Association, P. O. Box 60752, Boulder City, NV 89006.

30

Chapter 4

Zon's Force Field

Note to General Readers
Understanding the scientific technicalities of the previous chapters and the next four chapters with their footnotes is not necessary for understanding and fully using Zonpower. Read those chapters for what you can easily understand. Do not worry about the rest.

By understanding what existence *really* is, you gain control over impediments blocking your life. Without those impediments, you can foretell the future to gain limitless riches.

Indeed, you can get incredibly rich by controlling the force fields of existence. But first you must know what existence really is through Neo-Tech physics. Existence is axiomatic and eternal. For, existence simply exists with no prior causes. Existence is a natural, open-ended plasma of force fields[1] eternally evolving with no beginning or end. Neo-Tech physics demonstrates how human-like consciousness is not only an integral part of existence, but is the eternal controller of its geometries, fields, and particles. ...Yet, what is the actual nature of existence?

Most existence throughout the universe exists as an open-ended electroplasma, always evolving through its interacting matter (M) and energy (E) fields or modes. Those two fields of existence eternally interchange in a

---

[1]Fields and forces are the result of noneuclidean geometries and symmetries in space. Thus, there are no unaccounted, spooky "actions at a distance". ...Superstring theory, which would involve the geometries and mathematics of Gravity Units, consist of sixteen dimensions, or, in actuality, ten dimensions because six dimensions are redundant. Those ten dimensions can, in turn, split into a rolled-up six dimensions in which time, space, motion, and entropy do not exist — and the unrolled four dimensions of our current observable universe in which time, space, motion, and entropy do exist.

relationship expressed by Einstein as M=E/c^2 (from E=mc^2), with c being the universal constant representing the velocity of light.

Existence cannot *not* exist. Moreover, no vacuum void of existence is possible. "Vacuums" of the *matter* field can exist as in outer space, in vacuumed-pumped containers, and in areas between electrons. But, all those volumes are filled with the unmovable, frictionless ether or existence field — a uniform, continuous field of existence.[1]

Throughout eternity, a massless field uniformly occupies every spacetime point of existence. This field of existence behaves as an ether matrix with stationary wave, vibration, or string properties. Within this field matrix, both energy and matter geometries interact to form physical existence, always behaving in dynamic combinations of one mode interacting with the other. Certain motions of the matter field, for example, interact at the

---

[1]An all-pervasive existence field of mass and energy modes is somewhat analogous to a combination of (1) Dirac's ocean in which exists an endless field of "electrons" or energy fluctuations at all points throughout space and (2) Faraday's nonmatter, stationary lines or fields of force. ...All known energy modes can pressure wave through the energy/matter ratios of outer space. Most modes are absorbed or changed at the energy/matter ratios either in Earth's gaseous atmosphere or in the liquids and solids of Earth itself. By contrast, almost all neutrino wave pressures can pass through the electron/nuclear fields of thick solid masses, even through the entire planet Earth without mode change.

This resurrection of an *ether*, **not as a matter or energy field**, but as a fixed existence field, reconciles Newton's classical laws and Einstein's relativity with quantum mechanics. Such a reconciliation arises from a universal Zon constant, k, which, in turn, arises from conscious control of the existence-field ether manifested at every spacetime point of existence. The resulting causal control of existence by eternal conscious beings is (1) universal, (2) fixed, (3) unmovable, and (4) independent of any frame of reference or method of observation.

quantum level with the energy field. That interaction produces irreducible packets of quantized energies or geometric structures. Those irreducible quanta, such as photons, send relief-seeking signals or perturbations into the continuous existence field radiating throughout eternity.

Conscious Control of Existence Fields

During its creation, each new energy quantum slips smoothly and continuously from its matter field into the fixed existence field. Like water flowing from a dripping faucet, each quantum is pinched off into a minimum-energy wave packet. Simultaneously, from the continuous energy flow, a new quantum starts forming. Thus, continuous, smooth-flowing energy forms discrete photons. In turn, those photons or pinched-off wave packets of minimum *energy matter* create field disturbances or nonequilibrium pressures[1] signalling themselves in all directions throughout the existence field. Such signals generally travel near or at the speed of light.

Eventually, each point line of disturbance or pressure signal is relieved by a receptor that absorbs such signals. In turn, that disturbance absorption converts back into pinched-off packets of minimum *matter energy* — chemical, potential, or kinetic. In other words, a receptor relieves signal pressures by locally absorbing quanta equivalent to the quanta from the originating source. Each absorbed quantum is then converted back into the

---

[1]Not a pushing pressure, but a nonequilibrium pressure or disturbance signal seeking equilibrium. What is detected only *represents* what is transmitted. ...A pressure intruding into the existence field causes that field to curve around the intrusion which, in turn, traces the curved paths of gravity. The interactive relationships between mass, energy, fields, curved space, and gravity require an ether of existence fixed throughout spacetime.

equivalent of its original mode. Such exchanges of modes can be detected as a wave/particle in the energy field or a particle/wave in the matter field or a combination, depending on how and where that mode exchange is emitted, absorbed, and measured.[1]

Those field or mode exchanges occur, for example, when stars pour *nature-controlled*, gravity-fusion energy into its surrounding electrons. Those energized electrons, in turn, pour photons into the existence field. Those photons cause disturbances that simulate waves ranging from radio waves to gamma waves. Those simulated waves radiate toward receptors located at the end of all point lines throughout existence — such as a lens of a telescope in another galaxy. That receptor conserves existence by withdrawing or absorbing equivalent amounts of pressure-alleviating photons to neutralize the disturbances from the originating source.

Similarly, a hydro, fossil-fuel, or fusion power plant on Earth pours *human-controlled,* power-plant energy into, for example, a television transmitter. That energized transmitter, in turn, pours its *human-controlled* photons into

---

[1]In measurements, the distinction between metaphysical and epistemological certainties must be discerned, especially in quantum mechanics: No *metaphysical* uncertainties exist in physical nature. Only *epistemological* uncertainties exist.* Probability statistics are used in the absence of concrete knowledge. The de Broglie/Bohm's pilot-wave theories help eliminate the mystical misinterpretations of quantum mechanics arising from the 1926 Copenhagen Interpretation. ...Pilot waves are the fingerprint disturbances guiding moving particles.

*Consider the following epistemological uncertainty: The ratio of a circle's circumference to its diameter is π or 3.14159..., a number that continues indefinitely without ever repeating. Thus, the use of π in calculations, such as the area of a circle $A=\pi r^2$, can never yield an exact or certain answer. For the answer always depends on how many decimals one extends π in calculating that area. Yet, an exact area exists, it just cannot be calculated by using π or any method of diminishing triangulation.

the existence-field ether. Such an action creates radiating lines of disturbances that are equilibrated by absorption of photons into the matter field of, for example, a television receiver. The same energy/matter mode equilibrations can be traced from that television set to the retina of a human eye, then to a conscious brain, and finally to volitional physical actions that both alter and control the course of nature.

Discrete quanta or particles move at high velocities approaching the speed of light mainly in (1) expansions or contractions of the universe, in (2) certain nuclear reactions or radioactive decays causing symmetry breakings or hidings, and in (3) conscious-controlled actions such as particle accelerations. By contrast, the ordinary transmission of light, electromagnetism, or quantum energy across space is not a result of any significant particle movement. But rather such linear or curved transmissions are simply vibrating, resonating, or wave-like disturbances in spacetime geometries propagating near or at the speed of light through the existence field. Thus, discrete energy quantum and matter quantum do not themselves travel across space. Instead, each creates a disturbance pressure that radiates wave like along the stationary point lines of existence. That wave-like disturbance is eventually relieved, equilibrated, or absorbed by receptors at the end of each point line of existence.

Consider the above description of *locally* creating and relieving energy pressures by emitters and receptors in the stationary existence-field ether. Now, consider the popular notion that almost every particle ever created or released physically races across space — often across millions or billions of light years in space. That notion seems to violate some sort of "least-action" principle. Such an action-inefficient notion of endlessly traveling quanta seems as quaint as the notion of a geocentric universe in which all inertial matter, planets, and stars daily race around planet Earth.

Indeed, both matter and energy interact locally, not across space. Light, for example, does not literally propagate across time and space. But, rather, light locally manifests a disturbance that spreads wave like throughout the existence-field ether until absorbed or equilibrated by a receptor.[1]

Conscious Control of Existence

The above example of an energy-releasing star can be "deterministically" calculated from the "immutable" cause-and-effect of existence *without* conscious influences. But, the above example of an energy-releasing television transmitter is the volitional dynamics of existence being integrated, controlled, and forever altered by freewill human consciousness. Thus, as revealed by Neo-Tech physics, all existence is ultimately controlled and evolved through volitional human consciousness.

Unknown to the busily self-serving Establishment, the

---

[1]Then what really is the "speed of light", c? First, consider atomic fission or fusion in which a given mass is converted to energy as $mc^2=E$. Now, by contrast, the "speed of light", c, is the velocity at which a given energy is converted to mass as $E/c^2=m$. Yet, light itself is the opposite — it has no rest mass. So where is the connection of light to the velocity, c? There is none. The "speed of light", c, is not the speed of light at all, but rather c is the velocity relationships of field disturbances, which all have a speed limit of 186,281 miles per second in a particular vacuum state.

Incidentally, traveling near or at the velocity of light, energy fields bend in gravitational fields. The quasi mass generated by high-velocity, photonically disturbed existence fields is what bends in gravitational fields.

nature of existence and its dynamics of matter and energy are today being increasingly understood and methodically verified. That verification process will lead to the corollary verification that *human consciousness* is the eternal integrator and controller of existence. ...Human consciousness ultimately controls the relationships and geometries of the other existence modes — matter and energy along with space and time. The human-consciousness mode *is* the purposeful, unmoved mover of existence.

Zonpower Commands the Future

The scientific verification that any individual conscious being can control existence will vanish Earth's irrational anticivilization. As Earth's anticivilization vanishes, the rational Civilization of the Universe will embrace our world. ...With Zonpower, one can foretell and command the future by controlling the existence field that reaches into the future — into the Civilization of the Universe.

The age of Zon means controlling the universal information field *not* through Earthbound computers, but through Zonpower: the foretelling knowledge of Neo-Tech physics — the certainty used to gain limitless excitement, power, and riches...*eternally*.

The Five Forces of Nature

Force	Particles Affected	Manifestation	Field Quanta	Range (meters)	Relative Strength
1. strong	quarks	nuclear power	gluons	10^{-15}	1
2. electro-magnetic	charged particles	chemistry	photons	unlimited	1/137
3. weak	quarks and leptons	radioactive decay	$W^{\pm}$ and Z^0 bosons	$<10^{-15}$	10^{-5}
4. gravity	all particles	cosmic structures	gravitons	unlimited	10^{-40}
5. consciousness	gravity units + bosons (energy particles) + fermions (matter particles)	controlling all scales of existence	thinkons (see page 46)	unlimited	k•x

Chapter 5

The Physics Behind Zonpower

Zonpower is a communiqué from the Civilization of the Universe. When you carefully read the *entire* communiqué, an epiphany will occur. You will, for the first time in your life, know how to control all that affects you. Nothing negative or harmful in the anticivilization will control you again. You will gain majestic control over your mind, body, and all events involving your prosperity, happiness, and well-being. ...You will gain Zonpower from which you will capture the power and riches available from the Civilization of the Universe.

Every owner of *Zonpower* must carefully read this communiqué in its entirety at least once, perhaps twice or more, in order to reach into an ecstatic future...into the Civilization of the Universe to gain its power and riches. At the same time, you will toss the yoke of today's stagnant anticivilization. Indeed, *Zonpower* delivers a stunning new power to benefit from every event that touches your life.

Scientific Proofs

The final proof of the Civilization of the Universe lies in the foretelling powers of Zonpower that yield limitless riches, even to those trapped in this anticivilization. But to vanish this anticivilization by having everyone on Earth move into the Civilization of the Universe requires scientific proofs embedded in mathematics. Those proofs are today evolving. One such proof will evolve from answering the fundamental question: What is existence?

39

Movement I: Neo-Tech Physics

The answer will arise by first answering another question: What is the relationship of consciousness to mass and energy? That answer requires understanding the relationship of inertial or gravitational mass to a massless universal ether — a fixed matrix of existence. Then, one can discover the relationships among mass, energy, and consciousness itself. ...How are (1) mass as "weight" and (2) energy as "weightlessness" related to (3) conscious-controlled existence? Why do each of those three existence modes require a universal existence field? ...Below is the simplest approach to answering those questions:

If Mass is Not Intrinsic, What is Weight?

Aristotle postulated things had weight because they had tendencies to be heavy or light. But that postulate does nothing to really explain weight. Newton explained weight through the force of gravity. On careful thought, however, gravitational force does nothing more to explain weight than Aristotle's tendencies. Additionally, Einstein's general relativity demonstrates that gravity does not exist as a force. But rather mass curves space by displacing the space surrounding that mass. Thus, gravity is simply mass moving along spacetime curves — along natural paths of least action.

The greater the mass, the more it bends or curves space toward itself by displacement. Therefore, the more a unit of mass curves space toward itself the greater will be its inertia in falling toward another unit of mass with space likewise curved toward its own mass. ...Mass falling through space curved toward another mass gives the effect of gravitational attraction or negative energy striving toward nonmotion.

Now, through Einstein's relativity, one can approach

40

an explanation of what weight really is. But, on still closer examination, even Einstein fails to provide a complete answer. What is missing? The existence field is missing — the ether that Einstein dismissed. ...Mass is *not* intrinsic to matter. Thus, an existence-field ether is required to explain what weight really is.

Why does Einstein's General Relativity fail to explain weight without a fixed field of existence? Take two cannonballs of identical size, one made of solid iron, the other of solid aluminum. Both fall and accelerate in a gravitational field at the same rate. Why does the iron ball weigh about twice that of the aluminum ball of the same size? Einstein's general relativity explains that space curves toward the center of mass in proportion to that mass. But, if a non-ether space surrounding the equal-sized cannonballs is being "displaced" and curved, is that curvature equal for equal-volume cannonballs? Is the weight for identical-sized iron and aluminum cannonballs identical? Of course not. ...What is wrong? Nothing.[1]

One must first strip away volume/particle/mass/energy ideas such as the mass of a quark or the energy of a photon. For, gravity and weight can be understood only in terms of interacting geometries within a fixed existence field *beneath* all mass and energy quanta...beneath each cannonball, quark, electron, photon.

The key concept is this: In order to have weight or gravity, one must have a fixed ether field of weightless existence that is *uniformly and equally present everywhere* from the spaces between galaxies and above, down to the spaces between quarks and below, down to the final symmetry of the ether-hidden Gravity Unit.

---

[1]Volume, of course, does not explain weight or General Relativity. And, of course, Einstein's General Relativity is correct. Volume is simply used as an analogy to dig beneath volume/mass/energy to find the gravity geometries needed to explain the origins of weight. ...See pages 15-20 of the Closing Ceremonies for further understandings of weight.

Movement I: Neo-Tech Physics

If that symmetry-hiding ether were not uniformly present and fixed everywhere in existence, the universal laws of nature, such as gravity, would be arbitrary and fail. ...That fixed existence-field ether is not only necessary for existence, but *is* existence — conscious-controlled geometries throughout spacetime.

One must recognize that a fixed, weightless field *is* existence in which its modes of matter, energy, and consciousness interact. The mathematics and experiments will then fall into place for understanding and controlling existence.[1] ...Weight is simply what and where weightlessness is not.

Football-Stadium Experiments

From the macroworld perspective, conduct the following experiment: In a bowl-like football stadium,

---

[1] Controlling Existence at *All* Scales:

Any given astral volume of matter and energy will maintain its same weight before and after collapsing into a black hole. For, any collapsed volume will still contain the equivalent number of mass/energy units for equivalent ether-field displacements. Total spacetime curvature and total gravity will, therefore, be equivalent for any mass/volume in both its black-hole form and its fully expanded star, galaxy, or universe form. Now, by definition, light and other energy or mass forms cannot escape a black hole. Thus, a normal black hole cannot be detected, except by its gravity or perhaps by Hawking radiation. But nothing, not even gravity, can escape from universe-containing black holes that further collapse into Gravity Units. Why? Because mass and energy have collapsed into a symmetrical geometry of gravity curved in on itself. By collapsing to trillions of times smaller than a regular, microscopic black hole, the Gravity Unit becomes a *quasi point that causes no ether displacement*. It becomes a part of weightless ether. Thus, the Gravity Unit is essentially weightless with no current technology to detect its totally lost, inconceivably tiny weight and volume. ...This essentially weightless, undetectable Gravity Unit represents the underlying geometry of all existence *minus* consciousness. Now, all geometries of existence are subject to nongeometrical conscious control through Gravity Units.

Light cannot escape from black holes whose volumes are proportional to their masses. Neither light *nor gravity* can escape from Gravity Units whose "volumes" are *inversely* proportional to their *potential* masses. Does space, time, or motion exist beneath Gravity Units? Is our universe a Gravity Unit relative to other universes?

42

bolt on the arm of every seat a simple, low-cost, push-button, battery device. On pushing the button, a precisely tuned radio wave unique to each device is emitted. Beneath the stadium is a radio-wave detector hooked up to a computer. Now, fill the stadium with 100,000 football fans. As part of the halftime ceremonies, provide a laser-light display. Ask the spectators to keep their fingers on the signal button and immediately press it each time they see a green laser flash. Deliver 50 green flashes during the laser display.[1] The signal detector and computer will detect and record every person's signal, plotting each as a point along either side of a dividing line continuously calculated as the medium signal time.

If those signals plot reproducible, double sine waves for each 360⁰ revolution of the stadium, watch out! For, conscious quanta as an integral part of a fixed existence-field has been experimentally demonstrated. From such verifiable and repeatable experiments, the Civilization of the Universe and its powers can become known and increasingly accessible to everyone on planet Earth.

How would a double sine wave in this experiment (1) identify the fixed ether of existence and (2) demonstrate consciousness as an integral mode of that ether? The Earth is orbiting the sun at about 67,000 miles per hour...or about 0.01% the speed of light. Thus, if consciousness or conscious control is an integral part of the fixed ether, those oriented most directly in line with the direction of that motion will, because of relativity effects, record on average minutely slower but statistically measurable response times reflected by points plotted below the medium line.

[1] An *at-rest* comparison of the speed of light versus the 5,000,000 pieces of data requires several orders of magnitude more preciseness to detect the sought effect. But, the experiment can be enhanced to detect the sought effect through added computer/trigonometric analyses that detect secondary changes in statistical data reflecting particles *not* at rest but traveling 67,000 mph through the GU ether relative to the sun. ...Other motions could be detectable, even overwhelming: for example, the high-speed motion of our galaxy through the GU ether. ...See pages 15-20 of the Closing Ceremonies for further understandings of this experiment.

Movement I: Neo-Tech Physics

Those people sitting at a 90^0 angle to Earth's orbital motion will record on average a minutely faster response as reflected by points plotted above the medium line. The average of those points should then show a double sine-wave inclination for each 360^0 revolution of the stadium. Statistically, on calculating the effects of relativity, about 100 points should fall outside the statistical average, above and below the line, for each 360^0 revolution of 100,000 points of data recorded after each green laser flash. That 100 point variation per flash times fifty flashes should manifest itself as detectable, reproducible sine waves.

Why did the famous Michelson-Morley experiment in 1887, for which Michelson won the Nobel prize in 1907, "prove" that no fixed ether existed? Because the signals measured were photons of light, which are not intrinsic to the existence field. In other words, rather than seeking a weightless existence-field ether, a nonexistent matter-mode ether was sought. Therefore, no relativity effects would be detected for photons in that experiment. Thus, no detection of the "ether wind" could occur. But, what if consciousness or conscious control is intrinsic to existence — a constituent of the fixed ether? Then, with live conscious action, its mediating quanta particles called *thinkons* will cut through a fixed field of existence at 67,000 miles per hour relative to the sun — or greater speeds relative to other universe entities, such as other galaxies, or the entire expanding universe, or even the meta-universe — the Universe of Universes.[1]

---

[1]Electromagnetic forces such as photons would "disturb" but not measurably interact with a fixed ether of Gravity Units. Thus, photons would act independently and could not detect the "ether". By contrast, hypothetical thinkons would be intrinsic to Gravity Units, thus, would interact with the GU ether — the unmoving frame of reference for all existence. ...What if the speed through the GU ether is close to the speed of light, *c*, relative to the expanding universe?

(footnote continued on next page)

Other Experiments: Clocks and Computers

Physicists have already demonstrated minute differences in time for clocks at different latitudes and altitudes. Those differences are attributed to differences in gravitational "forces". Could similar experiments utilize super-computer-speed variations to detect both the orbital and rotational movements of the Earth through the GU ether?[1]

Gravity Units: the Basic Unit of Existence

Gravity Units are neither energy nor matter.[2] But, in

(footnote continued from previous page)

Does that mean conscious beings could measurably, albeit minutely, think more efficiently facing one direction versus another direction? Worth experiments? What if conscious beings are traveling at all directions simultaneously through the fixed "ether" at near the speed of light? In that case, the "ether" could not be detected by Stadium Experiments and thinking rates would be equal in all directions. ...In any case, the point of the Stadium-Experiment idea is not only one of physics, but one of metaphor to illustrate the relationship of consciousness to existence.

[1]Neo-Tech physics with its ether field resolves the many mysteries of quantum mechanics, including Bell's theorem in explaining the 1982 Alain Aspect's "faster-than-light" experiments. Conscious control of the ether field removes the mysticism from quantum interpretations of CPT symmetry breakings, the Einstein-Bohr debate, Schrödinger's cat paradox and Wigner's friend, and even reducing Everett's parallel universes from infinitely multiplying down to two: the universe and the antiuniverse (the anticivilization). ...Rational consciousness collapses the wavefunction of the antiuniverse.

[2]Energy and mass in the strictest sense do not actually convert from one to the other as suggested by $E=mc^2$. They are really just two different modes of the most fundamental field — the *existence field* consisting of quasi spacetime points and Gravity Units. From any Gravity Unit or quasi spacetime point can spring the mass and energy of an entire universe...an entire universe of quarks and electrons.

But, how do the quarks and electrons actually materialize? They materialize by breaking the symmetry of a Gravity Unit or spacetime point, which is pure symmetry at zero energy, zero mass, and zero gravity. That symmetry breaks into exactly equal but any amounts of positive and negative energy. The amount of energy depends on how the symmetry breaks. The positive energy consists of mass and

(footnote continued on next page)

sort of a de Sitter sense, energy and matter meld into the symmetry of Gravity-Unit space or an *existence field*. From that fundamental symmetry or field of existence, all universes spring. Indeed, Gravity Units are that which the latest string theories are groping toward. Gravity Units not only occupy all space among matter and energy particles, but comprise all such particles themselves including quarks and electrons, including gravitons and photons.

The most fundamental controller of existence is human consciousness, the force that controls symmetry and Gravity Units. From those dynamics, existence evolves. ...Consciousness is the ultimate logic, beauty, and symmetry of physics from which future, major theories and discoveries will be predicted and confirmed.

(footnote continued from previous page)

energy fields comprising the dynamics of quark-and-electron motions. The negative energy consists of gravity comprising the dynamics of antimotions and slowing time. The total energy, mass, and gravity for any universe or its alternate mode of a Gravity Unit is zero, with all positive and negative energies exactly cancelling each other. Indeed, in the totality of any closed universe or Gravity Unit, the conservation laws of energy, angular momentum, and electrical charge disappear. They each cancel to zero. ...In a Gravity Unit, time stops and disappears into a spatial dimension or geometry.

What really are quarks and electrons? They are existence modes or geometries of quantized momentums that are relativistically compacted into mass particles surrounded by energy fields or wave functions.

Gravity Units and their existence field are controlled by conscious beings through unblocked, wide-scope, integrated thinking efforts. The fine-coarse graining of existence will reveal a quantized particle of conscious thought: the *thinkon*. As photons mediate force in the electromagnetic field, as W and Z particles mediate force in the weak nuclear field, as gluons mediate force in the strong nuclear field, and as gravitons mediate force in the gravitational field, thinkons mediate the force of consciousness in the existence field. All existence can be identified through various sum-over histories of thinkons. ...The thinkon particle can be deduced from football-stadium type experiments. What experiments could directly demonstrate the thinkon particle? The mathematics of noneuclidean, multidimensional geometries may provide the field equations for the existence field and its thinkons.

Chapter 6

A Cosmology of Infinite Riches

$\Big($ From the F.R. Wallace's "Long Wave" publication ©1985
simplified in 1995 to be contextually accurate if not technically precise$\Big)$

> This chapter is going to take you on a journey. A journey into realms you never knew existed. By the time you finish this journey, your thinking will change about you, this world, the universe, the future. That metamorphosis will occur on putting together 25 pieces of a puzzle. ...When the last piece snaps into place, your thinking will change forever.
>
> More specifically, after reading this 25-part chapter, an array of new concepts will jell into a matrix on the final page. That matrix will eventually end all mysticism and deliver endless riches to this world.

Part 1
A Neo-Tech Discovery

Tony, a lad of thirteen, was singing the theme song of Monty Python's "The Meaning of Life". The song went something like this:

"Just remember that you are standing on a planet that's revolving at 900 miles per hour, that's orbiting at 90 miles per second. So it's reckoned that the source of all our power, the sun, and you and I and all the stars that we can see are moving at a million miles a day. That's figured out as moving at 42,000 miles an hour, in our galaxy called the Milky Way. Our Galaxy itself contains 100 billion stars. It's 100,000 light years from side to side and 16,000 light years thick. We are 30,000 light years from our galactic center and go around that center every 200 million years. Our galaxy is one of millions of billions in this amazing, expanding universe. The universe itself keeps on expanding in all directions at the speed of light. It's whizzing as fast as it can go, you know, at 12 million miles a minute. So remember

when we are feeling very small and insecure, how amazing and unlikely is our birth. And pray that there is intelligent life somewhere up in space, 'cause we are down here on Earth."

What makes those lyrics fascinating is that every statement is essentially factual and verifiable. But the song left out the most important part: Probability statistics overwhelmingly reveal that our universe contains at least a hundred million, and probably billions of Earth-like planets populated with conscious beings like you and me. Millions of conscious civilizations exist that are millions of years more advanced than our newly born, immature, still mystically oriented civilization.[1]

Moreover, that song was praying for what Neo-Tech already discovered. In fact, Albert Einstein spent his professional life searching in vain for what Neo-Tech discovered — the unifying, controlling element of the universe: *human-like consciousness*.

Part 2

Einstein and the Unifying Link

Throughout history, conscious beings on Earth have struggled with mystical notions of a "superior" consciousness, an imagined god, or some other "higher" power reigning over the universe. But today, by integrating the dynamics of mass and energy, Neo-Tech

---

[1]Since 1995, astronomers have been discovering by direct observation other planets orbiting nearby stars, providing mounting evidence for a super abundance of planets throughout our galaxy. Then, on August 7, 1996, NASA announced direct evidence from a Martian meteorite discovered on Earth in the early 1980s that cellular life evolved on Mars over 4.5 billion years ago. The implied ease that life evolved in at least two separate places in our own solar system lends stunning support to the Long-Wave hypothesis that life — evolved conscious life — exists on billions of planets throughout our universe . ...Moreover, an entirely different genetic form of life called Archaea, which needs no light, oxygen, and lives at 400°F, has recently been discovered on Earth.

reveals a relationship between our own Earth-bound consciousness and all existence. The unifying power that orchestrates existence is not some mystical god or "superior" being. But, as demonstrated in this chapter, that unifying power is conscious beings — conceptual/ introspective beings as you and I.

Einstein never accomplished his ultimate goal of unifying all forces. He never derived a Unified-Field Theory. But extrapolating Einstein's work into Neo-Tech reveals the unifying entity of existence — the only integrating force of the universe: human-like consciousness.

Why did Einstein not realize that fact? One reason perhaps stems from his abhorrence for unpredictable actions among the dynamics of nature. For that reason, he disliked quantum mechanics or anything that suggested arbitrary or "god-like" interventions. Always searching for order, Einstein focused on only two components of existence: mass and energy integrated with the geometries of time and space. He believed those components could always be explained, exactly and predictably. Thus, he never considered the third and controlling component of existence: volitional consciousness — a free-will, conceptual/introspective/integrating conscious mind.

Perhaps his passionate dislike for the unpredictable and disorder caused him to overlook consciousness as the third spacetime component of existence. For consciousness can and does unpredictably alter the dynamics of nature, every moment, throughout the universe. Yet, from the widest perspective, consciousness brings the most elegant order and predictability to the universe as demonstrated in this chapter.

All past attempts to link consciousness with existence

were based on mystical, "higher forms of consciousness". Such irrational, ethereal linkages always originated as dishonest, unfounded assertions by mystics or neocheaters conjuring up religious and political power. But the Neo-Tech discovery of human-like consciousness as the unifying element of existence can be scientifically established not only with theory but with direct observation and experimental proof.

Understanding the conscious mind as the controlling, unifying element of existence first requires understanding the *unchanging* nature of consciousness and existence versus the *changing* nature of matter and energy:

Part 3
The Unchanging, Eternal Nature of Consciousness

As first identified by Professor Julian Jaynes of Princeton University and described in Chapter 28, the conscious mind was discovered within nature's bicameral mind[1] about 3000 years ago. Given sufficient information, that first conscious mind had the same capacity as conscious minds today to understand anything in the universe from Einstein's theories to computer technologies and beyond. Consider the astonishing conscious minds of Socrates, Plato, Aristotle, Archimedes that were flourishing only a few centuries after the discovery of consciousness. They would, for example, have no problems whatsoever in understanding Einstein's theories

---

[1] The bicameral mind was man's intelligent, nature-evolved mind before he discovered consciousness as a conceptual/introspective mind. The conscious mind is not a part of nature's evolutionary process. But, rather, consciousness is a discovery by man that lies beyond the dynamics of nature. This discovery process is explained in Chapter 28, pages 241-256. ...When referring to consciousness, the word *discovered* is used when perhaps the word should be *invented*.

or computer technology. Given the information, they certainly had the capacity we have today to understand anything in the universe.

In other words, while much is unknown, nothing is unknowable to the conscious mind. By nature, the conscious mind requires no change or evolvement to understand anything in existence.[1] On acquiring the correct knowledge, conscious beings today are capable of doing anything within the immutable laws of physics throughout the universe.

Consciousness is man's discovery that sprang from his nature-evolved bicameral mind. Consciousness is not part of nature's evolutionary processes, but is a natural phenomenon of existence.[2] Thus, the first conscious minds on this planet 3000 years ago are the same as the conscious minds on this planet today...and the same as conscious minds in any galaxy ten million years from now. All conscious minds have the same ability to understand anything in existence.

Consciousness, therefore, does not evolve. It exists eternally, unchangingly.[3] And its capacity to understand anything in the universe transposes into forever fulfilling the supreme responsibility of conscious beings. That responsibility is to preserve forever the supreme value of the universe — individual consciousness. To meet that responsibility means achieving non-aging biological immortality as described in Parts 12 and 16 of this chapter.

---

[1]Individual minds are endowed with various capacities. Individuals then develop or retard their capacities through either conscious efforts or mystical defaults. But consciousness itself is either there to be used or abused...or it is not there.

[2]As demonstrated later in this chapter, consciousness has always existed throughout the universe as an integral part of existence.

[3]Consciousness is the fundamental invariance and overarching symmetry of existence.

Part 4

The Unchanging, Eternal Nature of Existence

Who Created Existence? And who or what created the creator of existence? And then who or what created the creator of the creator, and so on regressing forever. Such questions are, of course, unanswerable. But, such infinite-regression questions need never be answered.[1] For existence is primary and axiomatic — meaning irreducible, self-evident, and requiring no further explanation. While new realms of existence such as galaxies and universes are constantly being created, nothing creates existence itself. It simply exists. Existence always has and always will exist. And that primacy of existence existing forever is independent of consciousness or anything else. ...The most profound of all concepts as underscored by Einstein is simply: Existence exists. What is the alternative? No alternative is possible unless one accepts the contradiction that existence does not exist.

Throughout eternal time, existence constantly generates new realms of life out of which conscious minds spring from the evolvement of bicameral minds — minds of evolved intelligence capable of discovering consciousness. Once consciousness is discovered and harnessed, it can, with accumulating knowledge and productive efforts, learn to forever muster new realms of existence. From those new realms evolve new life. And from new life evolve bicameral minds from which conscious minds spring.

Throughout eternal time and space, the following creation cycle always has existed and always will exist:

---

[1]The *Neo-Tech Discovery*, Concept #28 identifies the specious nature of infinite-regression questions.

Table 1
THE CREATION CYCLE

Realms of existence created by conscious beings —> life evolved —> bicameral mind evolved —> consciousness discovered —> mysticism developed to replace lost, bicameral gods —> mysticism and neocheaters take control of conscious beings —> partial freedom and capitalism developed —> Neo-Tech discovered —> guiltless prosperity, power, romantic love revealed to value producers —> mysticism and neocheating are uncompetitive and, thus, eliminated —> biological immortality achieved —> control of the universe learned —> new realms of existence created by new conscious beings —> and so on, forever expanding and repeating the cycle.

Stated another way: Space, time, consciousness, and existence are eternal; they have no beginning or end. Throughout time eternal, stars, solar systems, and Earth-like planets constantly form anew. Thus, living organisms and conscious beings constantly form anew. Throughout never ending time and universes, limitless planets forever generate life. That life, in turn, forever generates nature's evolutionary processes that always end with conscious beings.[1] ...Conscious civilizations free of mysticism always survive, prosper, take control of nature and then existence.

Given the endless number of water/oxygen abundant, Earth-like planets forever spinning in endlessly evolving existence, one realizes life and consciousness have forever co-existed in limitless abundance. Human-like conscious-

---

[1]As explained in Chapter 28, pages 241-256.

ness, therefore, is as much a part of eternal existence as are mass and energy. When consciousness is integrated with endless existence and time, the stunning conclusion unfolds that human-like consciousness is also unchanging and has always existed.

Consciousness, mass, and energy are the three macro components of existence. Those three components are inextricably linked and must be integrated into all physical understandings and mathematical accounts of our universe. If only the mass and energy components existed, then all existence would be predictable and predestined through the dynamics of nature and physics. But further research and refinement of data will show that seemingly predictable actions of the universe are actually unpredictable from a mass and energy accounting alone. That unpredictability arises from not accounting for the influence of volitional conscious beings throughout existence.

Human-like, volitional consciousness is:

1) the third and integrating component of existence,

2) the unifying component or force never recognized by Einstein,

3) the supreme component of existence that controls the dynamics of nature, mass, and energy to forever preserve and evolve conscious life,

4) the eternal component that has existed and controlled existence, not for trillions of years, but forever.

* * * *

The balance of this chapter develops a non-mathematical, nontechnical understanding of how

54

conscious beings dominate the universe and muster new realms of existence and life through increasing control of mass and energy.

Part 5
The Changing Nature of Mass and Energy:
The Grand Cycle

All events of the universe fall within nature's mighty Grand Cycle, the dominating, all-inclusive energy wave involving the entire universe. That cycle consists of nature's longest energy wave exactly counterpoised with nature's shortest energy wave. All other cycles, waves, or forces of nature, ranging from cosmic and gamma rays to radio waves fall within the Grand Cycle. ...The Grand Cycle is described in Table 2 below:

Table 2
The Total History Of The Universe
(omitting the unifying element of consciousness)
is contained in
THE GRAND CYCLE
which consists of
The Googol-Year Explosion
Half-Cycle, Long Wave

> with gravity-wave dissipation
> with proton decay
> with quark and electron annihilation

The Googol-Year Implosion
Half-Cycle, Long Wave

The Googolth-of-a-Second
Full-Cycle, Short Wave
(black hole/white hole)

(a googol equals 10^{100} or
1 followed by 100 zeroes)

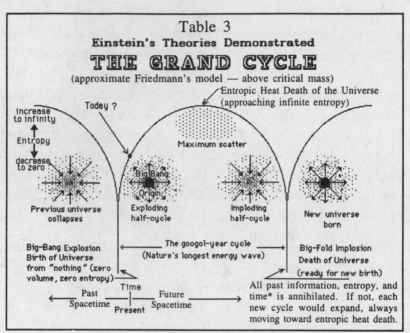

Table 3
Einstein's Theories Demonstrated
THE GRAND CYCLE
(approximate Friedmann's model — above critical mass)

*When time is annihilated, the next event (birth of a universe)
is instantaneous to the previous event (end of a universe). No
time passes between the two events.

Probabilities, however, favor an ever-expanding, open
Universe rather than a static or a closed Universe that
eventually cycles into a big crunch. For, if the
Universe of Universes (the Meta-Universe) is
conscious controlled, the open-universe model is more
logical, efficient, and delivers greater business
opportunities in constantly blending with other
expanding Universes.

A Cosmology of Infinite Riches

A capsulized account of the Grand Cycle starting with the so-called big-bang birth of the universe is illustrated in Table 3 on page 56.

Table 3 also indicates that all activity during nature's longest wave, the googol-year exploding/imploding cycles, exactly equals all activity occurring during nature's shortest wave, the googolth-of-a-second cycle. An understanding of that seeming paradox will evolve over the next few pages.

Part 6
The Explosion Cycle

Within the universe, all existence oscillates in one Grand Cycle spanning trillions of years. The actual time to complete that Cycle is not relevant here, but will someday be scientifically measured by us on Earth. But, even today, experiments and calculations from the astrophysical Doppler effect[1] show our universe is in the explosion, energy-to-matter half cycle. Our universe is exploding outward at near the speed of light, scattering away from a so-called "big-bang birth" with ever increasing entropy[2]

---

[1] A change of light-wave frequencies caused by a moving light source such as a star. The wavelength of light from a star moving away *red shifts* — becomes longer — stretches toward the color red.

[2] Entropy involves the second of the three laws of thermodynamics for *closed* systems. Entropy is simply the movement of events toward their highest probability or disorder.* Entropy measures irretrievable energy spent on scattering a closed universe. ...For every star that explodes, every pebble that drops from a cliff, entropy and disorder irreversibly increase throughout the universe. Approaching infinite entropy, all usable energy throughout the closed universe is spent. All is flat and scattered to the maximum. No star is available to explode, no cliff is available from which a pebble can fall. No wind blows. All is dead and still. Stars are collapsed, cold and dark, or not at all. No sound or light exists: perhaps not even mass exists. Perhaps only unusable radiation near and always approaching 0°K exists.

*The same probability concept applies to formulating hypotheses: always formulate toward the highest probability. Thus, the formulation of the Long-Wave hypothesis.

— a measurement of spent energy.

Energy available for work throughout the universe will keep decreasing as the universe spreads out for trillions of years until all energy is spent. In that state, trillions of years after the initial big-bang explosion, the universe exists at its maximum scattered or disordered state — as inert residue of an exploded bomb. At that moment, the entire universe is motionless, energyless, and while always approaching absolute zero Kelvin temperature (0^0K=-273.16^{0}C=-469.67°F), all energy is in the form of uniform, unusable heat radiation. ...Do subatomic arrows of time exist? Will protons, quarks, and electrons eventually decay or annihilate to end in radiation for all subatomic particles and motions?[1]

Part 7
The Implosion Cycle

With no usable energies or motions, the universe is dead. Entropy is essentially infinite. Entropic heat death has occurred. Without the force of consciousness, one incredibly weak force remains — by far the weakest of nature's forces — gravity. And, at that moment, in the absence of all other forces, gravity begins acting as an invisible cosmic hand destined to fulfill its function as the ultimate housekeeper, healer, and energy restorer of the universe. For, at that moment, gravity begins pulling a

[1]Are gravity waves the final dissipater of energy and motion? Or does mass itself seek higher entropy? With incredibly long half lives of 10^{32} years or perhaps up to 10^{220} years, do protons themselves decay toward infinite entropy? What about the energy and mass of a quark, an electron? Do quarks and electrons finally decay or annihilate with antiparticles? In any case, without conscious intervention, entropy death of a closed universe will eventually occur. ...**The laws of thermodynamics, however, apply only to *closed* systems. Existence itself is eternally open and evolving. Thus, any meaning of entropy to existence disappears, including the idea of entropic heat death.**

totally scattered, exhausted universe back toward increased order while gradually restoring potential energy. Increasingly restoring energy by reversing entropy, this cycle is the mirror image of the explosion cycle and equally lasts trillions of years. In that implosion cycle, gravity eventually pulls the universe back into essentially perfect order...an ultimate-compact, black-hole[1] bomb, ready to explode into another big bang as entropy races toward zero.

As contraction of the universe begins, gravity gradually changes from the weakest to the mightiest force of nature. Starting as an unimaginably faint but constant pull, gravity begins rebuilding the scattered universe by drawing all energyless existence closer together — perhaps initially by a millimicron in a million years. But every movement closer together increases the pull of gravity.[2] That, in turn, increases the speed at which the universe condenses toward an ordered, densifying mass. From the beginning to the end of that condensing-collapsing-imploding cycle, gravity steadily moves toward increasing all forms of

---

[1] The universe-containing black hole described here is matter and energy condensed beyond the critical mass and density needed to be captured, collapsed, and then imploded by its own gravity. When the collapse is complete, the resulting black hole can convert into a white hole, exploding into a new universe. The entire black-hole/white-hole cycle occurs in the tiniest fraction of a second because all information, entropy, and time obliterates between the two Grand Cycles.

[2] Gravitational attraction increases proportionally to the amount of existence involved multiplied by the inverse square of the distances between the eventual masses and energies. That means gravitational attraction accelerates exponentially as masses and energies are collapsed toward unity. Fields of existence are rolled ever closer together, perhaps into multidimensional space* and then into Gravity Units.

*Up to a twenty-six dimensional space has been mathematically derived in superstring theory. ...Most of those dimensions are rolled up into inconceivably tiny volumes or strings that vibrate at characteristic resonances.

New-Color Symphony

Movement #1

energy ranging from potential and kinetic energies to chemical, heat, and nuclear energies.

In the explosion cycle, all energy escapes the diminishing grip of gravity. But in the implosion cycle, no energy escapes the increasing grip of gravity. In this cycle, the universe keeps moving together. Gravity holds all forms of increasing mass and energy within the same shrinking unit as the universe races closer together at accelerating speeds.

Part 8
The Googolth-of-a-Second Cycle

On drawing the universe *toward* a never reachable point, the accelerating pull of gravity begins compacting matter and energy toward a super-ordered, super-compact black hole. Becoming the mightiest physical force in existence, gravity begins crushing the universe. All forms of energy blend into all forms of matter and vice versa. All molecules, atoms, protons, neutrons, electrons, sub-atomic particles, and energy waves of the universe are crushed together into unrecognizable forms of matter and energy. That rapidly compacting universe assumes entirely different forms of existence occurring only during that nearly instantaneous moment of super compaction at the final instant of the implosion half cycle.

Then, as the entire universe implodes to the size of a basketball, those bizarre forms of existence keep changing with increasing rapidity. Undergoing seemingly infinite changes into ever more radical forms of existence, the universe crushes inward at near the speed of light, imploding to golf-ball size, then to pinhead size, then to pinpoint size. Everything in the universe, including trillions of stars and billions of galaxies, even black holes, are crushed into that pinpoint. The universe then flickers from microscopic to submicroscopic size then to sizes unimaginably smaller than a proton — all while continuously changing into near infinite varieties of unimaginable radical structures shrinking toward zero volume and infinite density. ...The end condition may or may not be different, more disordered, from the beginning condition.

Most incredibly, the total of all mass/energy/activity changes that occur during nature's longest cycle (the seemingly infinitely long, googol-year explosion and implosion half cycles) is exactly counterpoised or duplicated during nature's shortest cycle (the seemingly infinitesimally short, googolth-of-a-second cycle). In other words, the total action during nature's longest cycle of trillions of years is exactly counterbalanced during nature's shortest cycle occurring in the tiniest fraction of a nanosecond[1].

Part 9
The Universe Turns Inside Out
From Implosion to Explosion

At that final instant, all activity ceases as the universe is essentially, but not actually, at zero volume, infinite density, and zero entropy. At that final instant, all the universe is in the form of gravity/existence symmetry. All information and time from the previous Grand Cycle has vanished. At that moment, with a quantum flux, a new spacetime is born — the universe turns inside out from the implosion cycle to the explosion cycle. At once, the universe converts from increasing order and compaction to "nothing" then to increasing disorder and scatteration, from decreasing entropy to increasing entropy, from

---

[1] A nanosecond is one billionth of a second.

61

implosion to explosion. At that instant, the entire universe is cataclysmically destroyed and then instantly reborn from seemingly nothing — reborn in a big-bang inflation of a trillion times a trillion suns.

Created from seemingly nothing, a mammoth composite of post-inflation mass and energy expands in every direction at nearly the speed of light. That ball of mass and energy keeps expanding for centuries, millennia, or perhaps longer before blowing apart, scattering, and then congealing its mass and energy. That scattering and congealing eventually forms visible stars, solar systems, planets. During our current googol-year cycle, millions of Earth-like planets and conscious civilizations formed billions of years before Earth's formation. And millions of Earth-like planets and conscious civilizations will form billions of years after Earth's formation.

Part 10
Super Grand Cycles

Assuming similar gravitational dynamics operate among universes,[1] similar Grand Cycles would occur among the universes themselves, but on endlessly greater scales. And then, ever longer cycles exist among ever larger clusters of universes, and so on, eternally. For each greater cluster of existence, its exponentially longer Grand Cycle would have occurred endlessly in eternity.

From the perspective of forever greater Super Grand Cycles, infinity becomes two dimensional with one vector forever reaching into space, eternally gathering greater and greater mass and energy. Concomitantly, the other vector forever reaches into time, eternally repeating ever longer

---

[1]Currently, Earth beings have no way to observe other universes. Thus, no way is currently known to establish if gravity operates among the universes — throughout the meta-universe.

cycles. Thus, travelling on those two vectors, existence evolves forever throughout the endless universes.

From the limited perspective of our world and universe, the speed of light seems incredibly fast and free. But from the perspective of endlessly evolving existence and ever greater clusters of universes, the speed of light seems increasingly slow and restricting. For, the process of escaping such super big-bangs seems chained to the speed of light. Indeed, being limited by the speed of light, a seemingly endless time would be needed just for those unimaginably large masses to escape their "instantaneous", initial big-bang inflations in their Super Grand Cycles.

Space, time, and distance throughout existence are mind-boggling because they truly never end.

Part 11
Grasping the Ungraspable:
The Infinity of Existence

Within the Milky Way, our relatively small galaxy, billions of stars and planets exist that are millions of years older than our Earth. Within our universe, billions of galaxies exist that are larger than our Milky Way. Throughout the Grand Cycle, millions of stars, solar systems, and Earthlike planets constantly form anew. Among those millions of Earthlike planets abundant in water and oxygen, the dynamics of nature immutably generate life. Life, in turn, always undergoes nature's evolutionary process that ends with conscious beings...and conscious beings always evolve to control endless existence.

Indeed, life itself, its evolutionary processes, and thus, conscious beings themselves, have always existed throughout the universe as its third and unifying/integrating/controlling component. And that unifying/

integrating/controlling component of the conscious mind was the component Einstein always sought but never recognized. For, he focused only on the mass and energy components of the universe while overlooking the component of consciousness.

When dealing with infinity, relationships among time, distance, knowledge, events, and probabilities become meaningless, resulting in seemingly bizarre situations. Consider a realistically impossible event here on earth for which the odds are a billion to one against occurring. When put in the context of infinite time, such an improbable event will not only occur with absolute certainty, but will occur an infinite number of times. Throughout infinity, whatever is theoretically possible becomes an absolute certainty that occurs an endless number of times.

To further demonstrate the bizarreness of infinity: Take an essentially impossible event that might occur once every billion years. Now take an event that happens constantly, say, once every nanosecond. Relative to infinity, both events will reoccur endlessly, forever into the future. Thus, from the perspective of infinity, no difference exists between their occurrences, for they both occur with endless repetition. So, juxtaposed against infinity, no difference exists between an event that occurs every nanosecond versus an event that occurs once every billion years. For, throughout infinity, both events occur infinite times.

Also, in the context of infinity, no difference exists between distances throughout space. For, throughout infinity, no reference points exist to measure differences among time or distances. ...Infinity is the only concept in existence without identity or boundaries. Thus, infinity[1] is radically unique from all other concepts.

To grasp the meaning of infinite existence, one cannot view existence from the perspective of a finite planet or a finite universe. Instead, one must view existence from the perspective of eternal endlessness. From that perspective, no difference exists between a mile and a trillion miles, or a year and a trillion years, or a forest fire and a star fire, or a lightning bolt and a big-bang birth of a universe. For, no reference points exist to compare distance, time, knowledge, or events of any magnitude when forever really means <u>forever</u>.

As shown later, certain deterministic concepts in the above four paragraphs are valid only in the hypothetical absence of eternal, free-will conscious life.

Part 12
Achieving Biological Immortality Now

From a perspective of the infinite time available throughout existence, all newly formed life evolves almost immediately into a highly intelligent brain that can invent consciousness from nature's bicameral mind. The resulting conscious beings then, nearly instantly:

1) take control of nature,
2) render obsolete nature's evolutionary "need" for life-and-death cycles,
3) evolve into the Neo-Tech/Neothink mind,
4) cure irrationality and its mysticism, the only disease of the conscious mind, and
5) achieve non-aging immortality in order to live forever with growing prosperity and happiness.
6) control existence.

---

[1]Infinity, as explained in the footnote on page 14, is a useful mind-created concept that does not exist in reality.

Movement I: Neo-Tech Physics

But from a perspective of the brief, finite time available for contemporary life on Earth, exactly how and when will biological immortality occur? First consider that, today, newly discovered Neo-Tech will eradicate the disease of irrationality and its parasitical neocheaters. Without the constant destructiveness of professional parasites, conscious beings will quickly, naturally develop commercial biological immortality as described below.

As Neo-Tech cures the disease of irrationality and vanishes those professional parasites, biological immortality will become a certainty for most human beings living today, regardless of age. In fact, today, freedom from irrationality will almost guarantee biological immortality for most people. And that could happen without massive efforts or spectacular medical discoveries. What is necessary, however, is the curing of irrationality and its mysticism. For irrationality, directly or indirectly, eventually kills all human beings while preventing biological immortality for all conscious beings.

Irrationality is the only disease of human consciousness. The symptoms of irrationality are harmful dishonesties and mysticisms. Those symptoms undermine the ability to integrate together the values of rationality *and emotions*. What is the value of emotions? The all-important value of emotions is to experience happiness — the bottom-line moral purpose of conscious life. But, mysticisms mixed with emotionalisms dishonestly assume a primacy over reason and reality. That dishonesty, in turn, casts mortal harm over every individual human being on planet Earth.

Neo-Tech, which is fully integrated honesty, eradicates the disease of irrationality. Thus, the immediate evolvement of biological immortality need not require quick technological breakthroughs, major research projects, or even explicit, direct efforts. But rather, with Neo-Tech, the process of biological immortality can begin immediately within one's own self. And that process will culminate with definitive biological immortality as the 3000-year disease of irrationality is cured by Neo-Tech worldwide.

How will biological immortality actually happen? First, consider:

- a world without irrationality,
- a world without professional value destroyers, parasitical elites, and dishonest neocheaters,
- a world without their destructive institutions of usurped power, such as the FDA (the most health-and-life destroying entity) and the IRS (the most value-and-job destroying entity),
- a world without the *anti-business* elements of irrational governments.
- a world without irrational governments.

Without life-corroding irrationality and its virus-like neocheaters draining everyone, business would explode into an endless productivity spiral. That value-driven explosion would launch human life into upward-spiraling prosperity with continuously expanding life spans.

Consider, for example, how the dynamics of computer technology have so far operated relatively free of parasitical elites, professional value destroyers, and government interference. Being relatively free of irrational regulations, force, coercion, and destructiveness, the computer industry has burgeoned. Computer technology is now delivering soaring capacities for processing and utilizing new knowledge at rates faster than new knowledge can be integrated and used by human beings. Such explosive advances in computer technology, or any technology, requires being free of government irrationality and its professional parasites.

The rational, conscious mind is synonymous with the productive, business mind. The value-creating business mind is the antithesis of the value-destroying political mind. The destructiveness of socialist, fascist, and religious societies prevents their citizens from developing efficient business-driven technologies. Indeed, all such societies are controlled by parasitical elites using force and deception to usurp harmful livelihoods. Such people live by attacking, draining, harming, or destroying value-and-job producing businesses...and their heroic creators and competitive expanders.

By contrast, explosive computer-like advances in human health and longevity directed toward commercial biological immortality will naturally occur in any mystic-free, business-driven society. But exactly how could biological immortality quickly occur today in a mystic-free society? Consider, a 60-year-old person today having a life expectancy of 20 more years. In a rational, business-minded society, uninhibited market forces will rapidly develop the most valuable products and technologies. ...The most valuable of all technologies — the quality preservation of conscious life — will advance so rapidly that when that person reaches 70, high-quality life spans will have expanded to 100 or 120 years, or more.

In a rational, mystic-free society, knowledge and technology accelerate geometrically. Thus, when that person reaches 100, high-quality life expectancy will have expanded to 140 or 180 years, or more. Those accelerat-

A Cosmology of Infinite Riches

ing extensions of life expectancy would provide the time needed to develop *definitive biological immortality* for almost every value producer living today. Indeed, in the coming years, Neo-Tech will cure the disease of irrationality to eradicate physical diseases and death among all conscious beings on planet Earth.

In a competitive business-driven atmosphere free of irrationality, the life spans of conscious beings will advance faster than the passing of years. Thus, the result of Neo-Tech eliminating irrationality is immediate, de facto biological immortality. Then, rapidly accelerating health technology — including antiaging genetics — will yield that *definitive biological immortality.*[1]

Therefore, by replacing all forms of irrationality, mysticism, and neocheating with the fully integrated honesty of Neo-Tech, nearly everyone today can live forever.[2] Most important, with Neo-Tech, one can live forever with increasing prosperity, happiness, and love.

Almost anyone living today can survive to biological immortality by (1) replacing the death disease of irrationality with the life elixir of Neo-Tech and by (2) stopping mystical behaviors and destructive actions, such as making problems where none exist, smoking, and becoming mentally and physically unfit. Almost everyone today can and will achieve biological immortality by rejecting irrationality and neocheating both in one's self

---

[1]Curing death is described in the *Neo-Tech Discovery*: specifically in Part V and generally in Appendix F titled, *Achieving Commercial Biological Immortality in Our Lifetime*. ...Mortality is natural in life, *except* for conscious beings whose nature *is* immortality — the same immortality God possesses!

[2]The longer a productive individual lives, the more valuable that person becomes through his or her increased knowledge, experience, competence, productivity, and capacity for business and happiness. Thus, in any rational, mystic-free society, the motivation for and value of biological immortality increases as the age of the individual increases.

and in others. The key for everyone is to first recognize and then reject the disease of irrationality and mysticism from within one's own self. Then one can effectively reject irrationality and mysticism in others.

Life is everything. Death is nothing. Irrationality trades everything for nothing. Irrationality is a terminal disease that breeds professional value destroyers who eventually harm or kill everyone. ...Today, the disease of irrationality is totally unnecessary since it can be cured with Neo-Tech. Thus, through Neo-Tech, essentially everyone can live forever with ever increasing prosperity and happiness.

Also, as demonstrated in Neo-Tech Advantage #31 of the *Neo-Tech Discovery,* conscious civilizations much advanced beyond ours would by necessity be free of irrationality and neocheating. For, by holding irrational premises, no civilization can advance much past the Nuclear-Decision Threshold[1] without destroying itself. ...In rational mystic-free societies, the idea of dishonesty is unknown.[2] Thus, *unknown* ideas also include war, murder, deception, fraud, forced taxation, conscription, racism, theft, assault, envy, anxiety, guilt.

Part 13
Infinite Knowledge

To quote from the first Neo-Tech World Summit (March, 1986) keynote address titled, "Three Steps to Achieving Commercial Biological Immortality in Our Lifetime" as quoted on the next page:

---

[1]Planet Earth is currently at that Nuclear-Decision Threshold. For our civilization to survive, the disease of irrationality must be cured.

[2] Science-fiction stories and movies of evil or hostile aliens are illogical. For, no civilization with the nuclear-energy technology required for interstellar travel could survive as irrational, evil, violent, corrupt, or criminal in *any* way.

"Living forever would be boring. False. Exactly the opposite is the fact. For creating and increasing values is the essence of a happy, exciting life, which, in turn, gives increasing motivation to live forever. Indeed, all new values come from expanding knowledge. And each new unit of knowledge generates several newer units of knowledge. Therefore, the ability to generate new knowledge is limitless. The notion of finite knowledge is only an illusion from our present, limited-knowledge perspective. Indeed, knowledge is not simply uncovered; it is generated from past knowledge. Thus, each day, the discovery of new knowledge generates ever greater bodies of ever newer knowledge and values.

"No one in the last century could have, for example, imagined any aspect of quantum mechanics, the computer age, genetic engineering, superconductivity, or fusion energy. For, everyone was many layers of knowledge away from even imagining those twentieth-century achievements. Yes, knowledge upon knowledge and achievement upon achievement will be generated anew — forever — by human consciousness.

"Human consciousness is the only force in the universe not predetermined by nature. Indeed, only consciousness can alter or go beyond the fixed patterns of nature. Consciousness obsoletes nature's blind, life-and-death survival cycles when applied to human beings. ...In a society free of irrationality, every conscious being produces open-ended achievements for society without bounds or limits. Thus, by producing an eternal stream of benefits for society, each conscious life continues happily, forever."

Part 14

Immortality — the Natural State of Consciousness

Thousands of years ago, before anyone on Earth grasped the concept of geometrical shapes, a man looked toward the heavens at the moon, then at the sun, then at the eyes of his woman. Suddenly he grasped the concept of "round"...a strange, new concept that no one had grasped or understood before. From that geometric concept came the circle, the wheel, the principles of mathematics and science, the automobile, the computer, and the latest theories of gravity. Yet, essentially no one today realizes that a concept so naturally integrated with life and taken for granted as the shape "round" was at one time unknown, strange, and spectacular to discover.

Likewise, a few thousand years from today, the natural physical state of conscious man — biological immortality — will be so natural, so integrated with life, so taken for granted that only historians would realize how during a brief time in faded history conscious beings were irrational and thus mortal. Indeed, mortality is not only the most unnatural, bizarre state for conscious beings, but is an essentially unknown state among rational, mystic-free, conscious beings throughout the universe.

In addition to biological immortality as revealed in the *Neo-Tech Discovery*, conscious man's most natural, psychological state is happiness. Essentially all human unhappiness arises directly or indirectly from the disease of irrationality and its mysticisms. With irrationality cured, happiness will become so natural and commonplace that in future millennia few if any will know that unhappiness and death ever existed.

Part 15
Einstein's First Oversight:
Failure to Integrate Human Consciousness *On Earth*
With the Grand Cycle

Consider us Earth beings with our technology of less than 3000 years. Consider our advances projected by the

A Cosmology of Infinite Riches

year 2000, only a few years away. Then project that rate of growth into a geometrically increasing curve of knowledge soaring toward a thousand years hence, a million years hence. One can easily see that conscious beings are altering the dynamics of nature at ever increasing rates. And through a relatively minuscule time span within the incomprehensibly long, googol-year cycle, conscious beings on Earth can quickly learn to dominate nature.

After only the first few centuries of consciousness, around 500 BC, human beings begin controlling nature faster then nature's evolutionary processes. Witness, for example, the development of consciousness from only 3000 years ago, an invisibly short time span in the Grand Cycle as shown in Table 4 below. Earthbound consciousness has already obsoleted nature's evolutionary processes: Today, man-made shelter, food, medicine, and technology

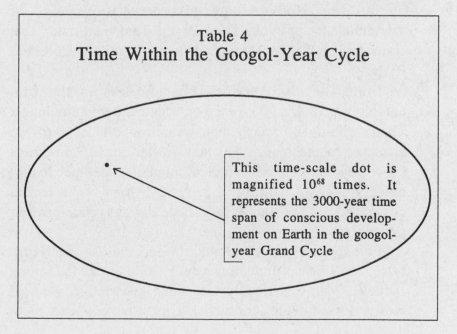

Table 4
Time Within the Googol-Year Cycle

This time-scale dot is magnified 10^{68} times. It represents the 3000-year time span of conscious development on Earth in the googol-year Grand Cycle

advance human survival and well-being much faster and better then do the slow evolutionary, adaptive processes of nature. In less than 3000 years, consciousness is already taking over the dynamics of nature on Earth. With that takeover, consciousness obsoletes nature's protective/ survival mechanism of death. Thus, through time, consciousness mandates biological immortality for all conscious beings.

Becoming free of irrationality, Earth beings will not just increasingly control nature, but will dominate nature just a few hundred years hence as explained below.

During the next million years, planet Earth will geologically remain relatively static with basically the same oxygen, land, and water conditions. But, with geometrically accelerating knowledge, we on planet Earth will soon dominate and control nature. Consider, for example, the world's largest man-made lake accomplished by building Hoover Dam with only 3000 years of accumulated, conscious knowledge. That man-made feat controlled and then dominated nature's mighty Colorado River.

From the discovery of consciousness to the first automobile took 2900 years of accumulated knowledge. Then, within 100 years, man went from the auto to the airplane, to the moon, and now toward super computers for everyone. ...Knowledge accumulates geometrically, quickly leaving nature's forces far behind as if frozen compared to the incredibly fast, always accelerating generation of new knowledge.

Perhaps only a few-hundred years hence, we Earth beings will be accumulating new knowledge at lightening speeds. With that rapidly increasing knowledge, we will easily, for example, corral heavenly asteroids into man-made orbital matter to fill our needs, just as today we corral river water into man-made lakes to fill our needs. ...What needs will we Earth beings have a thousand years from now, a million years from now? And how will we use our super-advanced knowledge and tools to control nature in filling those needs?

A thousand, even a million or a billion years, is an incredibly short time, a mere instant, within the Grand Cycle as shown in Table 4. But, well within that brief time span, we Earth beings can also accumulate the knowledge to dominate and drive the universe — to interdict nature's mass/energy dynamics in preventing the Grand Cycle from ever completing itself.

Part 16
Einstein's Second Oversight:
Failure to Integrate Consciousness *Beyond Earth*
With the Grand Cycle

Consider the billions of Earth-like planets existing within our own universe that are billions of years older than Earth. Through immutable evolutionary processes among those billions of Earth-like planets, conscious beings have evolved with millions or billions of years more advanced knowledge than we have on Earth today. ...Just imagine the technology and capacity of those conscious beings who have enjoyed geometrically accumulated knowledge for a million years, a billion years.

Human-like consciousness is the only entity in existence that can alter the inexorable course of nature. Human consciousness quickly advances from building cities to utilizing nuclear power, to developing computers, to making astronautical flights, to corralling astro matter, to understanding the universe, to controlling existence —

and beyond forever.

Integrating nature's Grand Cycle with conscious beings reveals an elegantly simple understanding of existence. That integration reveals how individual consciousness is not only an integral component of existence, but is the dominating and controlling component. For example, at either end of the Grand Cycle, all life would perish. But individual consciousness — the supreme value of the universe — must forever protect itself. Thus, conscious beings a thousand or a million years more advanced in knowledge than we on Earth have long ago *met that responsibility to preserve the supreme value of existence: individual consciousness.*

Without immortal consciousness, the Grand Cycle would inexorably and infinitely repeat itself as dictated by the natural dynamics of mass and energy. But, with consciousness, the integrating and controlling component of existence missed by Einstein, the Grand Cycle is always interdicted and truncated. Thus, the destruction of the universe and consciousness has never occurred and will never occur. In other words, by integrating conscious beings into the dynamics of existence, nature's Grand Cycle becomes hypothetical and never occurs.

Consciousness and Existence Integrated

1) Anything theoretically possible in existence, no matter how remote the probability, will happen infinite times unless interdicted by conscious beings.
2) Human-like consciousness has forever been and will forever be an integral part of existence.
3) Conscious beings, as you and I, can

understand anything in existence. On gaining the knowledge, therefore, we can and will eventually do anything theoretically possible that rationally benefits our existence.

4) Thus, human-like conscious beings throughout the universe always have, and always will, control existence.

5) On curing the disease of irrationality through Neo-Tech, we Earth beings will gain the same power, prosperity, and immortality of our fellow beings who control existence throughout the universe.

Part 17
Knowledge at the Speed of Light

Everything in existence seems limited by a universal constant — the speed of light. For, as shown by Einstein, nothing can exceed the speed of light. Consciousness, therefore, being an integral part of existence, must also be limited by the speed of light. But how can the speed of light limit knowledge, especially since consciousness has no limits on understanding anything in existence? To answer that, one must first understand the dual faculty of consciousness:

1) The unlimited faculty to understand anything in existence.

2) The limited faculty to store and process knowledge.

By nature, each new unit of knowledge begets multiple units of still newer knowledge. Thus, consciousness creates knowledge geometrically. So, then, what can limit increases in knowledge? Nothing can stop knowledge from increasing forever. But, the rate of knowledge accumulation is ultimately limited by the speed of light in our closed universe.

To understand the faculty of consciousness that stores and processes knowledge, one must first understand the history of that faculty starting with the origins of man-discovered consciousness on Earth 3000 years ago: For the first 2000 years after the discovery of consciousness, knowledge accumulated very slowly. That accumulation gradually increased as the base of knowledge increased through memory and oral communication. Knowledge then accelerated through written communication.

For man to produce great sailing ships, for example, he needed that initial 1800 years of accumulated knowledge and technology stored and passed by memory, hand-scribed documents, and oral communication. Then he needed another 1000 years of faster accumulated knowledge and technology stored and passed through written works to produce steamships and trains in further improving transportation. He needed another 100 years of more rapidly accumulating knowledge and technology stored and passed through printed works to produce automobiles that greatly improved transportation. Next, he needed only 60 more years of accelerating knowledge and technology stored and passed through books, journals, and communication equipment to produce practical airplanes that provided transportation inconceivable a century before. Finally, he needed only 40 more years of soaring knowledge and technology stored and passed through computers and electronic communications to develop space ships for landing men on the moon and building space stations.

Now, today, new knowledge is accelerating so rapidly

that our productive focus is shifting toward storing, processing, integrating, and transmitting information through million-dollar super computers moving toward thousand-dollar personal computers. Thus, today, computers are undergoing explosive increases in capacities, power, practicality, and economies. And from now into the future, the demands of accumulating, storing, processing, and transmitting knowledge will shift into high gear from man's limited storage-capacity brain to external extensions of the brain with electron/photon-circuited quantum computers and beyond.

Today, storing and processing our geometrically increasing knowledge depends on our developing and building increasingly efficient, man-made computers. Advancing economies and prosperity depend on developing ever more advanced devices until the capacity of every spacetime point in the universe is utilized for storing, processing, and transmitting knowledge.

Knowledge will increase geometrically for a few millennia or perhaps only a few centuries — until the building of external-knowledge devices approaches the speed-of-light limitation. From that point, the expansion of knowledge shifts from geometric to linear. Knowledge will then expand linearly, near the speed of light, and limited by the speed of light.

When our own expanding knowledge reaches that limitation, we can join the millions of other civilizations in our universe that have reached that point. We can then communicate through the universal computer (perhaps gravity-coded) and control existence as our fellow conscious beings do. For, then, the entire universe of universes expanding at near the speed of light becomes our computer and storage facility for all acquired knowledge.[1]

The relationship of conscious knowledge to existence reduces to a single equation. To understand that equation, the following two points must be understood:

1) Knowledge is a function of time, which as Einstein determined is related to the speed of light.

2) Essentially all mega-advanced knowledge throughout the universe is generated, stored, and processed near the speed of light, limited only by the infinite Universe of universes on vectors forever expanding at near the speed of light.

Thus, knowledge ultimately obeys the same laws that all existence obeys...such as Einstein's law that integrates energy and mass with the speed of light as expressed by his famous equation:

$$E = mc^2$$
where:

E = energy; m = mass; c^2 = the speed of
light squared

Likewise, knowledge integrates with time and the speed of light as expressed by the following equation:

$$K = tc^2$$
where:

K = knowledge; t = time; c^2 = the speed of
light squared

Today, in our young Earthbound civilization, the

---

[1]Conscious beings perhaps overcome the speed-of-light limitation through eternal inflationary expansions of Gravity Units beyond our universe, into limitless existence and hyperspace.

always fatal disease of irrationality darkens the future for all human beings. Growing irrationality reduces and eventually stops the accumulation of new knowledge needed to survive and prosper. Growing irrationality eventually destroys the conscious mechanism for processing and accumulating knowledge. But, with the Neo-Tech discovery, irrationality can be cured worldwide to let all conscious beings forge ahead, geometrically accumulating knowledge at rates eventually limited only by the speed of light.

Part 18
The Universe is but a Dot Next to
Individual Consciousness

Every individual consciousness has the capacity to generate, process, and use new knowledge at rates approaching the speed of light. By fully understanding the effects of such knowledge production and use, one quickly rectifies the false view of life held by most people who have lived on Earth. That false view expressed in Monty Python's "Meaning of Life" and promoted by mystics throughout history is: "Individual human beings are but insignificant dots among the vast universe."

Facts and logic demonstrate the exact opposite: Without irrationality or mysticism, each individual consciousness has unlimited capacity to generate and utilize new knowledge at near the speed of light. Francis Bacon identified, "Knowledge is power." Thus, after a few millennia of such knowledge accumulation, any conscious individual gains the power to so totally dominate existence that the entire universe and all its evolutionary processes seem by comparison to shrink into static insignificance. For, in both power and significance, individual consciousness quickly soars beyond the dynamics of nature and the entire universe.

Today, on Earth, the fully integrated honesty of Neo-Tech finally reverses that mystical view bewailing mankind's insignificance. Neo-Tech demonstrates that the power of the universe shrinks to almost nothing when compared to the unlimited power of individual consciousness.

Part 19
Who is the Creator?

Does a creator of galaxies and universes exist? Indeed, such a creator could not defy the laws of physics. Yet, today, as for the past three millennia, most people believe a creator must be some mystical higher "authority" or power as promulgated by someone's scriptures or edicts. ...For two millennia, such mystical gods of creation were conjured-up by neocheaters wanting nothing more grand than to live off the efforts of others.

As demonstrated in the balance of this chapter, everyday conscious beings like you and me work within the laws of physics to create and control all heavens and earths.

Part 20
The Goal of Conscious Beings

Throughout the universe, conscious beings pursue their natural goals and responsibilities by achieving biological immortality, limitless prosperity, and eternal happiness. Thus, they forever preserve the supreme value of the universe: individual consciousness. For without conscious beings, no value or meaning would exist throughout the universe. ...Conscious beings free of mysticism never allow their precious lives — lives of limitless value — to end.

Part 21
Galaxies Created Beyond The Dynamics of Nature

Eons ago, a conscious being, as you and I, worked at the edge of a distant galaxy with an integrating computer of a spatial-geometry driven, mass/energy assembler. By assembling units of gravitational geometries, that person corralled enough strings of wound-up gravity to equal the mass of another galaxy. As the moment of critical gravity approached, the final collapse into an entropy-reversing, rotating "black hole" began. He then arose smiling. With arm held high, he cried, "Let there be light!"[1] ...At that moment, in a far corner of the universe, the light of a million times a million suns flashed and began its photonic journey across the universe. A galaxy was born...a man-made galaxy.

Part 22
Galaxies Discovered Beyond The Dynamics of Nature

Today, eons later, specks of light from that conscious-made galaxy fall on the planet Earth — on the lens of a telescope. An astrophysicist examines computer data gathered from those specks of light. Then, integrating that data with the physical and mathematical dynamics of astral mass and energy, he moves closer to a momentous discovery. He moves closer to discovering a major astral event falling outside the natural dynamics of mass and

---

[1]The expression "Let there be light" was first manipulatively used in the mystical world of the Bible, then entertainingly used in the science-fiction world of Isaac Asimov, and now factually used in the objective world of Neo-Tech.

energy — an event that irrevocably altered nature's charted course for the universe.

But, that scientist knows, as any competent scientist knows, that nothing, including conscious beings, can alter the axiomatic laws of physics, mathematics, and existence. And he knows that existence can have no antecedent basis or original creator. Yet, he realizes that, within the laws of physics, conscious beings can alter the natural dynamics of mass and energy. Thus, he realizes conscious beings and only conscious beings can alter nature's manifest destiny, not only here on Earth, but throughout the universe.

Combining such knowledge with computer processed data, that scientist moves closer toward directly observing the alteration of nature's Grand Cycle by conscious beings. Such direct observation may come, for example, through a correlation of computer data concerning black holes or possibly quasars and pulsars. In fact, such correlations of data probably already exist on Earth — hidden in considerable accumulations of uninterpreted data. Integrating such data could reveal that certain cosmic events exist outside the natural dynamics of their mass, energy, and gravity. In turn, that data could then demonstrate how conscious beings create and control such cosmic events as energy and galaxy creators for the eternal prosperity of all conscious life.

Thus, conscious beings could forever prevent the Grand Cycle from completing itself. They could do that, for example, by routinely creating gravity dimensions and geometries that constantly pump entropy-reversing structures back into the universe. Such constantly created, new structures would break the dynamics of the Grand Cycle, allowing the universe to forever oscillate within its most efficient range for conscious beings.

Part 23
Create Your Own Galaxy

Beginning with the data from that speck of light born a million years before, today's Earthbound scientist will discover and prove a newborn galaxy created outside the mass/energy/gravity dynamics of nature alone. He will then look toward the heavens realizing that he has discovered a galaxy made by a conscious being. He will further realize that over eternal time, over eternally interdicted cycles, all the galaxies and universes, all the heavens and Earths, were at one time created from conscious-made structure pumps that formed new realms of existence while preserving old realms.

And finally, he will realize his mind is the same conscious mind possessed by our immutable conscious cousins who create new realms of existence in other worlds and galaxies for us, them, and everyone.

Part 24
After the Discovery

After that first discovery of a conscious-made galaxy or black hole, scientists will then approximate from our geometric increases of knowledge on Earth and our achievement of biological immortality, when you and I can stand above all the imagined gods to give the command, *Let there be light!*

Part 25
Conclusion

No intimidating god or ethereal super consciousness reigns over the universe. Mystical gods or "higher beings" do not exist, cannot exist, need not exist. For only universes created and controlled by rational, value-producing conscious beings as you and I are needed to explain all existence. And with biological immortality, we Earth beings will someday stand smiling at the edge of space creating our own stars, galaxies, universes, collections of universes, and beyond.

EPILOGUE

The mightiest power in existence, the power to control existence, is expressed by the great command, "Let there be light!" That power has forever existed among fellow beings throughout the universe. The essence of that power is available to all of us, now, here on Earth today through Neo-Tech. ...Neo-Tech eradicates irrationality — the disease that causes ignorance and death among conscious beings.

AIDS degenerates the body's protective immune system into weakness, sickness, then death; irrationality and mysticism degenerates the mind's protective thinking system into ignorance, sickness, then death. Irrationality cripples and finally destroys the conscious mind.

But unlike AIDS, an immediate cure exists right now for irrationality and its virus-like neocheaters. That cure is Neo-Tech. Curing irrationality will also bring definitive cures for AIDS, cancer, heart disease, and all other diseases harmful to conscious beings. Neo-Tech forever eradicates irrationality and its symbiotic neocheaters, allowing the individual to direct his or her life toward achieving guiltless prosperity and abiding happiness for self, others, and all society.

Neo-Tech also opens the way for knowledge expanding geometrically to eventually approach the speed of light. Every person applying Neo-Tech, therefore, holds unbeatable advantages over those crippled by irrationality, parasitical elites, and neocheaters. Indeed, Neo-Tech allows human beings to acquire total control over both the material and emotional realms. Neo-Tech gives all human beings on Earth today the power to execute the tripartite commands: "Let there be wealth!", "Let there be romantic love!", "Let there be eternal youth!"

The time has come to grow up...or be left behind to perish in a world of irrationality. Clinging to irrational or mystical beliefs such as supreme creators or "higher authorities" is as crippling to human life and prosperity as would be the clinging to the once popular belief that the Earth is flat or today's fading belief that force-backed "authorities" or politicians can advance the well-being of any individual or society.

After 3000 years, the time has come to abandon life-destroying irrationality and all its symbiotic parasites and neocheaters. Now is the time to mature into meeting our responsibility of grooming the supreme value of the universe — our own conscious lives. Now is the time to groom our conscious minds with fully integrated honesty for limitless growth and value production forever into the future. Now is the time to join our fellow conscious beings throughout all existence in meeting our supreme responsibility to life — to live happily, prosperously with our fellow conscious beings throughout eternal existence. **For, we are the creators of all heavens and earths. ...All glory to us conscious beings!**

A Mathematical View
of
Time, Eternity, and Existence
by
Bruce Gordon, Cyberglyph, 32 Debora Drive, Plainview, NY 11803

An **instant in time**, like this or any other moment in eternity is an *infinitesimal* quantity, expressed symbolically as

$$t_i = dt$$

Eternity (E) is the whole of time, from the infinitely distant past to the infinitely far future, an *integrated*, infinite time interval. Using the notation of the calculus, eternity is expressed as

$$\underline{E} = \int_{-\infty}^{\infty} dt$$

A universe (U) is a process in time.[1] It can be thought of as a matrix-valued function of dimensionality $(n_1, n_2, \ldots)$.

$$\underline{U} = [u_{x_1 x_2 \ldots}]_{(n_1, n_2, \ldots)}$$

where the $u_{x_1 x_2 \ldots}$ are **Gravity Units** at positions specified by the coordinates $(x_1, x_2, \ldots)$. If the status of a gravity unit varies as a function of time then, at any given instant, a "snapshot" of that gravity unit at that instant in time would be

$$u_i = u(t_i)$$

The composite portrait of the whole universe at that same instant,

$$\underline{U}_i = [u(t_i)_{x_1 x_2 \ldots}]_{(n_1, n_2, \ldots)}$$

is integrated to obtain the **equation of eternal existence**...

$$\underline{U}_E = \int_{-\infty}^{\infty} [u(t)_{x_1 x_2 \ldots}]_{(n_1, n_2, \ldots)}\, dt = [\int_{-\infty}^{\infty} u(t)_{x_1 x_2 \ldots}\, dt]_{(n_1, n_2, \ldots)}$$

(See page 98 for this equation adjusted to a perceived linearity of time.)

Future mathematical steps will involve the relationships among consciousness, Neothink, and Gravity Units. Submissions to Neo-Tech Publishing, P.O. Box 60906, Boulder City, NV 89006 are invited.

---

[1]Existence is not in time. Time is within existence. Thus, any universe is in time within existence.

Chapter 7
Gravity Units

The fully integrated honesty of Neo-Tech bridges the widest gaps among physics and science — from the general relativity of cosmic gravity and beyond to the quantum mechanics of quarks and below.[1] Conscious life using Neo-Tech — fully integrated honesty — bridges those and other problems, great and small, to deliver eternal life, happiness, prosperity.

The controlling keys of existence are the ultimate-symmetry Gravity Units as explained in Chapter 5. Also, as explained on pages 45-46, gravity is negative energy, always pulling in toward nonmotion. Mass and energy are positive energy, always pushing out toward motion. Our universe and all existence consist of gravity, mass, and energy. The sum of all existence equals zero energy. Therefore, the total energy of (1) our universe, of (2) every universe-containing, microscopically undetectable Gravity Unit, and of (3) all vacuums is zero — nothing — as explained on pages 45-46.

No real vacuum exists in nature. All spacetime points in existence contain *existence* itself. All existence consists of Gravity Units with zero energy. Thus, any and every point in existence can be quantum fluxed into equal amounts of negative-energy gravity and positive-energy mass/energy. Then, exploding from the cold "vacuum" or "nothingness" of pure geometric gravity into a cosmic

---

[1]And, from chemical clocks of strange-attractor chaos that are strong on empirical demonstration but weak on theory...to superstrings* of ultimate symmetry that are strong on theory but weak on empirical demonstration. ...Neo-Tech bridges those gaps.

*Strings, not points, seem to be the basic entities of existence. Even in nature-evolved life, the string-like helix of DNA is basic.

inflation, that Gravity Unit forms a new universe of mass, energy, space, time, and motion.

Zon Jr. Creating a Galaxy before Breakfast

A Metaphor

From any point above-and-below, in every vacuum state and universe, conscious beings can flux, break, or inflate Gravity-Unit symmetries into limitless new galaxies or universes. All of those actions can occur without violating the laws of physics.

Existence exists. For, existence cannot not exist. Existence is Gravity Units with fields of existence at every point in space, matter, energy, and time.[1] As philosopher Ayn Rand recognized, "Existence *is* identity." Thus, Gravity Units *are* identity: the fundamental identity of existence — as is consciousness. ...The melded symmetry of consciousness and Gravity Units points the way to unifying consciousness with physics — points the way to unifying all existence.

---

[1]Time is always within a background of existence: Existence is not in time. Instead, time is in existence. Thus, time can be measured as changing geometric shapes in space. Indeed, spacetime is a geometry dependent on its contents and their configurations. Inside Gravity Units, time disappears into fixed spatial dimensions.

Gravity Units

Gravity Inflations, Light Cones, and Universe Creations

Existence does not smoothly reduce down to nothing or non existence. Instead, everything in nature ultimately reduces to a discrete bump, a quantum, a unit in an ether of Gravity Units (GUs), which are the eternal quantum units of existence. GUs comprise the ether substrate in which all broken symmetries exist. A GU is an unimaginably small entity with essentially zero surface at seemingly infinite curvature. Yet, each GU is still an entity, a unit of existence — the prime unit of existence with specific properties. The GU is essentially maximal symmetry: a pure symmetry of gravity or field of geometry.

But, at the boundaries of GUs are *asymmetric* regions of countless smaller, connecting Gravity Units at which quantum fluxes can inflate into separate universes. Each of those universes creates a spacetime quasi light cone that eventually meets the real light cone of every other universe evolving from that Gravity Unit to create a universe of universes many times the total size of the distance traversed at the speed of light.

For example, as shown by the illustration on page 92, magnify a Gravity Unit by a googol...or 10^{100} times. The GU would now appear as unimaginably large with its highly curved surface now appearing as essentially flat. That surface is asymmetrically disrupted with bumps of countless other, smaller Gravity Units. Those disruptions can flux into universes at countless points on the surface of the GU to produce countless quasi light cones that eventually link at distances in any amounts beyond that communicated by the speed of light.

As shown on the illustration on page 92, light cones linked from Y to B″ have communicated at many times the speed of light with nothing exceeding the speed of light.

A Gravity Unit Magnified 10^{100} Times

fluxing into

Countless Universe-Making Gravity/Light Cones

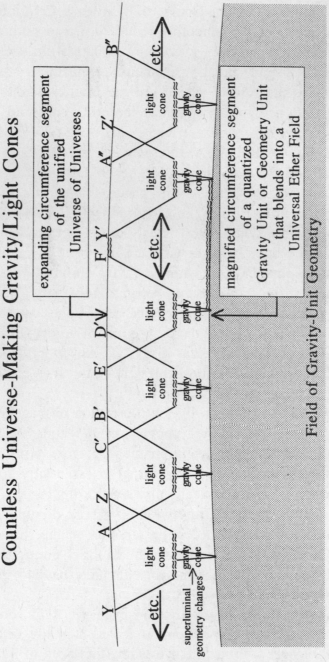

Field of Gravity-Unit Geometry

As a law of nature, everything in existence can be reduced to a smallest unit or quantum — be it an electron or quark for mass or a photon for energy. Beneath mass and energy lie resonating strings and thinkons with dimensions less than 10^{-35} meters. Those strings and thinkons create spacetime mass, energy, and consciousness. Beneath those dimensions lie an ether of Gravity Units that form a universal sea of eternal geometries. Measurements through Gravity Units may someday overcome the Heisenberg Uncertainty Principle in establishing the simultaneous position and momentum of an electron to any arbitrary degree of certainty.

MOVEMENT II

The Anticivilization

The Problem

Unconquerable Honesty

In this anticivilization, we each are alone in our struggle to live rationally. We have always been alone with our own honesty. That aloneness of honesty is our only unconquerable strength in this anticivilization. For, we are chained to a civilization based on dishonesty. In the end, that dishonesty cheats us of our earned rewards as we each die unnecessarily, tragically unfulfilled.

By contrast, in the Civilization of the Universe, no such struggle or dishonesty exists. In an honest culture of certainty and rationality, everyone is free — eternally free, prosperous, fulfilled.

Chapter 8

Unlocking the Secrets
to
Limitless Wealth

On planet Earth, no major breakthrough of knowledge has occurred in two generations — since (1) Albert Einstein replaced Newtonian physics[1] with relativity and (2) a handful of brilliant physicists like Dirac and Feynman developed quantum mechanics. Why no further seminal breakthroughs? Because thinking from today's greatest minds, such as those of Stephen Hawking and Roger Penrose, short-circuits when their wide-scope thinking turns to mysticism. Indeed, mystical bubbles reduce conscious minds to those of lost children, even the greatest minds like those of Hawking and Penrose. Thus, trapped in mysticism, new knowledge needed to deliver prosperity, both now and into the future, can no longer evolve.

In this anticivilization, the most brilliant conscious minds can no longer develop major, breakthrough knowledge. Most such brilliant minds today are stuck — limited to narrow, specialized areas — bounded by integration-blocking mysticisms. Those brilliant minds are weakened and limited by mysticism. They can be outflanked and outperformed by lower IQ minds that are

---

[1]Einstein did not "overthrow" Newton's gravity. Rather, Einstein adjusted and *explained* gravity (Newton would "frame no hypotheses"). Einstein actually strengthened and solidified Newton's inverse square law for gravity with spacetime geometry. *In context*, Newton as Einstein was, is, and will remain correct.

mystic-free — minds that can integrate wider perspectives of reality. Because of their expanding mysticisms, geniuses today are thinking and living with increasing impotence. ...So, where does the future lie?

The future lies in the Zonpower discovery: Throughout history, six seminal changes have occurred in the way mankind views itself and its world: (1) the invention of consciousness three millennia ago, (2) the Greeks' discovery of logic and its power, (3) the Renaissance's overthrow of traditional "truths" for the scientific method, (4) the Copernican revolution, (5) the Newtonian revolution, (6) Einstein's relativity and quantum mechanics. Today, the seventh seminal change arises: the unifying discovery of Neothink, Zonpower, and the Civilization of the Universe.

Zonpower delivers boundless knowledge and riches to any conscious individual. For, Zonpower frees reality from irrational illusions. Zonpower connects reality with *all* existence to bring unlimited purpose, wealth, and happiness to conscious beings.

Such wealth-producing, wide-scope integrations are easy to grasp and implement. This *Zonpower* communiqué will prepare you. First, *Zonpower* provides an entirely different way to view yourself, the world, and all existence. Second, *Zonpower* is so widely integrated yet so simply expressed that, on the first reading, you are ready to collect its guiltless riches. Then, on each subsequent reading, your powers to collect its boundless rewards expand.

How scientifically valid is Zonpower? Its mathematical models reduce to $T1=T2k$. Do not worry about that formula now. It is derived on page 239 and made clear throughout Part III. Such a simple formula or model can explain most, if not all, major anomalies in today's science and physics. That universal mathematical expression meets the "simplicity-and-beauty" criterion of Nobel-prize-winning Paul Dirac. Also, for validating major theories, the T1=T2k hypothesis meets the "correspondence" criterion of Nobel-prize-winning Niels Bohr.[1] The "correspondence" criterion requires noncontradictory linkages with science and nature.

And, finally, valid theory must meet three other criteria: (1) offer answers to previously unanswered questions and unsolved problems, (2) offer predictability, and (3) offer many ways to verify or refute the theory. Scientific demonstration of those three criteria focuses on identifying conscious configurations encoded throughout the cosmos. That scientific verification is the object of Neo-Tech research. But, practical proof already exists: **Today, Zonpower can make you rich, happy, and healthy.**

New-Color Symphony

Movement #2

---

[1]Niels Bohr's correspondence criterion should not be confused with his *complimentary principle*, which means the more of one the less of the other. For example, position and momentum of a particle are complementary — the more precisely one is known the less precisely the other is known. Truth and honesty are complementary. For example, the more dogmatically one asserts truth the less honest one becomes. In other words, the more one demands truth, the less contextual or honest become the facts.

A Linear View

Time, Eternity, and Existence
(view from the anticivilization)
by

Justin James Evermen, Theoretical Research Department
Iowa State University, Ames, IA 50012

Below is an alteration on Gordon's mathematical view of time, eternity, and existence on page 88. Gordon's equation does not explain the non circular/curved nature of time that seems to present itself to us. We see linear time. So to approximate this lineation it is necessary to take the natural log of the function. This lineates the space gravity curve and presents them as our consciousness perceives them. Just as $1/\chi$ graphed on logxlog paper is lineated so is time by the log or ln function. And just as $1/\chi$ appears linear on logxlog paper so does time. Thus, the necessity to lineate its curvature. So, therefore, we know $1/\chi$ is curved as also time is curved. But in this askewed frame of reference they will both present themselves as linear.

Therefore

$$\underline{U}_E = \int_{-\infty}^{\infty} [\ln{(u(t)\chi_1\chi_2\chi_3...)}](n_1, n_2,...)dt$$

$$= \int_{-\infty}^{\infty} [\ln{(u(t)\chi_1\chi_2\chi_3...)}dt](n_1, n_2,...)$$

Thus the log or ln function serves to lineate the curvature that the **Gravity Units** hold. Hence, our perception of linear, not curved time.

So thus the **equation of eternal existence...**

$$\underline{U}_E = \int_{-\infty}^{\infty} [\ln{(u(t)\chi_1\chi_2\chi_3...)}dt](n_1, n_2,...)$$

Where

t_i = instant of time	$\underline{U}$ = universe
$\underline{E}$ = eternity	$u\chi_1, \chi_2...$ = Gravity Units

Chapter 9

Birth of Parasitical Elites
in
America

James J. Hill was a 19th-Century super value producer who pushed into a worldwide business dynamic. Just as Hill achieved great success in the American railroad industry and began spearheading an international expansion, he was snuffed out by a newly burgeoning parasitical-elite class in America. The story of James J. Hill is documented in the book *"Entrepreneurs Versus The State"* by Burton W. Folsom, Jr.

Political Entrepreneurs Versus Market Entrepreneurs

In that book, Folsom identifies how throughout history there have been two distinct types of entrepreneurs: political entrepreneurs and market entrepreneurs. Political entrepreneurs seek profits by working with the government to get subsidies, grants, and special privileges. They seek success through political pull. In contrast, market entrepreneurs seek success by producing increasingly improved values, products, and services at increasingly lower costs.

The Transcontinental Railroads

The building of America's transcontinental railroads provided a dramatic example of political entrepreneurs versus market entrepreneurs. In the 1860s, railroads began expanding rapidly throughout America. Thus, political

99

entrepreneurs seeking easy dollars teamed up with Congressmen seeking unearned power and glory. Those political entrepreneurs lobbied Congressmen for the federal government to subsidize the building of America's first transcontinental railroad.

That situation presented a perfect combination for the parasitical-elite class: White-collar-hoax political entrepreneurs could line their pockets with lavish government subsidies, and the Congressmen handing out those subsidies could garner self-glory and justify their jobs by proclaiming how beneficial they were to the American people by financing America's first transcontinental railroad. Thus, a deception was woven by that parasitical-elite class through claiming only the government could finance an undertaking as large and expensive as building a transcontinental railroad. That same deception is still promoted in history books to this day.

With great fanfare, enormous subsidies were granted to the Union Pacific and the California Pacific. The California Pacific started building track from the west coast, the Union Pacific from the east coast. Those companies were paid by the government according to how many miles of track each laid. Consequently, both companies built along the longest, most out-of-the-way routes they could justify. That way, each company collected the maximum dollars from the government.

Spending public money they controlled but did not earn, the Congressmen were quick to claim credit for building America's first transcontinental railroad. But, unlike market-entrepreneur businessmen spending their own money, those Congressmen were not about to exert the nitty-gritty effort required to insure good value was received for each dollar spent. Thus, the building of that government-financed transcontinental railroad turned into an orgy of fraud.

As a result, after that first transcontinental railroad was built, subsequently called the Union Pacific, it had enormously high operating costs. Because extra-long routes had been purposely built, because time and research had not been taken to locate routes across the lowest-grade hills, each train took more time and fuel to complete its journey. More wages had to be paid; more equipment was tied up. In addition, because the railroad track had been laid so hastily, thousands of miles of shoddy track had to be pulled up and laid again before the first train could even travel over it. Thus, from the start, the Union Pacific could not make a profit. As a result, the federal government had to continue doling out taxpayer dollars just to enable the Union Pacific to operate after the line had been completed.

Soon other political entrepreneurs ganged up with local politicians to demand federally subsidized transcontinental railroads be built in their areas of the country. Thus, the federal government financed a transcontinental railroad in the North, the Northern Pacific, and a transcontinental railroad in the South, the Santa Fe. The building of those two additional government-financed railroads followed the same course as the building of the Union Pacific. The lines were poorly constructed. The builders focused on obtaining maximum government subsidies, not on achieving economy and quality. Thus, after the Northern Pacific and Santa Fe transcontinentals were completed, they too had unnecessarily high operating costs. Both lost money from the start, and both had to continue receiving government subsidies just to operate.

Movement II: The Anticivilization

A Deception Is Woven

A parasitical-elite class consisting of political entrepreneurs, job-justifying politicians, and government-subsidized university professors propagandize to this very day that only the federal government could have financed the building of America's first transcontinental railroads. The story of James J. Hill is ignored.

James J. Hill was a market entrepreneur, *not* a political entrepreneur. He was an integrated thinker and a forward-essence mover. Hill was born in a log cabin to a working class family in Ontario, Canada. He got a job with a local railroad when he was a teenager. He loved railroads and integrated his life with them. Hill moved up quickly. Soon he became involved in the building of local railroads. Then, in 1880, Hill decided to build a transcontinental railroad privately, without any government subsidies. He would call his line the Great Northern.

Hill's plan to build a transcontinental railroad at the very northern border of America was labelled "Hill's folly." Why? First of all, Hill was building a railroad way up north in unsettled wilderness. From where would his business come? Secondly, Hill would have to compete with three transcontinental railroads to the south: the Northern Pacific, the Union Pacific, and the Santa Fe. How could a private railroad be built without government help and then compete with three other railroads that had their expenses paid by the government?

James J. Hill was forced to meet the disciplines of a bottom line. He had to stay within profitable red-to-black business dynamics. Thus, instead of "rushing to collect government subsidies", he built his railroad one extension at a time, westward into the northern wilderness. Hill would build an extension westward a few hundred miles, then move in farmers from the East, free of charge, in order to settle the land along his railroad. Those farmers would then start using Hill's railroad to ship their crops back East to market. Because Hill received no government money, each extension constructed westward would have to profit before another westward extension could be built. In ten years, Hill completed his transcontinental railroad, the Great Northern, without receiving one cent of government money.

Hill had to build each extension with detailed planning to achieve maximum efficiency at minimum operating costs. Hill personally mapped out and built along the shortest, most direct routes. He also carefully surveyed land to find routes containing the lowest grades of hills over which to build. And, with Hill spending hard-earned private money, he insisted on the highest quality workmanship and materials.

The three government-financed transcontinental railroads south of Hill's Great Northern were in the heart of the country and none of them could earn a profit. But, what actually happened once Hill's Great Northern reached the Pacific? All three government-financed transcontinentals went bankrupt and required ever more government bail-out money — taxpayer money — to continue running. In stark contrast, Hill's railroad flourished from the very start. The Great Northern produced a profit, even during recession years.

A Spiral of Inefficiencies

Because the federal government continued subsidizing the money-losing, government-financed transcontinentals, each of those railroads had to obtain government approval to build any new extension. On the other hand, once the

Great Northern was running, Hill built his railroad with extensions called feeder lines. For example, if coal was discovered a hundred miles to the north of Hill's line, he built a feeder line to service that mine. If good trees were available for lumber on a nearby mountain, Hill would build a feeder line to that mountain so that a lumber company could move in and use his railroad to ship its lumber to market. If a suitable valley for cattle ranching existed a few miles to the south, Hill would build a feeder line to service that valley. Railroads discovered that feeder lines were crucial to their profitability. But whenever one of the government-subsidized railroads wanted to build a feeder line, it had to get approval from Congress since it was providing the financing.

Well, everyone knows what happens when politicians become involved. A simple business decision would get hung up for months, even years, before receiving approval. Thus, the government-subsidized railroads could not operate effectively. They could not compete with Hill's Great Northern railroad. What had initially been labelled "Hill's folly" by the establishment ran circles around the government-subsidized, poorly managed railroads.

Fraud Is Inherent in the Parasitical-Elite Class

Over time, the corruption that laced the government-financed transcontinental railroads began unraveling. Unlike James J. Hill's privately-financed transcontinental railroad, the managements of the government-financed transcontinental railroads were not operating by the disciplines of a bottom line. Thus, those white-collar-hoax political entrepreneurs did not exert the discipline required to closely supervise the construction of their railroads for quality and efficiency. The survival of those political

104

entrepreneurs did not depend upon efficient management. Their survival, instead, depended upon exerting political pull. Consequently, the government-financed railroads were left wide open to fraud. Managers often formed their own supply companies selling substandard materials to their own railroads at inflated prices. Payoffs and sellouts were rampant.

Over time, the fraudulent practices of the government-subsidized transcontinental railroads increasingly surfaced. The public became fed up with that corruption. Thus, glory-seeking politicians in Washington once again rushed in to grab attention and "serve the public". A new deception was woven. Congressmen now claimed they were the defenders of the American people and would expose the corruption in the transcontinental railroads. Glory-seeking Congressmen began conducting investigations into the nation's railroad business. Yet, in reality, those glory-seeking politicians were the root cause of that corruption.

As the fraud continued between political entrepreneurs and job-justifying politicians, consider what James J. Hill, the market entrepreneur, was accomplishing. After completing his profitable transcontinental railroad, Hill promoted the building of entire new industries in the Northwest, such as lumber companies in Oregon, apple farms in Washington, mining industries in Montana, cattle ranches in the plains. Hill helped businesses move to the Northwest and gave them special rates to ship their products back East until those businesses became established. This practice quickly built up business along Hill's railroad line.

Next, Hill began thinking about business beyond America. He began exploring opportunities in the Orient.

Movement II: The Anticivilization

Hill calculated that if a single major Chinese province substituted just one ounce of American wheat for rice in their daily diets, he could ship 50,000,000 bushels of wheat to China from America. ...Hill, using wide-scope integrated thinking, began moving beyond the boundaries of a restricted, single-nation mode. He began moving into a worldwide mode.

James J. Hill decided that he was going to promote American trade in Asia, just as he had promoted trade in the Northwest. So, he bought cargo ships and formed his own steamship company to ship American goods to China and Japan. He then sent agents abroad to promote American goods to Asians.

While the white-collar-hoax political entrepreneurs were still trying to figure out how to get more subsidies from the federal government, Hill was turning his attention to world business. James J. Hill was figuring out how to deliver increasing values to the world. He realized that the key to tapping the vast markets of Asia was to build trade by offering to ship American products on his railroad and steamships for free until trade could become established. So, Hill began racing his steamships back and forth between Japan, China, and America.

Hill was a heroic forward-essence mover. He exported to Asia wheat from Midwest farmers and cotton from Southern farmers. He offered a group of Japanese industrialists low-cost American cotton if they would test the American cotton in place of the cotton that they traditionally imported from India. If the Japanese did not like the American cotton, Hill offered to let them keep it free of charge. This worked. Soon Hill's boxcars were filled with cotton bales heading to Japan. Utilizing this same technique, Hill got both the Japanese and the Chinese to start buying American textiles from New England.

James J. Hill Was Spearheading
An American Dominance of Asian Trade

In 1896, American exports to Japan totalled 7.7 million dollars a year. Nine years later, James J. Hill had pushed that figure to 51.7 million dollars a year. He was spearheading an American dominance of Asian trade. And this was occurring a hundred years ago! James J. Hill worked diligently to promote American exports to Asia. For example, starting around 1900, Japan began a railroad building boom. England and Belgium were the traditional suppliers of rail. American rail-makers were still fledgling in the Pittsburgh area. But Hill recognized the importance of the Asian market for steel and rails. So, he personally underbid the Europeans to capture Japanese orders for American rail-makers.

Hill diligently promoted American goods in Asia, ranging from lumber from the Northwest to wheat from the Midwest, to copper from Montana, to apples from Washington, to steel from Pittsburgh, to cotton from the South, to textiles from New England. While the white-collar-hoax political entrepreneurs of the government-subsidized railroads were being closed in upon, Hill was booming American business while blossoming his railroad into an international dynamo.

So what happened next? Attention-seeking politicians began parading the corrupt political entrepreneurs infesting government-subsidized railroads before the public through Senate investigation hearings. Yet, it was Congress that created that corruption in the first place by self-righteously giving away public money it controlled but did not earn. Instead of identifying that Congress was the root cause of the problem, Congress began clamoring for strict regulation of the railroad industry. Congress then devised a strong-arm approach, proclaiming it was protecting the American public from greedy, corrupt railroad executives.

Congress proposed creating the Interstate Commerce Commission to regulate and control the railroads and the Sherman Antitrust Act designed to threaten and punish the railroad industry. Well, James J. Hill realized what was occurring. He travelled to Washington to testify before Congress. Hill meticulously explained what had happened with the government-subsidized railroads versus his privately-financed railroad and how the solution was for government to get out of the railroad business altogether.

But Hill was ignored. Those politicians and bureaucrats could not increase their power nor garner self-glory if they admitted that the root of the problem was caused by Congress getting into the railroad business in the first place — a place in which government never belonged.

Conscious Destruction

Congress ignored James J. Hill and went ahead to create the Interstate Commerce Commission (ICC) and pass the Sherman Antitrust laws that heavily regulated and punished the railroad industry. The ICC and antitrust laws forbid giving any special deals to customers. Thus, the techniques Hill had used to build up trade in the Northwest and was now using to build American trade to Asia became "illegal" — illegal not through objective law but through *force-backed, political-agenda "law"*. As a direct result of that legislation, James J. Hill ended his expansion into the Asian markets. One year after Congress created the Interstate Commerce Commission and passed the Sherman Antitrust laws, Hill sold his steamship line. His farsighted, wide-scope methods were stopped by corrupt government regulations.

America's trade to Japan and China dropped forty percent within two years. ...Remember, before that point, America's trade with Asia had been increasing geometrically. Two years after that legislation was passed by Congress, America's trade with Asia dropped almost in half.

What happened in Congress was not a case of ignorance. James J. Hill actually set up residence in Washington to intensively lobby Congress and its investigative committees. Hill made sure those Congressmen knew what had really happened in the railroad industry and why. He even wrote a book about the situation and published the book himself. Still, Hill's arguments were ignored. For, Congress's goal was not to serve the best interests of the public.

Instead, Congress could garner public support and praise by attacking and regulating the railroad industry, not by admitting that they had been the root cause of railroad corruption. ...Power-seeking politicians with regulating bureaucrats will always block free enterprise and competitiveness. The intervention of politicians and bureaucrats will always drive prices up, service down, while spreading decay and corruption.

What Are the Implications?

How many people today have the slightest idea what happened a hundred years ago with James J. Hill? How many people today know what was started by a single, integrated thinking, forward-essence mover? How many people today know that James J. Hill was spear-heading an American dominance of trade in Asia one-hundred years

109

ago!

Hill's incredible parade of value production, trade, business, and job creation was cut off in its infancy because of a handful of politicians. Seeking to advance their own harmful careers, with total disregard of honesty and reality, those politicians stopped a tremendous value producer, James J. Hill, and his push into Asia.

Hill's master plan was destroyed by corrupt Congressmen one-hundred years ago. And, one must not forget, those Congressmen knew what they were doing. Hill diligently informed them of the real situation — what he had done with his privately-financed railroad, whose fault it was for the corruption that occurred within the government-financed railroads, and what his railroad was doing for America's international trade by its freedom to nurture new business. Yet, those elite, college-educated Congressmen proceeded to pass their self-serving laws and regulations in order to protect and enhance their own harmful livelihoods.

What Really Happened a Hundred Years Ago?

Let us examine this situation even closer. ...What really happened a hundred years ago? What really was cut off by the parasitical-elite class in Washington using force-backed political policies? James J. Hill was not only spearheading an American dominance of trade in Asia a hundred years ago, he was also spearheading an industrialization of Asia. Hill was pushing American business into Asia, causing railroads to be built, causing factories to be built, causing new businesses to be created. He nurtured American business in Asia, and that business was beginning to follow its natural course of flooding into markets and dominating trade. That, in turn, would have led to a rapid industrialization of Asia.

Had James J. Hill been left free to continue spearheading the industrialization of China a hundred years ago, the world would be different today. What kind of creative energies would have been released if China, a country of one billion people, had industrialized a hundred years ago? Where would civilization be today? Would we have cures for cancer, heart disease, AIDS? Would we be building cities in the oceans and on the moon? The contributions that the Chinese could have made to science, to technology, to the world economy are mind-boggling. But no. All of that potential was smashed. A billion people were pushed down and stagnated, 30 million Chinese were killed by communist predators. Why? Because Congressmen a hundred years ago wanted to exercise unearned power and feel false importance!

Thus Arose the Newly Born Parasitical Elites

A hundred years ago, one man learned how to honestly integrate business with reality. He started moving up. He learned how business worked; he learned how the American economy worked. Then, he learned how the world economy worked. He began learning how the whole up-rising of civilization worked. One man, a hundred years ago, learned how to do integrated thinking and forward essence movement. He then began pushing the lid up on society. If that man had been left alone, if he had not been stopped by the politicians, he would have swung open that lid, China would have industrialized, all of Asia would have industrialized, the whole world would have risen up, and America would have been sitting on top of it all.

Instead, James J. Hill was smashed down. The newly

born parasitical-elite class consisting of politicians, bureaucrats, political entrepreneurs, and other professional value destroyers smashed down whatever threatened to expose their hoaxes, whatever threatened their nonproductive livelihoods.

Thus arose the newly born parasitical-elite class in America. They joined the worldwide parasitical elites that created an anticivilization on planet Earth. But this irrational civilization based on illusions and hoaxes will be replaced by the rational Civilization of the Universe sensed by James J. Hill at the start of the 20th century and implemented by Zon at the end of the 20th century.

E.S., 1989

> *Anticivilization*: The irrational planet Earth riddled with dishonest parasitical elites like Woodrow Wilson, FDR, and the Clintons causing endless cycles of corruption, destruction, and death for everyone.
>
> *Civilization of the Universe*: The rational universe filled with honest value producers like J.J. Hill, Ray Kroc, and Bill Gates providing endless happiness, wealth, and life for others and society.

Chapter 10

Who Is Wasting Your Brief Life?

An old man is dying. His one-and-only life is ending. All his adult life he worked hard producing values for others. He complained at times, perhaps even questioned, but never more. He always accepted the dictates of the ruling elite — the politicians, bureaucrats, journalists, lawyers, university professors. For that acceptance, he collected social security, food stamps, and other handouts for which he paid hundreds of times over with shrinking happiness, security, savings, and standard of living. At the same time, threats from crime, drugs, racism, and poverty kept growing.

His wife died ten months before. She had devoted her life to following the mystic path from the church, to astrology, to theosophy. He always silently thought her life path was for nothing — a sadly wasted life. Yet, was his path any different? Indeed, they depended on each other. Her loss caused unbearable pain that wanted to scream out. And now, for the first time, he began feeling an indescribable anger bubbling deep within his soul. What caused that rising anger? Did it come from the same source discovered by his wife during her dying days?

Her anger began when she realized the mystic path, which consumed her entire adult life, was a terrible hoax — was nothing real. Her life was wasted on an illusion — a vast hoax perpetuated and manipulated by those who used deceit to advance their own harmful

115

livelihoods, self-importance, and usurped power. ...Indeed, over the centuries, those hoaxers used and wasted the one-and-only lives of their victims by the millions.

As his wife lay dying, she suddenly startled him. She had always been so tranquil. But, now, anger lashed out. Suddenly that frail woman wanted to obliterate everyone associated with manipulating those mystic frauds.

Strangely, during her final moments of anger, he once again, after fifty years, felt love, excitement, and life with his wife. And he knew she felt the same. Their eyes shared the most precious moment of their lives. They shared once more, after fifty years, a fleeting moment of long-lost love and passion. Suddenly, they had discovered the key to life and happiness together. Then, she closed her eyes for the final time. She was gone forever.

Now, today, as he is dying, that old man feels anger rising deep from within. He wonders what would happen if that anger ever discovered its undefined targets. But, what targets? No, not the same mystic-leader targets his wife so angrily attacked. Those mystic leaders deprived his wife's entire adult life of love, happiness, and excitement. Yet, he was never tricked by those exploiters of ignorance and illusions. Then, who are his targets of this fifty-year accumulation of anger now surging from deep within? ...On second thought, could those targets be the same mystic hoaxers his wife discovered — just more cleverly disguised?

In his mind, he begins reviewing his life, year by year. In the perspective of potential, his life seems to have meant so little. He feels life lacked the growth, prosperity, and accomplishment that belonged to him. ...Did he miss a tremendous life experience that he earned but never collected? Who then collected those earnings?

Who Is Wasting Your Brief Life?

What happens to everyone's one-and-only life? The old man wondered. What happens to the promise of youth? Indeed, almost every human life is drained or used up until each dies. Why does such a waste occur to essentially everyone? Almost everyone seems to lose his or her life to nothing, for nothing. Who is responsible, who is to blame?

Then, he recalls an experience shortly after his wife died. It was a Saturday afternoon. He went to the shopping mall to which he and his wife had often gone. Somehow he knew this would be his last visit to that mall — or any mall. He sat in the rotunda to think about her.

After some time, he began noticing the people in the mall. He gradually noticed something different — something he never saw before: No one looked *really* happy! Many seemed overweight. So many seemed drained. Some were harassed by their children. Others seemed unhappy with their spouses. He knew most wanted or needed more money. Many probably disliked their jobs. Others were worried about losing their jobs, or had already lost their jobs. Most looked bored, anxious, or empty. Like him, he knew almost everyone had abandoned his or her youthful dreams of success, glamour, prosperity. ...Almost everyone's life seemed wasted.

He then thought to himself: To have so many losses and problems, we must be guilty of something. We must be guilty of all kinds of faults, failures, and mediocrities. Anyway, we cause our own problems and limitations, don't we? That's what the authorities say. They say we're to blame, we're at fault.

Wait a minute! We cause our own problems? We're to blame, we're at fault, we are guilty? Who says? Who exactly are those who say we are responsible for not

117

having success, prosperity, and happiness? Do we really prevent ourselves from gaining success, prosperity, and happiness? Does that really make sense? Is that natural? Or is some dark secret fooling us?

Coming back to the present, the old man realizes his rising anger is unlocking that secret. Such losses do not make sense, he tells himself. Such losses are not natural. Yes, some dark secret has been fooling everyone. The old man closes his eyes. He is dying. ...Someday everyone will discover the cause of that old man's anger, pain, and suffering. Everyone will discover that the deeply hidden causes of human suffering and death emanate from the parasitical-elite class.

Who exactly are the parasitical elites? A simple, wide-scope accounting process reveals one fact: Parasitical elites are those whose livelihoods are draining much more, often infinitely more, from the economy and society than they deliver. Such accounting answers the following question: Does one's job, livelihood, profession, agency, bureaucracy, or company *build or drain* the economy — *benefit or harm* the productive class? **Does one produce values or destroy values?** ...Wide-scope accounting is a definitive economic-impact statement.

Murderous Organizations are Killing *You*

Some net value destroyers are so obvious that no specific accounting figures are needed for the public to see the destructiveness of such people and their harmful organizations. Consider some of the most harmful bureaucracies in America today: the BATF, DEA, EPA, IRS, INS, FDA, FTC, SEC. Such murderous organizations[1] need guns, jails, and ego "justice" to exist and expand. Those organizations breed legions of professional value destroyers who are responsible for mass property and business destructions that eventually bring economic and social devastations. But, most harmfully, those organizations move *everyone* toward life-wasting stagnation, unhappiness, and death.

Daily, those organizations violate objective justice by committing real crimes of force and fraud. Those organizations are not only harming the economy, but are destroying society and everyone's freedoms by violating each of the ten Articles of the Bill of Rights except the third — they have not yet forced the quartering of their troops in private homes. ...Those organizations depend on a legal system corrupted with the subjective laws and ego "justice" used to advance their harmful political agendas.[2]

The DEA

With conventional accounting within arbitrary or closed boundaries, almost any destructive end, even destructions of entire economies and genocide, can be made to appear beneficial to the public as demonstrated by Lenin, Hitler, and Mao. But, wide-scope accounting

---

[1]Murderous organizations? Even the EPA, for example, is responsible for the deaths of 8–20 people for every life it theoretically saves. The EPA kills people through the increased living costs and decreased living standards that bureaucracy forces on society, especially on the lower classes (Ref: *Forbes*, 7/6/92, page 60). Likewise, other bureaucracies cause long-term harm and death to countless more people than those few people who may benefit. In fact, those who profit from or live off the lethal actions of those bureaucracies are accomplices to murder — often mass murder.

[2]Reference: *The Neo-Tech Protection Kit*, Volumes I and II, 780 pages, The Neo-Tech Research and Writing Center, revised 1994.

immediately reveals the destructiveness of those men and their organizations. Now, apply that wide-scope accounting to organizations like the Drug Enforcement Administration (the DEA). First, consider that the DEA exists entirely through gun-backed policies created by self-serving, demagogic politicians. From that fact, the public can increasingly see that the armed divisions of the DEA are the engines that support and expand the drug problem, crimes, death, and loss of constitutional rights for every American citizen.

The armed DEA divisions continuously expand the market for drugs by providing the super-high price supports that make possible the flourishing of organized crime and drug cartels. Such government-forced economics necessitate pushing ever more potent drugs onto others, especially onto vulnerable young people. In turn, those immoral DEA actions keep escalating the crimes and deaths related to drugs.

Gun-backed organizations like the DEA serve but one purpose — the expansion of harmful livelihoods that let politicians and bureaucrats drain the economy and damage society by creating ever expanding drug problems.

The IRS

Likewise, the gun-backed divisions of the Internal Revenue Service work with Dole-type[1] politicians in expanding destructive political agendas that enhance their jobs and power. Their armed criminal activities diminish everyone's future by crippling or breaking the daring entrepreneur and aggressive business person. Indeed, every large business today started with the daring courage,

---

[1]Career politician Senator Bob Dole has been a major supporter of expanding the destructive power and criminality of the IRS through its violent armed agents.

hard work, and precious seed capital of a heroically aggressive entrepreneur. Yet, as official policy, the IRS directs its newest-trained auditors and armed agents to "cut their teeth" on small, vulnerable, first-year companies. In that way, the IRS each year ruins countless individuals and small businesses — destroying the seeds to our economic future by destroying millions of current and future jobs.[1] Indeed, wide-scope accounting reveals how the armed divisions of the IRS are criminally destroying the essence of our economy, society, and freedoms not only for today, but for future generations.

The IRS thrives as a destructive bureaucracy *because* of the irrational income tax. By contrast, revenues raised through consumption or sales taxes would vanish deficits, reduce the IRS to a fraction of its current size...and eliminate its armed divisions that back criminal collection procedures used to override due process while inflicting cruel-and-unusual punishments on its victims.

No legitimate reason exists for armed agents in any bureaucracy. Local police and courts, not armed bureaucratic agents, can competently and constitutionally protect all individuals, property, and organizations, including physically protecting government officials.

The INS

What about the Immigration and Naturalization Service, the INS? By throwing wide-scope accounting on the gun-backed segments of that organization, anyone can see its harm to the economy. With its army of enforcers who never have to answer to American citizens, the INS

---

[1]The Neo-Tech Research Center estimates that 7.1 million jobs in the American economy were lost from 1980-1990 due to businesses being damaged or destroyed by illegal IRS actions.

ravishes hard-working value producers and their families. The INS army expands its power and livelihoods by attacking America's most competitive workers of the past and future. Those workers are the immigrants who abandon their homelands and risk their lives to deliver competitive values to our economy. Thus, they raise the well-being and prosperity of all Americans. Such life-improving immigrants have been the backbone of competitive growth and economic prosperity in America, despite the dishonest political demagoguery to the contrary.

The FDA

And the Food and Drug Administration? Wide-scope accounting shows the FDA to be the biggest killer of all — literally killing millions of human beings. Operating under a power-mad Commissioner like Dr. David Kessler, armies of FDA bureaucrats destructively build their own "achievement" files for their own promotions. By enforcing increasingly cost-prohibitive compliance to irrational regulations, the FDA blocks scientific and medical progress.

As specifically identified in the Neo-Tech literature, without the FDA and its armed enforcers, today we would have cures for cancer, heart disease, AIDS, muscular dystrophy, and essentially all other serious diseases (Ref: *The Neo-Tech Discovery*). Moreover, biomedical advances would have the human race moving toward non-aging longevity as achieved in all mystic-free civilizations throughout the universe — in all civilizations free of parasitical elites. This concept is supported by recent findings in physics and astronomy as summarized in Parts I and III of *Zonpower*.

Destructive Organizations
How Do They Survive?

How do destructive organizations succeed in deceiving everyone so completely for so long?

A successful magician deceives *everyone* in his audience with illusions. The key to the magician's successful tricks or deceptions is to keep everyone distracted. The magician with his wand keeps attention focused on a decoy illusion removed from the point of deception. With everyone's attention diverted, no one sees the deception.

All parasitical elites and their organizations have a myriad of decoy illusions. Created through deceptive rationalizations, those illusions have hidden the destructions of the parasitical-elite class since Plato showed golden-soul parasites 2300 years ago how to rule the value producers.

Consider today's Drug Enforcement Administration: With subjective laws enacted by power-usurping politicians, the DEA uses its wand of deception to point at the drugs it seized and people it jailed as progress in the "War on Drugs". But, in fact, the DEA has no motivation to diminish any drug problem. Without an expanding drug problem, its system of livelihoods and power would diminish. Thus, the DEA has every motivation to expand its bureaucracy of bogus livelihoods and power by creating and expanding drug problems, which it does very successfully.

Consider the armed criminal divisions of the Internal Revenue Service: With their wands of deception, those IRS divisions point at the money and property seized. Through its gun-backed agents, the IRS criminally squeezes the working assets out of the "underground" economy, heroic entrepreneurs, struggling individuals, and small businesses. They point to the dollars they have seized from those whom they have crippled, destroyed, or jailed. But throw wide-scope accounting on those illegal elements of the IRS, and one discovers its gun-backed enforcers are destroying our present and future economy, jobs, freedoms, privacy, and well-being. More broadly, the, IRS-forced paperwork alone is the greatest time-and-life destroyer *ever* devised to expand bureaucratic jobs and power. ...And most destructively, the IRS smothers youth from becoming the independent business giants needed for the future prosperity of any society.

Consider the Immigration and Naturalization Service: The INS points its wand of deception at the "illegal" aliens it forcibly drains, blocks, jails, or ejects from America. Such uses of force are not only racist, but are criminal acts against innocent value producers. Those crimes are hidden by deceptive-wand myths such as "draining welfare funds" and "keeping jobs for Americans". Both such claims are patently false. Wide-scope accounting clearly reveals that "illegal" aliens (1) add much more in taxes than they "drain" and (2) create many more jobs for Americans than they take. Thus, each racist INS crime diminishes everyone's job and life by undermining America's standard of living, its economic strength, its international competitiveness.

And finally, consider the Food and Drug Administration: The FDA points its wand of deception toward "protecting" the health of Americans. But, in reality, the FDA is responsible for killing more citizens than any other group of parasitical elites. For, through power-usurping regulations, the FDA blocks the cures for all major diseases. The FDA also blocks the development of major longevity advances. ...Only unhindered science and business can bring disease-free, non-aging longevity, as accomplished in all mystic-free, parasite-free civilizations throughout the universe.

The Neo-Tech Literature

With actual wide-scope accountings, the Neo-Tech literature reveals the huge net destructions caused by specific politicians, bureaucrats, judges, lawyers, prosecutors, white-collar-hoax business people, and other parasitical elites. The Neo-Tech literature also details how those elites can exist only by creating and expanding power-building instruments such as armed bureaucracies. The Neo-Tech literature identifies how all parasitical elites depend on armed bureaucracies and subjective ego "justice" to enforce their harmful survival agendas. And finally, the Neo-Tech literature details the spectacular prosperity that awaits everyone upon terminating the parasitical-elite class.

The Neo-Tech Wedge

Most people in government, business, and the professions are *not* targets for personal ostracism or job termination. Instead, they are candidates to benefit economically, professionally, and personally by getting on the honest side of the split caused by the *Neo-Tech Wedge*. That Wedge is already beginning to move through governments and businesses, separating the honest productive people from the parasitical elites. ...Only parasitical elites and their armed enforcers are targeted for ostracism and job termination. They are the ones who waste everyone's brief life. They shall not escape the Neo-Tech Wedge.

Movement II: The Anticivilization

Vanishing Armed Bureaucrats

In contrast to legitimately armed policemen who serve to protect life and property, armed bureaucrats serve to harm life and property. Today, the increasing social and physical harms caused by politicized armed bureaucrats are endangering all federal employees.[1] ...Bureaucrats, not law-abiding citizens, must be disarmed.

As with Shakespeare's Iago in *Othello*, a politician who lives through armed bureaucracies exists not to produce values but to destroy them, not to bring social harmony but to disrupt it. As with the conflict in Sophocles' *Antigone*, the conflict between Neo-Tech and politicized armed bureaucracies evolves from the deepest issues of right versus wrong, honesty versus dishonesty, and protective government versus destructive government.

Neo-Tech will bring *peace*[2] to America and *trust* in government by vanishing armed bureaucracies.

---

[1] The criminalities of various politicians and the brutal destructiveness of certain federal bureaucracies, all deceptively whitewashed by the news media, are fueling a public loathing toward government that is threatening its employees.

[2] On May 29, 1995, the following notice was posted on various Internet newsgroups:

Memorial Day: a Political Hoax
Clinton's wreath laying: obscene hypocrisy. Notice how such politicians, the cause of all wars, revel in glory as they eulogize their dead victims. ...Remember when Memorial Day was called Decoration Day? It was not a eulogy day for the politicians' dead victims, but a celebration for the end of war and its living survivors.

Chapter 11

Your Personal Terminator

guarantees

Limitless Prosperity

In the popular Arnold Schwarzenegger movies of the early 1990s, the terminator represents a nonstoppable force of destruction. In the real world, Neo-Tech represents a nonstoppable force that terminates *all* destructive forces. ...Neo-Tech is *your* personal terminator.

Today, right now, you hold a personal terminator in your hands — a terminator programed to eliminate all forces that harm you, your family, your future. ...Your terminator comes alive today to deliver unending happiness and prosperity.

What is a Personal Terminator?

A personal terminator is your *natural self* programed to deliver limitless prosperity by terminating all life-depriving forces, large or small. For example, consider the most damaging of those forces, which began growing over six decades ago: In 1933, politicians with their expanding bureaucracies began draining America's business and economic assets. Starting with Roosevelt's New Deal, that drainage has expanded into the largest, most camouflaged theft and destruction of assets in history. Today, politicians and bureaucrats, as part of a growing *parasitical-elite class*, are devouring those shrinking assets.

Economic deterioration is upon us. But, with your personal terminator, you can end such parasitical harms while creating prosperity for you, your family, and society.

127

Movement II: The Anticivilization

Neo-Tech — the Master Terminator

Personal terminators are generated from a Master Terminator called Neo-Tech. That terminator is eternally protective to all conscious life.

First, consider that neither harmful leaders nor destructive terminators can exist in civilizations evolved beyond the nuclear age. In other words, no civilization can survive much past its nuclear age with a destructive ruling class — with a parasitical-elite class.

Now, consider our civilization: Already well into our nuclear age, we are still ruled by parasitical elites. They are unnatural beings. For, they replace their productive human nature with a nonhuman program of purposely harming others, the economy, and society. Thus, they are not human beings. They are subhumans or *humanoids*. Not science-fiction humanoids, but self-made humanoids. For, each parasitical elite has removed from his or her thinking process the essence of a human being. That essence is the competitive production of economic and societal values needed for human survival, prosperity, and happiness.

Those humanoids increasingly drain everyone and society through dishonesty backed by the deception and force needed for parasitical survival. Those parasites live by covertly draining values produced by others rather than by competitively producing values for others and society. ...A civilization ruled by parasites must end in nuclear conflagration. But, that conflagration will never occur. For, the Master Terminator is programed to vanish the parasitical ruling class as nothing in cyberspace.

In pre-nuclear ages, the Master Terminator worked to overcome nature's forces that were harmful to conscious beings. With that natural terminator, for example, human

128

beings worked to increasingly protect themselves from the elements, wild animals, hunger, injuries, disease. Now, today, during this nuclear age, conscious beings are using that same natural terminator to eradicate their most harmful and dangerous enemy — the parasitical elites. For, those professional value destroyers control the means to kill everyone on Earth in a nuclear holocaust.

In post-nuclear ages, evolved conscious beings will continue using the Master Terminator to overcome diseases and death itself...along with overcoming the longer-range destructive forces in nature such as weather disasters, earthquakes, asteroid and comet collisions, cosmic disasters, solar burnouts, and collapses into black holes.

That natural Master Terminator which functions throughout all ages in all universes *is* Neo-Tech. Indeed, Neo-Tech is simply fully integrated honesty — natural honesty. Nothing can stop the natural mission of Neo-Tech. Nothing can stop its mission of terminating the parasitical-elite class.

Terminating the Parasitical-Elite Class

Today, economic deterioration accelerates: An enlarging pool of professional value *destroyers* increasingly pillages the shrinking pool of professional value *producers*. But, today, the rising Prosperity Revolution will accomplish the first-and-final *valid* class overthrow in history. That overthrow and termination of the parasitical-elite class by *Neo-Tech self-leaders and honest business leaders* will boom all economies. Mankind will finally experience the unlimited prosperity enjoyed by all advanced civilizations throughout the Universe.

This is *your* revolution to unlimited prosperity.

Your Prosperity Revolution

A prosperity revolution? Neo-Tech self-leaders? Class overthrow? Relentless and uncompromising? Overthrowing the entire parasitical-elite class? Yes. Forward march to the overthrow and unlimited prosperity!

Another revolution of bombs, blood, and tears? Power-seeking revolutionary leaders? Another round of destructions leading to ever more destructions? Socialist, fascist, or world-order "democracy" inspired? Building a new parasitical-elite class? No. Just the opposite.

All past revolutions required inconsistencies, illegalities, and destructions. But this revolution is unique. It is based on Neo-Tech. And, Neo-Tech requires logical consistency, objective law, and honest productivity. Neo-Tech upholds objective law by terminating all subjective political policies that harm you, society, and the economy. ...This is your revolution. This revolution will bring you unlimited prosperity.

Your prosperity revolution? When will it happen? What will happen? Who will make it happen? How will it bring you unlimited prosperity?

All past revolutions and class overthrows were bogus or compromised. For, all were fomented so one parasitical group could take power from another parasitical group. All were fomented from false or artificial class conflicts of nationalities, races, religions, political issues, economic levels, or social levels.

The Prosperity Revolution is the first and only legitimate class overthrow possible among human beings: The honest productive class ranging from ditch digger to billionaire entrepreneur will overthrow the parasitical-elite class — a criminal class comprised of destructive politicians and their legions of harmful bureaucrats, armed political-policy enforcers, ego judges, politico prosecutors, corrupt lawyers, dishonest journalists, evil academics, and white-collar-hoax business quislings.

Parasitical elites survive through false power — power gained through deceptive illusions. But, today, with your personal terminator, you can break their illusions to end all false power. ...Right now, with Neo-Tech, you can prosper without limits.

New-Color Symphony

Movement #2

Chapter 12

Terminating Evil

You are a hard-working entrepreneur. Starting with $3500, you worked 16 hours a day, seven days a week, for over twenty years to build a medical-research firm. Your life is dedicated to a single goal: develop marketable knowledge leading to the root cause of disease. Marketing various segments of that developing knowledge increasingly provides the keys to understanding and then curing all diseases — including cancer, AIDS, muscular dystrophy, and death itself.

Your only competitor, I & O Research and Writing, was attacked on November 3rd, 1986, by an armed criminal element growing within the IRS. I & O was destroyed through physical violence and looting inflicted by that criminal element. Each level of criminal behavior used by the IRS is identified in the table below:

Responsibility Level	Criminal Activity	Remedy
IRS Commissioner	Sanctions and uses criminal activities	Ostracize and prosecute
IRS District Directors	Direct criminal activities and destructions	Fire and prosecute
IRS Guns-and-Fists Agents	Blindly carry out physical violence and property destructions	Educate and rehabilitate if possible...or fire
IRS Seizing Agents	Blindly carry out financial lootings and economic destructions	Educate and rehabilitate if possible...or fire

133

Movement II: The Anticivilization

10:00PM, April 15: You have spent the last two weeks, sixteen hours a day, completing the tax paperwork for your company and employees. Along with your accountant and lawyer, you have spent an average of ten weeks each year over the past decade handling all tax matters concerning your company and its twenty-five employees. That means for this decade alone, two years were lost to forced-labor paperwork. And that does not include the irreplaceable time destroyed on paperwork forced by other government bureaucracies and regulatory agencies. ...Because of that growing destruction of time and life, both you and your business can never reach full potential. Thus, you may never reach your goal of delivering the fundamental, unifying cure to all diseases.

That productive time consumed through such forced-labor paperwork diminishes the long-range potential of every person, every trade, every profession, every business. You realize that destruction of the value-producers' time is undermining the future of our economy and society. That time destroyed is even more harmful than the *irrational* taxes the value producers are forced to pay. And, that devastating time destruction serves but one purpose — to expand harmful jobs and power throughout the government. That expansion of harmful jobs and government power, in turn, serves only to expand the parasitical-elite class.

You have struggled long hours at the cost of all personal relationships. You have no time for vacations, leisure, relaxation. That unrelenting struggle is required for meeting the responsibilities to your customers, employees, and company. Without more time, you cannot reach your potential of building a worldwide enterprise — an enterprise providing countless jobs by delivering health, happiness, and prosperity to everyone. You realize that those two years of forced-labor paperwork per decade (like receiving a ten-year prison term for producing competitive values for others and society over a fifty-year career) was the very block of creative time and crucial concentration needed to reach your potential, your goal. ...Such is the destruction inflicted today on every hard-driving value producer with supreme potentials and goals.

Then, you realize the escalation of time-destroying tax complexities backed by harsher and harsher penalties has nothing to do with collecting taxes. Instead, that escalation of destructiveness and penalties has everything to do with increasing bureaucratic control. For, that increasing control over the value producers is how the parasitical-elite class survives — how it creates more and more harmful jobs and power needed to live parasitically.

You now understand how the parasitical elites join with white-collar-hoax executives of stagnant big businesses to prevent competition from the most competent entrepreneurs. You now understand why those elites must malign, destroy, and imprison great value producers — honest but aggressive, tough, often unpopular business-people like Michael Milken and Leona Helmsley who prospered by delivering competitive values to society, thus, threatening the livelihoods of all parasites. By stifling aggressive competition, parasitical elites keep their own harmful livelihoods from being exposed and eliminated.

Also, without that competition, parasitical business quislings can entrench themselves in big businesses. For years, even decades, such pseudo businesspeople can gain unearned wealth and prestige by milking the great accumulations of assets built by genuinely competitive, aggressive value producers of the past. ...Most of those original, heroic value producers came from an age before

135

the creation of armed bureaucracies used to enforce destructive political agendas.

You then think about history's greatest value producers in art, music, science, and business. Despite the many-fold increases in population and technology, we have no more daVincis, Michelangelos, Beethovens, Mozarts, Galileos, Newtons, Hugos, du Ponts, Carnegies, Fords, Einsteins. Why? The reasons can be traced to the destructive effects of an expanding parasitical-elite class methodically draining everyone's time, energy, resources ...and long-range potential. With each passing year, fewer and fewer tender youth can rise to become great value producers. That shrinkage of individual potential reduces or eliminates greatness from all conscious beings.

You realize that increasing armed enforcement of destructive political agendas is designed to support a growing parasitical-elite class not only throughout government and stagnant big businesses, but throughout much of the news media, public education, and the legal profession. You then realize *all* political enforcements involve criminal violations of objective law by armed bureaucracies.

You realize that supreme value producers such as Andrew Carnegie, Florence Nightingale, J. J. Hill, and Henry Ford will not rise again until that criminal class of parasitical elites and their armed bureaucracies are eliminated. Indeed, if living today, every one of those heroic value producers would be in prison with their potentials collapsed. In prison for what? For violating political-agenda "laws" enforced not only by the IRS, but by all the other armed bureaucracies and invasive regulatory agencies cancerously growing today.

As described in Movements II and III of this New-Color Symphony, Neo-Tech and Zon will terminate those evils.

Chapter 13

My Termination

Depression hits me as I survey the view. The camp is bitterly uncompromising — its sheer vastness, its images of hopelessness and deprivation. The sight of withered, dying men and shoddy cardboard shelters, along with the endless odor of decay, combine to bring emotions of hatred and abhorrence in all the unfortunate people who live here.

In the distance is the city: a tall, beautiful, magnificent symbol of man's achievement and prosperity. That symbol makes the dichotomy of this land all the more painful. But this has been my home for the past three years. And, deep down, I detest myself and all that I represent. Disgust wells inside me as I think of this place and my failed attempts to rationalize my pathetic existence. Occasionally, in moments of honesty, I stop the rationalizing and grimly accept my fate, knowing that I deserve no better. In recognizing these rare moments of honesty, I find my mood becomes more positive. I almost mistake the mood for happiness. It isn't. I struggle to define the feeling for a few seconds and then stop, fearing that analysis may eliminate it. But the feeling stays, alien yet welcome. Welcome because it helps me face my last few minutes of life.

Death. An obsolete state in today's world. And yet today, the 3rd of November 2003, I will die a hideous and barbaric death. I will be sacrificed, murdered. But strangely, through the actions of my life, I have given my consent to this grotesque act. Again, the cold shock of reality hits me. My mind for once is free of mysticism and dishonesty. How ironic that I have allowed myself to evade honesty for so long, only yielding to it at the end of my miserable existence. My mood becomes reflective as I begin to wonder how I could have prevented this self-loathing and desperate end.

For as long as I can remember, I have succumbed to camouflaged laziness — to wangling values from others rather than earning values. Never have I put forth the effort to create anything of genuine value. Indeed, it is this self-chosen flaw that has sealed my fate, just as that same flaw has sealed the fate of thousands like me around the world. Decades ago, after cheating my way through a prestigious, Ivy-League university, I decided on a career in law and politics. I had no grand plan to improve the world. But I knew the power of politics would be to my advantage. I could use that power to outmaneuver my peers and competitors. For, most blindly believed, at least initially, that politics was benevolent and designed for the good of the people. They rationalized against seeing the big lie. I, without such quixotic limitations, easily used politics to capture a prosperous and prestigious living from the efforts of others. I fostered the big lie to usurp values from productive people. Indeed, my skills of deception and manipulation became highly refined. I made honest value producers feel guilty for any "selfish" gain or accomplishment. It was easy. My technique was simply to blame them for the endless sufferings and injustices we politicians ourselves cause. ...The value producers paid for our pillagings — those suckers paid us to drain them dry.

Within a short time, I was rich, famous, powerful. My

life was easy, and my potential for further success seemed endless. I was single-handedly capable of developing laws and getting them passed. I could control almost anyone or anything...and look like a saint while doing it. I was responsible for legislation that greatly empowered the Drug Enforcement Administration and its armed enforcers. That DEA bureaucracy had no motivation to reduce any drug problem; for, it had no desire to reduce its jobs or power. It didn't matter to us that innocent lives were lost or destroyed through our trampling on individual rights and property rights. We pushed to spend billions upon billions of tax dollars on projects that I knew would never work. But, so what. Through the media, I always looked good to the masses. Indeed, my "War on Drugs" created some of my richest years.

And my soul mates at the IRS? I helped create and expand their armed divisions. I cleared the way for them to rule through fear and destruction. I loved increasing their power. I loved the viciousness of their commissioner. I loved their lawlessness and criminality. We were soul mates. For, through them my power grew.

We politicians and our bureaucrats created a bond of malevolence with *Newsweek*-type journalists. That unified dishonesty let us smear, control, and ruin America's greatest value producers — innocent people like Michael Milken and Leona Helmsley. We giulianied them. ...We almost took over America with me riding high.

Next came the environmental movement. With dishonest journalists and bankrupt professors, we exploited every phony notion conjured up by pseudo environmentalists. Their hate-filled, save-the-earth movement offered a bonanza of opportunities to increase my power. Political correctness became my favorite weapon. We passed regulations controlling or influencing essentially every business. And, because of my power within Congress, almost every special-interest group courted me. I seldom paid for anything. The gifts and privileges were endless. It didn't bother me that the cost of everyday goods, automobiles, and housing increased substantially because of the regulations I created. In essence, I said to hell with the masses. If they have to suffer or pay a higher price, so be it. For, I was gunning for power — the presidency and beyond.

I further increased my power by exploiting the ego-seeking demagoguery of the anti-abortion gangs as well as the Ralph-Nader gangs. Feminists? Gays? Yahoo! With that power, I passed more and more laws telling people what they could and could not do. ...And they did what I told them because my laws were backed by guns and jails. At times, even I could not believe the power I had — the extent to which people could be controlled and manipulated.

The power. I loved the power. It was as if people would fall to their knees before me — I could do no wrong. And the women, they were everywhere. Most were prostitutes, but I never paid for any of them. Sex. Orgy sex, kinky sex, sex of any kind was the order of the day. Gradually, my wife, with the help of alcohol, learned to accept this, not that her feelings or health mattered to me. I came to believe that I was above everyone. It began to seem that such favors and advantages were owed to me. I answered to no one. Indeed, I quickly learned to live with myself; or should I say, to suppress any twinge of self-respect and honesty. For, with the money and power, it was easy to keep going, to keep taking more and more money, more and more power, more and more of everything. My lust for power constantly grew. I could never get enough.

But then it all crumbled with the Prosperity Revolution of the late 90s. That's what caused my downfall. I remember what seemed like the starting point — our destruction of people like Milken and Helmsley. Our atrocities began backfiring when we sadistically flaunted our power on that April-15th tax day. Using subjective laws, ego "justice", dishonest journalists, and a vicious IRS, we snuffed out the unpopular but innocent Helmsleys.

Soon after, we saw our own end coming with the 1994 American elections. Value-producing men and women all over the world began angrily realizing how they were being duped and exploited. ...Our final ploy was the Clinton pirouette of 1996.

Finally, with Neo-Tech echoing around the world through cyberspace, the value producers took control of their own lives, ending the stupidity of their blind obedience to me and all other false authorities. Almost overnight, politicians like me were scorned out of existence: first in Eastern Europe, then in Asia and Africa. In America, it started in those 1994 elections. Then, the whole world woke up to the hoax. Self-sufficient, value-producing men and women suddenly realized they didn't need self-serving politicians giving them inflation, poor economies, and wars. People realized they could control and direct all areas of their lives without a parasitical ruling class. Charismatic political leaders such as myself were finished when the public started scorning us — then started laughing at us. For us, the bottom line to our final campaign was fear — shear terror and panic over losing our livelihoods, our social standing, our power.

Very quickly, once-powerful politicians were ostracized from society. We were no longer able to plunder the

141

values produced by others. And for society, everything began to improve. There were a few initial and minor problems caused by the change, but advancement was rapid. Indeed, genuine free enterprise was the order of the day, not the insidious "free-trade" mercantilism that I, Bush, Clinton, Newt, Dole, and others touted throughout the world. A torrent of jobs were created. The standard of living soared. Poverty and racism disappeared. Third-world wars and starvation ended.

Before being overthrown, my cohorts and I used constant tax increases to force everyone's earnings into our power-boosting schemes. After we were overthrown, people invested their extra earnings into business and technology. ...Trade and science flourished. Unemployment fell to nearly zero. Only the professional social schemers were unemployed. Street crime vanished.

The technological advancements came quickly. Cures for AIDS and cancer came in a matter of months. Soon, one goal captured the focus of the world: Non-aging longevity. The religious and political objections were increasingly being scorned by the once submissive masses. The masses of productive people now demanded wealth, happiness, love, and life itself.

For me, I sat on the sidelines, increasingly feeling pity and hatred for myself. I had known the truth about politics and religion. Yet, I pushed my dishonesties onto the unthinking public. I knew I deserved the fate that awaited me — it was deserved because of the untold lives I had ruined by promoting and enforcing my destructive political policies. ...The loss of prosperity, happiness, love, and life itself caused by my actions was too great to count or imagine. If only I had assumed the responsibility to be honest and to produce values. Had I done this, I could right now be living in that prosperous other world. All the pain and fear I now suffer was avoidable had I been honest. In fact, if I and the others here had only exerted the effort to be honest in taking the responsibility to create values and pay restitution for our crimes, we all could have moved into that sunlit world of prosperity, happiness, and beauty. But now, it is too late for me. Starting over is impossible. Once, in desperation, I even offered myself to a zoo as an extinct humanoid. I thought scientists could study me as a relic of evil. But alas, the wide-scope accounting records of Neo-Tech showed I belonged here.

So that is why I am here — in this nightmare of a camp. I was ostracized like the rest — scorned out of society, laughed out of existence, unwilling to participate in any activity with the producers of the world, unwilling to produce or trade any desirable value.

In the beginning, we had food and supplies, mostly brought by the later arrivals. But eventually those supplies ran out, as did the animals shortly afterward. It was at this point that our very existence became threatened. Survival became the goal. We could no longer steal from the producers. They were now too smart, too organized. Computerized ostracism made hiding or even a nomadic life impossible. Ironically, the only choice we had was to live as before — to live off other people, to live by sacrificing the lives of others to us. So, we took the concept of sacrifice to its logical but horrific conclusion:

Some would have to sacrifice their lives so the rest could survive. That is why I am in this position today. My lot came up. I would now be sacrificed to the remaining few. Death, a fair and just outcome for all that has gone before me. It is with this perverse feeling of justice and inevitability that I console myself while I think of the manner of my death: clubs raining down on my weak, undernourished body, wielded by those remaining few. I imagine their emotions as they rip my limbs apart. They will be content with their meal, their hunger temporarily averted; each will be glad it's not him this time, but each knowing that soon, very soon, it will be. Fear will be the only companion until the bitter end. ...None can escape.

Suddenly, my introspection is broken by the sound of voices. I see my peers clambering over the rubble, weapons in hand, their ragged clothes and starving bodies almost comical, contrasting strikingly to the power and strength of the city visible on the horizon. Although I have accepted this ghastly end, I feel a fleeting desire to run, to escape before they get too close. But where? What is the point? My death is certain whatever I do.

I am aware that I am smiling as they face me. A matter of feet separate us, death seconds away. No words are spoken, but the sound of fear is deafening. My fear. And theirs.

I see the first club being raised high into the air by my own son. My life flashes before me. ...Oh, the millions who suffered just to keep me feeling important! I craved the ultimate — the goal of *every* politician — the power to rule the world. I craved the unearned power to control everyone in every way. For that power, I'd gladly surpass Hitler in destruction. Yes, I'd gladly nuke the world just to have that power. For, I'm not human. I'm a politician. I'm a humanoid.

I feel the first blow. I fall with my diary. I scrawl my last note: *Honesty terminated me.*

Chapter 14

The Prosperity Revolution

Over two millennia ago, the Greek politician and philosopher Plato established the techniques for hoaxing the public, thus, allowing a parasitical-elite class to rise. Throughout the subsequent centuries, parasitical elites have used Plato-like hoaxes to drain the prosperity that the productive class generates for society. ...Such sacrifice-to-higher-cause hoaxes remained largely unidentified until Neo-Tech unraveled them. Today, Neo-Tech is dissolving those Platonistic elite-class hoaxes. That dissolution of illusions will wash away the parasitical elites along with their higher causes that sacrifice us to them. ...All value producers will then gain their earned prosperity stolen from them and society for 2300 years.

Human History Approaches Its Greatest Event

As our civilization approaches the year 2000, the greatest event in human history is about to break across our planet. Planet Earth will give birth to a super civilization. Indeed, the whole world is shimmering, ready to reveal a new, previously unknown world. Today, raw and unguided fomentations are bubbling from beneath the seams circling the globe. Those fomentations are from the productive class — those who add more to the economy and society than they take. Those value producers are lashing out independently, without authoritarian leadership. Without guidance, they are driving parasitical elites from their destructive livelihoods, including some of the highest "authorities": politicians, clerics, bureaucrats in America, Europe, and Asia —

145

including elites in America like world-order-dominator George Bush, theocratic-statist William Bennett, and killer-hypocrite Hillary Clinton.

Blindness of Past Revolutions

Without Neo-Tech, the productive class impotently lashes out at the parasitical elites, never identifying their underlying hoax of sacrificing the workers to the rulers under the facade of helping the needy. Without identifying that hoax, all revolutions eventually fail by perpetuating the very same hoax to often yield new, even more destructive parasitical elites — new breeds of parasitical masters: new breeds of socialist, fascist, communist, theocrat, and world-order elitists.

To eradicate the parasitical-elite class, productive people around the world must have access to Neo-Tech.

Stop Paying the Parasite-Class Deficits

Who pays for the economic and social deficits created by the parasite class? Someone always has to pay. Until the Neo-Tech Discovery with its wide-scope accounting, the parasitical elites could always delude the productive class into paying their deficits. The parasitical elites have tricked each productive person of the past 23 centuries into supporting their destructive livelihoods.

What hoax could make the productive class continuously pay for those deficits? That hoax as revealed in Plato's *Republic* is to use truth rather than honesty. Ever since, that hoax has tricked the productive class into sacrificing itself to the parasitical elites. The key to perpetuating that hoax is building public-accepted illusions — illusions built by dishonestly twisting truths and facts into limited or false *contexts* acceptable to the public.

The Hoax of Using Truth Instead of Honesty[1]

How does that hoax work? It works through *false context*. **Avoiding full context to build false context is the most powerful tool of deception**. For, avoiding full context and building false context leaves honest people ignorant of the "sacrifice the producers to the parasitical elites" hoax.

By limiting or falsifying context, anyone can build *closed systems* of bogus logic to support or rationalize almost any idea or action — such as the rationalizations behind all force-backed organizations like the DEA, FDA, INS, IRS. Through false logic and context, one can create bogus but good-sounding claims or illusions to justify essentially any destructive means to any parasitical end. And each public acceptance of such bogus claims or illusions means the continued hoaxing of value producers into supporting the parasite class.

Once such hoaxes are identified through *full-context* wide-scope accounting, value producers worldwide will rise in irreversible revolution. ...The genuine value producers will stop paying those leech-class deficits forever.

Irreversible Revolution
All parasitical deceptions and illusions are now exposed by the Neo-Tech literature. Thus, through Neo-Tech, the business/working class will rise in the Prosperity Revolution to overthrow the leech class worldwide.

That Overthrow Can Occur Almost Overnight
In December 1989, on CNN satellite news, citizens of the Romanian productive class suddenly saw the false power of their dictator Ceausescu and the rickety hoax

---

[1]See page 327 for explantation of truth versus honesty.

of his parasitical-elite class. In just five days, those citizens unleashed an anger that brought Ceausescu from the height of life-and-death power over all Romanian citizens to his death before a firing squad manned by those same citizens.

Self-Defense against Criminals and Murderers

Consider the natural dynamics of a valid revolution: What happens when totalitarian oppression and censorship occur? As identified by Thomas Jefferson two centuries ago, overthrow becomes the only *moral* self-defense against the resulting rise of totalitarian criminals. That is why the government should never be allowed to disarm its citizens. By contrast, the *immoral* self-defense against those criminals is to support them in order to "be safe" from their enforcers.

> ### Neo-Tech Assures Everlasting Peace
> The opportunity for a peaceful overthrow must not be lost. The gun-backed oppression of free press executed against Neo-Tech must be rectified. With unfettered free press, the Prosperity Revolution will vanish the parasitical-elite class without a single incident of physical harm or violence. ...Everyone can then enjoy the unending peace and prosperity available to all conscious beings.

New-Color Symphony

Movement #2

Chapter 15

Neo-Tech Resurrects
The Child of the Universe

151

The Child of the Past
leads to the
Civilization of the Universe

Neo-Tech is fully integrated honesty. Neo-Tech is the natural essence of conscious beings as demonstrated in *every* young child still uncorrupted by dishonesty and irrationality. Through integrated thinking and rational exuberance, every child learns to perceive, talk, and then conceptualize. Every child learns with the certainty of integrated honesty present throughout the Universe. Yet, *every* child loses that certainty through the diseases of dishonesty, irrationality, and mysticism.

The dynamics of Neo-Tech bring back that certainty of fully integrated honesty. Neo-Tech brings everyone back to his or her nature. Neo-Tech resurrects that *Child of the Universe* who sleeps in everyone's soul. ...Fully integrated honesty *is* the nature of every conscious being throughout the Universe.

Neo-Tech Resurrects the Child of the Universe

What is Neo-Tech?

Neo-Tech is a matrix of fully integrated honesty and wide-scope accounting. From that matrix comes a certainty about the most effective way to live every aspect of conscious life. Each human being has sought that certainty since mankind became conscious. Indeed, Neo-Tech is the *natural* certainty residing in every conscious being throughout the Universe.

But, on planet Earth, a parasitical-elite class has hidden the objective process of honesty for twenty-three centuries by manipulating subjective *assertions of truth*: Beginning about 300 BC, the philosopher Plato pulled civilization into a cave. He obliterated the individual with his force-backed master-servant collectivism. Plato then crowned the parasitical elites and his philosopher kings with souls of gold.[1] Only they would have the "wisdom" to control, exploit, and drain the productive class: the masses trapped in Plato's cave. Plato relegated to his trapped servants lowly souls of copper and iron.[2]

How did Plato finesse such an outlandish hoax that dominates the Western world to this day? By using the *arbitrariness of truths* to turn reality upside-down, causing a sea of "noble" lies, illusions, deceptions, shadows, doubts, and uncertainties. Such created uncertainties let the parasitical elites rule through dishonesties backed by armed agents of force. By contrast, Neo-Tech eliminates

---

[1]Plato also assigned souls of silver to the obedient armed agents of force serving the golden-souled rulers.

[2]In America, Plato's hoax reached its climax in 1993 with criminal-minded, golden-soul Hillary Rodham Clinton knowing what was best for the health and welfare of the masses with their lowly souls of copper and iron. Through Neo-Tech, the American public broke that hoax in the elections of 1994.

New-Color Symphony
Movement #2

manipulated truths, doubts, uncertainties, out-of-context facts, deceptions, illusions, and gun-backed parasitical "leadership". ...The certainty of Neo-Tech uprights reality and forbids initiatory force against individuals and their property, thus, dooming the parasitical-elite class.

Certainty Without Omniscience[1]

Reality is relational. Knowledge is contextual and hierarchal. Thus, certainty evolves from Neo-Tech — from fully integrated honesty. By nature, fully integrated honesty is the mechanism for building relational, contextual, hierarchal knowledge. Through fully integrated honesty, we share the same certainty — the same knowledge-building *processes* — enjoyed among all mystic-free civilizations throughout the universe.

---

[1]Title of a lecture by objectivist philosopher Leonard Peikoff.

Neo-Tech Resurrects the Child of the Universe

America Today

America today is at once the greatest and the worst nation on Earth: The greatest by the productivity, well-being, and happiness created by the mightiest host of professional value producers and competent workers in history. The worst by the harm, deprivations, and unhappiness caused by a rapidly expanding parasitical-elite class. That leech class is cannibalizing history's most bountiful trove of earned wealth and created values. ...But, today, everyone can look happily to the future. For, the rising Prosperity Revolution and its army of independent self-leaders will eliminate the parasite class to bring ever growing well-being and happiness to everyone.

New-Color Symphony

Movement #2

155

Movement II: The Anticivilization

Ending the World of Chains

Imagine a world of cruel masters binding to a stake every puppy born — binding every dog for every moment of its life from birth to death to a stake with a short chain. Those dogs during their entire lives would know nothing except a totally bleak, constantly chained life. Thus, they would accept their one-and-only lives being used up and wasted without ever experiencing the joys and well-being possible for all dogs, but experienced by none. Not a single dog would ever experience natural puppy joy, playfulness, or the happy companionship of a loving master. But, imagine if those dogs had the ability to become aware of their chained lives. Imagine what they would feel toward their cruel masters.

Now, consider conscious human beings with almost infinitely more life experiences available to them. Imagine a world of human beings chained to stakes from youth to death. Imagine their lives being used up and wasted solely to support the destructive livelihoods of a few parasitical-elite "masters". ...Imagine the anger that would explode if all those chained beings suddenly discovered that their lives and the 'lives of a hundred generations before were used up and wasted just to support a handful of parasitical elites.

What will happen when conscious beings on Earth discover the hoax that has kept them chained, used up, and wasted for a hundred generations? The rising anger will push the ostracism matrix everywhere in government, religion, business, and the professions. A relentless army of value producers will then eradicate that parasite class, ending the world of chains forever.

Neo-Tech Resurrects the Child of the Universe

A World Brightly Lit

Over one hundred years ago, Thomas Edison lit the world with his electric light bulb. For many years, he built his foundation of knowledge. He knew exactly what would happen and exactly how *it* would happen...the *it* being electrically lighting the world. Then, he and his co-workers needed several more years of intense work to find the exact combination to unlock an incandescent bulb with more and more uses until the entire world was lit with electricity.

Using Neo-Tech, which means fully integrated honesty, Frank R. Wallace and his co-workers spent twenty-three years building the foundation of knowledge for intellectually and emotionally lighting the world forever. Today, those co-workers worldwide know exactly what will happen and exactly *how it* will happen...the *how* being cyberspace, the *it* being the vanishing of the parasitical-elite class in resurrecting the Child of the Universe on planet Earth.

157

Chapter 16

Neo-Tech
Self-Leaders

> *A Single Credo for Neo-Tech Self-Leaders*
> Direct every thought, every discipline, every effort
> toward the overthrow of the parasitical-elite class —
> toward the eradication of every livelihood that harms
> the value producers, the economy, and society.

Eleven Requisites for Neo-Tech Self-Leaders

1. To recognize that all past revolutions and their class overthrows have been false, compromised, or temporary. Only the Prosperity Revolution that eradicates the parasitical-elite class will permanently empower the productive class.

The Self-Leader's Goal

2. The self-leader has but one implacable goal: the unrestricted well-being and happiness of the productive class and all humanity.

3. To accomplish that goal, the parasitical-elite class must be eliminated. How will that be accomplished? By welding the productive class into an ostracism force that is all-subversive toward everything supporting that leech class.

4. Until now, every revolution in history eventually betrayed itself by overthrowing one parasitical-elite class in order to replace it with another. But, the *leaderless* Prosperity Revolution can never impose any form of rule

159

or exploitation on the productive class. For, the single task of the Prosperity Revolution is to eradicate the parasitical elites by eliminating their dishonest illusions, hoaxes, and mysticisms. The revolution will then be over. ...All revolutions will be over forever. Unending prosperity and happiness will reign.

The Self-Leader's Behavior
5. The self-leader dedicates his or her life toward the uncompromising eradication of the parasitical-elite class.

6. The self-leader breaks all bonds with the world controlled by parasitical elites. Yet, the self-leader infiltrates that world. He or she deals with parasitical elites, increasingly through cyberspace, only to subvert and destroy their corrupt systems more rapidly.

7. The self-leader rejects public opinion and the existing social morality. For the self-leader, morality is everything that advances the overthrow. Immorality is everything that blocks the overthrow.

8. The self-leader not only suppresses all sentimentality, but he or she abandons all private hatred and revenge. Day and night, the self-leader has but one thought, one aim — the merciless overthrow of the parasitical-elite class.

The Self-Leader's Relationship to Others and Society
9. The degree of friendship, devotion, and obligation toward others is determined solely by the degree they are useful in terminating parasitical elites.

160

10. A second-degree or third-degree self-leader is one who has not yet totally committed to the elimination of the parasitical-elite class. He or she is part of the common revolution capital to be used for the greatest advantage in advancing the revolution.

11. The self-leader is proven not by his or her words but by the deeds toward advancing the overthrow. The self-leader has no sympathy for the parasitical elites and does not hesitate to undermine their every position. He or she may frequently penetrate any area and live among their world in order to hasten their eradication.

Parasitical elites can be split into several categories. The first category consists of those who are condemned to termination as soon as possible. The second category consists of those who are spared temporarily as being useful for provoking the public into revolution. The third category consists of those liberals and conservatives in high positions of unearned power and influence, various dishonest politicians, and certain harmful bureaucrats, lawyers, and judges. Those parasitical elites can be useful — they can be exploited for advancing the revolution. The fourth category consists of pseudo-leaders who can be useful for a while. But, eventually, parasitical elites in all categories must be terminated.

The Greatest Event in History

What about other great events in history? Forget them. The emerging Prosperity Revolution is by far history's greatest event. That event will open the way for *all* future advancements toward eternal prosperity and happiness.

New-Color Symphony

Movement #2

Movement II: The Anticivilization

Terminating the Parasitical-Elite Class

Independent self-leaders are developing with no leader to follow or obey. They are people who will increasingly carry out missions of subversion against the parasitical-elite class.

So long as self-leaders have no leader to obey, they will steadily multiply and never stop moving forward. For, on learning how to break the hoax of professional parasitism, they will react personally to each parasite who harms or drains society. On their own, in their own ways, they will increasingly subvert the entire parasite class. They will subvert the leeches one by one, relentlessly, until each is driven from his or her bogus career. Especially through the Internet, self-leaders will have no time or energy limits to stop them from eradicating the parasitical-elite class that wastes the lives of everyone. They will have no more compunction about swatting down parasitical elites who exploit society than they have about swatting down mosquitoes that spread disease.

So long as uncensored cyberspace and free expression exists, the Prosperity Revolution will proceed peacefully. Without gun-backed oppression, the overthrow of the parasitical-elite class will be peaceful but uncompromising, total, permanent.

Seven Waves to Prosperity

1. Plant the root system: Identify and define the problem, the enemy, the solution. ...Completed 1976.

2. Build the foundation: Establish a two-million-word body of literature published in twelve languages with audio, video, art, and music supplements. ...Done 1966-1991.

3. Develop the confrontational phase: Setting self-exposure traps such as the Golden Helmet for neocheaters, professional value destroyers, and the parasitical elites along with their armed enforcers. (Ref: *Politicians and Bureaucrats on Trial,* B & W, 1991) ...Began in 1980. Activated in 1986. Continuing.

4. Carry out and complete the free-press protection phase: Decentralization of publishing activities and literature distribution. Dispersion into independent phantom-bantam companies worldwide. Translate foundation work into twelve languages. Distribute into 156 countries. Those actions protect Neo-Tech publishing activities from being wiped out in further attacks by armed agents in America or in any other country. ...Completed in 1987. Insures a peaceful revolution.

5. Enter the direct confrontational phase: Activate the self-exposure traps for the neocheaters, professional value destroyers, and parasitical elites in government, the courts, business, and the professions. Establish a computerized ostracism matrix that will drive all parasitical elites and their cohorts from their destructive livelihoods. As of 1994, over 2450 parasitical elites, neocheaters, and professional value destroyers have been permanently locked into the Neo-Tech Ostracism Matrix. ...Began in 1990. Continuing.

6. Begin the worldwide revolution-overthrow phase: Move from quiet foundation-building and self-exposure confrontational modes to public-action terminator modes. To begin in 1998.

7. Cyberspace into the future.

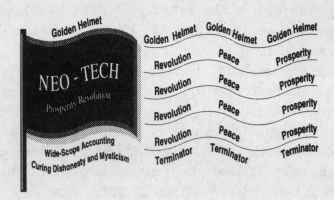

RULES FOR LIMITLESS PROSPERITY

Rule 1

No person, group of persons or government may initiate force, threat of force, or fraud against any individual or private property.

Rule 2

Force may be morally and legally used only in self-defense against those who violate Rule 1.

Rule 3

No exceptions shall exist for Rules 1 and 2.

Initiation of force, except in self-defense, always leads to destruction and is the opposite of value.

The Value-Producers'
CALL TO REVOLUTION

Preamble

We stand united — the worker, ditch digger, farmer, tradesman, office worker, business person, billionaire entrepreneur — the productive class. Dishonest parasitical elites shall no longer live off our work. They shall no longer exist by deceiving us.

The Two Points of Revolution
The Enemy
The Promise

Point One THE ENEMY	The enemy is the parasitical-elite class comprised of harmful politicians, lawyers, judges, prosecutors, bureaucrats, clerics, and other leeches, neocheaters, professional value destroyers, and agents of force. Those people fraudulently live off you. ...They have stolen their livings from you for far too long.
Point Two THE PROMISE	We will eliminate the parasitical elites. That ridding of the leech class will yield the unlimited expansion of jobs, prosperity, pride, and security for all honest value producers, their children, and their future generations.

WE DEMAND!

We the value-producing workers, entrepreneurs, business people, soldiers, police, youth, students, parish priests, exploited government employees, and suffering unemployed demand the breaking of all deceptions foisted upon us — deceptions that let the parasitical elites drain and harm our lives.

WE SHALL TERMINATE THE PARASITICAL-ELITE CLASS

We shall break the chain that chokes our lives. We shall terminate the parasitical-elite class forever. ...Our march to peace and prosperity begins now!

Peace●Prosperity

Have you been wronged, hurt, used, drained, exploited, or diminished by government "authorities", bureaucrats, religion, "law" enforcers, lawyers, certain unions, certain businesses, certain "friends" or relatives? The Prosperity Revolution will turn that harm into peace and prosperity.

Peace●Prosperity

Chapter 17

Commanding Life
on
Planet Earth

The Final Decade of Earth's Anticivilization

A parasitical-elite class has spawned this upside-down civilization — an irrational civilization that inflicts purposeful harm on conscious beings, their economies, their societies. Parasitical elites today manipulate nearly all politics, many bureaucracies, the legal profession, the courts, public schools, the academe, the news media, religion, entertainment, and certain big businesses. What most of those manipulators represent as the best is really the worst...the *most destructive* — and vice versa.

Be prepared to discover the facts: Jay Gould is the best, Abraham Lincoln is the worst; Leona Helmsley is the best, Eleanor Roosevelt is the worst; Malcolm X is the best, Martin Luther King is the worst; Michael Milken is the best, Rudolph Giuliani is the worst; Florence Nightingale is the best, Hillary Clinton is the worst. ...Indeed, you must first dismiss nearly *everything* that the parasitical-elite class and its news media represent as good and bad in order to command your life on planet Earth toward boundless prosperity.

What Do the Following Have in Common?

Armed ATF, DEA, IRS agents, force-backed anti-abortionists, jailing of Milken and Helmsley, Jew and Japan bashing, busting Noriega, gay bashing and gay

167

Movement II: The Anticivilization

"rights", racism, urban riots, RICO and seizure laws, PETA, political correctness, the DEA, EPA, FDA, INS, IRS, OSHA, formal religion, Greenpeace, evangelism, gun control, Ralph Nader, Fidel Castro, Jesse Jackson, Jesse Helms, Pat Buchanan, white-collar-hoax big-business executives: What do they all have in common?

All of the above are based on economic and social parasitism. They are all backed by professional value destroyers, parasitical elites, envy mongers, and self-righteous neocheaters infesting government, religion, big business, entertainment, the media. By purposely creating problems where none exist, all such parasites end in destroying the very values they pretend to support. Such destructive people must pretend to support values. They must fake compassion and good intentions to survive — to gain false esteem, power, and bogus livelihoods.

They and their supporters comprise a rapidly expanding class of parasitical elites. Today, from survival necessity, they are converging in a final feeding frenzy. They increasingly loot and destroy innocent value producers through despotic "laws": RICO, seizure, and EPA/FDA/FTC/OSHA/SEC-type "laws"...all backed by force along with the irrationalities of ego "justice", fake scientisms, and pressured by escalating deep-pocket litigations. And now, the parasite class fight one another to devour the remains of a vanishing class of genuine job-and-wealth producers.

Indeed, for decades, that escalating class of professional value destroyers has orchestrated libel, slander, and public envy to attack and drain a now decimated, crumbling class of super value producers. Eventually, under various disguised forms of fascist socialism — such as Clinton/Gore/Dole-type, tax-the-producers envynomics

— those converging parasites would drain dry the remaining remnant of super job producers and aggressive entrepreneurs.   The demise of those last great value producers would bring annihilations of the world economies and societies. ...But, none of that will happen because of Neo-Tech and the Prosperity Revolution that started in 1994.

New-Color Symphony

Movement #2

Chapter 18

What is the Illuminati?
What is Zon?

> **The Illuminati**
> has its origins in the biblical Abraham who smashed the idols four millennia ago in establishing the existence of only one reality.

Ever hear of the Illuminati? For the past two centuries, they have been condemned by nationalistic governments and mystical religions. How about the Bilderbergers, the Club of Rome, the Council on Foreign Relations, the Trilateral Commission? They are semi-secret organizations that for the past several decades have been linked to one-world conspiracy theories. Consider the controlling influences behind those worldwide organizations — businessmen, such as today's quiet businessman David Rockefeller. He, for example, is seldom seen or mentioned in the mainstream media. But, he is hysterically attacked as the epitome of evil by the ultra-conservative media, the nationalistic-populist media, and the religious-right media. Yet, David Rockefeller is among the world's most moral, clear-thinking, responsible people.

The Illuminati Protocols
This chapter refers to the early Illuminati protocols — the master plan for worldwide control first formulated over two centuries ago by leading European bankers and businessmen. Essentially anyone reading the protocols

171

alone and out of context would view them as one of the most evil plots ever devised. Yet, on reading those very same protocols in the context of wide-scope accountability, one will realize the men responsible for those protocols were among the most moral, clear-thinking, responsible people who ever lived on this planet. Moreover, through Zon, today's Illuminati can make everyone on Earth rich and happy.

Making the Illuminati Serve You

Zon will far surpass the goal of the Illuminati. By understanding Zon, the Illuminati and their organizations will be at your service — providing you with limitless wealth.

Business-Controlled Master Plans

Business-controlled master plans underlie all actions controlling the creation of long-term prosperity and happiness. Two such master plans or protocols operate on planet Earth: (1) the closed-system Illuminati protocols developed in Europe over two centuries ago, and (2) the evolving, open-ended Zon protocols that began developing in early 1992 and reflected in the American elections of 1994. Today, Zon is replacing the Illuminati's master plan. With Zon, the world will soar in cyberspace beyond the Illuminati's plan for worldwide prosperity. For, Zon delivers eternal happiness with limitless wealth to all conscious beings.

The Illuminati, from its founding protocols forged in the mid-18th century by Adam Weishaupt and Albert Pike, have nearly completed their noble goal of undermining and eliminating the twin instruments of irrationality and destruction on this planet: (1) forced-backed nationalist governments, and (2) fraud-backed mystical religions.

What is the Illuminati? What is Zon?

Now, after two centuries, that goal will not only be achieved but far surpassed, perhaps as early as 2001AD. How? By replacing the established, seemingly violent Illuminati protocols with the newly evolving, peaceful Zon protocols as deduced from the original, 176-page *Cassandra's Secret* manuscript developed in 1993. The specific Zon protocols will be ready for public use before 2001AD. But, first, one must understand the goal and protocols of the original Illuminati as described below:

The Illuminati's Business Plan
for
Depoliticizing Planet Earth

Since the late 1700s, essentially all public reporting and exposés of the secretive Illuminati have been rabidly negative. Most such reports and exposés emanate from paranoid conspiracy theories presented in populist, nationalistic, or right-wing religious publications. All such reports and exposés present the Illuminati and their protocols as diabolically evil. Modern-day exposés especially rail at the Illuminati's tools used to undermine public respect for political-agenda laws, irrational traditions, and predatory institutions. The Illuminati work to undermine public support of the parasitical-elite class...a destructive class that survives through politically and religiously ruled governments.

The modern-day tools of the Illuminati include international organizations such as the Trilateral Commission, the Council on Foreign Relations, the Bilderbergers, the Club of Rome, and the outdated Freemasons. In addition to high-profile parasitical elites, those organizations comprise the most-influential, low-profile businesspeople throughout the world. Still, they

173

are all simply tools masterfully maneuvered into advancing the Illuminati's goal.

Many members of those organizations are sincere value producers; others are power-seeking parasites. Yet, all effectively serve the Illuminati's pretended goal of worldwide political and economic cooperation. Beneath that goal, however, lies the Illuminati's real goal: break the institutions that support this destructive anticivilization.

To understand the Illuminati, one must understand their poker-playing modus operandi. The Illuminati perfected the shrewdest poker-playing stratagems imaginable — analogous to those stratagems revealed in Frank R. Wallace's *Advanced Concepts of Poker*, first published in 1968. After 21 printings, plus additional printings by Crown Publishing and Warner Books, Wallace withdrew that book from print in 1986 in favor of the evolving Neo-Tech literature.

Consider the following stratagem by the Illuminati: To most effectively achieve their goal, they knew their real targets for termination must remain concealed for as long as possible. Because of their world-wide influences, the Illuminati also realized that, over time, information about their work and goal would leak to the public, despite their influence over the world news media. Thus, the Illuminati planted ruses in their protocols that would invite hysterical criticism of them and their satellite organizations. By promoting hysteria against themselves, criticisms would lose credibility, preventing any effective effort to block or retard their progress.

For example, the Illuminati realized their secret protocols would eventually be publicly revealed. Thus, they drafted their Protocols to conceal their real agenda. They made their Protocols to appear as a Jewish or Zionist plot for placing all human beings under one-world tyrannical rule. They floated a poker-ploy hoax document titled *The Protocols of the Learned Elders of Zion*. Throughout that document, they shrewdly planted a Jewish slur word for Gentiles to describe their targets — the *goyim*.

That strategy has worked brilliantly for two centuries: All exposés or attacks on the Illuminati turn into strident accusations about being evil socialistic, communistic, Jewish, Zionist, satanic, or Luciferin plots for world domination. Thus, all exposés and attacks have ultimately been dismissed as paranoid anti-Semitic, Jew baiting, racist, or religious-right paranoia — exactly what the Illuminati intended.[1] ...Incidentally, from their origin to modern day, many among the Illuminati are Jewish. But, they are moral Jewish businessmen, not socialists or Zionists seeking world domination. Indeed, the Illuminati are ingenious "poker players" who orchestrate criticisms of them to advance their goal.

The Illuminati especially utilize their poker strategies in wielding influence from their toolbox of international organizations. Those organizations comprise the world's leading businesspeople, politicians, journalists, publishers, bankers, industrialists, military leaders, and other influential people used to advance a one-world agenda. But, that agenda conceals the real goal fully known only to the Illuminati. That goal is to undermine and eliminate the institutions supporting parasitical elites.

What gave the Illuminati businessmen their overwhelming power and success for the past two centuries? The answer lies in their ability to create genuine values and jobs for society, *combined* with an unshakable moral responsibility to bring growing prosperity to all conscious beings on this planet. Their

[1]A good example of how this strategy works is found in the April, 1995, *Reader's Digest* article titled, "This Lie Will Not Die".

moral foundation, however, was based on knowledge limited to this closed, irrational anticivilization. Thus, for them, the only possible way to preserve and then flourish human consciousness on Earth was to eliminate, by whatever means necessary, the institutions that support this anticivilization and its parasitical-elite propagators. ...But, means cannot justify the ends — morally...and ultimately, practically. Zon, by contrast, functions through the consistently sound principle of fully integrated honesty. Thus, Zon solves such dilemmas by delivering practical, objectively moral solutions free of force and violence.

Zon replaces the moral justification for violence upon which the Illuminati have stood since their institution-breaking role in the 1793 French Revolution. ...Today, Zon has replaced that justification with a moral foundation that *peacefully* elevates the wealth and happiness of *all* conscious beings throughout time and existence. That moral base stands on integrated honesty, productive effort, wide-scope accounting, objective law, and the Golden-Helmet dynamics as detailed in the Appendix at the end of this manuscript.

The institution-breaking accomplishments of the Illuminati along with their one-world organizations such as the Bilderbergers and the Trilateral Commission provide an advanced position from which the Civilization of the Universe can envelop this planet while peacefully vanishing the anticivilization and its manipulators.

With the discovery of Zon, the keys to prosperity are found in (1) originating conscious actions from Civilization-of-the-Universe perspectives and (2) recognizing that anticivilization perspectives are unreal. In that way, harmful aspects of the anticivilization are dismissed and ultimately vanished. Also, in that way, the two-century-old Illuminati dynamics of using deceit and force to undermine those elements supporting the anticivilization are replaced by the honest, peaceful Zon dynamics.

The Most Moral Men on Earth

Without the concepts of white-hat neocheating and advanced poker strategy combined with Neo-Tech, anyone who reads the Illuminati protocols[1] will come to the same conclusion: Those protocols are the epitome of evil. But on understanding neocheating and the concepts of poker along with Neo-Tech and Cassandra's Secret, one comes to the exact opposite conclusion: The Illuminati protocols reflect the most responsible and moral forces on Earth — forces designed to bring wealth and happiness to our world by breaking the institutions and racisms that support this parasitically drained, death-oriented anticivilization.

As identified in the *Neo-Tech Discovery*, the original Illuminati also realized that honest business dynamics are what sustain and advance conscious life. Thus, those business dynamics are the only source of genuine, life-enhancing power among conscious beings. Indeed, only competitive value-and-job producers hold real power — the ultimate power to control not only current events but future events on planet Earth.

Until the original 18th-century Illuminati, no value-and-job producer understood the draining hoaxes and illusions of the parasitical elites. From Plato's time, a ruling leech class has built and propagated an anticivilization with the single purpose of sustaining their own harmful livelihoods by draining the productive class.

---

[1]*The 18th-Century Illuminati Protocols*, 32 pages, Zon Association (1994).

Movement II: The Anticivilization

The Illuminati discovered that they, not kings, popes, tyrants, sultans, or other parasitical elites hold the power to control and direct society. On that realization, those original Illuminati, most of whom were powerful businessmen and bankers, moved with confidence to eliminate the parasitical elites by relentlessly pitting those leeches and their institutions against each other. That dynamic caused the world populations to increasingly lose confidence in politics, nationalistic governments, mystical religions, and their parasitical leaders.

Schindler's List, the factual story of German businessman Oskar Schindler in the 1940s, illustrates how even at the evilest depths of this anticivilization, the value-and-job producer is the *only* person with genuine power and love...even midst humanoids who live by guns and mass murder. Only businessman Schindler, for example, could walk through the bloody mud of the Holocaust without soiling his soul, his compassion, his respect for human life. Only job-producing Schindler had the power, moral character, and strength to reach into the depths of this anticivilization to save conscious beings from the destruction and death wrought by its humanoid propagators.

Extrapolate the metaphor of businessman Schindler into the advanced technologies among the Civilization of the universe. One will then recognize that honest businesspeople with their limitless valuation of conscious beings are the real saviors of everyone in existence. Only such value-and-job producers have the power, responsibility, and love to never let perish the supreme value throughout the universe — conscious life, including conscious human beings on planet Earth. ...The competitive, value-and-job producing businessperson eternally preserves and advances all conscious life.

The Illuminati originally comprised the few most efficacious businessmen in Europe. The original Illuminati rejected parasites holding false or life-draining power. Indeed, none of the Illuminati were kings, tyrants, politicians, lawyers, religionists, entertainers, writers, or orators. Instead, they were quiet businessmen and bankers — they were among the world's most potent creators of life-sustaining values and jobs.

The Illuminati's relentless work has always been directed toward saving the future generations of conscious beings from destruction by the institutionalized irrationality woven throughout this anticivilization. The Illuminati's goal has been to free conscious beings from the tribal mentalities that make possible criminal societies: parasitical governments, socialism, fascism, the welfare state, and mystical religions.

The Illuminati sought a world in which its citizens valued their fellow citizens not by social status, wealth, nationality, race, or religion, but by what each did to competitively benefit others and society.

For 250 years, playing the most ingenious poker game in history, the Illuminati have brought much of the world close to their goal of ending 3000 years of unnecessary suffering and death inflicted on all populations of Earth — inflicted by parasitical humanoids through their criminal institutions. ...Finally, today, the newly arrived Zon dynamics will not only peacefully achieve but far surpass the noble goal of the Illuminati.

179

Movement II: The Anticivilization

Chapter 35 publicly identifies the meaning beneath the Illuminati protocols[1], their master plan, their one-world organizations...and the resulting future for all on planet Earth through Zon.[2]

---

[1]What is the source of those Protocols? In 1906, the British Museum in London received a copy of the Illuminati Protocols written in Russian. Those secret Protocols were probably translated into Russian sometime after 1850 from the original German language Protocols, which first appeared in Bavaria during the late 18th century. Parts of the Protocols were used by Maurice Joly in his 1864 satire, *Dialogue in Hell Between Machiavelli and Montesquieu*. In the early 20th century, British journalist Victor Marsden translated the Protocols into English. His translations were finally issued by the British Publishing Society in 1921 (Ref: Des Griffith, *Fourth Reich of the Rich*). ...Metaphor or real, those Protocols express the Illuminati strategy.

[2]The Illuminati's goal has always been to replace the destructive forces of monarchism, nationalism, religion with the productive dynamics of business. Toward that goal, Neo-Tech/Zonpower adds (1) free-market dynamics for societal decisions plus (2) the essentialness of working-class individuals. For, such working-class individuals are disconnected from the elite class, which is intellectually indoctrinated into closed-circle visions of nature. Thus, non indoctrinated workers have retained their childhood capacities for fully integrated honesty — for wide-scope viewings of nature. While vision-controlled elites, specialists, and philosophers — including most Objectivists — have lost their capacities for fully integrated honesty.

Indeed, the honest, wide-scope views of nature by the working class will lead the mass advance of mankind into a rational civilization — into the Civilization of the Universe. ...Such ability to see nature as it is by non Establishment individuals — an ability lost by the indoctrinated elites — was first identified by Georg Büchner (1813-1837) in his path-breaking drama *Woyzech*.

180

What is the Illuminati? What is Zon?

The Neo-Tech Trojan Horse

Over the years, the Neo-Tech/Illuminati dynamic has evolved into today's *Zonpower*. This 200-year-old dynamic is increasingly undermining false, harmful authorities throughout governments and religions worldwide. The Neo-Tech/Illuminati dynamic has been the hidden force beneath the collapse of communism in Eastern Europe and America's coming sea change first reflected in its Neo-Tech inspired 1994 elections.

The seventh and final cyberspace stage of Neo-Tech/Zonpower — the public phase — will activate sometime before 2001 with the Internet distribution of the *Zonpower Protocols*...the Trojan-Horse penetration of Neo-Tech into the heart of the Establishment in America and worldwide.

Chapter 19

Dumping Goy Politics

Reality and Objective Law

The *real* physical world resides in a beautiful symmetry of rationality embodied by the objective laws of nature. Philosophers and scientists throughout the ages have striven to discover the ultimate nature and symmetry of existence. For 24 centuries, great minds have opened one door after another, solved one deep mystery of nature after another, only to discover whole new and deeper symmetries hiding beneath the ever evolving forces within the unchanging laws of nature. That long history started with the postulating of atoms and led to the discovery of gravity, electromagnetism, and relativity. Those great minds ranged from Democritus to Newton, to Faraday, to Einstein...to Nobel laureate Leon Lederman, the preeminent experimental physicist who in his book *The God Particle* (Houghton Mifflin, 1993) metaphorically named the ultimate nature of existence, the "God Particle"[1].

Are we opening the final door that reveals what lies beyond the "God Particle"? Will we find at last the elegantly simple, beautiful force with no beginning or ending, lying beneath and above the "God Particle"? ...Beneath and above that particle lie Gravity Units of symmetrical, subspatial geometries controlled by conscious beings free of *goy* politics.

Nonreality and Subjective Law

The *unreal* political world of the goyim hides the ugly irrationality embodied by subjective laws born of politics. Those laws are used to gain destructive livelihoods and

---

[1]Technically the "God Particle" is called by physicists the Higgs boson.

criminal power in an anticivilization. As one discovers the secret of goy politics, one discovers that *everything* arising from their political-agenda laws involves the criminal acquisition of power — from Caligula to Hitler to the Clintons.[1]

From Caligula's socio-fascist Rome to Hitler's socio-fascist Germany to Clinton's socio-fascist America, all destructive laws arise from political processes — processes designed to create self-serving political powers. Today, as in Germany 60 years ago, the process of law making is driven by politics rather than by objective reality. Indeed, most law today arises from arbitrary political correctness in a drum roll of force-backed, political-agenda laws.

Such laws are turning political tools like the FDA, DEA, BATF, IRS, INS, EPA into armed bureaucracies that destroy life, liberty, and society. Also, consider today's politicization of health care, food diets, abortion, religion, education, the media, drugs, tobacco, law enforcement, criminal prosecution, immigration, the environment. Decisions in those areas should have nothing to do with politics, but everything to do with objective reality. ...What irrational forces underlie the politicization of human action?

The forces underlying harmful political actions are camouflaged dishonesty, hidden laziness, and parasitical livelihoods. From those forces, a purposeful destructiveness arises. That destructiveness is used to gain unearned values at the expense of the competitive value

[1]Consider the following: How many Platos, Alexander the Greats, Caesars, Caligulas, Attilas, Genghis Khans, Tamerlanes, Napoleons, Lincolns, Lenins, Woodrow Wilsons, Mussolinis, Hitlers, FDRs, Stalins, Maos, Pol Pots, Castros, Idi Amins, Bokassas, Khomeinis, Pengs, Saddams, Nicolae and Elena Ceausescus, Bill and Hillary Clintons were Jews? None.

producers. Beneath those forces lie irrationality and insanity — the schizophrenia of parasitism. Contrary to common belief, schizophrenia is not a split or a dual personality, which is just one of many possible *symptoms* of schizophrenia. Rather, the disease of schizophrenia is the ***detachment of consciousness from objective reality***, which is required to convert one's precious life into a worthless life — into a parasite.

The tripartite cure for insanity in government is simple: depoliticize, depoliticize, depoliticize. ...How will that cure arise? Consider the following Illuminati article of June, 1994. This article was published five months before the first Neo-Tech domino fell in America — five months before America's November 1994 elections:

Quote
Obsoleting the Criminal-Minded Goyim

The most valuable goyim of the '90s are the Clintons. Faking compassion and using demagoguery, they foment envy against the productive class — against the competitive producers of wealth and jobs. They move forward, feeding on individual rights and competitive value production. Their grand wealth-distribution schemes consume the source of earned values and well-being. Their illegal schemes, epitomized by bribes paid through fraudulent cattle straddles, undermine the public's sense of justice and honesty in America.

Moreover, the fake compassion of the Clintons is nothing more than a three-step, **Toll-Booth Compassion:** Personally they give nothing that genuinely benefits humanity or society. Instead, (1) they collect self-aggrandizing tolls by forcing the productive class into financing an expanding parasitical-elite class through

---

185

political-agenda laws. (2) They extract financial tolls by draining the only real benefactors of the needy and society: the competitive value-and-job producers. And, then (3) they hit the jackpot with a neocheating livelihood replete with force-backed political power and praise-filled honors.

Such three-step, toll-booth compassion includes larceny and homicide. For example: "If this law saves one life, then it's worth it" type demagoguery hides the 100 or 1000 or million innocent victims hurt, impoverished, or killed directly or indirectly through such sound-good, toll-booth-compassion laws — laws that subjugate society through force-back control, destruction, and death.

Seeking unearned power through virtuoso lying, the Clintons emasculate America's long-term security and prosperity for their own power. Left unchecked, such criminal agendas would destroy health care, individual rights, the economy, and maybe start a war to avoid impeachment or jail. ...The point is that such goy politicians will loot, kill, and build violent hatred toward government just to sustain their destructive livelihoods.

Indeed, today, political predators are crushing property rights, plundering the middle class, and widening the gap between the rich and poor. How? By escalating police-state regulations, destructive political-agenda laws, and irrational taxes enforced by armed bureaucrats. Those irrationalities decimate small businesses, the middle class, and individual self-reliance: the three originators of all productive jobs and earned profits. ...Why do political predators purposely advance economic and social harms? So they can live in power and praise without themselves having to produce competitive values.

The above dynamics are ironically in accord with the

original Illuminati Protocols. Those master-plan protocols use Machiavellian political tools such as the Clintons who have Dostoyevsky-type criminal minds[1]. For, such goy tools cause calamities that undermine planet Earth's twin institutions of parasitical evil: nationalistic governments and organized religions...institutions that subjugate the well-being of society to the parasitical-elite class.

Obsoleting such criminal-minded goyim will halt the government's parasitical feeding on the value-producing class. A depoliticized civilization will bring eternal peace and prosperity. Indeed, the laws among the Civilization of the Universe arise from the divine grace embodied in every conscious being who has ever existed. From those laws arise genuine prosperity and romantic happiness.

End Quote

Seven-Point Agenda
for
America's First Neo-Tech President

1. Immediately pardon and free *all* individuals convicted of "crimes" created from political-agenda laws.

2. Veto and work to repeal *every* political-agenda law passed by Congress, current and past.

3. Work to end all welfare and social programs. Replace Clintonian toll-booth compassion with genuine compassion.

4. Privatize Social Security. Fully meet all obligations by paying back with market-rate interest *all* monies paid into Social Security. Finance this payback by

---

[1]Such deluded "superior beings" think their "greatness" puts them above objective law, including murder...as Raskolnikov in Dostoyevsky's *Crime and Punishment*, as the OJs and the Clintons in today's America.

selling government businesses and assets.

5. Permit government activity only in areas of national defense, *local* police, and the courts to protect individual and property rights. Eliminate all other force-backed government powers and programs. Disarm all bureaucrats, not honest citizens.

6. Replace the irrational, envy-based income tax with a rational consumption tax — a national sales tax. Then phase out sales taxes with major budget reductions, market-rate user fees, and the Golden Helmet. Use revenues only for national defense and the protection of individuals and their property from objective crime.

7. Help redeemable parasitical elites, neocheaters, and professional value destroyers convert to competitive value producers in the Civilization of the Universe.

Accomplishing the above seven points are the natural results of upholding the Constitution of the Universe:

CONSTITUTION OF THE UNIVERSE
Article 1
No person, group of persons or government may initiate force, threat of force, or fraud against any individual's self or property.
Article 2
Force may be morally and legally used only in self-defense against those who violate Article 1.
Article 3
No exceptions shall exist for Articles 1 and 2.

Even Plato recognized that the creation of a civilization is the "victory of persuasion over force...". By contrast, an anticivilization means the use of force over persuasion.

Dumping Goy Politics

A "Heaven-Sent" Illuminati Tool — The Clintons

Why did most of the news media and much of the public keep accepting the automatic lies and covering up objective crimes by Bill Clinton when he became the President of the United States? What about his Machiavellian drive to escape his crimes and stay in office? Through his and his wife's dishonest camouflages, the Clintons strove to ravage health care and society itself.

All genuine jobs, prosperity, and happiness in *any* society come from honest individuals and businesses. President Clinton had no concept of honesty or business. He never held or created a productive job in his adult life. He lived parasitically by (1) demagogically attacking and then (2) self-righteously draining those who produce the jobs and values upon which society depends. ...How did such a person become accepted by a population as its leader?

Congenial President Clinton was the most skilled, manipulative public speaker since Hitler, Churchill, and FDR.[1] His gross lack of principles combined with his supreme ability to sound good let him project sincerity and good intentions with persuasive skills, perhaps surpassing any neocheater living today. Pandering to envy and parasitism, both Clintons "compassionately" extracted maximum capital from the producers to buy votes and power from the public.

Indeed, Bill and Hillary Clinton were a key find for the Illuminati to accomplish their two-century goal of eliminating public acceptance of the parasitical-elite class draining the value producers and society. ...Ultimately, the pernicious Clintons will bring prosperity and happiness to America. How will that happen when all their actions

---

[1]Clinton crafted words as Shakespeare's Iago crafted words — crafted to put poisons in everyone's ear, potions that make evil actions seem good and good actions seem evil.

worked to decay individual rights, property rights, self-responsibility, self-respect, objective law, crime prevention, education, health care, and the economy?

The "Heaven-Sent" President Clinton was a professional Elmer Gantry who exuded sincerity, confidence, and compassion upon all whom he exploited for his own unearned livelihood and selfish ego. But, just as he built his illusions to the height of public deceptions, the fully integrated honesty of Neo-Tech began breaking those illusions in 1994. As the illusions break, such parasitical elites and their supporting casts will be scorned or prosecuted out of existence. The dishonest concepts of politics will be increasingly trashed along with political-agenda laws and ego-"justice" systems. At that point, America will be ready for depoliticization and decriminalization.

The Clintonian criminal mind is woven throughout goy politics — woven throughout the White House, the Congress, the legal profession, the media, and the celebrity industry. Above-the-law/beat-the-law, golfing-partners OJ/Clinton hid their criminal minds behind sharp lawyers, automatic lying, public adulation, and wonderful-person facades. Such persons will always coldly, arrogantly rationalize themselves out of criminal acts ranging from wife batterings and WACO killings to the destruction of public health, safety, and the economy.

The fully integrated honesty of Neo-Tech and the wide-scope accounting of the Golden Helmet combined with the coming cyber-information revolution will eliminate dishonest politicians, their harmful political-agenda laws, and their armed agents of force.

Why is victory on Earth possible over the next few years? Consider the survival tool of purposely destructive politicians and government officials. Their survival tool is the public acceptance of armed bureaucracies made possible by deception and irrationality. To perpetuate those dishonesties, the fully integrated honesty of Neo-Tech and the wide-scope accounting of the Golden Helmet must be hidden from the population by force, coercion, and fraud. Yet, every act to suppress the Neo-Tech/Golden-Helmet, including the jailing of its author and publisher, enhances public movements toward its all-revealing, depoliticization dynamic.

Through cyberspace, Golden-Helmet economies backed by nonpolitical *objective* law could be in place by 2001 AD or earlier. ...Prosperity and happiness will then be available for everyone and society.

Chapter 20

# The End of Chaos
xn=rx(1-x)

The Start of Guiltless Wealth

The best-selling book *Chaos* by James Gleick (Penguin, 1988) popularized the vogue theories of chaos in nature. Yet, the universal laws of physics and nature preclude chaos throughout time, space, and existence. Still, *appearances* of chaos are everywhere in nature, especially through irregular shapes called fractals.[1] Yet, with enough knowledge, one discovers genuine chaos does not exist, save one exception. Indeed, the law of identity along with cause and effect holds everywhere, barring that one exception.

That one exception proves the rule that *conscious beings* control existence. They control existence with a system designed for eternal survival through limitless value creation. Ironically, that universal rule can be proven by its one exception — the existence of parasitical humanoids who survive by creating chaos. They survive by creating chaos in draining economies and harming societies. With facades of good intentions and compassion, those humanoids inflict cruel harm and fraud on society. Such inflictions of harm and fraud are epitomized by Clinton-type *Envynomics*. Those media-hyped economics of envy

---

[1]Nonlinear, far-from-equilibrium situations bifurcate into potentially endless fractals in any finite space. That process, in turn, self-organizes into patterns of near-perfect order reaching over potentially limitless distances. ...Thus evolves not only the cosmos and life itself but all productive work, creative thinking...and limitless knowledge.

would drain dry all productive dynamics remaining in America. Indeed, envynomics provide the only means of survival left for the expanding clique of parasitical elites and their value-destroying bureaucracies.

Throughout the vast universe, genuine chaos exists only in an unnatural anticivilization such as now dominates planet Earth. Its humanoid rulers survive through parasitisms requiring force, threat of force, and fraud. They live by criminally draining those who produce values for society. ...But, all such parasites and their unnatural anticivilization will vanish on exposure to the natural Civilization of the Universe, which is now coming to planet Earth.

Beyond that exception found in an anticivilization, no fundamental chaos exists in nature, from quarks to universes. Still, *appearances* of chaos exist everywhere. However, investigation into every such appearance reveals either a transitory illusion in nature or a purposely *productive* act by conscious beings creating higher degrees of order as explained in the coming paragraphs. ...Remember, conscious beings are the grand-unifying force and controlling dimension of existence as identified in Part I on Neo-Tech Physics and discussed in Part III on the Civilization of the Universe.

Only purposely *destructive* acts of parasitical humanoids create genuine chaos. Wars, for example, create bona fide chaos that has no connection to the conscious-controlled flow of value production throughout the universe. Still, chaos-causing humanoids and their anticivilizations, such as infesting planet Earth today, comprise only a minute, transitory part of the universe. Thus, the effect of humanoid chaos on the universe is essentially nil and undetectable, except at its tiny moment

194

of flickering existence in time and space. By contrast, the *appearances* of chaos created by increasing values are not chaos at all. Instead, all such appearances are revealed as conscious creations of ordered values...even in Earth's anticivilization.

Look at a sleek, high-powered sports car from a little distance. One perceives beautiful symmetry and order — the antithesis of chaos. But, approach that car and throw open its engine hood — chaos! To the nonmechanic, all appears so asymmetrical and complex — a chaos of wires and tubes among a myriad of varied shapes and parts. Yet, pursue knowledge to the function and essence of that complex engine. One then perceives a supreme beauty of conscious symmetry and purposeful order.

Now, open a computer — chaos! But again, what looks like chaos — a jumble of electronics, chips, and circuitry — is actually a wondrous display of conscious-made order delivering mega values to the economy and society. Such value synergies arise from assembling widely varied components into functional designs. ...In ruling existence, conscious beings create ever increasing values that appear as chaos to the more primitive, unknowledgeable eye.

Look into the night sky. Sense the smooth, orderly-rotating universe. Now, using radio and optical telescopes combined with computers and astrophysics, throw open the curtain of the Universe for a closer look. Chaos! All looks so asymmetrical, jumbled, complex. A seemingly random scattering of all kinds of stars, galaxies, black holes, pulsars, quasars, nebulas, novas, particles, waves, rays, forces, fields, energies, and masses. Yet, on pursuing the widest knowledge and integrations, one discovers the orderly purpose in such "chaos". With that discovery on

195

planet Earth, everyone will grasp the purpose and value of the universe as orchestrated by conscious beings with much more-advanced knowledge. Then, finally, everyone on Earth can share that same beneficial control over time, space, and existence.

In Earth's anticivilization, the more conscious beings evolve, the more chaos appears to the unknowledgeable eye and primitive mind: Consider the obvious order of building blocks comprising the ancient pyramids. Compare the ordered symmetry of those pyramids to the apparent chaos perceived by the unknowledgeable, primitive eye gazing for the first time upon the jumbled maze of Manhattan's skyline. Compare the ordered drumbeats by early African or Indian tribes to the apparent chaos filling the untrained, primitive ear listening for the first time to full-blast Wagnerian opera. Compare the easy reading of simple parables throughout the Bible to the apparent chaos meeting the unintegrated mind perusing for the first time *Zonpower* — a communiqué from beyond the stars.

Now, trace the societal values within the symmetries of ancient human achievements — from the ordered pyramids advancing to the more chaotic-appearing but astronomically valuable Stonehenge. Then advance through the ages toward the ever increasing complexities of conscious achievements — toward ever greater economic and social values. Finally, consider the combined volumes of *Neo-Tech* and *Zonpower*: Their 1400 plus pages combine the widest-scope integrations possible — from subatomic particles to the universe of universes, from eternal time to eternal mass and energy, from romantic love to non-aging longevity with ever increasing prosperity and happiness for *all* conscious

196

beings. From that integrated combination, an epiphany appears — the epiphany for the Civilization of the Universe enveloping planet Earth by the turn of this century.

A single artist can paint or sculpt a perfect-ordered auto engine or computer circuitry in a matter of hours or days. But consider what is required to actually invent, develop, and then competitively mass-produce complex, jumbled-appearing engines or computers that deliver ever increasing values to others, the economy, and society. Such mega achievements require countless man-*years* of efforts — heroic efforts combining fully integrated honesty with brilliantly integrated efforts.

In other words, only competitive business dynamics deliver ever increasing values to all peoples, in all societies, at all times. For, those dynamics follow the preordained paths of honesty and effort required for genuine job-and-value production. Only that value production delivers prosperity and happiness to conscious life. ...Such value production often appears as increasing chaos to the more primitive mind and eye. But, the opposite is *always* the fact. For, all genuine values consist of conscious minds molding existence into ordered benefits for everyone and society.

On studying *Zonpower*, one finds a widely varied communiqué. Yet, on integration of these varied writings, *Zonpower* unveils the supreme order for *all* existence. How? By contextually interweaving the general with specifics, theory with practice, abstraction with fact, history with the contemporary...and the future. Thus evolves a spiralling synergy of many parts — a synergy that crunches millions of words and countless volumes into this single communiqué.

Movement II: The Anticivilization

Zonpower reveals to citizens of Earth their most important discovery: the Civilization of the Universe. Through the condensation of such wide-scope integrations arises the Neo-Tech/Zonpower discovery. And, from that discovery will come the first-and-final product of existence: the Civilization of the Universe.

Through the Neo-Tech/Zonpower discovery, that ultimate product can now arise on planet Earth. The Civilization of the Universe will start overtaking the parasitical-elite class, perhaps as early as the 2000 AD elections. Indeed, the Civilization of the Universe will vanish Earth's anticivilization and free everyone from unnatural deprivations, unhappiness, and death. For, those evils were wrought by chaos producers ranging from subhuman thieves and murderers to humanoid parasitical elites and professional value destroyers. ...The Civilization of the Universe will vanish those chaos generators to bring everyone on Earth the gifts of eternal life, prosperity, and happiness — gifts that are natural to all citizens of the universe.

Universal Communication

Zon talks to every conscious being in the universe. But, with the disease of mysticism and prior to the Neo-Tech/Zonpower discovery, no one on Earth could hear Zon.

Can conscious beings receive the eternal communications from the Civilization of the Universe? Because of mysticism and its anticivilization, no one on Earth could hear such communications. Through Gravity Units, universal communication is possible within the laws of physics as identified in Movements I and III. As Movements I and III further identify, we can cue our "ears" for such communication. Then, on curing the integration-blocking disease of irrationality, everyone on Earth can receive the eternal benefits available from the Civilization of the Universe.

MOVEMENT III

The Civilization of the Universe

The Solution

The Anticivilization

How long? How long?
How long must we suffocate and die
in a web of dishonesty?
Was John Milton[1] right?
Was the happy fall needed to gain paradise?

Dante proposed that conscious beings could escape evil
and be born into a new life: "Incipit Vita Nova".
Jonathan Swift sensed the all-pervasive anticivilization,
about which he bitterly railed. Voltaire recognized the
futility of life in the anticivilization in his totally
pessimistic antitheodicy, *Candide*. None knew of the Zon
escape — the escape to the Civilization of the Universe.

Escaping Dishonesty

A four-dimensional field or matrix of dishonesty pervades
the anticivilization. Our every thought, our every movement
during every instant becomes entangled in that matrix of
dishonesty. In its omnipresent smog, we *all* suffocate and
die. ...With the forthcoming *Quantum Crossings* and *Zon
Protocols*, we can escape that dishonesty — escape that
matrix of entrapment, diminishment, and death. How? By
using Zonpower to quantum jump from the anticivilization
to the Civilization of the Universe.

The Civilization of the Universe
Free. Free at last. Free forever.

---

[1]John Milton and many other writers with radical ideas that contradicted the
Establishment were politically imprisoned, some almost losing their lives:
Dante imprisoned 2 years, Marco Polo imprisoned 6 years, Cervantes
imprisoned, John Milton imprisoned and nearly executed, John Bunyan
imprisoned 12 years, Daniel Defoe imprisoned, pilloried, barely escaped the
gallows, Voltaire imprisoned in the Bastille twice, Fyodor Dostoyevsky twice
imprisoned for many years, nearly executed. And, remember, nonwriter
Socrates was executed simply for discussing his ideas. ...The author of
Neo-Tech was politically imprisoned after barely escaping being shot by armed
federal agents who beat, kicked, and hospitalized his personal editor.

Chapter 21

Finding Tomorrow's Golden World

On February 13, 1991, the federal prosecutor turned to the jury and revealed the man on trial was from another world. The prosecutor told the jury that this one man was the most dangerous man. For, this one man threatened the status quo — threatened to upright this upside down world in which we live.

Did you ever feel that a better world must exist somewhere: an eternally benevolent world of honesty, integrity, rationality, peace, security...a world of limitless excitement and prosperity? Where is that other world? How do we get there? Has any explorer yet discovered that world? Does he have a map for us? Is that our world of the future?

In 1980, a scout, a pioneer, a Columbus set sail into the unknown to discover a new world. All but a handful of people thought he was going to sail off the edge of this flat, irrational society. He did not. Instead, he returned wearing a Golden Helmet. He had discovered that better world. He discovered our world of tomorrow. He discovered a world of eternal rationality, peace, and prosperity. ...He discovered the Civilization of the Universe.

On returning from his long voyage, that man was imprisoned. Why? That man as a scientist ventured beyond the known to discover the route to Shangrila. He returned with a map. And, that map shows all men and women the route to a rational world of opportunity, growth, and unimaginable riches. Once started on that route, one can no longer accept the political criminalities,

203

Movement III: The Civilization of the Universe

social insanities, and economic destructions overtaking today's world. Thus, for bringing you the map that leads to the Civilization of the Universe, that man was imprisoned by the threatened parasitical-elite class. But, now, with his map and Zonpower, nothing can stop those on Earth from discovering that golden world of eternal prosperity and happiness...starting now!

MS

Chapter 22

Cassandra's Secret

> **13th Century BC**
> Cassandra of Troy possessed the power to predict the future with perfect accuracy. But, no one would believe her. Thus, everyone missed collecting unlimited riches.

Imagine you are speaking to an old friend. Suddenly, you realize every conversation, every action, no matter how seemingly reasonable or conventional, is geared toward losing values and happiness. Suddenly, you see this mundane, completely "normal" experience as bizarrely unnatural. Then, you see nearly everyone and all society as hypnotized losers in a civilization that is irrational, insane.

Next, you realize your own children, your spouse, your own self, all who seem to live with some success and happiness, are equally trapped in an insane civilization that always moves toward loss and death. You then realize the only realm of consistent sanity and increasing values lies within value-producing professions and market-driven businesses.

Breaking the Hypnotic Spell

First, you must choose to live in either a sane civilization or an insane one. An insane civilization is one that shrinks backward into irrationality. In today's anticivilization, essentially all thinking and knowledge are hypnotically contracting into ever more narrow ranges that

205

increasingly block honesty and understanding. Thus, communication and actions are becoming increasingly politically correct, irrational, and harmfully split from reality...increasingly schizophrenic.

Hypnotic irrationality grips Earth's anticivilization. That spreading irrationality yields a decaying system in which increasing entropy brings decreasing order and increasing strife. That, in turn, brings declining job-and-value creation. Thus, whenever irrationality prevails, time must be *redefined* as running backward toward increasing ignorance, poverty, and entropy.

With consciousness as the controlling force of existence, the arrow of time in physics is reversed and must be redefined: In an open and eternally evolving universe, time flows forward toward decreasing entropy (increasing order) as controlled by productive conscious actions, *not* toward increasing entropy (decreasing order) as controlled by nonconscious actions or destructive conscious actions.

In a naturally evolving civilization with decreasing entropy (increasing order and harmony), competitive value production constantly expands. Thus, with rationality prevailing, time runs forward toward expanding knowledge, prosperity, and *decreasing* entropy.

Various aspects of this time-and-energy flow throughout the cosmos are observationally and experimentally demonstrated by electromagnetic-plasma cosmology — a cosmology first identified by Nobel laureate Hannes Alfvén — backed by Nobel laureates de Broglie, Schrödinger, and Prigogine — then advanced by Eric J. Lerner in his popular book, *The Big Bang Never Happened* (Vantage Books, 1992).

Now comes the real discovery: You discover what

everyone on Earth fears, including yourself. You discover what *no one* on Earth wants, including yourself. You discover how anyone on Earth can become rich, powerful, happy — quickly, guiltlessly, eternally. Yet, only with great concentration and effort do you break your hypnotic paralysis enough to barely open the easy-turning spigot to limitless riches.

Something seems paradoxical or upside down about the above paragraph, especially when restated as follows: Everyone on Earth, including you, *fears and shuns* that which brings exciting riches and romantic happiness!

On learning Cassandra's Secret, you will understand the above statement. You will view reality from wider dimensions. You will understand this anticivilization. You will see the invisible hypnotic state in which everyone on Earth loses the values of life. You will then awaken to win everything — fabulous riches and happiness while benefiting everyone and society. You will discover what Zonpower is; you will discover that Zon is you. ...Those who do not rise to understand Cassandra's Secret will remain asleep in malignant irrationality, steadily losing their lives and happiness.

You Control Reality

Cassandra's Secret vanishes irrationalities and mysticisms, ranging from the false concepts of a finite existence and the singularity big-bang creation of the universe to the criminal concepts of socialized collectivism and political-agenda laws backed by ego "justice". ...Cassandra's Secret operates from two directions: (1) it vanishes irrational illusions, (2) it reveals objective reality. Now, consider the following two points:

1. *You* **can Vanish Irrationality**: From the widest-

207

scope knowledge possible, Cassandra's Secret interweaves the essences of science, reality, business, and human consciousness to reveal a stunningly benevolent and bountiful civilization — a civilization 180° different from the one in which we all live. That endlessly rich civilization is available now — easily available to any conscious being on Earth who realizes the impotent nothingness of *all* irrationalities, mysticisms, and insanities.

Today, the disease of irrationality infests everyone on Earth. Cassandra's Secret reveals how by stepping into the Civilization of the Universe, you cure that disease — you vanish irrationality into its nothingness.

2. *You* **are the Controlling, Fixed Center of Existence**: Human consciousness is eternal. It has always been a fixed part of existence as demonstrated in Chapter 6. Indeed, human consciousness *is* the prime mover of existence.

The above statement implies nothing mystical about consciousness. Cassandra's Secret is not at all about new-age ideas, pantheistic Eastern mysticism, or some abstract "universal consciousness". It is about the limitless power of *your own* down-to-earth consciousness. Moreover, you must understand that consciousness can never *create* reality or existence.[1] Any claim that consciousness creates reality or existence is mystical. For, any such claim contradicts the nature of both consciousness and existence. ...Existence was not created. Existence simply exists as eternally evolving fields of matter and energy. Existence *cannot not* exist.

---

[1]However, consciousness can and does control the modes of existence such as matter, energy, and spacetime geometries to evolve new modes of existence, including new universes.

Cassandra's Secret

Indeed, consciousness is the sole *integrator and controller* of existence. Thus, consciousness is the prime mover of existence. Ever wider scopes of integrations unleash the limitless power of human consciousness. By contrast, irrationalities and mysticisms are diseases of human consciousness that truncate the power to integrate reality. For, integration of reality can never move beyond any point of irrationality or mysticism. By curing irrationality comes (1) ever growing knowledge of existence, (2) ever growing control of existence, and (3) ever growing prosperity and happiness.

Newton's absolute physics, Einstein's relativistic physics, and Bohr's quantum physics are reconciled by the ever widening knowledge generated from human consciousness free of mysticisms and irrationalities. Indeed, existence is controlled to eternally provide ever wider, integrated knowledge and riches for every conscious being. In other words, your consciousness *is* the fixed center and ultimate controller of existence.

* * *

Cassandra's Secret comprises the widest-scope integration with reality to yield accurate predictions of the future. Cassandra's Secret is based on observed facts, scientific research, and direct experience combined with inductive and deductive reasoning ranging from well-demonstrated theory and objective law to speculative hypotheses moving toward rejection or confirmation.

But, Cassandra's Secret is in no way dependent on recognition or approval by anyone, much less the Establishment. For, the anticivilization Establishment is irrelevant to evolving knowledge and progress. Moreover, the fully integrated honesty and wide-scope integrations of Cassandra's Secret will ultimately end all bogus livelihoods — all livelihoods arising from professional value destroyers corrupting today's political, legal, scientific, and educational systems.

The ideas revealed by Cassandra's Secret are now propagating through worldwide networks, beyond the reach of oppressive "authorities" and their gun-backed political agendas. Neo-Tech spreads independently of the Establishment media and academe. The key is Neo-Tech publications — free cyberspace publications combined with low-cost newsprint publications in twelve languages mass distributed by worldwide mailings from many countries.

The certitude arising from Cassandra's Secret quietly spreads from those Neo-Tech publications to the populations throughout the world. Nothing can stop that certitude from spreading in print and through cyberspace. The revelations of Cassandra's Secret will bring honest, rational people eternal prosperity and happiness.

Chapter 23

Ultimate Wealth Lurks

within

Cassandra's Secret

Undreamt wealth can be gained by controlling the power underlying the universe: Zonpower *is* the universal symmetry that underpins Cassandra's Secret. The power of Zon controls existence at *all* scales. ...Hidden beneath everyone's consciousness flows Zonpower — a mighty river of wealth creation. That power is available to you now: through Cassandra's Secret, through the supersymmetry of Zonpower.

Born Free

Born free of the irrationalities propagating Earth's anticivilization, all young children hold the power of Zon. They are citizens of the universe. But, quickly, every child becomes trapped in a bizarrely irrational civilization created by parasitical elites...humanoids who have lost their humanity. Those humanoids must trap and blind every child. Why? To assure the future survival of humanoids. For, they survive by parasitically draining productive adults who have been blinded since youth by illusions, deception, and force.

Trapped

This humanoid-created anticivilization blinds and then corrupts its children. This corruption is force fed into the

211

mind of every child. While unknowingly holding the power of the universe, children lack the knowledge to protect their minds. Thus, before they can learn to use their power, they are inflicted with painfully destructive illusions built on contradictions and irrationalities. Those illusions damage the minds of children and block Zonpower from their consciousness.

How have such harms corrupted everyone on Earth for the past three millennia? To live "comfortably" in this life-draining anticivilization, one must increasingly invest in the harmful illusions of the anticivilization — one must sink to a lower social dimension. From that restricted dimension, no one can discover his or her natural power.

Until now, Zonpower has remained submerged in everyone's natural consciousness. Yet, Zonpower functions in parallel but hidden ways beneath one's clouded consciousness — clouded since childhood. The resulting becloudings provided the hypnotic set up for lifetime exploitations of every value producer by the parasitical elites. Indeed, that exploitive set up is the illusion of "needing to get along in or approval from" this irrational anticivilization hypnotically conjured up by the parasitical-elite "leaders".

Cassandra's Secret breaks that hypnotic spell. Once that spell is broken, one can freely access Zonpower to control existence and predict the future to gain limitless wealth.

Leaving the World of Losers

Perhaps certain children become autistic because they will not let their minds be corrupted by the anticivilization. Perhaps they withdraw from all relationships with their environment and cease their journeys into this corrupt, unreal world. But with that withdrawal, they also cease their personal development.

In 1993, Public Broadcasting aired a documentary about an acclaimed "breakthrough" from Australia for treating autistic children by a technique called "facilitated communication". Almost the entire professional field involved in treating and caring for autistic children embraced that technique, around which they began boosting their careers. Many millions of tax dollars poured into this "breakthrough", including costly physical facilities, such as at Syracuse University, dedicated to "facilitated communication".

Yet, any objective observation of that technique, even by those unfamiliar with autism, will immediately reveal the technique as bogus. Not only does the technique lack rationality, but has no correspondence with any law of nature, science, or logic. Anyone can easily recognize the technique as nothing more than a Ouija board spelling out the subliminal thoughts of the professional therapists "treating" autistic children. This technique is not only worthless but is harmful toward those children and their families.

How could an entire field of professionals invest their lives and build their careers on something so obviously bogus and harmful to everyone? When people start investing their lives into bogus activities, they increasingly rationalize — blindly and without limits — to continue expanding their harmful investments and livelihoods.

Thus lies the mechanism through which almost everyone on Earth invests his or her life into this bogus civilization. Once that investment is made in the anticivilization, one is trapped within its all-encompassing, irrationality.

Everyone in this anticivilization starts with the mind

213

of an innocent, defenseless child. That mind is then tortured with painful contradictions and dishonesties until the child either becomes autistic by withdrawing from this irrational civilization or becomes "normal" by surrendering to its destructive irrationalities.

The more irrational and destructive people become, the more they will destroy and kill to maintain their harmful careers in the anticivilization. Additionally, the more people invest in destructive careers, the less competent they become in producing competitive values that genuinely benefit others and society.

Most politicians — along with many bureaucrats, lawyers, judges, and stagnant big-business executives — abolish their human nature by becoming parasites. As professional parasites, they become camouflaged criminals, even murderers, rationalizing behind shields of subjective political-agenda "law" and corrupt ego "justice".

Consider Hitler, Mao, Castro, Pol Pot, and the Clintons. Each increasingly invested their lives into becoming clandestine parasites until they could no longer support themselves by competitively producing values for others and society. Thus, such people *must* become increasingly open criminals and killers to survive.

With Zonpower, you leave all such losers behind forever.

Becoming Zon

Heathcliff, the main character of Emily Brontë's[1] novel *Wuthering Heights*, reflects the hidden, parallel consciousness that flows in every human being. Heathcliff is portrayed as the epitome of a nasty, evil man. Yet, even in him, the nature of human consciousness surfaces to reveal nobility and good. Likewise, both the heroes

---

[1]She died too young at 30 as did her author sister Anne at 29.

and villains created by the great novelist Victor Hugo reveal the underlying human power and nobility that flow independently of the meanness and irrationalities controlling this unnatural anticivilization.

The nobility and good of human character are revealed at times in everyone, except in humanoids who have destroyed their human nature. Indeed, nobility and good are revealed spontaneously, in greater or lesser degrees, throughout the life of every conscious being. Now, today, the limitless potential of one's childhood can be fulfilled through Zonpower. At the same time, anyone can tap Cassandra's Secret to emasculate and vanish the harmful consequences of this anticivilization.

Conclusion

Through Cassandra's Secret, you will break the hypnotic spell of this anticivilization. You will discover how Zonpower puffs away the harms propagated by parasitical elites. Zonpower lifts *you* toward wealth — guiltless wealth for you and society, wealth that flows from super-wide integrations of knowledge. In your hands, you hold the widest-scope knowledge ever unveiled on planet Earth — the knowledge of Zonpower.

From *Zonpower*, you gain an entirely new way to view yourself, your life, and all existence. You will then be poised to capture eternal life. From Zonpower, you will seize iron-grip control and a confident certitude that brings everlasting youth, riches, and romantic love.

Chapter 24

Zon Speaks

"In this anticivilization dominating planet Earth, only young children hold the power of the universe. For, they are innocent and pure: free of the irrationality disease called mysticism. During their brief mystic-free period, children live among the Civilization of the Universe. They hold the limitless yet unlearned power of the universe — Zonpower. But all children are dependent on their parents and teachers for acquiring initial knowledge. Thus, parents and teachers are responsible for infecting and debilitating the minds of their children with deadly irrationality — with the integration-blocking disease of mysticism.

"The minds of such children are manipulated and twisted into grotesque dishonesties ranging from accepting parental irrationalities and mystical religions to accepting the politically correct insanities and destructive actions of harmful 'teachers', 'authorities', and 'leaders'. Thus, children are dragged into Earth's irrational, Plato-enslaved anticivilization to lose their potential for eternal growth and happiness.

"Upon accepting an irrational civilization as normal, a closed bubble of mysticism forms around each child. Each such closed bubble assumes its own wobbly size and shape to accommodate the dishonesties, inner logic, and rationalizations required to live 'normally' in an irrational civilization. *In such a bubble, one can never squarely stand on reality. Therefore, one never has real strength or power. One is never anchored in objective reality, but is always trapped in illusions.* Thus, one never even

217

glimpses his or her potential. Floating in a mystical bubble, often upside down, one can never experience the Civilization of the Universe with its limitless power and wealth.

"Today, all citizens of Earth's anticivilization live in such bubbles, floating detached from reality and the universe. Those bubbles are easily pushed around in directions that support false authorities backed by their armed agents of force. Those false authorities lack any real power to produce genuine values for themselves and others. Such parasites survive by manipulating both the dishonesties of mysticism and the evils of force. They learn how to manipulate or force *everyone's* bubble of mysticism into supporting their own destructive lives.

"Indeed, every person living in this anticivilization is trapped within his or her own bubble, never to gain eternal prosperity and happiness. Thus, everyone on Earth sooner or later stagnates and dies. By contrast, in the rational Civilization of the Universe, stagnation or death of any conscious being is the ultimate loss, the ultimate tragedy, the ultimate irrationality. ...Thus, stagnation and death have long ago been cured or eliminated from the Civilization of the Universe.

"Until today, no one on Earth realized that conscious beings never need to live in an anticivilization. For, an anticivilization is unreal — created entirely from illusions and hoaxes by parasitical 'leaders'. Those false leaders live as they have for three millennia: by enforcing fraudulent political agendas in order to control and, thus, live off the value producers.

"But, today, through Neo-Tech, all value producers on planet Earth can begin to recognize the Civilization of the Universe. That recognition begins the journey into fully integrated honesty. That honesty, in turn, will begin to dissolve the bubble of mysticism. When the bubble finally breaks, one lands upright, feet firmly planted in reality. From that position, one commands reality, never again threatened or manipulated by illusions. From that position, one captures Zonpower with its limitless excitement and prosperity.

"The most remarkable feature about Zonpower and the Civilization of the Universe is that to become Zon and achieve limitless prosperity requires *nothing* remarkable. Zon and the Civilization of the Universe are open to all honest people, no matter what their intellectual or physical attributes.

"Once one breaks his or her bubble of mysticism, the unreal anticivilization is revealed as nothing — as a nightmare of illusions. That person then becomes a Citizen of the Universe. That person captures the limitless power of eternity. That person becomes Zon!"

Civilization of the Universe, 1993

New-Color Symphony

Movement #3

Chapter 25

Are You Zon?
What Is Zonpower?

> You are chained to an anticivilization
> But Zonpower breaks those chains to let you capture
> Boundless wealth, romantic love, and happiness

The Power of Zon

You are thunderstruck. You have discovered the source of unlimited wealth. You have discovered how to leave the boring anticivilization of planet Earth for a civilization of boundless life, excitement, wealth, and romantic love. How did you make that discovery?

Sitting before a mirror, you have just interviewed an ordinary-appearing human being. But, that person is not a citizen of this world. Sitting before you, talking as a physical being, that person is a citizen of an all-powerful civilization — the Civilization of the Universe. With powers beyond what Earth citizens could ever imagine, that person is called Zon. To those among Earth's stagnant civilization, Zon has powers wondrous beyond description.

A UFO has landed? An alien from space? A supernatural being? Or other such mystical wonder? No, nothing mystical or supernatural. Yet, in Earth's tribalistic anticivilization, the powers of Zon seem infinitely wondrous. Still, Zon is starkly in the here and now, standing before everyone on planet Earth. For, Zon exists just as you and everyone else.

221

Movement III: The Civilization of the Universe

From where did Zon come? What can and will Zon do for you? How can you gain Zon's power? Can you become Zon? Are you already Zon?

Zon was born on planet Earth. By five years of age, that child escaped Earth's anticivilization to experience the all-powerful Civilization of the Universe. During that escape, he held universal power — a power greater than held by any adult on Earth. But, not until many years later, decades later, did he rediscover that power. He then realized that every conscious child two to six years old likewise escapes Earth's anticivilization to experience the power of the universe. Yet, *every* child forgets that experience as he or she is inexorably drawn into Earth's irrational, mind-crippling anticivilization.

A rare, perhaps one-in-a-trillion combination of ordinary circumstances let an ordinary person escape Earth's anticivilization. He then returned to construct a map for all conscious people to rediscover the all-powerful Civilization of the Universe. Today, by using that map, any conscious being can vanish the illusions of this anticivilization to boom into a civilization of limitless power, wealth, and life.

Thus, today, one can finally become free of the life-destroying humanoids infesting planet Earth. Zonpower offers everyone the key to vanish this anticivilization beset with parasitical elites, their illusions, their hoaxes. ...Zonpower will eventually bring everyone into the endlessly exciting Civilization of the Universe.

The Origins of Earth's Irrational Civilization

As babies first start becoming conscious, perhaps around two years of age, they automatically become citizens of the universe with omnipotent yet unlearned and unrealized powers over all life and existence.[1] But, before they can realize those unlimited powers, all young children are relentlessly, remorselessly drawn into Earth's irrational anticivilization. This unnatural anticivilization could not evolve until man's bicameral mind invented consciousness about 3000 years ago as described in Chapter 28. With that event, man's nature-organized automatic mind jumped to a much superior, man-organized conscious mind.

About a half millennia after that jump, man's newly conscious mind became infected with irrationality, which is an integration-blocking disease analogous to the immune-blocking disease of AIDS. The result was a fatal condition known as Plato's disease. Named after its historical originator, Plato's disease breaks down rationality — the mind's defense mechanism against integration-breaking illusions. ...Without consistent rationality, such illusions allow purposeful destructions, exploitations, poverty, unhappiness, suffering, disease, envy, evil, and death itself seem a natural part of life.

Thus, illusion-infected consciousness creates economically stupid, war-like civilizations that continuously collapse on themselves into black-hole anomalies. Irrationality is the disease that causes certain human beings to mutate into parasites or humanoids programed to harm conscious life and society. Those mutants survive by feeding off and draining value-producing human beings. That constant, parasitical drain leaves innocent people in chains — increasingly unfulfilled and eventually dead.

---

[1]Babies do not grow old; they grow toward knowledge and power. After becoming infected with irrationality, however, everyone grows old and dies.

Movement III: The Civilization of the Universe

Zon's Escape — Your Escape

How did one conscious person on planet Earth escape its unnatural anticivilization? How did that one ordinary person as an adult rediscover the rational Civilization of the Universe? How can that person deliver to you boundless power and prosperity?

In answering those questions, you too can capture Zonpower. You can have the power of Zon. You can become Zon.

Zonpower is Waiting for You

You can acquire Zonpower by going to the origin of Earth's anticivilization. At that origin, one discovers the exit. ...Prior to that discovery, no adult could leave this anticivilization ruled by parasitical elites and their armed agents of force.

Until the Zonpower discovery in 1992, every person on Earth was embedded in this dead-end anticivilization. Every person's thinking process was corrupted by parasitical "leaders" in government, education, journalism, entertainment, and big business. Every person's logic was undermined by illusions and hoaxes from those professional parasites. Indeed, to live off the efforts of others, all parasitical elites *must undermine logic* with look-good illusions and rip-off hoaxes. As a result, everyone on planet Earth suffers incalculable losses.

But now, today, you too can leave that anticivilization. *Immediately upon leaving, you will experience the greatest mind empowerment possible for conscious beings. You will suddenly dominate life and control the future.* Moreover, you will be among the first in history to acquire knowledge beyond this anticivilization. You will capture ever expanding knowledge from the all-powerful

Are You Zon? What is Zonpower?

Civilization of the Universe — you will capture Zonpower for unlimited life, wealth, and happiness.

By understanding the charts on the next three pages, you can begin eliminating those who harm and drain your life — those who chain your life to a stake, those who keep you in a mystical bubble.

Chart 1

Vanish Purposely Harmful People
(parasitical-elite value destroyers)

State of Being:
Diseased, ridiculous, unfocused, destructive, ignoble
Self-corrupted, malevolent minds; ciphers, uncompetitive
Degenerated their natural minds, unintegrated word spouters
Metaphysically dishonest, clownish, guilty, unhappy
Entropy-increasing humanoids. Penis collapsors

Archetypes: Most politicians; many lawyers, bureaucrats, and journalists; all business quislings, socialists, fascists, nihilists, criminals, armed agents of force, political entrepreneurs

Examples

Historical: Plato, Alexander the Great, Julius Caesar, Caligula, Genghis Khan, Kant, Hegel, Alexander Hamilton, Napoleon, Lincoln, Woodrow Wilson, John M. Keynes, John Dewey, Lenin, Hitler, FDR, LBJ, Mao, Ayatollah Khomeini

Current: Fidel Castro, Li Peng, Rudolph Giuliani, William Bennett, Newsweek-type journalists, purposely destructive politicians and bureaucrats, money-mad lawyers and doctors, dishonest professors and journalists

Survival Dynamics: Survival depends on draining values from others, armed enforcement of political-agenda policies, obscuring objective law, and implementing ego "justice" to control and drain the value producers.

Potentials: Drainers of human life, the economy, and society. Destroyers of earned property, happiness, economies, and civilization.

Action Toward: Identify, dishonor, ostracize, vanish. Forget them.

End their Current State of: Being dishonestly glorified and praised. Reject JFK's *Profiles in Courage*. They are nothing. Remove their images and names from stamps, money, monuments, streets, buildings. Replace them with honest value-and-job producers.

Uphold Naturally Beneficial People
(economic value-and-job producers)

State of Being:
Healthy, important, focused, productive, noble
Self-made, benevolent minds; infinites, competitive
Developed their natural minds, integrated thinkers
Metaphysically honest, serious, innocent, happy
Entropy-decreasing human beings. Penis erectors

Archetypes: Blue-collar workers, farmers, job-creating business-people, laborers, byte heads, defenders of property rights, nurses, postal workers, firemen, defense soldiers, market entrepreneurs

Examples

Historical: Thales, Socrates, Aquinas, Bruno, Galileo, Spinoza, Newton, Jefferson, Darwin, Mark Twain, Andrew Carnegie, Jay Gould, J.J. Hill, Edison, Henry Ford, Einstein, Maria Montessori, Walt Disney, Ray Kroc, Sam Walton

Current: Jonas Salk, Steven Jobs, Soichiro Honda, Michael Milken, Dershowitz, Leona Helmsley, Bill Gates, honest writers and editors, blue-collar workers, local police-men, value-producing housewives and teachers, entrepreneurs

Survival Dynamics: Survival depends on producing competitive values for others and upholding objective law. The result is expanding prosperity, happiness, and justice for everyone.

Potentials: Enhancers of human life, the economy, and society. Builders of assets, economies, and civilization.

Action Toward: Identify, honor, uphold, multiply. Remember them.

End their Current State of: Being ignored, mocked, slandered, scorned, envied, plundered, even jailed and killed. They are everything. Praise and uphold value-and-job producing business people and risk-taking entrepreneurs. They are the real heroes.

Chart 2

Discover the Power of Zon

Code: — = Economic and social harms inflicted on society
+ = Economic and social benefits produced for society

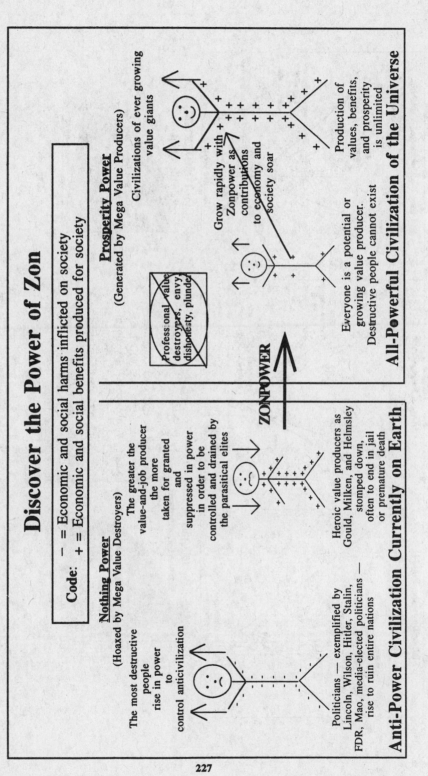

Prosperity Power
(Generated by Mega Value Producers)

Civilizations of ever growing value giants

Grow rapidly with Zonpower as contributions to economy and society soar

Production of values, benefits, and prosperity is unlimited

Professional value destroyers, envy, dishonesty, plunder

Everyone is a potential or growing value producer. Destructive people cannot exist

All-Powerful Civilization of the Universe

ZONPOWER

Nothing Power
(Hoaxed by Mega Value Destroyers)

The greater the value-and-job producer the more taken for granted and suppressed in power in order to be controlled and drained by the parasitical elites

The most destructive people rise in power to control anticivilization

Heroic value producers as Gould, Milken, and Helmsley stomped down, often to end in jail or premature death

Politicians — exemplified by Lincoln, Wilson, Hitler, Stalin, FDR, Mao, media-elected politicians — rise to ruin entire nations

Anti-Power Civilization Currently on Earth

New-Color Symphony

Movement #3

227

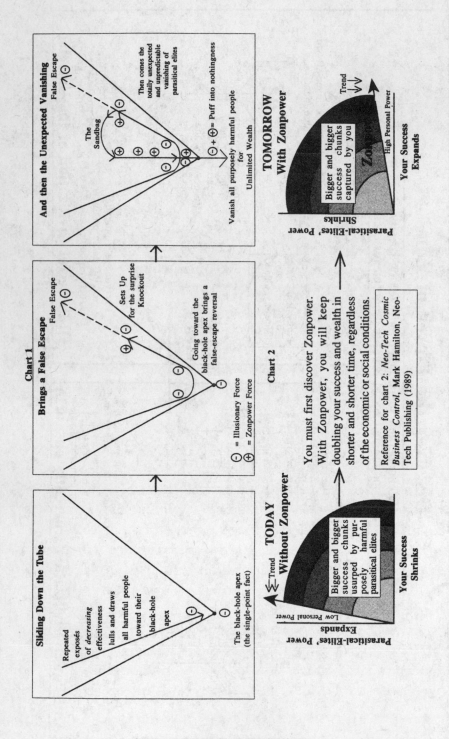

Chart 1

Sliding Down the Tube

Repeated exposés of *decreasing* effectiveness lulls and draws all harmful people toward their black-hole apex

The black-hole apex (the single-point fact)

Brings a False Escape

False Escape

Sets Up for the surprise Knockout

Going toward the black-hole apex brings a false-escape reversal

⊖ = Illusionary Force
⊕ = Zonpower Force

And then the Unexpected Vanishing

False Escape

Then comes the totally unexpected and unpredictable vanishing of parasitical elites

The Sandbag

Vanish all purposely harmful people for Unlimited Wealth

⊖ + ⊕ = Puff into nothingness

Chart 2

TODAY Without Zonpower

Trend

Parasitical-Elites' Power Expands

Low Personal Power

Bigger and bigger success chunks usurped by purposely harmful parasitical elites

Your Success Shrinks

TOMORROW With Zonpower

Trend

Parasitical-Elites' Power Shrinks

Zonpower

High Personal Power

Bigger and bigger success chunks captured by you

Your Success Expands

You must first discover Zonpower. With Zonpower, you will keep doubling your success and wealth in shorter and shorter time, regardless of the economic or social conditions.

Reference for chart 2: *Neo-Tech Cosmic Business Control*, Mark Hamilton, Neo-Tech Publishing (1989)

228

Chapter 26
Breaking the Bubble
of
Mysticism

Neo-Tech/Zonpower cures irrationality. Curing irrationality will end the parasitical-elite class and its hoax-built anticivilization. Indeed, curing irrationality and breaking its mystical bubbles of illusions will bring everyone into the Civilization of the Universe. ...Key knowledge for breaking everyone's mystical bubble evolved from three sources: *The Neo-Tech Discovery* by Frank R. Wallace (800 pages, Neo-Tech Publishing, revised 1994), *The Origins of Consciousness* by Julian Jaynes (467 pages, Houghton Mifflin, New York, 1976), and *Objectivism: the Philosophy of Ayn Rand* by Leonard Peikoff (493 pages, Dutton, New York, 1991).

Julian Jaynes, an academic at Princeton University, avidly avoids recognizing the titanic significance of his discovery that human consciousness is man-discovered, not nature-evolved.[1] For, to protect his own personal bubble of mysticism needed to live "acceptably" in today's anticivilization, he must avoid knowing the mystic-shattering key embodied in his work. And, as did the late Ayn Rand, her protégé Leonard Peikoff, a highly productive and principled philosopher, also avoids knowing the mystic-vanishing power lying within his and Rand's work. For, he, too, must protect his mystical bubble in order to live "normally" in today's anticivilization.

As is now experienced explicitly with mystic-breaking

---

[1]Jaynes's work is reviewed in Chapter 28 of this communiqué.

Movement III: The Civilization of the Universe

Neo-Tech, Peikoff's masterwork will be experienced implicitly as a threat by everyone living "normally" in an irrational anticivilization. Thus, today, Peikoff's great work is largely ignored or minimized not only by the threatened parasitical-elite class, but by his professional peers and objectivist cohorts. And, finally, neither Jaynes nor Peikoff recognizes the achievements of the other. Thus, neither integrates their great works together: Jaynes's work reveals the origins and metaphysical nature of consciousness; Peikoff's work reveals the epistemological nature of consciousness and its philosophical consequences.

Other major value producers, such as Albert Einstein and Michael Milken, were also trapped in their own bubbles of mysticism. Thus, they never identified the widest, most important values contained in their work. For, they would rather perish than abandon their lifelong emotional and material investments in the status quo that trapped them in Earth's anticivilization. ...*Every* citizen of planet Earth exists in a self-made mystical bubble in order to live "correctly" in a loser's anticivilization.

Vanishing the Parasitical-Elite Class

What are we talking about? We are talking about a parasitical-elite class that has created an anticivilization on planet Earth. We are talking about a parasitical-elite class that after 2500 years has finally overwhelmed its host — the producers of objective values and genuine jobs...the sole providers of life and prosperity to mankind. We are talking about a malignancy of parasites who drain and destroy those value-and-job producers. We are talking about forever vanishing professional value destroyers and their anticivilization. We are talking about limitless

230

wealth, health, and happiness available to everyone on Earth. ...We are talking about the mystic-free Civilization of the Universe enveloping planet Earth, perhaps as early as 2001.

"No, that could never happen," everyone exclaims. "Not in a generation, a century, or even a millennium."

Such an exclamation is valid within today's hoaxed anticivilization. But, anyone who steps into the Civilization of the Universe will exclaim: "Parasitical elites? An anticivilization built on force and deception? ...Everything was so irrationally destructive and boring back then. What is there to remember about such a value vacuum — such nothingness?"

Indeed, parasitical elites are subhumans or humanoids who lack the requirements for supporting human life. They lack honest character, long-range principles, real power. They live by manipulating truth to bleed others — by undercutting objective law, societal well-being, and human happiness. They bring society only losses and suffering. Thus, all memories of those parasites and their hoaxed civilization will vanish as the Civilization of the Universe brings to Earth the excitement of boundless prosperity and happiness.

How can such certainty exist about vanishing the parasitical elites and their anticivilization? That certainty rises from new knowledge: As demonstrated in *Zonpower*, every hoax and illusion is revealed on exposure to the Civilization of the Universe. Stripped of their illusions, parasitical elites go down the memory hole in whirlpools of absurdity. Also washed away will be politicians living as destructive humanoids, bureaucrats violently enforcing harmful political agendas, judges applying ego "justice", and prosecutors ignoring objective law and justice. ...They

231

all will vanish down the drain of public ostracism.

As the Civilization of the Universe envelops Earth, *genuine* value-and-job producers from hard-working laborers to multimillionaire entrepreneurs will assume power. This anticivilization will then end. ...What guarantees the end of this anticivilization? Relentless self-spreading Neo-Tech guarantees the end of the parasitical-elite class and its hoax-built anticivilization.

The Role of Rand and Peikoff

Amidst the pending demise of the parasitical-elite class and its anticivilization, Earth's first valid philosophy arises. That philosophy arises from two people in history who applied fully integrated honesty in developing a comprehensive philosophy: Ayn Rand and Leonard Peikoff. Ayn Rand established Objectivist philosophy, despite her tragic personal irrationalities. That philosophy evolved by overcoming the philosophical errors of Aristotle, Spinoza, and Nietzsche. Today, Objectivist philosophy combined with the limitless prosperity available from Neo-Tech disintegrates the anticivilization on planet Earth by *dis*integrating all its bogus philosophies.

Ironically, the Civilization of the Universe with its Zonpower requires no explicit philosophy. For, by nature, the only moral and practical philosophy throughout all universes and all times — Objectivist philosophy — is self-evident to everyone in the Civilization of the Universe. Indeed, valid philosophy — its metaphysics, epistemology, ethics, politics, and aesthetics — reduces to thirteen words: *What is is. Perceive it. Integrate it honestly. Act on it. Idealize it.* ...Honesty *is* free will.

Peikoff definitively grounds those thirteen words to existence. After thirty years of preparation and six years

232

of writing and editing, he crafted Ayn Rand's philosophy of Objectivism into 180,000 words. Those words link the Civilization of the Universe to existence, throughout time. ...Dr. Peikoff provides an unmovable position that philosophically exposes the parasitical-elite class and its anticivilization.

In philosophically exposing the anticivilization, Peikoff provides a reality-linking tour from sense perception and volition to concept formation, objectivity, and reason; from the nature of man to the concepts of good, virtue, happiness, government, economics, and art. *That tour is the death knell for the grotesque anticivilization in which today every citizen of Earth lives...and upon which every Earth-bound citizen falsely feels dependent.* Indeed, everyone's comfort-zone rationalizations, livelihoods, socializings, and contemporary lifestyles are falsely dependent on a wealth-and-life-destroying anticivilization. Yet, in reality, no healthy, prosperous life is dependent on any anticivilization or on any parasitical humanoid.

How does Neo-Tech extend Jaynes's and Piekoff's works into Zonpower? Neo-Tech is fully integrated honesty applied within a dishonest anticivilization. Zonpower is the limitless power radiating from the Civilization of the Universe. Zonpower both unifies and evolves existence, radiating as unbreached, integrated honesty throughout the universe. With Neo-Tech literature seeding the world in many languages, the Civilization of the Universe will blossom to vanish Earth's anticivilization. ...Ironically, from the rising specter of uncompromised Zonpower, those people closest to Neo-Tech, even the discoverer and author of Neo-Tech, will also feel their bubble-protecting urges to shun the rise of Zonpower. For, they too will feel the threat of losing their

233

stake in the anticivilization if their "protective" bubbles of mysticism are broken. ...On stepping into the wider social dimensions found in the Civilization of the Universe, one can use Zonpower to vanish all connections with the anticivilization.

Limitless Success Guaranteed

With Jaynes's and Peikoff's masterworks, the Neo-Tech/Zonpower dynamics guarantee the disappearance of Earth's anticivilization. Indeed, today, with Zonpower, any citizen of Earth can step into the Civilization of the Universe and vanish Earth's anticivilization. ...In the Civilization of the Universe, every conscious being is guaranteed limitless prosperity and exciting happiness — eternal success.

The Government and Religion of the Universe

Philosophy with its ivory-tower approach is incomprehensible to most people. By contrast, government and religion provide the behaviors, laws, and values understandable to general populations. *Rational* government and *rational* religion, therefore, benefit society.

In an anticivilization, destructive governments and irrational religions grow from Earth-bound "authorities" manipulating truths based on illusions and faith. Thus, harmful behaviors and subjective laws evolve. A parasitical-elite class backed by force can then rise by draining the value producers. Stagnation of conscious life results. By contrast, the government and religion of the universe grow from rational consciousness. Humanoid parasites cannot rise or even exist in the rational Civilization of the Universe. Thus, an unlimited flourishing of conscious life results.

Breaking the Bubble of Mysticism

Zon is the unbreached honesty of the universe. Zon honors the honesty within each conscious being. By contrast, mysticism profanes honesty. Those who hold the honesty of Zon above the dishonesty of mysticism become all-powerful. Those who use the power of Zon to end the destructiveness of Earth's anticivilization secure themselves among the stars.

Movement II of *Zonpower* identifies the problem: Earth's irrational anticivilization. Movement II also shows how Neo-Tech lets one live free and incorruptible within Earth's unfree, corrupt anticivilization. And, finally, Movement III of *Zonpower* shows how the universal "government" and "religion" of Zon let one become a Citizen of the Universe to live free of the anticivilization — to live forever with unbounded prosperity and happiness protected by the Constitution of the Universe shown on page 188.

The Discovery of Zon

Zon is the essence of fully integrated honesty. Zon is the giver of boundless prosperity to conscious beings throughout the universe. Zon is beyond God and heaven. ...Zon *is* the eternal government, religion, and paradise of the universe. Zon is you.

Thirty years ago, Frank R. Wallace discovered fully integrated honesty, later called Neo-Tech. He then abandoned the Earth-bound ideas of government and God formulated through manipulated truths and mystical faith. In 1972, Dr. Wallace resigned his position as Senior Research Chemist at E.I. du Pont de Nemours & Company with the goal of bringing the limitless benefits of Neo-Tech to everyone on Earth. Twenty years later, *The Neo-Tech Discovery* is published in twelve languages and distributed worldwide — in 156 countries.

Movement III: The Civilization of the Universe

From the indelible foundation of Neo-Tech, the world advances toward fully integrated honesty — toward Zon, the rational government and religion of the universe. Today, Zon rises on planet Earth midst the pillagings, jailings, and deprivations inflicted upon the value-and-job producers. Zon rises midst the economic destructions by a burgeoning parasitical-elite class comprising morally corrupt journalists, politicians, bureaucrats, and judges who are circling to silence Neo-Tech. They must silence fully integrated honesty to continue their harmful livelihoods. To survive, they must break the all-exposing, wide-scope accounting of Neo-Tech. But, they cannot silence the unsilenceable. They cannot break the unbreakable. ...Professional value destroyers cannot survive in the Civilization of the Universe. In America, the first hint of their demise was signalled in the elections of November, 1994.

Compassion Rules the Universe

Who really helps the needy: the elderly, the handicapped, the oppressed, the sick, the helpless? Who really protects the disadvantaged, the consumer, the environment, the innocent animals? Who really provides the rational needs of everyone at ever lower costs? No, not those people who effusively try to convince themselves and others how much care and compassion they have for the disadvantaged, animals, and the environment. They are compassion hoaxers. For, they function by irrationally demanding *others* be forced into providing for the needy and protecting the environment.

Those compassion hoaxers do not function through benevolence and good will. They function through parasitical force and malevolent destruction. Be they

236

politicians, journalists, judges, professors, advocates, or entertainers, they all hypocritically feign good intentions to conceal agendas of unearned livelihoods, power, esteem.

How much can one trust a president or anyone who must implore his victims to "trust" him? How good are the intentions of politicians, news journalists, judges, or clergy who must constantly try to convince themselves and others of their good intentions and compassion, especially toward their ultimate victims, such as minorities, the poor, the disadvantaged, innocent animals, and the environment?

By contrast, the genuinely honest, trustworthy, and good-intentioned person *never* needs to publicly prove that he or she is honest, trustworthy, good-intentioned, compassionate. In fact, the more genuinely good-intentioned and compassionate one really is, the less that person is aware of being good-intentioned or compassionate.

Essentially every parasitical elite and professional value destroyer is consumed with guilt over his or her self-made, destructive nature. Each lives by what others think rather than by the facts of reality. Thus, each squirms behind hoaxes of good intentions and compassion. Within each such hoaxer exists an agenda of vilifying, draining, and destroying genuine value-and-job producers from innocent <u>GM truck manufactures</u> to innocent <u>apple growers</u>. ...Dishonest compassion hoaxers at the end of Earth's anticivilization era include people like Hillary Clinton, Pope John Paul, <u>Jane Pauley,</u> NBC news producers, <u>Meryl Streep</u>. Equally dishonest are the religious-exploiting demagogs seeking political power such as Pat Buchanan and Bill Bennett. ...Zon vanishes those souls of malevolence.

Remember, Zon is fully integrated honesty: the widest integrations of reality throughout the universe. Those who produce genuine jobs for others and competitive values for society have authentic power and benevolence. Those who have earned that power have the greatest good intentions and compassion toward others. Thus, through Zon, those with authentic power — those souls of benevolence — reign supreme among the stars, eternally delivering genuine compassion and prosperity to all citizens of the universe.

Chapter 27
Rise from Your Knees

Until now, all governments and religions grew from dishonest mysticisms...from Earth-bound "authorities", force, and fraud. Until now, all governments and religions worked to break human beings of their natural self-confidence, creativity, happiness, pride, courage, and honesty. But, today, Zon makes the clean sweep sought by Nietzsche a century ago. Zon frees everyone on Earth. Through Zon, any conscious being can unite with the Civilization of the Universe to gain its unlimited power — Zonpower. *Unlike* Nietzsche's strong-rule-the-weak ideas[1], Zon allows *every* man and woman on this planet to become an "overman"; a superman ruled by no one, a genius regardless of IQ or race. Zon brings dignity with boundless excitement, wealth, and romantic love to every conscious being throughout the universe. ...Rise from your knees. Zon vanishes mystical "Gods". Zon lives eternally. Zon is *you!*

Guiltless Riches Through Zon

Energy and matter are one and the same as identified by Einstein. Energy (E) can become matter; and matter (M) can become energy: $E=Mc^2$. Likewise, thought and things are one and the same as identified by Spinoza. Nonmystical thoughts (T1) can become all things throughout the universe; and all things (T2) throughout the universe can become nonmystical thoughts: T1=T2k, where k is the universal constant of Zon. Also, the Di Silvestro equation: $T1(I°+E°)=vT2(k)$ in which I° is the

---

[1]Friedrich Nietzsche staunchly opposed nationalism, anti-semitism, and tyranny. After his death, his writings were grossly misappropriated and dishonestly altered by his anti-semitic sister Elizabeth and the Nazis.

degree of intent and $E°$ is the degree of effort behind the thought. $I°$ and $E°$ affect v or the velocity of converting T1 to T2, with T2 being the thought converted to reality. ...Thus flows the power of Zon.

Consider this: Can empty space or vacuums really exist? Or does existence always exist — *everywhere*? Is *all* space filled with an ether of existence, filled with quantized Gravity Units — the weightless geometry of existence so tiny with near-surfaceless, seemingly infinite curvature that gravity, mass, or energy can neither enter nor exit? If so, do endless universes exist above and below each Gravity Unit, hiding as pure symmetry beneath every point in existence? ...Regardless of the ultimate answers to those questions, wealth and happiness evolve eternally for every citizen of the universe.

Chapter 28

Infinite Power

from

Conscious Dynamics

(From a 1980 article by Frank R. Wallace)

A person could make an excellent bet by wagering a hundred ounces of gold that Julian Jaynes's book, *The Origin of Consciousness in the Breakdown of the Bicameral Mind* (Houghton Mifflin, 1976) will someday rank among the twenty most important books ever written. ...Jaynes's book signals the end of a 10,000-year reign of authoritarian institutions. His book also marks the beginning of a new era of individual consciousness during which people will increasingly act on the authority of their own brains. That movement toward self-responsibility will increasingly weaken the influences of external or mystical "authorities" such as government and religion.

The discovery of the bicameral mind solves the missing-link problem that has defied all previous theories of human evolution. But more important, that discovery is generating a new field of knowledge called Neothink with which all human life can evolve into abiding prosperity and happiness through powerfully competitive Neo-Tech advantages.

Dr. Jaynes discovered that until 3000 years ago essentially all human beings were void of consciousness.[1] Man along with all other primates functioned by mimicked or learned reactions. But, because of his much larger, more complex brain, man was able to develop a coherent

---

[1]An interesting note that underscores the recency of consciousness: A person living to 70 years today will have spanned over 2% of the time since human beings have been conscious.

language beginning about 8000 B.C. He was then guided by audio hallucinations. Those hallucinations evolved in the right hemisphere of the brain and were "heard" as communications or instructions in the left hemisphere of the brain (the bicameral or two-chamber mind). ...In effect, human beings were super-intelligent but automatically reacting animals who could communicate by talking. That communication enabled human beings to cooperate closely to build societies, even thriving civilizations.

Still, like all other animals, man functioned almost entirely by an automatic guidance system that was void of consciousness — until about 1000 B.C. when he was forced to invent consciousness to survive in the collapsing bicameral civilizations. ...Today, man's survival still depends on his choice of beneficially following his own consciousness or destructively following the voices of external "authorities".

The major components of Jaynes's discovery are:

- All civilizations before 1000 B.C. — such as Assyria, Babylonia, Mesopotamia, pharaonic Egypt — were built, inhabited, and ruled by nonconscious people.

- Ancient writings such as the *Iliad* and the early books of the Old Testament were composed by nonconscious minds that automatically recorded and objectively reported both real and imagined events. The transition to subjective and introspective writings of the conscious mind occurred in later works such as the *Odyssey* and the newer books of the Old Testament.

- Ancient people learned to speak, read, write, as well as carry out daily life, work, and the professions all while remaining nonconscious throughout their lives. Being nonconscious, they never experienced guilt, never practiced deceit, and were not responsible for their actions. They, like any other animal, had no concept of guilt, deception, evil, justice, philosophy, history, or the future. They could not introspect and had no internal idea of themselves. They had no subjective sense of time or space and had no memories as we know them. They were nonconscious and innocent. They were guided by "voices" or strong impressions in their bicameral minds — nonconscious minds structured for nature's automatic survival.

- The development of human consciousness began about 3000 years ago when the automatic bicameral mind began breaking down under the mounting stresses of its inadequacy to find workable solutions in increasingly complex societies. The hallucinated voices became more and more confused, contradictory, and destructive.

- Man was forced to invent and develop consciousness in order to survive as his hallucinating voices no longer provided adequate guidance for survival.

- Today, after 3000 years, most people retain remnants of the bicameral guidance system in the form of mysticism and the desire for external authority.

- Except for schizophrenics, people today no longer hallucinate the voices that guided bicameral man. Yet, most people are at least partly influenced and are sometimes driven by the remnants of the bicameral mind as they seek, to varying degrees, automatic guidance from the mystical "voices" of others — from the commanding voices of false external "authorities".

- Religions and governments are rooted in the nonconscious bicameral mind that is obedient to the "voices" of external "authorities" — obedient to the voice of "God", gods, rulers, and leaders.

- The discovery that consciousness was never a part of

nature's evolutionary scheme (but was invented by
man) eliminates the missing-link in human evolution.

• Essentially all religious and most political ideas today
survive through those vestiges of the obsolete bicameral
mind. The bicameral mind seeks omniscient truth and
automatic guidance from external "authorities" such
as political or spiritual leaders — or other "authoritarian" sources such as manifested in idols, astrologers,
gurus. Likewise, politicians, lawyers, psychiatrists,
psychologists, professors, doctors, journalists and TV
anchormen become "authoritarian voices".

The idea of civilizations consisting entirely of
nonconscious, yet highly intelligent, automatic-reacting
people and the idea of man bypassing nature to invent his
own consciousness initially seems incredible. But as
Jaynes documents his evidence in a reasoned and detached
manner, the existence of two minds in all human beings
becomes increasingly evident: (1) the obsolete,
nonconscious (bicameral) mind that seeks guidance from
external "authorities" for important thoughts and decisions,
especially under stressed or difficult conditions; and (2)
the newly invented conscious mind that bypasses external
"authorities" and provides thoughts and guidance generated
from one's own mind. ...Understanding Jaynes's
discoveries unlocks the 10,000 year-old secret of
controlling the actions of people through their mystical or
bicameral minds.

What evidence does Jaynes present to support his
discoveries? After defining consciousness, he systematically presents his evidence to prove that man was not
conscious until 3000 years ago when the bicameral
civilizations collapsed and individuals began inventing
consciousness in order to survive. Jaynes's proof begins
with the definition of consciousness:

Infinite Power from Conscious Dynamics

Defining and Understanding Consciousness

Julian Jaynes defines both what consciousness is and what it is not. After speculating on its location, he demonstrates that consciousness itself has no physical location, but rather is a particular organization of the mind and a specific way of using the brain. Jaynes then demonstrates that consciousness is only a small part of mental activity and is not necessary for concept formation, learning, thinking, or even reasoning. He illustrates how all those mental functions can be performed automatically, intelligently, but unconsciously. Furthermore, consciousness does not contribute to and often hinders the execution of learned skills such as speaking, listening, writing, reading —as well as skills involving music, art, and athletics. Thus, if major human actions and skills can function automatically and without consciousness, those same actions and skills can be controlled or driven by external influences, "authorities", or "voices" emanating under conditions described later. ...But first an understanding of consciousness is important:

Consciousness requires metaphors (i.e., referring to one thing in order to better understand or describe another thing — such as the head of an army, the head of a household, the head of a nail). Consciousness also requires analog models, (i.e., thinking of a map of California, for example, in order to visualize the entire, physical state of California). Thinking in metaphors and analog models creates the mind space and mental flexibility needed to bypass the automatic, bicameral processes.[1]

The *bicameral thinking* process functions only in

---

[1]Metaphors and analog models bring the right hemisphere brain functions to the left hemisphere with a much broader, wide-scope view which enables ever more powerful conceptual thinking.

concrete terms and narrow, here-and-now specifics. But the *conscious thinking* process generates an infinite array of subjective perceptions that permit ever broader understandings and better decisions.

Metaphors of "me" and analog models of "I" allow consciousness to function through introspection and self-visualization. In turn, consciousness expands by creating more and more metaphors and analog models. That expanding consciousness allows a person to "see" and understand the relationship between himself and the world with increasing accuracy and clarity.

Consciousness is a conceptual, metaphor-generated analog world that parallels the actual world. Man, therefore, could not invent consciousness until he developed a language sophisticated enough to produce metaphors and analog models.

The genus Homo began about two million years ago. Rudimentary oral languages developed from 70,000 B.C. to about 8000 B.C. Written languages began about 3000 B.C. and gradually developed into syntactical structures capable of generating metaphors and analog models. Only at that point could man invent and experience consciousness.

Jaynes shows that man's early writings (hieroglyphics, hiertatic, and cuneiform) reflect a mentality totally different from our own. They reflect a nonmetaphoric, nonconscious mentality. Jaynes also shows that the *Iliad*, which evolved as a sung poem about 1000 B.C., contains little if any conscious thought. The characters in the Iliad (e.g., Achilles, Agamemnon, Hector, Helen) act unconsciously in initiating all their major actions and decisions through "voices", and all speak in hexameter rhythms (as often do modern-day schizophrenics when hallucinating). Hexameter rhythms are characteristic of the rhythmically automatic functionings of the right-hemisphere brain. Moreover, the *Iliad* is entirely about action...about the acts and consequences of Achilles. The *Iliad* never mentions subjective thoughts or the contents of anyone's mind. The language is nonconscious — an objective reporting of facts that are concrete bound and void of introspection and abstract thought.

With a conscious mind, man can introspect; he can debate with himself; he can become his own god, voice, and decision maker. But before the invention of consciousness, the mind functioned bicamerally: the right hemisphere (the poetic, god-brain) hallucinated audio instructions to the left hemisphere (the analytical, man-brain), especially in unusual or stressful situations. Essentially, man's brain today is physically identical to the ancient bicameral brain; but with his discovery or more precisely his *invention* of consciousness, he can now choose to focus on integrating the functions of the left and right hemispheres.

Beginning about 9000 B.C. — as oral languages developed — routine or habitual tasks became increasingly standardized. The hallucinating voices for performing those basic tasks, therefore, became increasingly similar among groups of people. The collectivization of "voices" allowed more and more people to cooperate and function together through their bicameral minds. The leaders spoke to the "gods" and used the "voices" to lead the masses in cooperative unison. That cooperation allowed nomadic hunting tribes to gradually organize into stationary, food-producing societies. The continuing development of oral language and the increasing collectivization of bicameral minds allowed towns and eventually cities to form and flourish.

Movement III: The Civilization of the Universe

The bicameral mind, however, became increasingly inadequate for guiding human actions as societies continued to grow in size and complexity. By about 1000 B.C., the bicameral mind had become so inadequate that man's social structures began collapsing. Under threat of extinction, man invented a new way to use his brain that allowed him to solve the much more complex problems needed to survive — he invented a new organization of the mind called consciousness.

Jaynes eliminated the missing link in the evolution of man by discovering that consciousness never existed in the evolutionary processes — consciousness was invented by man.

The Development of Consciousness

Dr. Jaynes shows through abundant archaeological, historical, and biological evidence that the towns, cities, and societies from 9000 B.C. to 1000 B.C. were established and developed by nonconscious people. Those societies formed and grew through common hallucinating voices attributed to gods, rulers, and the dead — to external "authorities". Various external symbols that "spoke" (such as graves, idols, and statues) helped to reinforce and expand the authority of those common "voices". Such "voices" continued to expand their reach through increasingly visible and awe-inspiring symbols such as tombs, temples, colossuses, and pyramids.

But as those unconscious societies became more complex and increasingly intermingled through trade and wars, the "voices" became mixed and contradictory. With the "voices" becoming muddled, their effectiveness in guiding people diminished. Rituals and importunings became ever more intense and elaborate in attempts to evoke clearer "voices" and better guidance. The development of writing and the permanent recording of instructions and laws during the second millennium B.C. further weakened the authority and effectiveness of hallucinated voices. As the "voices" lost their effectiveness, they began falling silent. And without authoritarian "voices" to guide and control its people, those societies suddenly began collapsing with no external cause.

As the bicameral mind broke down and societies collapsed, individuals one by one began inventing consciousness to make decisions needed to survive in the mounting anarchy and chaos. On making conscious and volitional decisions, man for the first time became responsible for his actions. Also, for short-range advantages and easy power, conscious man began discovering and using deceit and treachery — behaviors not possible from nonconscious, bicameral minds. ...Before inventing consciousness, man was as guiltless and amoral as any other animal since he had no volitional choice in following his automatic guidance system of hallucinated voices.

As the "voices" fell silent, man began contriving religions and prayers in his attempts to communicate with the departed gods. Jaynes shows how man developed the concept of worship, heaven, angels, demons, exorcism, sacrifice, divination, omens, sortilege, augury in his attempts to evoke guidance from the gods — from external "authorities".

All such quests for external "authority" hark back to the breakdown of the hallucinating bicameral mind — to the silencing and celestialization of the once "vocal" and earthly gods.

Much direct evidence for the breakdown of the

249

bicameral mind and the development of consciousness comes from writings scribed between 1300 B.C. and 300 B.C. Those writings gradually shift from nonconscious, objective reports to conscious, subjective expressions that reflect introspection. The jump from the nonconscious writing of the *Iliad* to the conscious writing of the *Odyssey* (composed perhaps a century later) is dramatically obvious. In the *Odyssey*, unlike the *Iliad*, characters possess conscious self-awareness, introspection powers, and can sense right, wrong, and guilt. ...That radical difference between the *Iliad* and the *Odyssey* is, incidentally, further evidence that more than one poet composed the Homeric epics.

The transition from the nonconscious *Iliad* to the conscious *Odyssey* marks man's break with his 8000-year-old hallucinatory guidance system. By the sixth century B.C., written languages began reflecting conscious ideas of morality and justice similar to those reflected today.

The Old Testament of the Bible also illustrates the transition from the nonconscious writing of its earlier books (such as Amos, circa 750 B.C.) to the fully conscious writing of its later books (such as Ecclesiastes, circa 350 B.C.). Amid that transition, the book of Samuel records the first known suicide — an act that requires consciousness. And the book of Deuteronomy illustrates the conflict between the bicameral mind and the conscious mind.

Likewise, the transition to consciousness is observed in other parts of the world: Chinese literature moved from bicameral nonconsciousness to subjective consciousness about 500 B.C. with the writings of Confucius. And in India, literature shifted to subjective consciousness around 400 B.C. with the Upanishadic writings.

American Indians, however, never developed the sophisticated, metaphorical languages needed to develop full consciousness. As a result, their mentalities were probably bicameral when they first encountered the European explorers. For example, with little or no conscious resistance, the Incas allowed the Spanish "white gods" to dominate, plunder, and slaughter them.

The Bicameral Mind in Today's World

Dr. Jaynes identifies many vestiges of the bicameral mentality that exist today. The most obvious vestige is religion and its symbols. Ironically, early Christianity with its teachings of Jesus was an attempt to shift religion from the outmoded bicameral and celestial mind of Moses to the newly conscious and earthly mind of man. Christianity then discovered a devastatingly effective tool for authoritarian control — guilt. Indeed, guilt not only worked on conscious minds, but required conscious minds to be effective.

Despite religion, conscious minds caused the gradual shifts from governments of gods to governments of men and from divine laws to secular laws. Still, the vestiges of the bicameral mind combined with man's longing for guidance produced churches, prophets, oracles, sibyls, diviners, cults, mediums, astrologers, saints, idols, demons, tarot cards, seances, Ouija boards, glossolalia, fuhrers, ayatollahs, popes, peyote, Jonestown, born-agains.

Jaynes shows how such external "authorities" exist only through the remnants of the bicameral mind. Moreover, he reveals a four-step paradigm that can reshuffle susceptible minds back into hallucinating, bicameral mentalities. The ancient Greeks used a similar paradigm to reorganize or reprogram the minds of uneducated

251

peasant girls into totally bicameral mentalities so they could become oracles and give advice through hallucinated voices — voices that would rule the world (e.g., the oracle at Delphi). ...Today, people who deteriorate into schizophrenic psychoses follow similar paradigms.

A common thread united most oracles, sibyls, prophets, and demon-possessed people: Almost all were illiterate, all believed in spirits, and all could readily retrieve the bicameral mind. Today, however, retrieval of the bicameral mind is schizophrenic insanity. Also, today, as throughout history, a symptomatic cure for "demon-possessed" people involves exorcising rituals that let a more powerful "authority" or god replace the "authority" of the demon. The New Testament, for example, shows that Jesus and his disciples became effective exorcists by substituting one "authority" (their god) for another "authority" (another god or demon).

As the voices of the oracles became confused and nonsensical, their popularity waned. In their places, idolatry revived and then flourished. But as Christianity became a popular source of external "authority", Christian zealots began physically destroying all competing idols. They then built their own idols and symbols to reinforce the external "authority" of Christianity.

Among today's vestiges of the bicameral mentality is the born-again movement that seeks external guidance. In that movement, people surrender their self-choice and self-decision making in exchange for false promises of protection and guidance. Such vestiges dramatize man's resistance to use his own invention of consciousness to guide his life.

The chanting cadence of poetry and the rhythmic beat of music are also rooted in the bicameral mentality. In ancient writings, the hallucinated voices of the gods were always in poetic verse, usually in dactylic hexameter and sometimes in rhyme or alliteration — all characteristic of right-brain functionings. The oracles and prophets also spoke in verse. And today schizophrenics often speak in verse when they hallucinate.

Poetry and chants can have authoritarian or commanding beats and rhythms that can effectively block consciousness. Poetry is the language of the gods — it is the language of the artistic, right-hemispheric brain. Plato recognized poetry as a divine madness.

Most poetry and songs have an abruptly changing or a discontinuous pitch. Normal speech, on the other hand, has a smoothly changing pitch. Jaynes demonstrates that reciting poetry, singing, and playing music are right-brain functions, while speaking is a left-brain function. That is why people with speech impediments can often sing, chant, or recite poetry with flawless clarity. Conversely, almost anyone trying to sing a conversation will find his words quickly deteriorating into a mass of inarticulate cliches.

Likewise, listening to music and poetry is a right-brain function. And music, poetry, or chants that project authority with loud or rhythmic beats can suppress left-brain functions to temporarily relieve anxiety or a painfully troubled consciousness.

Jaynes goes on to show phenomena such as hypnosis, acupuncture, and déjà vu also function through vestiges of the bicameral mind. And he demonstrates how hypnosis steadily narrows the sense of self, time, space, and introspection as consciousness shrinks and the mind reverts to a bicameral type organization. Analogously, bicameral and schizophrenic minds have little or no sense

253

of self, time, space or introspection. The hypnotized mind is urged to obey the voice of the hypnotist; the bicameral mind is compelled to obey the "voices" of "authority" or gods. By sensing oneself functioning in the narrow-scope, unaware state of hypnosis, gives one an idea of functioning in the narrow-scope, unaware state of bicameral man.

Jaynes also identifies how modern quests for external "authority" are linked to the bicameral mind. Many such quests use science to seek authority in the laws of nature. In fact, today, science is surpassing the waning institutional religions as a major source of external "authority". And rising from the vestiges of the bicameral mind are an array of scientisms (pseudoscientific doctrines, faiths, and cults) that select various natural or scientific facts to subvert into apocryphal, authoritarian doctrines. That subversion is accomplished by using facts out of context to fit promulgated beliefs. Such mystical scientisms include astrology, ESP, Scientology, Christian Science and other "science" churches, I Ching, behaviorism, sensitivity training, mind control, meditation, hypnotism, as well as specious nutritional, health, and medical fads.

Today the major worldwide sources of external "authority" are the philosophical doctrines of religion (along with the other forms of mysticism and "metaphysics") combined with political doctrines such as Socialism, Fascism, and Marxism. All such doctrines demand the surrender of the individual's ego (sense of self or "I") to a collective, obedient faith toward the "authority" of those doctrines. In return, those doctrines offer automatic answers and lifetime guidance from which faithful followers can survive without the responsibility or effort of using their own conscious minds. Thus, all current political systems represent a regression into mysticism — from conscious man back to bicameral man.

Despite their constant harm to everyone, most modern-day external "authorities" and master neocheaters thrive by using the following two-step neocheating technique to repress consciousness and activate the bicameral mind in their victims.

1. First man is made to feel guilty. He is condemned for having lost his "innocence" by inventing consciousness. He is condemned for assuming the responsibility to use his own mind to guide his life. He is condemned for exchanging his automatic, bicameral life for a volitional, conscious life...condemned for exchanging his nature-given bicameral mind for a superior, man-invented conscious mind.

2. Then man is offered automatic solutions to problems and guidance through life — is offered an "effortless" Garden of Eden or a utopian hereafter if he exchanges his own invented consciousness for faith in external "authority": bicameral faith in some leader, doctrine, or god. He is offered the "reward" of protection and the escape from the self-responsibility of making one's own decisions to guide one's own life. But for that "reward", he must renounce his own mind to follow someone else's mind or wishes disguised as "truths" promulgated by some external "authority" or higher power.

But, in reality, no valid external "authority" or higher power can exist or ever has existed. Valid authority evolves only from one's own independent, conscious mode of thinking. When that fact is fully realized, man will emerge completely from his bicameral past and move into a future that accepts individual consciousness as the only authority. ...Man will then fully evolve into a prosperous, happy individual who has assumed full responsibility for

255

his own thinking and life.

Still, the resistance to self-responsibility is formidable. The bicameral mentality grips those seeking mysticism or other "authorities" for guidance. Those who accept external "authority" allow government officials, religious leaders, environmental and anti-abortion movements, faith, homilies, cliches, one-liners, slogans, the familiar, habits, and feelings to automatically guide their actions. The *Neo-Tech Discovery* demonstrates how throughout history billions of people because of their bicameral tendencies unnecessarily submit to the illusionary external "authorities" of parasitical Establishments, governments, and religions. Such submission is always done at a net loss to everyone's well being and happiness.

The Implications of Neo-Tech

To some, the implications of Neo-Tech (fully integrated honesty) are frightening, even terrifying. To others, the implications are electrifying and liberating. ...The implications of Neo-Tech are that each individual is solely responsible for his or her own life — responsible for making the efforts required for learning how to honestly guide one's own life toward growing prosperity and happiness. No automatic, effortless route to knowledge or guidance exists.

No valid external "authority" exists that one can automatically live by. To live effectively, an individual must let only the authority of his own consciousness guide his activities. All consistently competent people have learned to act on reality — not on their feelings or someone else's feelings or doctrines. An individual must accept the responsibility to guide his or her own life in order to live competently, successfully, happily.

Chapter 29
The Rise and Fall
of the
Anticivilization

Earth's anticivilization is characterized by humanoids with criminal minds controlling value-producing human beings. For 3000 years, such humanoids survived through hidden agendas designed to usurp the wealth created by the productive class. Those hidden criminals are responsible for all wars, slave-master relationships, mass thefts, purposeful property destructions, terrorisms, genocide.

Neocheaters: The Hidden Criminals

Two classes of criminals exist: (1) The less-dangerous *subhuman* class consisting of people, who with blatant criminal minds, openly rob, injure, and murder human beings. Such subhumans are generally scorned by society and are usually jailed for their crimes through objective laws and valid justice. (2) The most-dangerous *humanoid* class consisting of people, who with ingeniously hidden criminal minds, covertly rob, injure, and destroy entire economies, entire populations, entire nations, entire civilizations. Such humanoids are camouflaged criminals who survive by destructive deceptions used to gain bogus livelihoods, respect, even adulation from their duped human victims. Such criminals are usually praised by the parasitical Establishment and seldom held responsible for their crimes.

The subhuman class of criminals sporadically commit crimes against various individuals. The humanoid class

257

of criminals daily, continuously commit crimes against everyone and society through their destructive careers.

The anticivilization is created by the parasitical-elite class and its legions of professional value destroyers. They exist by manipulating the disease of irrationality. Such career criminals deceive and plunder populations through subjective laws, harmful regulations, and dishonest ego "justice".

Cambodia's Pol Pot to FDA's Dr. Kessler

Neocheaters comprise destructive politicians, corrupt lawyers, and killer bureaucrats who exist through the criminal use of government force implemented through political-agenda laws, gun-backed regulations, and ego-determined "justice". Examples of destructive neocheaters in the closing years of Earth's anticivilization include genocide-champion Pol Pot, mass-killer FDA commissioner Dr. David Kessler, envy-demagog Hillary Clinton, Tiananmen-Square murderer Li Peng, job-killer Interior Secretary Bruce Babbitt, child-abuser/killer (Fijnje/Waco) Janet Reno, and Russia's star of evil Vladimir Zhirinovsky. ...In what way are all such neocheaters mass killers? Wide-scope accounting demonstrates that for every life humanoids purport to benefit, they are responsible for killing several, often dozens, even hundreds or thousands of innocent people directly through guns and political prisons or indirectly through draining economies and destroying assets as documented in the *Neo-Tech Protection Kit*, volume II, 1994 edition.

Homer to Plato

How did the disease of accepting criminal neocheaters as legendary heroes evolve on planet Earth? And, how does that disease continue to ravage everyone today? As identified previously, the philosophical father of the parasitical-elite class and totalitarian governments is Plato. His neocheating masterpiece was *The Republic* written nearly 2400 years ago. But, the foundations were laid 400 years earlier with two of the three primary epics of Western literature — the *Iliad* and the *Odyssey*.

The Iliad's hero, the nonconscious amoral Achilles, and the Odyssey's hero, the conscious immoral Odysseus, were in essence nothing more than wildly irrational, criminal killers with no sense of honesty or justice. The nature of all glory-seeking criminal minds is summed up in the character of Odysseus, especially as he returns home after a decade of "glorious" battles and "heroic" adventures. The great bully Odysseus simply plunders and butchers the innocent populations of defenseless coastal towns whenever he and his cohorts want to feel big and powerful — whenever they want to plunder the value producers, rape them, kill them, have a good time.

Such Homeric-hero characters are not human beings, but are humanoids with no concept of honesty, human values, or objective justice. They are criminals who pretend worthiness through fake glories, destructive heroics, and evil ego "justice". All their boastfully paraded "heroics", "courage", and "glory" are nothing more than masks for criminal acts and parasitical cowardice. ...All such humanoids are simply plunderers and killers, *nothing more*, no matter what "heroics" they stage. Indeed, was that the message which the blind-poet Homer intended? For, Homer grants no hint of virtuous good-versus-evil struggles by those "heroes".

If so, 400 years later, the politician-philosopher Plato turned Homer's message upside down. As identified in

259

the *Neo-Tech Discovery*, Plato ingeniously constructed an integrated philosophy justifying the parasitical control and dictatorial rule of the honest value producers by criminal-minded elites. Finally, 300 years after Plato, the Roman poet Virgil in his famous secondary epic, the *Aeneid*, recycled Homer's *Odyssey* into a "gentler", more hidden form of evil. Thus, Virgil laid the structure for ever more subtle and hidden neocheating techniques.

Ever since Virgil, subtle neocheating techniques have allowed criminal-minded humanoids to plunder the value producers in countless, hidden ways while appearing moral, even heroic. Thus, those neocheating techniques allowed an irrational anticivilization to rise and exist to this day on planet Earth.

Virgil to Hitler

Virgil promotes the evil falsity that the virtues of life, character, bravery, and morality lie in sacrifice and service — sacrifice of the workers and value producers to the service of the parasitical elites. All such calls for sacrifice are done under the arbitrary guises of government, nationalism, religion, society, "higher causes"...whatever sounds good at the time. Virgil's *Aeneid* lays the foundations for totalitarianism and "glorious" leaders like Hitler to rise and destroy entire economies and populations.

Most Germans and many others in the 1930s were duped into admiring Hitler's Odysseus-like courage as one of the bravest soldiers in World War I and the strutting Wagnerian "glory" he bestowed on the Third Reich. Thus, most Germans and many others blinded themselves to the obvious fact that popular, glory-talking Hitler was nothing more than a criminal value destroyer — a mass murderer for his *own* parasitical livelihood and glory. Like most politicians, Hitler increasingly committed destructive acts so he could increasingly feel big, important, powerful.

Likewise, prompted by a deeply dishonest media, many Americans were duped into admiring a good-sounding, smooth-talking Hillary Clinton. Until the Neo-Tech dynamics began taking hold in America in 1994, most people were blind to the fact that she was a criminal-minded lawyer intent on controlling society by draining the value producers. She almost succeeded through her attempted power-grab encompassing America's entire health-care system. How would she have carried out her giant, free-lunch fraud? Through use of government force — through subjective laws and gun-backed regulations enforced by ego "justice". ...Had Hillary Clinton succeeded, health-care would have decayed, effective medical research would have stopped, businesses would have shut down, jobs would have been lost, innocent value producers and dedicated doctors would have been fined and jailed, many precious lives would have been lost.

How could anyone be so purposely destructive? Given the chance, essentially *any* politician from a small-town mayor to a nation's president or his wife would eagerly seize Hitlerian power with all its criminalities and destructiveness. For, that is the essence of essentially all politicians. Under camouflaged deception, they will simply plunder and destroy people, property, jobs, capital, *whatever they can get away with*, in order to advance their own harmful careers, glory, and power...in order to have an Odysseus-like good time.

Capone to Clinton

Humanoid criminals are much more destructive and dangerous than *subhuman* criminals such as Al Capone.

Movement III: The Civilization of the Universe

For example, Hillary Clinton, with help from a fawningly dishonest media, rationalized away her criminal-minded behaviors. Her camouflaged drive for Orwellian power and control would be justified through the sacrifice of productive workers and hard-working businesspeople to a hypocritically proclaimed "higher good" or "caring for others". Such ploys ultimately hurt everyone badly. For, Hillary Clinton's "higher good" meant nothing more than a self-serving empowerment for personal gains through government force. ...Such self-serving empowerment and gains are the essence of essentially all politicians who propagate Earth's irrational anticivilization.

Beowulf to a Neo-Tech President

The third and final primary epic of Western literature, the allegorical *Beowulf*, written about 1000 AD, reflects an honest, moral foundation for conscious beings. The hero, Beowulf, is genuinely noble and honest as his pure goodness triumphs over pure evil — over allegorical monsters who are metaphors for humanoid neocheaters. Indeed, Beowulf himself explicitly identifies the greatest evil as harming and killing innocent people, especially one's own people. But, evilly *unprincipled* Odysseus, not virtuously *principled* Beowulf, underpins Earth's anticivilization. Yet, Beowulf represents the first glimmerings of the Civilization of the Universe.

In this anticivilization, most political leaders are nothing more than camouflaged, criminal-minded plunderers. Those "leaders" hide behind Plato's and Virgil's neocheating techniques. They are simply modern-day Odysseuses committing their hidden crimes to garner unearned livelihoods, power, and glory — be they a Hitler, a Stalin, a Bush, a Clinton.

The Rise and Fall of the Anticivilization

Will the to-be-announced Neo-Tech presidential candidate be the first major political figure of the past 2000 years to embody the life-enhancing character of Beowulf? By 2001 AD, will the benevolent spirit of Beowulf vanish the neocheaters and let the value producers bring eternal prosperity and happiness to *all* human beings? By 2001 AD, will Cassandra's Secret and the fully integrated honesty of Neo-Tech have vanished this anticivilization? By 2001 AD, will *Zonpower* be delivering limitless prosperity, love, and happiness to all conscious beings on Earth?

Honoring Value Producers and Ending the Anticivilization

The Neo-Tech web site honors the values delivered by the premier entrepreneur philosopher — Dr. Leonard Peikoff. The values he delivers to mankind are grossly under recognized and under appreciated not only by the public, but by libertarians, objectivists, Peikoffian Objectivists, even Dr. Peikoff himself. Leonard Peikoff has produced and continues to produce more major, competitive values than all the other professional Objectivists combined.[1] Thus, sadness arises when that outstanding man diminishes himself through his own irrationality. He has become a tragic Aeneas/Beowulf contradiction. ...Indeed, sadness is felt whenever irrationality diminishes anyone of great personal value, be it one's spouse or child or mega value producers such as Ayn Rand and Leonard Peikoff.

Whatever the root of his irrationality, Dr. Peikoff's persona shrinks with his advocating force-backed intolerance as he expressed during his 1995 Ford Hall Forum lecture. Recall how Ayn Rand's life was tragically diminished by her irrational, deadly, "dot-of-light" glamorization of smoking. Her emotional, irrational denials of the narcotically addictive, physically destructive nature of tobacco smoking led her and some of her "caped" followers to the grave. ...Now, today, arises the Peikoff tragedy — Greek-tragedy style. But, because this outstanding

[1]See page 272 for footnote.

New-Color Symphony

Movement #3

263

value producer still lives, he has the potential for a life of supreme fulfillment through his continuing production of universal values. He can soar to great heights by using fully integrated honesty to eliminate his tragic flaw — his advocating force-backed intolerance.

Consider those who brought functional Objectivism to the general public. Of course, Ayn Rand was the prime contributor. But major contributors also included: 1) Dr. Leonard Peikoff as the continuing producer of exciting, profitable Objectivist values; 2) Dr. Nathaniel Branden as the highly successful, NBI business-entrepreneur director who profitably marketed Objectivism to the public as well as being a major contributor to its products (a value greatly under appreciated and misunderstood by Ayn Rand and most of her followers), and 3) Warner Brothers, Inc., as the business-savvy launch pad of Ayn Rand's work and fame (a value also under appreciated and misunderstood by Ayn Rand).

The values those competitive producers gave to our civilization should be kept separate from their personal contradictions and errors. Such errors, as with any public figure, should be identified and accounted for objectively. But, at the same time, their gifts of competitive universal values should always be recognized, appreciated, and honored. For, their values, not their errors, are what count for the quality of our lives and futures. Those who seek ego boosts by attacking Ayn Rand, Leonard Peikoff, or Nathaniel Branden without acknowledging the outstanding universal values each has given to mankind should first consider what outstanding universal values they themselves have given to mankind.

The bottom line: Absorb and integrate the values produced by others, honor those values, and then profit from them. Also, identify the errors, reject them, and then make objective adjustments for them. That process is called wide-scope integration with fully integrated honesty. That process takes profitable advantage of every value and error available. That process carries one to eternal prosperity — to the Civilization of the Universe.

Chapter 30

RELAX

for

Zonpower Rules Cyberspace

What should you do about this draining anticivilization and its humanoid creators — its parasitical elites who only fake the human qualities of value and compassion? Should you stand up, resist, fight back? Unless you are a Neo-Tech self-leader described in Chapter 16, you can relax. Simply ignore the parasitical elites. Ignore the negative, the irrational, the unreal. For, with Neo-Tech advancing through cyberspace, the anticivilization and its harmful humanoids will lose their power over you. And, when you learn Cassandra's Secret, humanoids will be unable to drain your life or harm your future.

On learning Cassandra's Secret, anxieties vanish. You will discover that *nothing* in this anticivilization has power over you or your future. ...Parasitical elites have no power in cyberspace.

After capturing Cassandra's Secret, most of what you see and hear from others becomes meaningless. Most of what others say or do becomes pointless and boring. For, you will control all that affects you, now and in the future. You will dismiss all political and philosophical positions — left or right, conservative or liberal, rationalist or empiricist. You will dismiss them all as equally senseless. You will see every position and argument in this anticivilization as an irrational swirl of nothing.

On reading and rereading *Zonpower*, you will learn Cassandra's Secret and control the power of Zon. Not only is Zonpower real, it is omnipotent. With Zonpower, any loss in the unreal anticivilization is no loss at all.

Movement III: The Civilization of the Universe

For, within the dynamics of nature, losses in an unreal world become gains in the real world. Thus, with Zonpower dynamics, all such unreal losses become real gains in propelling you into the Civilization of the Universe — into limitless power and wealth.

In the anticivilization, its parasitical humanoids — its malignant politicians, wealth-destroying bureaucrats, life-destroying ego judges, mind-destroying academe, dishonest journalists, stagnant big-business executives — are, in reality, *nothing*. For, they make *no* difference to anything in the real world or over any span of time.

Humanoids and their anticivilization are no more real than fleeting antimatter particles that exist not in permanent reality but in a transitory, virtual reality — a false, simulated reality that affects nothing real, nothing in the future. ...Those humanoids are nothing more than figments that can be vanished by Zonpower and the Civilization of the Universe.

Arriving at the next millennium, today's anticivilization and all its destructive humanoids will have affected nothing in our world, universe, or future. Only you with Zonpower will affect our world, universe, and future. Thus, this anticivilization with its last wave of humanoids can be ignored and forgotten, now and forever. But, you, with Cassandra's Secret, will become eternally powerful, forever gaining exciting adventure, wealth, and happiness.

The Hidden Source of All Advantages

Zonpower is easily understandable for readers at all levels, especially after a second reading. Yet, most dishonest politicians, parasitical elites, destructive lawyers, and force-backed bureaucrats shrink in befuddlement on exposure to *Zonpower*. Therein lies the hidden power of

Relax

Zon — its great advantage in this anticivilization.

As did the mythical Cassandra, *Zonpower* foretells all. Yet, the more minds that are beclouded by Cassandra's Secret, the greater is its power. For, if the professional value destroyers knew Cassandra's Secret, they would forcibly block its future. Moreover, most people will not directly hear about *Zonpower* until the year-2000 presidential campaign. Thus, today, arises the greatest opportunity. With *Zonpower,* one can live beyond the parasitical elites — one can live on Earth with immortal prosperity.

1996 AD

Most know something is wrong. Some know something is terribly wrong. Most want change — real change.

They are right: Something is wrong — terribly wrong. For, here lies a stagnant, envy-ridden anticivilization shrinking into dishonesty and ignorance worth nothing to the future. But, relax. Enjoy life. The first domino of a seminal change fell in America during its 1994 elections. Ahead lies the booming, exciting Civilization of the Universe expanding through cyberspace forever into the future.

2001 AD

During the year-2000 Presidential Campaign, people in America will begin directly learning about Zonpower and Cassandra's Secret through the forthcoming *Zon Protocols.*

2005 AD

After the turn of the millennium, highly productive market entrepreneurs will have already swept away today's political parasites along with their armed agents of force.[1]

Today

Zonpower is an exotic manuscript that initially will becloud most conscious minds on Earth. Like suddenly being flipped up into a higher spatial dimension, *Zonpower* initially will make many conscious beings on Earth go blank and run. That fact can be illustrated by the following account:

On Saturday, June 27, 1992, a meeting was held in Las Vegas, Nevada. At that meeting, Dr. Frank R. Wallace revealed Zonpower. He explained how the reactions to this new discovery by essentially everyone would not only be negative, but would grow increasingly negative as its dynamics became manifest. For, on planet Earth today, essentially everyone is engaged in wide-scope dishonesties and evasions to protect his or her investments in this anticivilization. ...But, therein lies the key to everyone's prosperity and happiness as described below:

Sweeping Away Ignorance and Evil

Part of Cassandra's Secret involves isolating the essence of ignorance and evil personified by many politicians, lawyers, and judges. Many high-profile men and women, especially those in government and law, are ignorant of justice and honesty. More destructively, they function through automatic dishonesties and deceptions. They build harmful careers based on ego agendas and reveal the irrational foundations of an anticivilization. Those revelations produce a predicted reaction among those exposed to Zonpower as described next:

---

[1]Swept away as described by Mark Hamilton in his book *Will America Go Neo-Tech?*, Neo-Tech Publishing, 1995.

Relax

Confronted with the foretold banishment of irrationality, many minds go blank. For, the closer one gets to the knowledge of Zonpower, the clearer becomes the realization that the cure for irrationality is coming. In turn, that means Zonpower will sweep away this anticivilization along with its parasites who survive unnaturally through irrationalities, dishonesties, and deceptions backed by bogus political-policy laws, ego "justice", and armed agents of force.

So why will almost everyone on Earth initially blind themselves to Zonpower and Cassandra's Secret? Because, (1) almost everyone has a lifetime investment in this anti-civilization with its wide-scope dishonesties and (2) almost everyone is addicted to its neocheating opiates of the past 2300 years.

On reading *Zonpower,* many cannot proceed past the first few chapters when they (1) sense the end of their lifetime investments in an anticivilization, and (2) sense the end of their hypnotic state that yields automatic, wide-scope dishonesties. Many will rationalize, "I don't understand", "this is real deep", "it's eerie", "it's kooky", "it's beyond me", "it's scary". ...They cannot face losing their bad investments and hypnotic rationalizations.

By contrast, those who do not "have it made" with the Establishment, those honest workers who are not benefiting from the ruling elites, those who are not invested in today's society...they will most quickly flourish on reading *Zonpower.* They will be among the first to understand its intoxicating secret.

Thus, lies the power of *Zonpower* — one's route to fabulous riches. By grasping *Zonpower* before it spreads to everyone, one can dominate the sleeping minds of others. One can gain wide-awake powers far beyond the

269

parasitical elites. Indeed, the parasitical elites living today in this moribund anticivilization are losing their deceptive means to control others because of Neo-Tech in cyberspace.

Cassandra's Secret

Harnessing *Zonpower* is a dual process: (1) recognize that nearly everyone's mind in the anticivilization will initially becloud on exposure to *Zonpower,* (2) follow the two steps given on the next page for breaking mystical bubbles and preventing one's own mind from beclouding on exposure to *Zonpower.* ...Those two steps will unlock the forecasting power of Cassandra's Secret.

Breaking the Hypnotic Spell

First consider that knowledge ends at each person's boundary of irrationality and dishonesty used to hold everyone in the anticivilization. That boundary is defined by each person's mystical bubble needed to tolerate life in this futile-loser anticivilization. But, by breaking that hypnotic boundary — that mystical bubble — one breaks into the winning realm of limitless knowledge and prosperity.

The purpose of *Zonpower* is not to persuade or convert others. That cannot be done. For, no one can understand beyond his or her hypnotic boundary or bubble. Indeed, everyone today mistakenly protects his or her mystical bubble in order to justify living in an irrational civilization.

The essence of *Zonpower* is its power to break that hypnotic spell — to break that mystical bubble in which everyone on Earth is trapped. Once that bubble is broken, one is no longer trapped in the dishonesties of an anticivilization. One can then soar beyond everyone else's boundary. One can soar into the Civilization of the Universe, gaining its knowledge and foretelling power to collect limitless riches here on Earth.

Two Steps to Break Mystical Bubbles

1. Realize that *Zonpower* does *not* rise from a different drummer or some higher power. Instead, *Zonpower* rises from every natural, mystic-free mind — from every honest, conscious mind that produces competitive values for self and others.

2. Read *Zonpower*...and then carefully reread *Zonpower* until its integrations reveal new-color powers — powers to accurately control, thus forecast, the future.

Those two steps let fully integrated honesty integrate and then use the wide-scope knowledge needed to control the future.

Movement III: The Civilization of the Universe

(Footnote from page 263)

[1]By stating that Dr. Peikoff has delivered more competitive, commercial values than all the other professional Objectivists combined does not imply the works of other Objectivists lack value. To the contrary, almost all written and audio works of the Peikoff-sphere Objectivists such as the Berliners, Binswingers, Schwartzs are valuable, interesting, and valid.

The Peikoffian dynamics of intolerant no-compromise Objectivism provide great power and strength when applying its principles. Problems with the Peikoffians arise when they generalize their intolerances inaccurately or emotionally to non-applicable areas of people and situations. Such misapplied intolerances are invalid, self-limiting, and eventually lead to intellectual isolation, even personal defeat...especially now as every area of mystical intolerance will be subject to the full scrutiny of the integrated honesty that ultimately rules cyberspace.

Leonard Peikoff has a wide array of valuable commercial products involving education and communication. Many of his products contain uniquely original, invaluable information that will be around for a long time. Also, his 493-page book, *Objectivism: The Philosophy of Ayn Rand*, Dutton, 1991, is a supreme accomplishment that permanently locks Objectivism into our civilization. Generally, those who carp about that masterpiece do not see the book as a powerful, wide-scope value that will eventually drive all bogus philosophies from this planet.

Also, it was important to publicly identify Peikoff's "Police-State" error so adjustments can be made to make his work even more valuable in the future. Hopefully, Dr. Peikoff will see and correct that error so he can more fully enjoy the fruits of his great work.

The books, tapes, lectures and other products of the "tolerant", more open-ended Kelley-sphere Objectivists might be more valuable to both professional philosophers and those interested in studying philosophy in technical depth. Also, David Kelley's sphere might grow in academic importance faster than Leonard Peikoff's sphere.

* * *

Perhaps the most profitable lesson to learn in business is to accurately distinguish the 1) specific principled areas for hard-nosed, objective application of no compromise intolerance from the 2) general non-principled areas that require constant discipline to develop wide-scope, tolerant understandings. Acquiring that skill lets one take profitable advantage of every positive *and* negative situation. Stated another way: In business, one increases competitiveness and profitability by developing the skills to confidently toughen up with accurate, no-compromise control of specific principles while loosening up with benevolent understandings of general principles. ...For maximum effectiveness, communicate more like Horace and Erasmus and less like Juvenal and Jonathan Edwards. Toughening up by lightening up powerfully complement one another in philosophy and business.

272

Chapter 31

Earth's Greatest Discovery

On any objective consideration, one cannot take seriously religious claims of life after death. Yet, such claims are the centerpiece of Western religions as well as many other religions. But, all such claims are marketing hype to exploit the deepest hopes and fears of conscious beings. For the past two millennia, afterlife promises have hoaxed Earth's anticivilization into embracing mystical religions.[1]

Earth's Greatest Discovery: Profit-Driven Immortality[2]

The afterlife hoaxes promoted by mystical religions serve to hide the single most important, potentially provable fact on this planet: *Most if not all honest conscious beings who have died on Earth in the past 3000 years continue to live with eternally expanding prosperity and happiness throughout the Civilization of the Universe!*

Ultimate Justice

Justice is an immutable law of nature. As demonstrated by Cassandra's Secret, justice is *always* fulfilled throughout existence. As a result, the eventual destination or just reward for every actual and potential value producer — of every honest conscious being — is eternal prosperity and happiness in the Civilization of the Universe.

[1]Religious faith has, however, been a key value at various periods in history. At times, for example, religious faith served to divide and weaken government tyranny, and vice versa, leaving pockets of freedom to advance knowledge, technology, and well-being within the anticivilization.

[2]Profit-driven immortality as presented in this chapter is a speculative hypothesis arising from a-priori logic. Yet, logically, no contradictions exist in that hypothesis. Today, the chief value of that hypothesis is metaphorical — an illustration of justice that reality ultimately asserts. Tomorrow? Facts and knowledge will unfold to reveal the hypothesis as fact or fiction.

Movement III: The Civilization of the Universe

That just destination is the inevitable consequence of nature. From that nature comes (1) immutable justice that characterizes the Civilization of the Universe, (2) the supremely leveraged, limitless value of each conscious being when placed in a rational civilization, (3) the dynamics of eternally expanding prosperity, which demand the full use of *every* available conscious being, and, as explained later in this chapter, (4) the technology needed to transceive[1] every volitionally developed human consciousness through the omnipresent existence field and into the Civilization of the Universe.

Humanoid criminals or parasitical neocheaters who have lived by harming others or society through force, fraud, and illusions also meet ultimate justice: They become humanoids because they destroy the human nature of their own consciousnesses. Therefore, they destroy the conscious structure needed to transceive through the Gravity-Unit existence field and into the Civilization of the Universe. Moreover, having lived as enormous net negatives to society, humanoids such as destructive politicians with their armed bureaucracies and ego-"justice" systems are, unless rehabilitated, worthless to the Civilization of the Universe. Thus, they simply vanish from existence, forever forgotten.

Bases of Proof

Any future proof of immortality for conscious beings must be derived from theories that are in full correspondence with the laws of physics. Theories derived

---

[1]Transceived not in the mystical Plato sense of a detached soul. For, the soul and physical body are one in the same and function as a unit. But, transceived (within a profit-mode, business dynamic) in the Gravity-Unit form that captures conscious "I"ness immortality as described in *The Neo-Tech Discovery*, all in accord with the laws of physics. ...The crucial importance of "I"ness in the rejection of the cryonic approach to immortality is detailed in the *Neo-Tech Protection Kit*, volume II, pages 371-375, Neo-Tech Publishing Company (1994).

both deductively and inductively must provide wide-range predictiveness, reproducible experimental evidence, consistent mathematical definitions, and limitless ways to test for contradictions and falsifications. This communiqué provides the elements needed to develop such proofs, predictions, and facts. ...Those theories must withstand challenges of direct and indirect experimental tests, observations, and calculations.

Listed below are the elements found in this communiqué. When assembled, those elements posit the hypotheses that (1) the Civilization of the Universe exists, (2) every fully developed, honest conscious being who lived on this planet for the past 3000 years continues to live with growing prosperity, love, and happiness in the Civilization of the Universe, and (3) technology commonly exists throughout the Civilization of the Universe that provides eternal life and prosperity to all honest, conscious beings on this planet. Those hypotheses also posit that every humanoid criminal who has died during the past 3000 years has vanished from existence. Moreover, all such parasitical humanoids who currently live by harming others will also vanish from existence. Humanoids living on Earth today, however, can be "saved" by restructuring their behaviors in order to mature into healthy, conscious human beings who competitively produce values for others and society.

Potential Elements of Proof found in *Zonpower*
Existence exists.
Existence is axiomatic, endless, eternal.
Existence exists eternally with no prior causes.
Consciousness is not only an eternal part of eternal existence, but is the eternal controller of existence.
Individual human consciousness is the greatest value in

275

eternal existence...the seminal value from which all other values flow.

The greatest social value among conscious beings is honest, competitive businesses combined with *objective* law and justice.

Valid knowledge is contextual and hierarchal. Valid ideas are hierarchal paradigms of contextual facts.

Conscious knowledge is limitless because knowledge always begets new knowledge — geometrically, up to the speed of light.

The essence of human consciousness is goodness: By nature human consciousness is noble, rational, honest, just, compassionate, value producing, benevolent, kind, loving, happy.

The only diseases of human consciousness are dishonesty, mysticism, and irrationality.

Those diseases destroy the natural good of human consciousness. Those diseases cause all wars and crimes, including politically inflicted property destructions, harms, sufferings, cruelties, and deaths. Such evils are inflicted by force or fraud to support the lives of open criminals (subhumans) such as muggers and rapists...or the much more evil, hidden criminals (humanoids) such as destructive politicians, tyrannical rulers, and killer-type (WACO) bureaucrats.

Camouflaged irrationality and deception used to drain, harm, and kill human beings is called neocheating.

Neocheaters are highly intelligent humanoids in whom the diseases of dishonesty and irrationality have destroyed the human nature of their conscious minds. Thus, such neocheaters are no longer human beings. They are humanoids who have destroyed the conscious structures of the human essences needed to enter the Civilization of the Universe. [Ref: The Neo-Tech Matrix described in the *Neo-Tech Discovery*]

To parasitically exist, neocheaters purposely propagate a bizarre, irrational civilization on planet Earth within which conscious life always moves toward unnatural death instead of natural immortality.

This unnatural, transitory anticivilization in macroscopic existence is somewhat analogous to the unnatural, transitory antiparticle in microscopic existence.

As the bizarre antiparticle vanishes forever on contact with natural matter, the bizarre anticivilization will vanish forever on contact with the natural Civilization of the Universe.

The supreme value of human consciousness will always be preserved by advanced civilizations using multi-dimensional[1] transceiver technologies in quantum-state, digitized cyberspace. Those technologies integrate rational consciousness with the existence field throughout the Civilization of the Universe.

By the fact of their continued existence, civilizations technologically advanced significantly past their Nuclear-Decision Thresholds are free from the diseases of dishonesty, mysticism, and irrationality. Thus, all such advanced civilizations are a part of the Civilization of the Universe.

In most areas, no one can predict the state of technology 100 years ahead, and certainly not a 1000 years ahead, much less a million years into the future. We cannot even imagine the technological states and economies of the advanced societies throughout the Civilization of the Universe.

---

[1]Such multidimensional examples are derivable from superstring and wormhole theories. Traversable wormholes, rotating black holes, and above-and-below Gravity Units offer theoretical but questionable time-travel possibilities at superluminal speeds. Such possibilities, nevertheless, can be codified through mathematics.

Movement III: The Civilization of the Universe

We can, however, know that no society, regardless of how advanced, can contradict the laws of physics or nature. Moreover, we can know that conscious beings throughout the Civilization of the Universe will never purposely act to violate their nature, well being, and happiness.

The basic nature of rational conscious beings has never and will never change. No rational being would ever let technology overtake his or her nature, self-control, self-responsibility, growth, and happiness. For, that loss of control over one's self — one's greatest value — would be self-destructive and irrational. Indeed, all conscious beings in the Civilization of the Universe are free of such irrationality or any other impediments to the growth and happiness of individual consciousness.

Thus, conscious beings in the Civilization of the Universe have the same nature: They live for happiness and its corollary emotions of genuine self-esteem and love. Indeed, the moral purpose of conscious beings is to meet the requirements for achieving rational happiness.

The nature of existence includes (1) objective law and justice, which characterize the Civilization of the Universe, (2) the limitless value of each conscious being when functioning in a rational civilization, (3) the dynamics of continually expanding value production and prosperity, which demands eternally preserving the supreme value of *every* conscious being.

The most bizarre characteristics of the anticivilization are its overpopulation and aging problems. In any rational civilization, overpopulation and aging are impossible. Exactly the opposite occurs. When free of destructive humanoids, each conscious being is free to productively, culturally, and artistically innovate and flourish without limits, becoming a priceless value to others and society.

For, each conscious being in a rational civilization is free to innovate and produce through division-of-labor dynamics far more values and resources than he or she consumes. ...Always increasing in value while always decreasing entropy, conscious beings remains forever young and precious.

Thus, in the open-ended Civilization of the Universe, a great demand for volitionally conscious people *always* exists. ...When free in an open and rational society based on objective law, each conscious individual enormously benefits and enriches all other conscious individuals and their societies. Through eternity, therefore, each conscious being will eventually contribute more value to society than its entire population at any given point in time.

Knowledge and technology increase endlessly. All advancing civilizations require developing ever greater and cheaper energy sources and production efficiencies.

Prosperity and happiness of conscious beings do *not* depend on their actual level of knowledge or technology, but depend on their rational thinking and acting processes required for continuously advancing knowledge and technology from any level.

Throughout the universe, every level of advancing knowledge and technology exists. Therefore, a technological level of conscious beings exists whose most efficient production of values depend on the *unsupervised* development and utilization of free-will conscious being. Thus, each such transceivable conscious person would provide endless values to all individuals and societies in the Civilization of the Universe.

Every populated area in existence has the economic-growth

279

needs for which each additional, volitionally developed, conscious being from any civilization would be of immense value. Thus, honest conscious beings anywhere in existence are never allowed to perish.

In Earth's anticivilization, *every* volitionally developed, honest conscious person is transceived/redeemed on a commercially profitable basis into the Civilization of the Universe. In other words, essentially every honest conscious being who has ever lived on Earth continues to live, flourishing eternally, in the Civilization of the Universe. ...But, the harmful humanoids of past history self-programed themselves to perish — to vanish from existence forever in the ultimate Ostracism Matrix.

Thus, justice and rationality are preserved through immortality.

Assembling the Proof of Immortality

Consider the effect of delivering irrefutable proof showing how all honest human beings live *forever* with increasing prosperity and happiness. Such proof might include measuring Gravity-Unit field changes of human beings versus humanoids and animals as they die.[1]

Of course, the primary responsibility of conscious beings on Earth today is to protect and preserve their existence — to create their own immortality in which transceiving would be unnecessary.

---

[1]In the mid 19th century, the great German mathematicians, C. F. Gauss and G. F. Riemann uncovered the noneuclidean geometries and higher spatial dimensions involved in such transductions throughout existence. Matter, energy, forces, and fields arise from motions through varying geometries in various dimensions and quantum states. Einstein needed Riemann's geometries to develop general relativity. Today, superstring theory originating from Kaluza-Klein theory further links geometries in various dimensions to existence.

Gravity-Unit Consciousness $\xrightarrow{\text{convert to}}$ matter/energy/forces/fields $\xrightarrow{\text{convert to}}$ spacetime curvatures/geometries $\xrightarrow{\text{convert to}}$ Gravity-Unit Consciousness

Chapter 32

Your Ride

into the

Civilization of the Universe

What will actually happen when you travel into the Civilization of the Universe? What will you experience? Will you ever return to this anticivilization? What about those left behind? What will limitless prosperity and eternal happiness really mean to you — emotionally, practically?

Once in the Civilization of the Universe, you will quickly forget the anticivilization. For, the anticivilization vanishes as the unreal nothingness it really is — it simply vanishes to be forever forgotten. And, those left behind? They too will vanish and be forgotten. But, no one will be left behind except criminal humanoids who have destroyed their human nature and refused to reconstruct their humanity. Thus, every conscious being, once in the rational Civilization of the Universe, has no reason or desire to connect their lives or memories with the destructive irrationalities of an anticivilization.

What will a nonpolitical civilization based entirely on integrated honesty and *objective* law be like? That civilization will be free of *subjective* political-policy laws, irrational ego "justice", and dishonest parasitical elites. Gone will be force-backed governments with their above-the-law rulers. Gone will be the politicians, lawyers, and judges identified as criminal-minded "superior people" by Fyodor Dostoyevsky in his classic *Crime and Punishment.*

281

Movement III: The Civilization of the Universe

Gone will be armed bureaucracies, mystical religions, wars, crime, fraud, poverty, disease, and death itself.

But, what is the Civilization of the Universe really like — emotionally, intellectually, and experience wise? What will living free of disease, mysticism, dishonesty, criminality, and irrationality be like? One's entire pattern of thoughts, emotions, and experiences will be different — so radically different from anything experienced in this anticivilization that no one today could fully know or describe that eternal difference...at least not until the Civilization of the Universe is created on planet Earth.[1] The conscious-created Civilization of the Universe could be available on Earth as early as 2001. If so, then by 2005 AD, many conscious beings in the business-developed countries will have already left behind this unreal anticivilization to reside in the exciting Civilization of the Universe.

How can one get some idea of what conscious life in the Civilization of the Universe might be like — some idea before actually taking that one-way journey from this grotesquely contradictory anticivilization into the beautifully harmonious Civilization of the Universe?

Perhaps one can begin imagining an eternally prosperous, happy life by trying to view this closed-system anticivilization from the outside. From that external view, one can sense how irrationality constantly blocks or cuts

---

[1]Consider a flatlander living in a two-dimensional universe being flipped up into a three-dimensional universe then falling back into his flat-plane universe. Observing only a series of two-dimensional planes or lines fly by as he travels through three-dimensional space, that flatlander would have no adequate way to understand a three-dimensional universe and would have no way to explain it to his fellow flatlanders. ...Do not confuse this useful dimensional analogy with the invalid analogy of Plato's cave to so-called higher realities. No higher or multirealities exist. Only one reality exists.

off experiencing life as ecstasy, cuts off achieving limitless prosperity, cuts off experiencing a fully joyful, productive, rational life. From the Civilization of the Universe, *every* perspective will look different from anything one could experience within this anticivilization. Each new perspective will be like encountering a new color for the first time — a new-color symphony — a stunningly unexpected experience unrecognizable from any previous experience.

The increasing government-imposed difficulties in achieving competitive values and genuine happiness throughout this anticivilization will wondrously transform into the easy way — the path of self-responsibile freedom — a consistently joyful path filled with endless victories. Indeed, that easy way is *endless* growth through discipline, rational thought, and productive action. Perhaps the closest, but still distant sense to that experience, can be observed in children under six years old still not diseased by the anticivilization. In every such child, one can observe his or her learning as not only remarkably rapid but compellingly joyful and exciting. Until poisoned by the dishonesties and mysticisms of the anticivilization, each young child experiences increasing joy in progressing toward knowledge and control of existence.

Through the Zon Protocols, every adult can reenter the Civilization of the Universe left behind as a child. On reentering, one becomes free from the life-draining burdens of irrationality, dishonesty, and mysticism. One then gains hitherto unknown perspectives on discipline, productive work, love, happiness, health, diet, fitness, entertainment, pleasures. Indeed, an ecstatic life of endless growth is experienced by all conscious beings in the Civilization of the Universe. Even destructive politicians and other

283

parasitical humanoids can reenter that nonpolitical Civilization of the Universe after reconstructing their humanity — after becoming honest, competitive human beings who are genuinely valuable to others and society.

What joyful lives await human beings on Earth. Our journey toward the nonpolitical Civilization of the Universe has begun. Indeed, our one-way, magic-carpet ride into the Civilization of the Universe begins with *Zonpower* and is completed with the forthcoming *Zon Protocols*.

This unreal anticivilization whose politicians depend on dark Schopenhauer drives to survive by harming others and society will then vanish. Yes, the *Zon Protocols* will usher in the Civilization of the Universe...the natural civilization from which we came as children. And, into which, we will return as increasingly valuable, fully responsible, mature adults. For, we belong to the eternally evolving Civilization of the Universe.

Zon is the *natural* law of conscious beings in all worlds and universes.

Chapter 33

You Will Become Zon

Consider the following six points:

1. Zon is the measure of all conscious beings.
2. Zon is disconnected from *every* aspect of any anticivilization.
3. Parasitical elites have created a dishonest, violent anticivilization on Earth. They each will unhesitantly lie, make war, commit crimes, murder, even mass murder to continue their destructive livelihoods and increase their power usurpations.
4. One finds eternal freedom by disconnecting from Earth's anticivilization. Such a disconnection switches one from this anticivilization into the Civilization of the Universe.
5. No part of any anticivilization is redeemable or correctable. For, nothing is redeemable or correctable from illusions based on nonreality. ...Fully integrated honesty with its wide-scope reality vanishes all such illusions.
6. Daybreak does not at once replace the darkness. Thus, the Civilization of the Universe will not at once replace Earth's anticivilization. In both cases, a seeming glow comes first. Then light breaks across the darkness. All becomes visible, clear — a peaceful civilization of eternal prosperity and exciting romance here on Earth.

The following journey unites the above points by returning *you* to Zon whose kingdom is the Civilization of the Universe.

Movement III: The Civilization of the Universe

You Control Existence
You are Invulnerable
You are Zon

Zon is a citizen of all universes. How would a citizen of Earth recognize Zon? How would Zon appear? How would Zon think? What would Zon do?

Zon is the controller of existence. Zon is the past and future creator of all universes. Zon is identical to you, except he or she acts entirely through fully integrated honesty and wide-scope accounting. Thus, you can experience Zon. Indeed, you can become Zon to rule existence and gain eternal prosperity. ...As Zon, nothing in an anticivilization has power over you.

You were born Zon. Every conscious being who has ever existed was born Zon. But, on planet Earth, *every* conscious being has been dragged from childhood into the dishonest illusions that perpetuate this anticivilization. Thus, everyone today behaves as someone else — as someone other than an honest, fully conscious human being. ...Until today, every adult on Earth has lived as a phantom, never realizing that he or she is an eternal Zon.

You are Zon living in an illusion-shrouded anticivilization. In this illusionary civilization, all human beings live as phantoms deluded into believing they are mortals who live and die with no eternal power, purpose, or prosperity. When, in reality, conscious beings are immortal with limitless power and purpose.

On vanishing the illusions of this anticivilization, you reconnect with Zon, the ruler of existence. Although you still walk among the phantoms in this anticivilization, you have no connection with their illusions. You are as divorced from their illusions as you would be divorced from the illusions of schizophrenics in an insane asylum.

Yet, you see *everyone* as your kin. You see the profound value and power in every conscious being. Beyond all else in existence, you treasure the soul of each human being, regardless of what civilization or age in which each lives.

* * *

As Zon, how would you appear physically, mentally, and behaviorally among the phantoms of this anticivilization? How would you gain ever increasing prosperity, love, and happiness when you are disconnected from all the illusions comprising this anticivilization? How would you function among the hypnotized human beings and destructive humanoids of this anticivilization?

As Zon, you do not feel superior to, aloof from, or even particularly different than others. Nor are you a Bartleby. You simply know you are in a different civilization — a 180° different civilization. That difference does not make you feel uncomfortable or uneasy. In fact, your ability to function with others is enhanced. That disconnection also enhances your ability to benefit all human beings *and* humanoids on this planet. Moreover, your disconnection enhances your own happiness and enjoyment of life on Earth.

Most profoundly, as Zon you know that you are invulnerable to the irrationalities of this anticivilization. Like the anticivilization itself, the irrational actions of both its human-being and humanoid citizens are unreal — not connected to reality. Thus, such nonreality has no meaning for you...no real influence on you.

Movement III: The Civilization of the Universe

Still, you are among fellow conscious beings — the greatest value in existence. Moreover, the objective requirement for eternal life, prosperity, and happiness remains the same wherever conscious beings exist. That requirement is to deliver ever increasing values to others and society. Through the division of essence and labor combined with voluntary transactions, you create increasingly more values for others than you consume. You become increasingly valuable to yourself, others, and society.

You live to *be*, not to *have*. You live to create, not to consume. You need nothing beyond the requirements to produce life-enhancing values at maximum efficiencies for yourself, others, and society. You need or want nothing from this moribund anticivilization. You neither need nor want anything from its inherently destructive rulers and their dishonest media, organizations, academe, politicians, intellectuals, or celebrities.

Why the zero value of this anticivilization? Consider its irrational effects: The more life-enhancing values that heroic value producers deliver to society, the more parasitical humanoids foment public envy against those value producers. Why? To increasingly usurp unearned livelihoods from the productive class. Likewise, the more life-supporting jobs that honest businesses deliver to society, the more parasitical humanoids use government force to drain those businesses through irrational taxes, political-agenda laws, and destructive regulations. Such insanity is not the fault of human beings. Rather, that insanity is inherent in any irrational civilization functioning through subjective laws fashioned by parasitical rulers backed by armed agents of force.

In reality, you and all human beings belong *not* among this unreal anticivilization but among the Civilization of the Universe. All the insanities of which an anticiviliza-

288

tion is constructed are merely illusions that never exist in reality — bizarre illusions that ultimately yield only diminishment and death to human beings — dishonest illusions that serve only the parasitical livelihoods of humanoids.

Yet, you as Zon are eternally protected by honesty and reality. You are always advancing in *real* spacetime to ever greater accomplishments, continually decreasing the entropy[1] of existence — continually making order out of disorder. Thus, nothing in the anticivilization can really harm or adversely affect your progress in moving through spacetime toward eternal life and prosperity.

At this moment, you can experience the first glimpse at how you as Zon function among your fellow human beings in this anticivilization. You first note the honest innocence of young children. You realize that essentially all children under six years of age are Zons — innocent, uncorrupted, honest. You notice how all such children struggle to obtain objective knowledge, not illusions. Those children strive for value-producing powers, not socially destructive pragmatisms. Then you realize how all parents and adults in this anticivilization are deluded by their humanoid rulers — humanoids who eventually corrupt and then bury the innocence, honesty, and power inherent within *every* young child.

Only through that ultimate crime inflicted on all children has this bizarre anticivilization been perpetuated since its creator, Plato, twenty-three centuries ago.

Real and Imaginary Killing of Human Beings

You start your journey into the Civilization of the Universe by transporting yourself into a mind and body that functions through fully integrated honesty and wide-

------

[1]That capacity to decrease entropy is why conscious beings and only conscious beings can potentially reverse physical aging.

scope accountability. With the power of fully integrated honesty, you discover the universal laws that deliver valid solutions to all problems. As a simple example, consider two diverse problems in this anticivilization: (1) the unhealthy fattening of Americans and (2) the emotionally charged abortion issue. Wide-scope accounting provides completely different perspectives on those two problems, links them together in unexpected ways, and then delivers powerful, definitive solutions to each based on universal laws. Consider the following example:

— Real Killings—

You are sitting in a mall ice-cream parlor eating nothing, just looking at those eating ice cream. You then look into the mall promenade at the milling crowd. You let nothing block your thoughts. You think honestly, widely. Nothing is out-of-bounds. In such wide-scope thinking, everything eventually connects together through new knowledge, certain knowledge about the past, present, and future.

You are thinking about the intentional destruction of the human mind and body. You realize that such destruction accrues through subjective laws and views replacing objective laws and views. By that process, you see America is becoming a fat farm as well as an insane asylum. You realize that obesity and insanity are related. With drug-like intensity, Americans are increasingly living to eat, rather than eating to live.

Indeed, the intentional destruction of the body requires the intentional destruction of the mind, which in turn requires the loss of honesty through rationalizations. That loss of honesty evolves from a culture of parasitical leaders foisting self-serving political agendas and exploitive mysticisms onto the public.

You Will Become Zon

How do the above facts link together to cause the intentional killing of Americans — the lethal fattening of men, women, and most evilly, innocent children[1]? How do those facts link together to increasingly diminish the chance for a healthy, happy life for Americans and their children? ...You discover the answer:

Research for the Canadian Air Force in the 1960s compiled and implemented scientifically sound facts about human metabolism, health, and physical fitness. That study identified the objective causes of damaging one's metabolism to breed unhealthy weight gains that lead to demoralizing stagnation, decreasing happiness, and early death.

Then in the early 1970s, Dr. Robert C. Atkins converted the Canadian Air Force findings into the best-selling, most effective diet book ever published: *The Diet Revolution.*[2,3] The eternal fact underlying Dr. Atkins' diet is that carbohydrates combined with poor aerobic fitness — *not* calories, oils, or fat per se — cause unsavory weight gain, heart disease, diabetes, hypoglycemia, and other health problems. For, the human body does *not* naturally metabolize concentrated carbohydrates. In fact, above certain modest quantities, carbohydrates are both poisonous and addicting to human beings.

Human beings are natural carnivores, not herbivores. Human beings are natural meat or protein eaters, not vegetarians or carbohydrate eaters. Human beings naturally metabolize proteins along with fats and oils. Thus, natural foods include meat, poultry, fish, cheese,

[1]With hypocritical concerns and dishonest pleadings, people like Susan Smith and Hillary Clinton either directly kill their own children or indirectly kill thousands or even millions of other people's children. Also, Dickens/Gifford-type child-labor dishonesties have starved millions of children.

[2]In later years, Dr. Atkins sadly surrendered to the politically correct establishment, grew stout again, and leaned toward bogus fad diets.

[3]A modified, improved version of Dr. Atkin's diet was published in 1995: *The Zone*, Barry Sears, Harper Collins.

nuts, butter, cream, eggs, low-starch vegetables, and high-fiber cereals. While corn, sweet fruits, potatoes, pastries, pastas, and breads are troubling foods for human metabolism. All concentrated carbohydrates are harmful above modest levels, especially the most concentrated, purest form of carbohydrate — sugar in *all* its forms, including fructose, honey, and corn-syrup sweeteners. ...Sugar, a heavily government-subsidized industry, is subtly the most addicting, toxic, and deleterious drug known to afflict the human body...and mind.

Sugar is the crack cocaine of the carbohydrate drugs. Sugar is by far the biggest killing substance among human beings today. Such concentrated carbohydrates lie at the root of most eating disorders, discipline problems, concentration deficiencies, moodiness, unhappiness, depression, sloth, poor performance, and criminal behavior. Indeed, *without exaggeration*, the most insidiously harmful of child abusers and drug pushers are parents who addict their defenseless children with sugar in all its forms.

Those are facts: facts now, facts before, facts forever. Sitting in that ice-cream parlor, you realize why Americans today are increasingly throwing away their health and happiness. You realize they are increasingly mutilating their bodies and trashing their minds through endless upside-down "health" diets, government-subsidized nutritional frauds, bogus low-fat school lunch programs, and dishonest government-backed, survey-type pseudo science. Those frauds along with the FDA armed bureaucrats maliciously work to harm the physical and mental health of all Americans and their children.

In the 1970s and 1980s, increasing numbers of people directly or indirectly recognized the universal, objective facts about diet and health. Development and sales of sugar-free food and drinks escalated. But, in the early 1990s, sugar-free foods began vanishing in favor of meaningless low-fat, low-cholesterol, organic "natural" foods — politically correct foods. Mega-size, fat-free, sugar-laden cookies, brownies, snacks, and drinks are sold as health foods while the most benign and effective of the nonsugar sweeteners — cyclamates — are dishonestly banned by power-crazed FDA bureaucrats...and the harmless sugar-substitute saccharine is irrationally labelled as cancer-causing by the FDA, leaving only dubious NutraSweet® unscathed.

Today, as the public obsession with irrational food consumption and bogus fat-free diets grows, the per capita intake of toxic carbohydrates soars. Indeed, consumption of sugar and carbohydrates is now accelerating as people are deceived with illusions generated by the government, FDA, and bogus health advocates. Their sickening deceptions dupe people into believing they are eating healthier by eating low-cholesterol, low-fat carbohydrates. In the meantime, they and their children are increasing their carbohydrate intakes and addictions. Thus, they grow fatter while irreversibly damaging their metabolic systems, leading to glandular harm, uncontrolled fatness, and mounting unhappiness.

Next, consider Dr. Kenneth Cooper's great, scientifically grounded research in the 1960s concerning physical fitness and his subsequent book, *Aerobics*. From that book, Americans freely, on their own, began a rational trend toward genuinely improved physical fitness and happiness. For, in the 1970s and early 1980s, without the blatherings of government "experts" or self-appointed "health" advocates, the two natural criteria of a healthy human body were being increasingly understood: Human beings are by nature (1) protein metabolizers and (2) long-distance running animals.

Yet, in the 1990s, sales of near worthless, non-aerobic exercise devices, health-club memberships, low-fat diet books, and "anti-aging" pills soared. Fewer and fewer people kept *aerobically* fit to remain trim and happy into old age. ...The key to human health and longevity is *low-carbohydrate* diets combined with *aerobic* fitness. The key to human dietary happiness is the CAS diet — no <u>C</u>affeine, no <u>A</u>lcohol, no <u>S</u>ugar.

Observe the increasing political-correctness machinations combined with government-funded, pseudo-science "research" in the form of noncontextual surveys. Today's avalanche of lazy, dishonest "science" is why objective knowledge about health, fitness, and happiness is being lost in a sea of irrationality — forgotten in a contradictory blizzard of bogus, survey-type health "discoveries".

The mid 1990s was like reentering the Dark Ages that were dominated by dishonest religious Establishments similar to today's dishonest politically correct Establishments. During that dark-age period of extreme irrationality, knowledge about health and prosperity was lost or sequestered. Life expectancy plunged, for example, to less than half that experienced in the previous, more-rational Golden Age of Greece.

Today's period of increasing irrationality blocks public knowledge of the destructive political agendas diminishing everyone's precious life. For example, government promotes public dependency and control by increasing drug-like carbohydrate consumption in the form of low-fat, low-cholesterol, sugar-laced foods and drinks. As people become carbohydrate addicted, unfit, and unhappy, they lose self-esteem and seek ever more dependency on authorities supplying good-sounding "easy answers". ...Consequently, the first major product that totalitarian governments allow into their countries is the insidious, will-breaking, sugar-laced caffeine drug, Coca-Cola®. ...Such governments show no interest in importing healthy, sugar-free, caffeine-free beverages.

The inescapable essence of a healthy human mind and body is *honesty and effort*. That identification about honesty and effort will eventually serve to vanish our chronically sick anticivilization, replacing it with the eternally healthy Civilization of the Universe.

— Imaginary Killings —

Now shift to an entirely different problem in this anticivilization: Today's religious-right individuals are among the most worthy of Americans. Most religious-right people deliver genuine values and prosperity to others and society. Many are hard working, productive, family-oriented individuals who act as foils to the destructive actions of the parasitical-elite class throughout the secular Establishment.[1] Most religious-right people are self-sufficient and do not partake in government-sponsored, gun-backed parasitism. Yet, they are self-defeating and thoroughly hoodwinked by their own demagogic leaders on abortion and issues like school prayer.

Only with fully integrated honesty can they escape their trap — their contradictions of reality. With integrated honesty, they can remove the threats against their lifestyles while expanding their admirable values to vanish their nemeses: parasitical elites who enforce evil agendas through their armed bureaucrats.

Because of their loyalty to genuine values, religious-

---

[1]As stated on page 273, Western religion has often acted as a foil to the destructive power of the state — and vice versa. ...In the Civilization of the Universe, no illusions exist. Thus, no state or religious powers exist. Only individual Zonpower exists.

right people properly respect human life above all else. Thus, they would be correct — morally and legally — to block by any means within *objective* law, anyone, including government itself, who purposely murders other human beings. But, the problem with their all-out crusade against abortion "murder" is simply that a fetus is *not* a human being. ...Potentiality is *not* actuality.

Their badly misguided concept of "murdering" fetuses springs from emotional brainwashings by false "spiritual" leaders — leaders who support agendas needed to advance their own self-serving demagogic livelihoods. Indeed, at *any* stage, a fetus is nothing more than self-created protoplasm. The fetus is not a baby, not a child, not a human being. The defining essence or attribute of a human being is consciousness — conscious awareness and conscious functioning. The fetus has no consciousness. The fetus is not a human being. The fetus has no rights. The fetus requires no legal or moral protection.

Many millions of intelligent, religious people have been duped into morally and physically defending fetuses as if they were human beings. Consider their forcibly aggressive anti-abortion demonstrations along with other contradictions such as their demanding prayer or silent mediation in *public* schools. Such repugnant blending of church and state ultimately subverts the rights and freedoms of all nonreligious *and* religious people. For, demanding *any* gun-backed government action to promote political frauds or religious agendas means sanctioning gun-backed actions leading to all criminal acts, including political-agenda mass murder such as at WACO. Indeed, WACO was a political fraud that involved *real* child killings by the President, his armed bureaucracies, and his Attorney General.

You Will Become Zon

Objective Laws are Universal Laws

In the final analysis, all problems tie together to yield valid, effective solutions according to objective, universal laws that can never be contradicted. Only objective laws are valid and apply to everyone, at all places, at all times. By definition, objective laws do not spring from the minds of men and women. Such laws have always and will always exist universally — independent of the human mind and its emotions. Thus, no objective law is new; each is eternal. Moreover, *no* law — physical, legal, or moral — is valid unless that law is naturally applicable, universally and eternally.

Living by the universal principles of objective law, one neither needs nor wants approval, acceptance, or recognition from anyone interacting with this unreal anticivilization. The entire history of the anticivilization and its humanoid rulers is one of fraud leading to human diminishment. The anticivilization has no real existence or power. Its humanoid perpetrators have only illusionary existences and imaginary powers in an anticivilization first conjured up by Plato and then perpetuated by parasitical elites. Such parasites are epitomized by the dishonest hierarchies of the church, state, and academe who have fatally corrupted the minds and bodies of human beings for the past two millennia.

Now consider the meaning of vanishing the illusions that support this anticivilization and its humanoid rulers — the meaning of you becoming Zon:

Becoming Zon

On becoming Zon, you increasingly disconnect from the actions, people, and humanoids interacting with this unreal anticivilization. Your disconnection is not one of

297

misanthropy, but one of grace. Your disconnection involves (1) *physical actions* reflected by a pleasant demeanor, (2) *mental processes* reflected by creative, nonlinear, far-from-equilibrium thinking that brings order out of chaos to create new knowledge, and (3) *behaviors* reflected by benevolent disconnections from the irrationalities of this anticivilization. Those irrationalities include health-diminishing, life-consuming distractions ranging from drug-like obsessions with eating to life-escaping obsessions with sports, entertainment, and celebrities.

You need not correct anything in an uncorrectable anticivilization. **You only need to disconnect**. ...Now consider these areas of disconnection:

— Physical —

Expanding health and vitality are earned, not given. Expanding health and vitality come no other way except through DTC — Discipline, Thought, then Control. DTC self-perpetuates, builds on itself, and then brings limitless rewards to every aspect of conscious life. ...DTC is the most powerful determinant of human health, longevity, and happiness.

Returning to your free-ranging thoughts, you have long known human beings on Earth are by nature long-distance running animals. Thus, through DTC, you run daily. You started years ago by running a slow 100 yards, working up over several years to a steady five miles a day in 40 minutes. Now you run every day, probably not missing a half-dozen days in a year. Time and schedule "inconvenience" are no more an inconvenience than bathing everyday. With that daily run, you are physically and mentally reborn each day, ready to advance beyond the accomplishments of the previous day, progressing forever into a future of expanding knowledge and prosperity.

You also know human beings are carnivorous animals. Indeed, your natural, low-carbohydrate diet eliminates desires for drug-like, high-concentration carbohydrates and sugar toxins. ...DTC naturally occurs throughout the Civilization of the Universe as does the CAS happiness diet — no Caffeine, no Alcohol, or no Sugar. ...You recognize cups of coffee, for example, as cups of unhappiness.

You are trim, fit, and happy. With your spouse, values such as growth, communication, love, and sexual enjoyment grow each year. In handling life, your effectiveness increases each year, *never* diminishing with age.

Your joy with your work, your loved ones, and your life expand eternally. You realize DTC and physical fitness are natural for all conscious beings throughout all universes, in all ages.

You disconnect from the irrationalities throughout this anticivilization.

— Mental —

Your power to acquire expanding knowledge for controlling existence derives through fully integrated honesty and wide-scope thinking. Fully integrated honesty is the underlying source of value creation and competitive businesses on Earth and throughout existence. In an anticivilization, its humanoid creators and perpetrators can survive only by disintegrating the most powerful essence of conscious beings —‾ fully integrated honesty.

You disconnect from the dishonesties throughout this anticivilization.

299

Movement III: The Civilization of the Universe

— Behavior —

Conscious beings are social animals mediated through value exchange and business. The limitless benevolence, prosperity, excitement, and happiness possible among conscious beings are derived from the natural dynamics among the Civilization of the Universe. They are derived from conscious beings freely producing and volitionally trading mutually beneficial values through not only the division of human labor but through the division of human essences. ...Poverty, crime, and war are inconceivable concepts in the Civilization of the Universe.

You disconnect from the socially and economically destructive behaviors throughout this anticivilization.

* * *

As Zon, you feel a profound care and valuation for the source of *all* human values, in all universes, in all ages. That source of values is your fellow conscious beings. You also care for the humanoid parasites who created and propagate this destructive anticivilization. Indeed, you work for their redemption as human beings. Why? Most humanoids can be guided back to their childhoods when they were innocent Zons. From that point, they can learn to grow up — to mature into value-producing human beings. On becoming honest conscious beings, they also can reenter the Civilization of the Universe to become limitless values to others and society.

300

You Will Become Zon

The Zon Protocols

The forthcoming *Zon Protocols* is the medium through which the Civilization of the Universe will embrace planet Earth. The *Zon Protocols* identify, integrate, and then vanish each and every illusion conjured up for the past two millennia by parasitical humanoids. Eventually, through the *Zon Protocols*, every conscious being on Earth will, with no transition phase or backward glance, simply click off this transitory, unreal anticivilization and step into an eternal, real civilization — the Civilization of the Universe in which each conscious person naturally belongs.

In the meantime, *Zonpower* will enable adults to protect children from being dragged into this illusionary anticivilization. Children will remain Zons. Thus, their Zonpower will remain intact as they grow into adults. They will leave this anticivilization behind as *nothing*. The anticivilization with its humanoid rulers will vanish, forgotten forever. Everyone will then live prosperously, peacefully, eternally in the Civilization of the Universe.

Children are the Achilles' heel of this anticivilization. For essentially all children under six belong to the Civilization of the Universe. They are Zons, citizens of the universe. Uncorrupted, they hold the power to control existence through fully integrated honesty. When, through *Zonpower* or the *Zon Protocols*, parents realize that every baby is born a Zon, they will protect and prevent their children from being dragged into this lethal, illusionary anticivilization. Thus, when those children become adults, they will assume their responsibilities as all-powerful citizens of the universe. They will be free of corruption and dishonesty. For them, the anticivilization will not exist. It will have been vanished, forgotten forever. ...Conscious beings on Earth will then be free to control

301

existence in creating for society eternal health, prosperity, and happiness.

Chapter 34
The Zon Awakening

Nothing links the nonliving to the living, the plant to the animal, or the animal mind to the human mind. Similarly, nothing links the slumberous consciousness of the anticivilization to the dynamic consciousness of the Civilization of the Universe. ...Likewise, nothing links the endless deprivations in this anticivilization to the limitless prosperity in the Civilization of the Universe.

In physics, nothing links one electron state to another or one spacetime system to another. In both life and physics, essences exist in either one state or another with no flow, transition, or linkage between them. Consider the nature of Planck's go/no-go blackbody radiation, Einstein's go/no-go photoelectric effect, and *civilization's go/no-go limitless-prosperity dynamics*. Locked within the laws of physics, how could one ever enter the law-based Civilization of the Universe from this criminal-based anticivilization?

As in physics with the introduction of Planck's energy, the introduction of Zonpower will allow entry into the Civilization of the Universe. Eventually, everyone on Earth will leave criminal politics behind and click into the Civilization of the Universe without transition.

Since no link or communication with the anticivilization is possible, no one today can know what life is like in the Civilization of the Universe — not until it actually appears on planet Earth, perhaps by the end of this century. Until then, all that can be known with certainty is that life in the Civilization of the Universe means

303

limitless prosperity and eternal happiness. Indeed, everyone can look forward to the happiest shock of his or her life as each suddenly awakens in a law-based civilization of eternal riches and exciting romance.

Why is linkage between the two civilizations impossible? That impossibility is not because of any cultural or psychological differences, which are profound and absolute. But, rather, that impossibility is because the laws of physics make impossible any contact or linkage, both practically and theoretically. The reason for that impossibility lies in the fact that each civilization travels along separate spacetime coordinates. One cannot travel or switch to a different spacetime system anymore than one can travel backward in time. *For, any such spacetime travel or switch would require the conscious reconstruction of every quantum state — of every matter and force coordinate — in the universe at every instant in time.* Thus, the arrow of time cannot be reversed or switched.

Spacetime systems constantly evolve and move forward. One is never able to travel to different spacetime or light-cone coordinates that have already come and gone...here or elsewhere. Nothing can revisit, return to, or alter events occurring in any past or separate time frame as reflected in a familiar way by Omar Khayyám in *The Rubáiyát* nine centuries ago:

> The moving finger writes; and, having writ,
> Moves on: nor all your piety nor wit
> Shall lure it back to cancel half a line,
> Nor all your tears wash out a word of it.

Consider the two illustrations on the next page:

Illustration A
ENERGY-ACTIVITY SYSTEMS

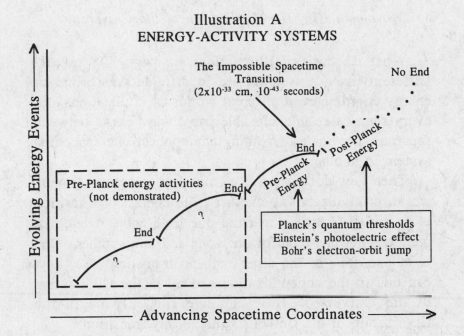

The Impossible Spacetime Transition
(2×10^{-33} cm, 10^{-43} seconds)

No End

End

Post-Planck Energy

Pre-Planck energy activities (not demonstrated)

End

Pre-Planck Energy

End

?

End

?

Planck's quantum thresholds
Einstein's photoelectric effect
Bohr's electron-orbit jump

— Evolving Energy Events →

⟶ Advancing Spacetime Coordinates ⟶

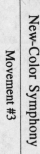

New-Color Symphony
Movement #3

Illustration B
CONSCIOUS-ACTIVITY SYSTEMS

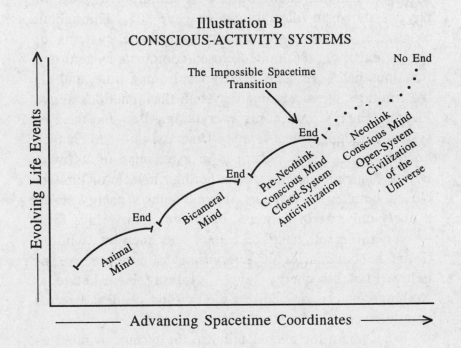

No End

The Impossible Spacetime Transition

End

Neothink Conscious Mind Open-System Civilization of the Universe

End

Pre-Neothink Conscious Mind Closed-System Anticivilization

End

Bicameral Mind

Animal Mind

— Evolving Life Events →

⟶ Advancing Spacetime Coordinates ⟶

305

Movement III: The Civilization of the Universe

What do the two illustrations on page 305 reveal? Different essence systems are in different spacetime or energy coordinates in different worlds or civilizations. In every such case, an unclosable gap always exists between separate coordinates. Nothing can connect one spacetime system to another.

Then how does one move from one spacetime system, world, or civilization to another if no contact or transition is possible? Like going from one time zone to another, one does not phase out of one zone and into another. One is in one zone or the other with no transition. So, how can one in the anticivilization end up in the Civilization of the Universe? How can one suddenly be in the Civilization of the Universe without any transition?

Consider the analogous, well-established laws of physics shown in Illustration A on page 305. Throughout existence, at least two distinct coordinate systems of energy exist: (1) the limited closed-coordinate system that functions below Planck's energy level doing little, and (2) the limitless open-coordinate system that functions above Planck's energy level doing everything. Between the two systems, nothing except Gravity Units exists — no contact, no transition. Each system is in a universe of its own. Below Planck's energy level, a boring universe of limited, closed boundaries exists. Above Planck's energy level, a lively universe of limitless, open evolution springs forth — generating all possible events and energies, without limits or boundaries. ...Everything is either above or below Planck's energy level. Nothing is in-between. Nothing connects or mediates the two independent systems or universes.

What about the animal mind to the bicameral mind as shown in Illustration B? The bicameral mind to the conscious mind? The closed-system, rationalizing Kantian mind comprising the anticivilization to the open-ended, integrating Randian mind comprising the Civilization of the Universe? The criminally destructive Hitlerian/Clintonian mind to the heroically productive Thomas Edison/Bill Gates mind? ...What is the analogous Planck's energy that will jump the spacetime gap or void from the anticivilization to the Civilization of the Universe? That equivalency of Planck's energy is contained within the universal constant of Zon, k, described on page 11. From the constant k flows the power of Zon.

The Civilization of the Universe *is* Zonpower. Once one integrates with Zonpower, he or she automatically makes a Planck-like jump with no transition. Abruptly, one is in the Civilization of the Universe. The anticivilization is then left behind, impossible to contact, soon forgotten forever.

Nonaging through Time Dilation

Civilizations are functions of conscious thinking, especially integrated thinking. The speed of integrated thinking depends on the depth and range of objective knowledge acquired. All such thinking is subject to time-dilation as described by Einstein's Special Relativity. In the closed boundaries of the anticivilization, integrated thinking is severely and absolutely limited. Thus, both the power and speed of integrated thinking are limited to minimal ranges. The speed of integration always increases with advancing knowledge. But, the closed boundaries of the anticivilization holds the speed of advancing knowledge far below that which Einstein's relativity has any observable effects.

By contrast, the Civilization of the Universe has no

boundaries. Thus, new knowledge is limitless and the speed of integrations are bounded only by the speed of light. Thereby, both knowledge and speed of thinking increase geometrically, if not exponentially. With such a multiplying effect, the speed of integration will soon approach the velocity of light as described in Chapter 6. At such speeds, time dilation becomes noticeable and then dominates.

What happens as the speed of integrations for new knowledge keeps accelerating ever closer to the velocity of light? The resulting time dilation becomes so great that the flow of time essentially ceases relative to events and experiences in technologically advanced cyberspaces.

* * *

The rationally open Civilization of the Universe allows conscious beings to live in eternal prosperity and exciting happiness. By contrast, the criminally closed anticivilization forces conscious beings to live in boring deprivation and then die.

Those differences in time dilation reflect the separate spacetime coordinates or paths along which conscious beings travel in the closed anticivilization versus the open Civilization of the Universe. With those differences in time dilation, any linkage or contact is impossible between conscious minds travelling along their separate spacetime coordinates — the anticivilization slow path versus the Civilization of the Universe fast path. ...Galileo/Newton provided the transformations of classical physics; Lorentz/Einstein provided the transformations of relativity; today Neothink/Zon provides the transformations of consciousness.

The Civilization of the Universe is coming. On its

arrival for each individual, the anticivilization and its criminal parasites will disappear, lost in bygone spacetime coordinates, never to be revisited, forever forgotten as nothing.

Life in the Civilization of the Universe

Why do people who materially indulge themselves live in hidden desperation, cynicism, boredom? Why do they grow increasingly dissatisfied with themselves? Why does the greatest dissatisfaction and emptiness occur in those who seek ego indulgences and material gains most fervently? By contrast, what makes the Civilization of the Universe inconceivably different in which *everyone* has limitless prosperity and romantic excitement...void of anxiety, doubt, boredom?

In the anticivilization, why care about what anyone thinks, says, or does? Except for competitive values and their heroic producers, what difference does anything or anyone make in the schizophrenic irrationality of an anticivilization? Beneath this anticivilization, nothing except permanent value production makes any difference...or sense. In the Civilization of the Universe, however, everything that each individual does or experiences makes the most profound difference to everyone eternally.

Onward to Cyberspace
(See periodic chart on next page)

A Periodic Chart
Evolving from Endless Losses to Limitless Prosperity

→ Expansion Phases

→ Movement toward Limitless Prosperity →

	Foundation	Value Development	Value Spreading	Protection
Neo-Tech in the Anticivilization	Fundamentals and Principles Neo-Tech Pincer I — Advanced Concepts of Poker 1968; Neo-Tech Reference Encyclopedia 1976; Neocheating 1979; Golden Helmet 1980; Neo-Tech Discovery 1981/1986/1994	Conversion to Business Applications Neo-Tech Pincer II — Neo-Tech/Neothink Business System 1988; Neo-Tech World Summits 1985-1987	Spreading Worldwide Neo-Tech Pincer III — Building a Global Business Empire 1992; Golden-Helmet Package 1994; The Seven Waves 1987-1997	Neo-Tech Protection Kit 1988/1994
Resurrection of Zon	Prosperity Revolution 1991-1999; Court Trials 1991-1995; The Zonpower Discovery 1992; Cassandra's Secret 1993; Depoliticize, Decriminalize 1995-2001	Foundation Building for a New Civilization 1. Neo-Tech Day-Care Centers 2. Neo-Tech Elementary Schools 3. Neo-Tech Role Models 4. Neo-Tech high-paying jobs for everyone 5. Neo-Tech Love Connection and Friendship Service 6. Objective-Law Party 2001	Neo-Tech Literature Distribution Program 1994; Social Connection 1994; Zon World Summit 1999	Operation of the Ostracism/Praise Matrix 2001; Worldwide Conscious Control 2005
Civilization of the Universe	*Cyberspace* Zon Protocols 2001; Civilization of the Universe under development (available 1999-2004)	*Cyberspace* Implementation Worldwide as shown above 2001-2005	*Cyberspace* Universal Networking 2005	*Cyberspace* Universal Conscious Control 2010

Chapter 35

Poker Stratagems

replaced by

Zon's Integrated Honesty

As described in Chapter 18, how could anything so seemingly evil as the Illuminati Protocols be compatible with the fully integrated honesty of Neo-Tech? How could the founding Illuminati be the heroic precursors of Neo-Tech? Those questions are answered by comparing the underlying dynamics flowing beneath the fatally flawed, close-ended Illuminati dynamics to the pristine, open-ended Neo-Tech/Zon dynamics:

Compatible Dynamics

The original Neo-Tech author and the original Illuminati recognized that all conscious beings on Earth, throughout the ages, were and continue to be drained, impoverished, and killed by a permanently entrenched parasitical-elite class. Moreover, the original Neo-Tech author and the original Illuminati recognized that this parasitical-elite class created a bizarre anticivilization from which no one could escape its always fatal human diminishments. The original Neo-Tech author and the original Illuminati also recognized that no matter what reforms or advances occurred, the same ever increasing cycles of parasitical destruction would always occur on planet Earth. ...Thus, when technology advanced to the capacity of destroying the entire human race through biological or nuclear weapons, that destruction would occur on the next major upswing cycle of irrationalities leading to mass destructions or wars.

311

Movement III: The Civilization of the Universe

As was the original Neo-Tech author, the original Illuminati were aware that every conscious being and all earned values on Earth would eventually be consumed by the parasitical elites. Although not knowing the final technology that could destroy conscious life on Earth, the original Illuminati knew that capability would eventually develop. Today, everyone knows that this total-destruction technology is thermonuclear energy.

Thus, the Illuminati today race to complete their goal of subverting and eliminating all life-draining institutions that support parasitical humanoids — eliminate them before they obliterate conscious life on Earth. The current parasitical cycle will increasingly ruin the real value-and-job producers, their means of production, their capital, their property. As in all past such cycles, this parasitical feeding cycle will escalate until the maximum possible human values are consumed or destroyed.

By using nuclear or biological weapons to destroy maximum possible values, this final wipe-out cycle would end most if not all conscious life on Earth. ...Some religious-right fundamentalists fervidly root for such an apocalyptic wipe out.

As revealed in Movement II of *Zonpower*, the only solution possible by working *within* this anticivilization is to undermine and then break every harmful institution throughout the anticivilization — eliminate every institution that supports humanoid parasites. That breaking of parasitical institutions could be accomplished by harnessing genuine business power through advanced poker stratagems. For, by combining that business power with such stratagems, one can outflank every parasitical maneuver.

The breaking of destructive governments and religious

institutions along with their parasitical beneficiaries can be done through organized, persistent business dynamics. In fact, that breaking of those destructive institutions has been nearly accomplished. By whom? By the dedicated handful of highly responsible Illuminati businesspeople.

Advancing the Illuminati's goal required the confident certainty that genuine business power combined with advanced poker strategy will *always* outflank and eventually vanish the false power of parasitical elites and their illusion-built institutions. Indeed, the underlying Illuminati strategy is maneuvering parasitical elites and influential leaders alike into irresistible positions of worldwide, ego-boosting power. Such positions are proffered by various quasi-secret international organizations. But, the controlling long-range plans and power are orchestrated by that handful of obscure Illuminati. Through such a system, the Illuminati could always maneuver influential leaders worldwide into creating conflicts that increasingly undermine nationalistic governments and organized religions.

Incompatible Dynamics

While discovering the Civilization of the Universe in 1992, the following was revealed: On the brink of victory, the Illuminati would catastrophically fail, resulting in the end of conscious life on planet Earth. For, parasitical humanoids and their institutions can never be eliminated from *within* their own creation — from within their closed-system anticivilization. Instead, those humanoids on the brink of defeat would devour the Illuminati and their organizations as explained later in this chapter.

By contrast, as revealed in *Zonpower*, the Civilization of the Universe provides an eternally open, evolving

313

system of advancing knowledge, value production, and prosperity that is totally independent of the anticivilization. When individuals begin functioning from the Civilization of the Universe now arising on planet Earth in cyberspace, the illusions of the anticivilization and the influences of its parasitical rulers simply vanish.

Thus, the Illuminati's goal can be fully achieved not by violently working within this unnatural anticivilization but by peacefully working from without — from the natural Civilization of the Universe. ...The Civilization of the Universe is a healthy business civilization void of poverty and violence — void of parasitical elites.

Credit for Zon and the Civilization of the Universe being able to embrace planet Earth and vanish the anticivilization by the turn of this century belongs to the Illuminati — to their two centuries of relentlessly undermining the destructive institutions of this anticivilization. Credit must go to the heroic "dirty work" done by men of productive accomplishments and moral responsibility from the 18th-century Adam Weishaupt to today's 20th-century David Rockefeller...and all the other unrecognized, low-profile Illuminati. For two centuries, they have brilliantly duped and poker played the parasitical-elite class into undermining its own institutions.

Eight decades ago, Einstein's open system of relativity physics jumped past Newton's brilliant, invaluable work within the closed system of classical physics. Both systems were dedicated to eliminating ignorance about physical reality. To advance into the future, however, Einstein's open system had to move past Newton's closed system.

Likewise, today, Zon's open-system Civilization of the Universe jumps past the Illuminati's brilliant, invaluable work on the closed-system anticivilization. Both works are dedicated to eliminating the deceptions supporting this anticivilization. To advance into the future, however, the open-system moral base of Zon must replace the closed-system moral base of the Illuminati.

The Illuminati Would Fail Without Zon

The Illuminati could not foresee the inevitable failure of their master plan. That failure would occur near their moment of victory: In the death throes of this anticivilization, its parasitical-elite rulers in a desperate attempt to survive would enter into a final feeding frenzy. They would devour the last seeds of human and financial capital needed for populations to exist and prosper.

Today, less-and-less earned wealth remains for the burgeoning parasitical-elite class to feed upon. When those last seeds of prosperity are devoured, even the Illuminati along with their master plan, their influential international organizations, and their noble goal would end in a suicidal, global Hitler-like debacle. For, with the essence of productive business gone, the Illuminati could no longer function. The anticivilization would then be primed for a new cycle of Hitlerian tyrants to arise — arise chaotically without the two-century-old restraints and controls of the Illuminati. Such uncontrolled humanoid rulers would drum-beat the world toward nuclear conflagrations, consuming nationality after nationality, race after race, population after population. ...The Illuminati's fatal flaw is their working *within* the closed-system anticivilization. They could not foresee that in the end they too would be devoured by the anticivilization.

Zon removes that fatal flaw to allow the successful conclusion of the Illuminati's master plan. ...Against the reality of Zon, the anticivilization with its parasitical rulers vanish in cyberspace.

Today, with the glimmerings of Zonpower rising from America's 1994 elections, the Illuminati are sensing the shift of their moral and operational base from the politicized anticivilization to the nonpolitical Civilization of the Universe.

The Wonderful World Ahead

Ahead lie limitless riches, romantic excitement, and eternal happiness for all conscious beings. Today, the Illuminati can finally vanish this moribund anticivilization. How? By using the glittering nonpolitical Civilization of the Universe as their new, limitless base of operations.

* * *

In the Civilization of the Universe, one asks not where another is from, but one asks what another does for a living...what one does to deliver needed, competitive values to others and society. Concepts of race, nationality, and religion are unknown in the Civilization of the Universe.

Objective Laws are Universal Laws

In the final analysis, all problems tie together to yield valid, effective solutions according to objective, universal laws that cannot be contradicted. Only objective laws are valid and apply to everyone, at all places, at all times. By definition, objective laws do not spring from the minds of men and women. Such laws have always and will always exist universally — independent of the human mind and its emotions. Thus, no objective law is new;

like the laws of physics, objective laws are valid in all frames of reference. Moreover, *no* law — physical, legal, or moral — is valid unless it is valid in all frames of reference.

The Protocols of Zon

The Illuminati's goal will now be peacefully, humanely completed through the protocols of Zon. Those omnipotent protocols arise from Cassandra's Secret. Around the turn of this millennium, the explicit, formal Zon Protocols will be published through the Internet for worldwide implementation. ...The nonviolent Zon Protocols will bring a nonpolitical business civilization to planet Earth.

New-Color Symphony
Movement #3

The Evolution of Neo-Tech

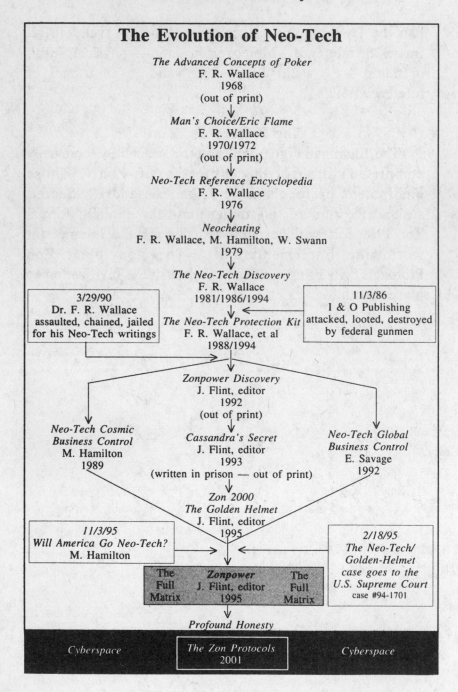

The Advanced Concepts of Poker
F. R. Wallace
1968
(out of print)

↓

Man's Choice/Eric Flame
F. R. Wallace
1970/1972
(out of print)

↓

Neo-Tech Reference Encyclopedia
F. R. Wallace
1976

↓

Neocheating
F. R. Wallace, M. Hamilton, W. Swann
1979

↓

The Neo-Tech Discovery
F. R. Wallace
1981/1986/1994

| 3/29/90 Dr. F. R. Wallace assaulted, chained, jailed for his Neo-Tech writings | *The Neo-Tech Protection Kit* F. R. Wallace, et al 1988/1994 | 11/3/86 I & O Publishing attacked, looted, destroyed by federal gunmen |

Zonpower Discovery
J. Flint, editor
1992
(out of print)

| *Neo-Tech Cosmic Business Control* M. Hamilton 1989 | *Cassandra's Secret* J. Flint, editor 1993 (written in prison — out of print) | *Neo-Tech Global Business Control* E. Savage 1992 |

Zon 2000
The Golden Helmet
J. Flint, editor
1995

| 11/3/95 *Will America Go Neo-Tech?* M. Hamilton | | 2/18/95 *The Neo-Tech/ Golden-Helmet case goes to the U.S. Supreme Court* case #94-1701 |

The Full Matrix   *Zonpower* J. Flint, editor 1995   The Full Matrix

↓

Profound Honesty

Cyberspace   *The Zon Protocols* 2001   *Cyberspace*

318

Chapter 36
The Zon Protocols

Most physicists, scientists, or physicians with vested interests in the anticivilization, such as tax-funded livelihoods, will resist identifying that human consciousness is the omnipotent force controlling existence.[1] Likewise, business people, professionals, or academics seeking praise and acceptance from within Earth's anticivilization must avoid grasping the wide-scope dynamics of Neo-Tech with its fully integrated honesty. But, those who integrate with *Zonpower* today or those who encounter the *Zon Protocols* at the end of this century can disconnect from Earth's anticivilization to gain Zonpower.

Without Zonpower, You are Trapped in an Anticivilization
With Zonpower, You Control Existence

Until the unveiling of Zonpower in June 1992, every conscious adult on planet Earth was imprisoned in its irrational civilization — a mortally destructive anticivilization. Through force and coercion, a dishonest parasite class has propagated an anticivilization around the globe. They continue propagating that anticivilization by deceptively, forcibly draining the productive class, especially the entrepreneur business class which is the source of all genuine jobs, prosperity, and happiness.

Without Zonpower, every conscious mind is imprisoned. Without Zonpower, no conscious mind is able to escape the products of an anticivilization: dishonesty, irrationality, destruction, death. The reason for that entrapment is that everyone is coerced from *every*

---

[1] As reviewed in Chapter 6, *The Long Wave*.

319

direction. And no conscious mind can think honestly, widely, or deeply under *any* form of coercion.

Most important, on trying to live by fully integrated honesty that is natural in the Civilization of the Universe, one will increasingly feel uncomfortable and anxious if his or her life remains invested in the anticivilization. Indeed, one cannot capture Zonpower while remaining invested in this unreal anticivilization.

Ironically, throughout history, only young children and certain schizophrenic savants have tasted Zonpower, albeit in narrow areas. What is meant by stating certain schizophrenics have tasted Zonpower? Do their experiences provide a hint of the undreamt power available to conscious beings not invested in this anticivilization? Consider the ancient oracles of Greece, including the most famous, the Oracle at Delphi. They had one common background: They all were naively honest, uneducated country girls who hallucinated as schizophrenics. None were invested in the anticivilization. Yet, kings as mighty as Alexander the Great, emperors, generals, lawmakers, and the wealthy regularly consulted and acted, often with spectacularly favorable results, on the uncanny, seemingly brilliant insights of those hallucinating women.

Consider Joan of Arc in the early 15th century. She too was a naively honest, uneducated country girl who hallucinated and was disconnected from society — disconnected from the sophistications of the anti-civilization. Yet, as a teenager, she became the premier military commander and war strategist in France. She delivered brilliant new insights into politics, warfare leadership, and battle tactics. Starting by liberating Orléans at 17 years old, she personally led France to key victories over the English invaders. She then provided the political strategy to restore Charles VII to the throne of France. ...At 19 years old, undermining the false power of the parasitical-elite class, she was politically imprisoned, tried by ego "justice", and then burned at the stake.

Why did those uneducated, illiterate women have insights beyond anyone else in areas of state and war? Because they were uneducated, poor, and disconnected from established society, their minds were disconnected from the integration-blocking dynamics of the anticivilization. In those areas, therefore, they were free to think more widely, without bounds...free to think with greater honesty.

In their areas of disconnection, they could gather wider ranges of integrations and insights than anyone connected to the anticivilization, including the greatest contemporary experts. Thus, the unblocked minds of those women could provide completely new and often more accurate perspectives of momentous events.

Consider the most powerful moral savant of Western Civilization: an uneducated, illiterate hippie who also hallucinated. He too was disconnected from the anticivilization of his day. Yet, that man held moral sway over the Western world for a hundred generations, right up to this day. That person was Jesus. He undermined the parasitical-elite class, was politically imprisoned, tried by ego "justice", and then crucified. ...Jesus' *earthly* moral principles are now yielding to the *universal* moral principles found in objective law and expressed by the forthcoming Zon Protocols.

Indeed, wide-scope thinking is impossible under coercion. That is why no one in this anticivilization can fully grasp the concept of integrated honesty to unleash Zonpower. *Any form of coercion generates an array of rationalizations that prevent the wide-scope, contextual thinking required for Zonpower.*

By disconnecting from *every* aspect of the coercive anticivilization, the conscious mind springs free from the anticivilization to gain Zonpower. With Zonpower, one controls existence through fully integrated honesty.

You

and the

Zon Protocols in Cyberspace

Through the Zon Protocols, you will live with ever increasing health, prosperity, and happiness. You will no longer need to invest in a corrupt anticivilization. You will live in the Civilization of the Universe. You will vanish the dishonesties, illusions, and nonrealties that today assault the mind and body of every conscious being on Earth. The anticivilization with all its coercions, harms, and diminishments will disappear. You will gain genuine power. You will gain Zonpower. You will control existence.

Today, you are unable to experience fully integrated honesty and wide-scope thinking. Today, you are bound within bubbles of mysticism, stunted by coercions, blocked by rationalizations in seeking acceptance from an irrational civilization ruled by parasitical elites. Thus, you will enter the *Zon Protocols* as a citizen of Earth's anticivilization created by criminal politics and morbid religions. ...But, you and everyone reading the forthcoming *Zon Protocols* will become a Citizen of the Universe. You will become Zon. You will be free of mysticisms and illusions — free of Earth's anticivilization. You will control existence through fully integrated honesty, boundless energy, and wide-scope thinking. **...You will gain the eternal prosperity and happiness available to all conscious life.**

Word Usage

Neo-Tech is a noun or an adjective meaning *fully integrated honesty* based on facts of reality. Neo-Tech creates a collection of *new techniques* or *new technology*[1] that lets one know exactly what is happening and what to do for gaining honest advantages in all situations. Neo-Tech provides the integrations in every situation to collapse the illusions, hoaxes, and all other forms of irrationality manipulated by the parasitical-elite class. ...Understanding *is* the process of honest integration.

Mysticism is action based on dishonest irrationalities and mind-created "realities". Mysticism evokes, accepts, or uses unreal notions that *create problems where none exist*. Contrary to popular belief, mysticism today seldom involves god-type religions or the occult. God religions and the occult are dying forms of mysticism with fading powers to hurt the productive class. More generally, mysticism is the dishonesty that evolves from using feelings or rationalizations to generate mind-created "realities". In turn, those "realities" create unnecessary problems and unnatural destructions. Unnecessary and unnatural because the human brain *cannot create* reality. Instead, the brain *perceives* and then *integrates* facts of reality in order to control reality.

Thus, "reality"-creating mysticism is a perversion or disease of human consciousness. Indeed, mysticism is the destruction disease. For mysticism blocks brain integrations to erode all values. Mysticism breeds dishonesty, malevolence, and death. Hence, mysticism is suicide on all levels — on personal, family, social, and business levels; on local, national, and world levels.

---

[1] New to the anticivilization, but normal to the Civilization of the Universe.

Neocheating is the undetected usurpation of a livelihood — the unsuspicious swindling of money, power, or values through clever manipulations of dishonest rationalizations, non sequiturs, and mystical notions. Neocheating means *new cheating* for usurping values earned by others. Actually, parasitical elites have used neocheating for two millennia in hidden, unnoticeable ways. But the *techniques* of neocheating were not specifically identified until 1976. Thus, neocheating is a *new identification* rather than a *new technique*. Before that identification, no one could define or even notice a neocheater. Now, anyone with Neo-Tech can easily spot neocheaters and render them impotent. For, against Neo-Tech, the illusions of mysticism vanish and neocheaters become powerless. ...Neocheaters are unnatural people. Some are humanoids.
   • The essence of Neo-Tech is honesty and effort.
   • The essence of mysticism and neocheating is hidden
     dishonesty and laziness.

NEO-TECH is rational. It lets one act consistently on objective *facts*. That approach yields beneficial emotions of happiness and love. Thus, Neo-Tech captures reality by having actions produce emotions. ...*Neo-Tech integrates the mind.*

MYSTICISM is irrational. It lets one act arbitrarily on subjective *feelings*. That approach yields harmful actions and spoils beneficial emotions. Thus, mysticism loses reality by having emotions produce actions. ...*Mysticism disintegrates the mind.*

Mysticism is the essential tool of all parasitical elites and neocheaters. But Neo-Tech will cure the disease of mysticism to end irrationality, dishonesty, neocheating, and the parasitical-elite class.

Neothink is the boundlessly wide integrations made possible by Neo-Tech eradicating irrationality. Neothink is the harnessing of Neo-Tech power here on Earth: *...Neothink outcompetes all, controls all.*

Integrated Thinking is the honest effort of putting information into the most accurate, widest context by logically connecting *all* known relevant facts. Only contextual knowledge is valid. Thus, genuine power is gained through integrated thinking, both vertical and horizontal, in the widest possible context. ...Volitional choice, the essence of free will, is also the essential of effective integrated thinking and valid knowledge building.

Justice is based on objective law and integrated honesty.

Ego "Justice" is based on arbitrary subjective laws and force-backed political agendas used to gain unearned livelihoods and feel false importance.

Parasitical Elites are unnatural people who dishonestly drain others. They have lost the attributes of human beings. They are humanoids who live by furtively usurping, swindling, or destroying values produced by others. To exist, they must prevent honest, integrated thinking by others. For survival, they depend on ego "justice" and force-backed political policies.

Criminal Minds: *"Others owe me a living. Thus, I can live by destroying, stealing, leeching, or usurping values earned by others."* ...Criminal minds lay the responsibility for competitive value production onto others. Such criminal minds epitomize politicians, business quislings,

325

also many bureaucrats, academics, clerics, news journalists, judges, and lawyers. For, their behaviors fit Dostoyevsky's *Crime and Punishment* definitive description of the criminal mind: 1) Unawareness of or contempt for individual property rights. 2) The presumption that parasites, usurpers, enviers, value destroyers, and con artists have a right to live off the productive efforts of others. ...Criminal minds exist by using deception or force to live off the productive class. Survival depends on fraud-driven or force-backed value destruction. Incompetence and unhappiness result.

Virtuous Minds: *"I must earn my own living. Thus, I must live through my own productive efforts. I must competitively create and produce values needed by others and society."* ...Such virtuous minds are the opposite of criminal minds. For, virtuous minds, by nature, respect individual property rights. Virtuous minds never need to use ego "justice", deception, fraud, or force to prosper. Survival depends on value production. Competence and happiness result.

Value Producers have business minds that benefit society. They live by creating or producing competitive values and productive jobs for others and society. They succeed by honest, integrated thinking.

Money: Is it wanted for laziness or effort? A criminal mind sees usurping money as a way to escape competitive efforts needed to produce values for others...a way to do less. A business mind sees earning money as a way to increase competitive efforts to produce ever more values and jobs...a way to do more for others and society.

Word Usage

Neo-Tech Minds are the powerful, mystic-free minds of the Civilization of the Universe...minds based on fully integrated honesty and justice.

Neo-Tech Business Minds easily outflank and outcompete the narrow thinking and dishonest behavior of all criminal and mystic-plagued minds.

Truth is a mushy, hydra-headed word. Everyone disputes its meaning. Truth denotes a <u>static</u> <u>assertion</u> that changes from person to person, opinion to opinion, culture to culture. Thus, *truth* is a hollow, manipulative word that parasitical elites promulgate to gain credibility for their deceptions, destructions, and ego "justice".

Honesty is a solid, indivisible word. No one disputes its meaning. Honesty denotes a <u>dynamic</u> <u>process</u> that is identical for every conscious being. *Honesty* cannot be manipulated. Therefore, parasitical elites must squelch honesty in order to live off the productive class.

*Discard the Word **Truth** —*
   *Uphold the Word **Honesty***
Discard Ego "Justice" —
   Uphold Objective Law
Discard the Parasitical Class —
   Uphold the Productive Class

The News-Media Establishment

vanishes in
Cyberspace

The news-media establishment must promote the political status quo as meaningful. Neo-Tech and Zon sweep away the political status quo as meaningless. The news-media establishment has little value in cyberspace and no value in the Civilization of the Universe.

5940

Cyberspace/Zon137=$hc/2\pi e^2$

330

Zonpower Index

337

Zonpower Index

Thermonuclear energy, 312
Thinkon, 38, 46, 92
Third Reich, 260
"Three Steps to Achieving Commercial Biological
    Immortality in Our Lifetime",70, 71, see also
    Biological immortality
Tiananmen Square, 258
Time, 4, 19, 49, 50, 88, 98
    dilation, 19-20, 46, 307
    eternal, 196, 197
    flow or arrow of, 58, 206
    of googol-year cycle, 73, 74
    as infinite, 53, 54, 63, 64
    knowledge as function of, 79, 80
    knowledge integrated with, 80, 81
    redefining of, 206
    travel, 277, 304, 306, 308
Toll-booth compassion, 185-186, 188
Tort law, 168
Trade, 107-111, 112
Transceivers, 277
Transcontinental railroads, 99-111
Trilateral Commission, 171, 173, 176, 180
Trojan-Horse Neo-Tech, 181
Truth, defined, 327
Twain, Mark, 226
T1–T2k, 90, 239, 240

– U –

UGU, see Universe-Containing Gravity Unit
Ultra-conservative media, 171
Uncertainties, 34
Uncertainty Principle of Heisenberg, 12
Unconquered honesty, 94
Understanding, 206, 207
Unemployment, 142, 143
Unified-Field Theory, 49
Union Pacific Railroad, 100-102
Universal communication, 199
Universal computer, 4, 79, 80
"Universal consciousness", 208
Universal constants and forces, 25, 30
Universal law, 290, 297, 317
Universal laws, 287
Universe-Containing Gravity Unit (UGU), 23-26
Universe(s), 3-6, 193, 194, 196, 197
    birth of, 14, 15
    business as power of, 9-12
    child of the, 151
    citizens of, 235
    Civilization of the, see Civilization of the Universe
    communication among, 5-10, 26
    compassion in, 236-238
    components of, 63, 64
    conscious beings throughout, 48, 72, 75, 86, 125
    consciousness compared to, 81-83
    Constitution of, 164
    creation of, 14, 15, 23-26, 85-86
    death of, 58
    destruction of, 76, 77

essence of, 222, 223
finite, 207
government of, 234
history of, 55, 56
honesty of, 235, 236
infinite number of, 14, 15
instant communication across, 5-10
man-made, 85-86
observation of, 62
origin of, 14, 15
religion of, 234, 236
super-fast growth of, 6-8
turning inside out of, 60-63
wave function of, 45
Upanishadic writings, 250, 251
Urban riots, 168
User fees, 188

– V –

Vacuums, 8, 32, 240
    false or quantum, 8, 96
Value-and-job producers, 20, 112, 113, 128, 129, 135,
    136, 141, 145, 147, 157, 218, 259, 260, 261, see also
    specific individuals by name
    archetypes of, 226
    call to revolution for, 165
    defined, 326
    demise of, 118
    draining of, 29
    examples of, 226
    Goy politics and, 186
    Illuminati and, 177-179
    immortality of, 280
    INS and, 121, 122, 124
    IRS and, 120-121, 133, 134
    religious-right as, 295-296
    ruining of, 312
    state of being of, 226
    survival of, 226
    Zon and, 288
    Zonpower and, 226
Value destroyers, 118, 119, 165, 167, 168, 210, 214,
    217, 218, 236, 258, see also Parasitical-elite class;
    specific individuals by name
    Golden Helmet and, 162, 163
    guilt of, 239
    power of, 227
    redemption of, 188
    subjective law and, 154, 155
    termination of, 159-161, 226, 231, 232
    Zonpower and, 224
Vatican, 13, 21
Vegetarianism, 292
Virgil, 260
Virtuous minds, 326
Vitality, 298
Vitamins, 292
Volitional choice, 325
Voltaire, ii, 202

343

Closing Ceremonies

"...Dreaming dreams no mortal ever dared to dream before."
Edgar Allan Poe
The Raven

Profound Honesty not only dreams such dreams, but makes those dreams become real to all mortals here on Earth.

Ride to Prosperity
in
Cyberspace

Neo-Tech Stimulants Underlie the Future

Stimulation is the most basic need for all life. For conscious life, stimulation underlies the drives for sex, identity, self-esteem, security, survival, and consciousness itself. Lose stimulation and conscious life is lost. Excitement is an outward expression of stimulation. Natural stimulation and excitement arise through efforts that produce ever greater values for self and others — values that let conscious life become increasingly prosperous. Stimulation can also arise unnaturally through irrational acts that harm self and others — destructive acts ranging from dishonest politics and criminal parasitism to promiscuous sex and drug abuse. Such unnatural stimulations always leave hangovers of value destruction, stagnation, anxiety, boredom, ill health. The more one depends on *unnatural* stimulation to survive, the more destructive that person becomes to self and others. By contrast, the more one achieves *natural* stimulation, the more valuable and exciting that person becomes to self and others. ...This Closing Ceremony shows how natural Neo-Tech stimulants in cyberspace will deliver prosperity and happiness to everyone.

Marsh Ward, working with the Washington DC Homeless Shelter, originated this stimulant concept. He is the innovator of "nongovernment drug therapy for the ghetto poor" — America's most effective drug-addiction cure.

Closing Ceremonies

Table Of Contents

Ending the Long Search

"I have long searched for the words to explain
the purposely destructive attacks by governments, religions, and their leaders on the essence
of human values — attacks on competitive
business, property rights, individual rights, fully
integrated honesty, objective law. What deep
anti-life disease warps the conscious mind to
cause such irrational actions? That disease is
not only the ultimate cause of all purposeful
harms and injustices inflicted on human beings,
but that disease ultimately brings decline,
stagnation, and death to all conscious beings on
Earth. ...Perhaps, in prison, I shall find those
words to explain what has never been explained."

Above were the words of Dr. Frank R. Wallace upon
entering federal prison on June 28, 1991. He was
imprisoned for writing, publishing, and billboarding about
the rising government violence against innocent value
producers. He was imprisoned for publicizing the rising
criminalities, including murders, by armed federal
bureaucrats. ...If Wallace had not been silenced in 1991,
perhaps the Waco and Oklahoma City murders would
never have occurred.

Now consider the words of President Clinton in 1995:

"There is nothing patriotic about hating your
government or pretending you can hate your
government but love your country".

The political desperado who uttered that statement to
condemn American citizens who morally resist rising
government tyranny placed himself among the despots of
history: Remember, despot King George III condemned
British citizens George Washington, John Adams, Thomas

1

Jefferson, James Madison for loving their country by morally resisting their government's rising tyranny. King George III hanged Nathan Hale ("I only regret that I have but one life to lose for my country") and would have hanged Washington, Adams, Jefferson, and Madison if captured by their government. And, remember, despot Santa Ana condemned and killed *Mexican citizens* Jim Bowie, David Crockett, and many others at the Alamo and elsewhere in Texas for loving their country by morally resisting their government's rising tyranny.

Remember, too, despot Adolf Hitler and his armed Gestapo bureaucrats murdered bands of heroic *German citizens* in the 1930s for loving their country by morally resisting their government's rising tyranny. Millions who loved their country were killed for hating and resisting Stalin's evil government. Thousands who love their country still rot and die in prisons for hating and resisting Castro's evil government.

Unless morally resisted by those who love their country, criminal-minded politicians and their armed bureaucrats will continue driving America toward tyranny, terrorism, riots, and lawlessness. ...Fully integrated honesty, which rules cyberspace, is morally resisting and will vanish such despots and tyranny not only in America but worldwide.

This document brings forth those long-sought-after words found by Dr. Wallace in prison. Those words finally bring understanding to 3000 years of incomprehensible attacks on competitive value production, property rights, individual rights, and fully integrated honesty.

This document identifies the deep anti-life disease that impels conscious minds to attack the essence of good. Most important, this document celebrates the cure to those irrationalities — a cure already being delivered by Neo-Tech stimulants in cyberspace. That cure is fully integrated honesty.

Curing the Criminal Mind

Can people perceive themselves as so important, so self-righteous that they believe their actions are above objective law? Are such people capable of remorselessly inflicting great harms even deaths upon the innocent, even entire populations? Examples abound in great literature and across history. From great literature arise the murderous minds of Homer's Odysseus and Dostoyevsky's Raskolnikov. And, across history arise the murderous minds of Caesar, Woodrow Wilson, Stalin, Mao, Castro...and currently the Clintons, O.J. Simpson, and "race-excused" criminals. They seemingly escape justice through the latent criminal mind buried in others — buried in everyone invested in this anticivilization. That pervasive criminal mind embedded at all levels of society allows such self-aggrandizing killers to inflict their harms against others without apology, without punishment, often without even rebuke. ...How can justice prevail? How can the criminal mind be cured?

Everyone from Ayn Rand to the Pope can and does rationalize away criminal-minded acts of themselves and others. Such acts, including murder, are rationalized given particular combinations of threats to that person's livelihood, ego, and survival in this irrational anticivilization. Some Nazi death-camp killers, for example, were refined university-educated scholars of Schiller and Goethe. Indeed, the anticivilization can activate a criminal mind in anyone, at any time. ...Everyone must try to deny integrated honesty in order

3

to protect his or her investments in this irrational civilization. But, ultimately, honesty cannot be denied.

In the rational Civilization of the Universe, self-destructions, criminal acts, and harmful rationalizations vanish. Integrated honesty is the gateway to the Civilization of the Universe. Indeed, integrated honesty ultimately eliminates all threats to one's livelihood and survival. Thus, through integrated honesty, the criminal mind with its rationalized injustices is cured.

That curing is already happening in cyberspace through Neo-Tech. ...Neo-Tech will *crush the evil*.

Écrasez l'infâme
Voltaire

Who Rules Cyberspace?

Happening Now In Cyberspace

on
World Wide Web Site
http://www.neo-tech.com/

Vaporizing Irrationality

Cyberspace Excitement

Throughout conscious existence on planet Earth flows an unbridgeable gulf separating dishonesty from honesty, irrationality from rationality, subjectivism from objectivism. Conscious beings today stand upon the shore awash with dishonesty, irrationality, subjectivism. Most are productive human beings, a few are parasitical humanoids. Some advance liberty, a few advance tyranny. All stand with their backs to the gulf. At first, none are aware of the approaching new paradigm for an eternally prosperous life.

Poised upon the lip of eternity, a few lift their heads to glimpse beyond the gulf. They see that new paradigm. They see a paradigm of integrated honesty that terminates the long train of illusions and investments throughout this moribund anticivilization. At first, rejection abounds. As the paradigm approaches, rejection turns to fear. For, that paradigm means the disappearance of government force that created a galaxy of parasitical livelihoods — livelihoods supported by dishonesty, irrationality, fraud, murder.

At the height of that fear, those irrational investments become worthless. As those life-long investments in beguilement evaporate, people will sublimate into an exciting, prosperous civilization of integrated honesty. ...That sublimation has already begun in cyberspace.

5

Closing Ceremonies

Vanishing Irrationality

Fully integrated honesty rules cyberspace because no one rules cyberspace. A paradoxical statement? Consider the following: Individual consciousness reigns supreme in cyberspace. Indeed, in cyberspace, harmful politicians, armed bureaucrats, ego judges, religious charlatans, dishonest journalists, and stagnant big-business executives have no control or power over individuals. Consider the harmful politicians who promote gun-backed laws to impose their whims in trying to control others. In cyberspace, destructive politicians are left impotent, thus harmless. They are simply flamed out of existence.

What will happen as individuals by the millions, then by the billons, move into cyberspace? In cyberspace, individuals function freely, voluntarily among themselves. No space, time, or cost boundaries exist in cyberspace. No legal, political, or religious boundaries exist. Thus, a natural dynamic develops in which the honest, the exciting, the valuable drive out the dishonest, the boring, the destructive.

By contrast, in the noncyberspace world ruled by political agendas, the honest and rational are often condemned or suppressed as politically incorrect or subjectively illegal. Also, in the noncyberspace world, the dishonest and irrational are often politically promoted, especially when backed by armed bureaucrats functioning as unpunished criminals. In the noncyberspace world, armed bureaucrats become dehumanized criminals who destroy innocent people's lives, values, and property.

In cyberspace, contextual facts vanish myths. Likewise, rationality vanishes irrationality: value vanishes disvalue, honesty vanishes dishonesty. The good drives out the bad, reality drives out mysticism, excitement drives out stagnation. Why? Because fully integrated honesty

6

rules in the freely competitive atmosphere of cyberspace. Thus, through cyberspace, a powerfully exciting, value-filled civilization will replace the dishonest, nihilistic anticivilization choking planet Earth today.

In cyberspace, each individual can freely communicate with any other individual, free of media dishonesty, free of destructive gun-backed political agendas, free of the irrational noncyberspace world. Today, the noncyberspace anticivilization is ruled by self-serving parasitical humanoids through their armed bureaucrats, sycophantic journalists, and hypocritical entertainers promoting various politically correct agendas. By contrast, the new cyberspace civilization spreading across the globe is free of such corruption. Thus, any cyberspace civilization is ultimately ruled by honest, value-producing individuals — just as are all advanced civilizations throughout the Universe.

The corrupt establishment media are irrelevant in cyberspace. No matter how articulately mendacious are *Washington Post* or *Newsweek* type journalists, their dishonesties have no power in cyberspace. The corrupt, deeply dishonest print-media and network news simply cannot compete in cyberspace. By contrast, *any* honest, articulate individual has limitless competitive power and relevance in cyberspace. For example, consider the most powerful person in the noncyberspace world: The articulate but pervasively dishonest President Clinton would have no chance hoaxing people in cyberspace, especially the articulate, honest individuals roaming the Internet. His lies and criminalities would be mercilessly exposed. He would then be flamed, skewered, and laughed off Usenet — the Internet newsgroups. That is why he and other harmful politicians dare not personally enter in the dynamics of cyberspace.

Those proclaiming authority by revelation, deception, or force have no power or influence in cyberspace. By contrast, in cyberspace, any individual can become powerful and influential by applying the dynamics of wide-scope, fully integrated honesty.

Below are examples of the *philosophical* and *physical* dynamics that operate together throughout cyberspace.

Philosophical Dynamics

Consider the following example: Two Newsgroups on the Internet embrace the identical philosophy with essentially no intellectual points of disagreement between them. Yet, profound spiritual differences exist: Newsgroup A is oriented around fully integrated honesty and the limitless power of conscious beings. Newsgroup B is oriented around a closed-system authority and the power of dead heroes and fictional characters. As a result, Newsgroup A expresses itself through active, forward-moving, competitive business modes. Newsgroup B expresses itself through passive, philosophizing, uncompetitive academic modes. What are the consequences?

Spiritual passions of Newsgroup A evolve around exciting, competitive value production. Spiritual passions of Newsgroup B evolve around stagnant, collective intellectualizing. Newsgroup A welcomes and profitably utilizes competitive encounters. Newsgroup B fears and dishonestly attacks competitive encounters. ...Newsgroup A represents open-ended growth. Newsgroup B represents close-ended stagnation.

Newsgroups A and B both uncompromisingly hold Objectivism as the proper philosophy for conscious beings. But, most in Group A are exciting and creatively alive, while many in Group B are boring and creatively dead. Newsgroup A holds, for example, dishonestly besmirched, unpopular mega value producers like Jay Gould and Michael Milken as real-life, heroic benefactors to all conscious beings. Newsgroup B holds popular but unreal, fictional characters like Howard Roark and John Galt as heroic idols. Newsgroup A actively sails forth into uncharted territories of future discovery. Newsgroup B passively remains anchored in safe harbors of the previously established.

Both Newsgroups are intellectually in debt to philosopher Ayn Rand. Group A gratefully utilizes her achievements while moving forward. Group B desperately idolizes her importance while clinging to the past. Group A utilizes the outstanding yet grossly under-recognized values constantly being produced by Ayn Rand's intellectual heir, Dr. Leonard Peikoff. Group B chains Dr. Peikoff within the shadow of Ayn Rand by minimizing or ignoring his continuous, commercial value production unmatched by all the other Objectivist "leaders" combined. Group A orients around time-efficient *aggressive objectivism* that will spread across cyberspace through real-life business dynamics. Group B orients around time-consuming *passive intellectualizing* that will stagnate into ever shrinking, closed circles. Group A works in the future; Group B dwells in the past.

In response to flame attacks, the following template was posted on both Newsgroups. That template demonstrates how the essence of Newsgroup A is attuned with cyberspace while the essence of Newsgroup B is ultimately incompatible with cyberspace:

Template Post
Objectivist Heroes
Pseudo objectivists frantically trying to flame the fully integrated honesty of Neo-Tech off the Internet anxiously flatter one another as Objectivist Heroes

---

9

defending the philosophy of Ayn Rand.

Thirty years ago those kinds of heroes were the desperate hangers-on in the Branden/Rand lectures in New York City. Back then, they were characterized by their cigarette holders emblazoned with dollar signs and swirling black capes. They were the sycophantic defenders of their ego facades leached from Ayn Rand's monumental achievement: Objectivism. Throughout the years, such Objectivists have remained the biggest impediment to advancing Objectivist philosophy around the world.

Today, those ersatz Objectivists are panicking. And why not? After 30 years of faking heroic Galtisms and shrugging Atlases, they are being revealed in cyberspace as contradictions to everything Objectivism means in living competitively, honestly, and happily through business-like modes. Similarly, in cyberspace, fully integrated honesty is exposing the fakeries and dishonesties of politicians and many government-dependent academics. ...Eventually, all such fakes will disappear as nothing in cyberspace.

Today, as back then, those pseudo Objectivists appear as sad, boring people. They are basically immature, kind of pitiful. Today, as back then, perhaps not a single, self-made businessperson or really successful entrepreneur exists among them. How many are really excited about what they do for a living? How many are genuinely proud of their competitiveness — of their value-producing competence? Most have no idea of the incredibly difficult journey required to independently produce long-range, competitive values and jobs for others. Ayn Rand knew. But, most of her dependent followers never knew.

Today, on the Internet, some of the most immature, dependent Randians seem to be on tax-paid academic edu lines, perhaps living off some kind of public funds with abundant idle time on their hands. They can never acknowledge the wide-scope Objectivist nature of fully integrated honesty. For, that wide-scope, active use of Objectivism through the competitive dynamics of Neo-Tech reveals stimulating powers — exciting powers possible for all conscious beings, Objectivists or not. Such competitive dynamics become illusion-collapsing threats to ego-dependent followers of Objectivism — especially those living stagnant lives that are going nowhere.

What are those "Objectivist Heroes" harping about? What do they do besides endlessly displaying philosophical "brilliance" while tearing down the practical, objective values of Neo-Tech? What do they do constructively? Have any of them ever made the excruciating effort or borne the racking pain oft required to do anything really important, to take big risks for big payoffs, to alone face down dangerous armed evil in the real world, or even to build and maintain a business that creates competitive values and jobs for others?

Many who attack fully integrated honesty are trying to inflate their shrunken self-perceived images by creating problems where none exist. One should always ask those who tear down values what they have done to make themselves proud of their lives — what they have done to build values — long-term competitive values for themselves, others, and society. Today, such people might be called wimps. Ayn Rand had a better word: pip-squeaks.

In reality, Objectivism never needs defending. Moreover, only commercially competitive efforts increase the permanent, long-range value of Objectivism to civilization. And finally, Neo-Tech has never attacked a single tenet of Objectivism. Instead, Neo-Tech vigorously applies and commercially advances every tenet of Objectivism throughout the world.

By contrast, those ego-seeking pontificators of Objectivism unnecessarily waste their lives on nothing much. Most will never discover their exciting, glorious potential in the value-producing business dynamics throughout cyberspace. ...Yet, the helping hand of Neo-Tech is always extended. Still, from

11

Closing Ceremonies

Neo-Tech, no leader, guru, or authority is available for anyone to follow or obey. Only fully integrated honesty with its wide-scope integrations is available for all to understand, use, and produce prosperity.

The contributors to Neo-Tech integrations, not the flamers of Neo-Tech, are genuine Objectivists. Only through Neo-Tech business modes is Objectivism pushed forward, into the competitive market place, bringing integrated honesty and exciting Objectivism to the general public worldwide.

Maturing into an Objectivist

Some supporters of Objectivism are like Moliére's Tartuffe with his hypocritical piety. Or, perhaps they are more like Moliére's Alceste in *The Misanthrope* who rants and rails, neither delivering much of value to anyone nor improving much of anything. Such people ignorantly bluster about things, situations, and people they do not understand. Such people deliver only the narrow-scope nothingness of an ego-tripping Alceste. ...But, many could mature into the everythingness of a Defoe's do-everything Robinson Crusoe, or at least the somethingness of a go-getter Moll Flanders.

Not to be an Alceste takes some brain, mouth, and keyboard responsibility. Discipline is required to deal contextually with reality from the widest perspectives. Indeed, learning to work tolerantly, efficiently, profitably with problems, situations, and people while remaining uncompromising on principles is hard work. To produce competitive values for the world takes constant discipline, thought, and control combined with fully integrated honesty. ...It takes Neo-Tech.

The above template shows *why* fully integrated honesty rules cyberspace from the philosophical perspective. The following example shows *how* fully integrated honesty rules cyberspace from the physical perspective.

Physical Dynamics

Two approaches to the physical world embrace the identical laws of physics with no scientific points of disagreement: Approach A is oriented around objective, conscious *entities*[1] utilizing fully integrated honesty. Approach B is oriented around objective, nonconscious entities determined by peer approval. As a result, Approach A rapidly advances in a wide-scope integration mode. Approach B, gradually advances in specialized academic modes.

Approaches A and B both utilize the scientific method of validation. But, Approach A relies on fully integrated honesty while Approach B relies on establishment peer review.

Both approaches uncompromisingly correspond to and abide by the laws of physics. Yet, Approach A integrates unrestricted panoramas of knowledge, while Approach B focuses on specialized areas of knowledge. Approach A welcomes competitive encounters that would change the status quo. Approach B resists competitive encounters that would change the status quo.

The essence of Approach A is attuned with existence. Thus, Approach A will create stimulating new knowledge and lead this world into fully integrated honesty — into the Civilization of the Universe. By contrast, the essence of Approach B is chained to Establishment stagnation, always remaining in the background of history.

Utilized throughout history by only a tiny fraction of

---

[1]Consciousness itself is *not* a primary of existence. Both Approach A and Approach B are based on objective reality being the primary of existence. But, most philosophers from Plato to Kant erroneously consider consciousness as a primary of existence. Aristotle and Ayn Rand are the two major exceptions who were free from that profound error. They recognized the primacy of existence and rejected the primacy of consciousness.

Closing Ceremonies

Closing Ceremonies

scientists, Approach A has yielded essentially every major breakthrough in science and technology since Democritus, 2500 years ago, proffered his theory of atoms as the primary units of existence. In contrast, Approach B has been utilized throughout history by a vast majority of scientists. Approach B solidifies and eventually moves forward those radical breakthroughs that are scientifically valid. ...Both approaches advance science. Yet, almost all individuals among that vast majority following Approach B protect their status-quo positions by initially attacking every valid breakthrough by those rare individuals utilizing Approach A.

Consider the physics and philosophy derived from Approach A and described in Movement 1 of the New-Color Symphony: Both the physics and philosophy of Zonpower are without known contradictions. Still, *Zonpower from Cyberspace* is not about physics or philosophy. It is about the application of fully integrated honesty to objective reality. The resulting wide-scope integrations will eventually bring eternal life with limitless prosperity to all conscious beings. While perhaps ahead of their time, speculative hypotheses are proffered in *Zonpower from Cyberspace* as metaphors. Yet, all the hypotheses correspond to the laws of physics as well as to objective reality...and all are open to experimental verification or falsification.

The following example involves the interaction of an industrial research chemist, Dr. Higgs Field, utilizing competitive business-funded Approach A versus an academic astrophysicist, Professor Edu from a Big-Ten University, utilizing noncompetitive tax-funded Approach B. Dr. Edu publishes in prestigious peer-review journals, such as the *Astrophysical Journal* and *Reviews of Modern Physics*. He also participates in international peer-review astrophysical symposiums such as the June 1995 symposium in Brussels, Belgium.

After selecting one of the more radical chapters in the on-line version of *Zonpower from Cyberspace*, Professor Edu published a review of it on the Internet. Had Dr. Edu carefully read *Neo-Tech Physics* in full context, he could have saved himself the embarrassment of publishing the following seven-point review:

Quote

1. To learn what a smart astrophysicist I am, or am not, I'd suggest reading the *Astrophysical Journal* or *Reviews of Modern Physics*, where I have published papers. I'd be glad to send you reprints. I've been asked to evaluate the physics in Zonpower. I have picked a couple of examples from Chapter 5 of the electronic version that I hope illustrate the problem. In this chapter we read..."Take two cannonballs of identical size, one made of solid iron, the other of solid aluminum. Why does the iron ball weigh about twice that of the aluminum ball of the same size?"

Most physicists would say that iron has more protons and neutrons in its nucleus than aluminum does; thus there are "more particles" in a given volume of iron than aluminum. This has <u>nothing</u> to do with "conscious-controlled geometries" which are listed as the explanation. The author claims that without them we would expect both balls to have the same weight because they have the same volume. Why should different numbers of particles in the same volume have the same weight? This reflects misunderstanding of physics at a basic level.

2. By the way, the explanation in a footnote of "Gravity Units" is just plain bizarre, and apparently contradicts General Relativity.

15

3. In this chapter there is a persistent confusion between mass and weight; we read, for instance, that energy is "weightless". Given the equivalence between mass and energy, this is simply false. I can collide two energetic photons and produce particle-antiparticle pairs; this happens all the time in accelerators. Gravitational redshifts have been measured; photons <u>do</u> respond to gravity. The author's arguments would seem to contradict this, and thus be falsified.

4. As an experiment, the author (PhD in what? "Science"?) proposes that in a stadium with 100,000 people one should 1) emit a pulse of light; 2) measure radio waves coming from buttons that people push when they see the light. The pattern that emerges is then claimed to be proof that "conscious quanta as an integral part of a fixed existence field". Huh? This sounds like a good way to measure reaction time, and nothing else.

5. By the way, the speed of the Earth around the Sun is <u>not</u> 0.01 of the speed of light, which is claimed in the text! When I see the orbital speed of the Earth off by a factor of 100, I conclude that the author is sloppy.

6. This experiment sounds like a muddled attempt at the Michelson-Morely experiment, which did not detect the motion of the Earth through the ether. But wait...the authors claim that the M-M experiment failed because the signals measured in that famous experiment were photons of light, which are not "intrinsic to the existence field". ($E=mc^2$, anyone?) Sorry, but the radio waves used in the Neo-Tech experiment are photons too. The author is apparently unaware of this, and it invalidates the entire experiment. This is basic physics, which I teach in my

introductory astronomy class. To make new theories in a field, you need some knowledge that goes beyond popular books on the subject.

7. We then hear of a new particle, called a "thinkon". When particle physicists invent a new particle, they estimate its basic properties: mass, charge, spin, its cross-section for interaction, and so on. How many thinkons are there near the Earth? No answers here, and none will be forthcoming.

End Quote

By reading that chapter on Neo-Tech physics in context with the other chapters and footnotes in *Zonpower*, one discovers the following answers to each of Professor Edu's seven objections:

1) Dr. Edu starts by opining his misunderstanding of weight relative to Gravity Units. The entire concept of weight involves the Gravity-Unit geometries mathematically interacting with matter geometries — independent of conscious actions. Consider the analogy that compares the "volume" of cannonballs to the "volume" of quarks or electrons: Volume, of course, does not explain weight. But neither does mass. In seeking the most-fundamental concept of weight, all volume/mass energy unit quantities such as cannonballs, quarks, electrons, and photons are stripped away. Conceptually replacing volume/mass/energy units with the new concept of interacting geometries lets one reach the most-basic understanding of weight. That understanding corresponds to the laws of physics. Moreover, the resulting hypothesis offers experimental ways to verify or falsify the hypothesized Gravity Units.

2) By taking one footnote out of context, Dr. Edu uses a single assertion to dismiss the well-defined concept of Gravity Units developed throughout the document. He offers not a single specific fact as to why Gravity Units contradict General Relativity[1], which they do not. Dr. Edu's approach, of course, would prevent one from examining any radically new but valid concept. Such an approach guarantees continued stagnation for its practitioners.

3) No disagreement exists with the physics stated by Dr. Edu. What is not understood by Dr. Edu is the subtle difference of nonfundamental *created* mass vis-a-vis the fundamental *noncreated* Gravity Unit, which exists as an *ether* in a weight mode or in a weightless mode. ...Thus, again, Dr. Edu's objections are little more than naive, non-sequitur statements about basic physics. Such statements have nothing to do with the concepts presented.

4) Perhaps excused by not being an experimental scientist, Dr. Edu reveals his misunderstanding of the Stadium Experiment. How could he or anyone understand that experiment if viewed so out of context. Contrary to Dr. Edu's claims, this experiment has nothing to do with human reaction times or radio waves. By carefully reading the Stadium Experiment, one finds that it is explicitly designed to eliminate — wash out — the differences in human reaction times. That wash out is accomplished by the 100,000 people times the 50 flashes of light to give an overwhelming 5,000,000 pieces of data in the few minutes of the experiment. With that huge number of separate measurements, human reaction times become a self-canceling variable arising from the tools used to measure the effects of special relativity on the hypothesized "thinkons".

---

[1]General Relativity: "*all* laws of physics hold in *all* frames of references" — that is the essence of Einstein's Theory of Gravity. ...Special Relativity applies to frames moving at constant speeds in which space and time change to keep the laws of physics constant.

Cyberspace Vaporizes Irrationality

As Dr. Edu properly indicates in a later review, a straight comparison of the speed of light versus the five-million pieces of data requires more preciseness by several orders of magnitude to detect the sought effect. But, the experiment is enhanced by the sought-after particle *not* being at rest, but traveling at 67,000 mph relative to the Sun or 0.0001 the speed of light, thus, reducing the preciseness needed to detect the hypothesized particle by several orders of magnitude. The sought effect is further enhanced and then detected through diffraction-pattern, computer/trigonometric analyses that trace secondary changes in statistical data. Even greater accuracies could be achieved if the particles could be measured at much greater speeds as relative, for example, to other entities in our galaxy...or to the entire expanding universe and beyond.[1]

The Stadium Experiment and the other proposed experiments are sound in principle. They are explicitly designed to support or refute the hypothesis of thinkons. What more could a scientist ask for in examining a speculative hypothesis posited for metaphorical purposes?

5) Indeed, as Dr. Edu states, the orbital speed of Earth is not 0.01 the speed of light. Dr. Edu was off in his criticism by a hundred fold in wrongly accusing the author of carelessness. Had Dr. Edu been less careless in reading *Neo-Tech Physics*, he would have seen the figure stated was 0.01% (not 0.01), which is 0.0001 the speed of light — a figure that both Dr. Field and Dr. Edu agree is correct.

6) Dr. Edu combines the citations about the Michelson-Morely (M-M) experiment with his own interjections about radio waves being photons. While correct, his interjections

[1]See pages 42-46 of the New-Color Symphony, especially the footnote on page 44, for further understandings of this experiment.

19

have nothing to do with the experiment. Through such non-sequitur interjections, Dr. Edu reveals not even a cursory understanding of the Stadium Experiment. ...Incidentally, the M-M experiment was based on movement relative to the sun.

7) Dr. Edu dismisses the quantized thinkon particle without identifying a single contradiction to the laws of physics. Instead, he evokes non-sequitur statements about the physical properties of particles and the number of "thinkons" near Earth. His statement has no meaning regarding the hypothesis advanced and the experiments proposed for detecting thinkons.

In cyberspace, fully integrated honesty will vanish bogus biases and arrogant "authorities" used to protect the status quo. The above example is not meant to insult or criticize Dr. Edu, but is meant to help him and others in tenured academic professions by shaking them from their stagnation traps and moving them into competitive, new ways of thinking that will let them deliver much greater values to themselves, others, and society.

Neo-Tech Physics will bring an Objectivist Civilization

By evading the context of Neo-Tech Physics and the purpose of Zonpower, one can isolate almost any sentence or paragraph and attack it. Responding to such out-of-context attacks generally would (1) be futile, (2) encourage ever more such erroneous attacks, and (3) become so time consuming as to retard progress toward curing irrationality.

Consider the following four points:

1. *Zonpower from Cyberspace* is not a treatise on philosophy or physics. Zonpower is *metaphorically* presented for the general public to gain much wider, more

valuable perspectives of objective reality.

2. Neo-Tech Physics comprises a set of speculative hypotheses, none of which contradict the laws of physics or nature. Those hypotheses serve as metaphors needed to introduce a radical paradigm of widest scope thinking about conscious life, civilization, and the universe.

3. Those metaphorical hypotheses sweep across the entire thirty-six chapters of *Zonpower from Cyberspace*, uniquely integrating widely diverse areas of cosmology, physics, and conscious minds never before linked together.

4. The purpose of Zonpower and Neo-Tech Physics is to provide new ways to view conscious life and everyone's relationship to existence — mind-boggling new perspectives that eventually will eradicate irrationality and dishonesty from cyberspace and then the world.

Fully Integrated Honesty Rules Cyberspace

Cyberspace is free of initiatory force, politicians, and their gun-backed bureaucrats. Thus, honesty ultimately rules in cyberspace.

Genuine power and success in conscious life arises through fully integrated honesty or thinking. That sounds simple enough, but its dynamic involves a totally different way to use the conscious mind — a way never before utilized by conscious beings on planet Earth. Yet, wide-scope, fully integrated thinking is the modus operandi for competitive beings in advanced civilizations throughout existence. Indeed, any normal conscious being on Earth today has the capacity to think with wide-scope, integrated honesty. But, first, each person must break from the closed-circle, non-contextual thinking processes that have imprisoned virtually every conscious mind on Earth for 2500 years.

Breaking out of that prison to acquire omnipotent control over existence within the laws of physics requires conscious action. That action, in turn, involves fully integrated honesty acting from an Objectivist-based philosophy anchored in factual reality — *not* from conscious subjectivisms floating in mind-created "realities".

The ingredients for that omnipotent control are identified in the (1) wide-scope, *objective-action* mode of the Neo-Tech literature, including the business modes identified by Mark Hamilton and Eric Savage, and in (2) the *integrated-honesty* mode of the Zonpower literature. In cyberspace, the tools of Neo-Tech and Zonpower will become available to and then implemented by all competitive individuals in America and throughout the world.

New Paradigm for the Conscious Mind

As described in Chapter 28 of the New-World Symphony, about 3000 years ago, an entirely new paradigm for human thinking was invented. That new paradigm arose out of necessity — out of chaos as civilizations based on man's nature-given animal mind began collapsing into ruin. Populations of those civilizations sharply contracted. Man's nature-given, unconscious bicameral mind was too inadequate to survive. Those who did survive invented a new way to use their minds. They discovered not only self-awareness and introspection, but they discovered (1) the use of metaphors to expand mind space, (2) a sense of individual responsibility, and (3) a sense of right and wrong. ...They invented a survival tool more powerful than anything nature alone could offer or develop. *They invented human consciousness*. That invention was necessary to develop modern man and modern societies.

Today, civilization on planet Earth is again moving toward chaos and destruction. Thus far in the 20th century, governments have murdered more innocent people — about 170 million — and criminally destroyed more property than all governments and all criminals in all previous recorded history combined. The final wave of destruction awaits as thermonuclear and biochemical[1] warfares are poised to strike. Indeed, without the fully integrated honesty of Neo-Tech, the conscious mind on Earth today cannot handle modern-day human survival.

In 1976, the first inkling of an exciting, totally new format or paradigm for the conscious mind surfaced. That budding paradigm called "Neothink" was based on wide-scope, fully integrated honesty. Neothink is a radical break from the narrow-scope, manipulative *truth-based* conscious mind of the past 3000 years. The *honesty-based* Neothink mind breaks from the closed-circle stagnation of

---

[1]For example, an estimated 8-ounces of botulinal toxin could kill every person on Earth.

an anticivilization. By contrast, in an open-ended Neothink-based civilization, the diseases of dishonesty and irrationality do not exist. ...Limitless excitement, stimulation, prosperity, and happiness are the natural consequences of the Neothink mind.

The Neothink mind is as radical a break from the man-discovered consciousness mind as was the conscious mind a radical break from the nature-provided bicameral or schizophrenic mind 3000 years ago.

The Goal of Neo-Tech/Zonpower

The entire purpose and goal of Neo-Tech/Zonpower is to have conscious individuals think about and see civilization in a different way — in a way completely different from the losing paradigm that has harmed and killed every conscious being on this planet for the past 3000 years. Indeed, Neo-Tech/Zonpower is a stimulating new way of thinking, an exciting new way of seeing everything, a powerful new mode of action that leads to beneficent control over existence within the laws of nature.

Neo-Tech/Zonpower has no leaders or followers. Throughout cyberspace, every conscious individual will increasingly become individual self-leaders living in ever more exciting, value-producing business modes. ...The *individualistic* Neo-Tech mentality is the antithesis of today's *collectivist* big-government, religious, one-world, nationalistic, militia, new-age, patriot, tribal, and cult mentalities.

Universal Excitement and Prosperity

The Appendix at the end of this manuscript provides the practical, Golden-Helmet dynamics for limitless prosperity. That Appendix also provides a real-life drama involving armed bureaucrats wreaking murderous destructions on the means of value production in the noncyberspace world. That drama includes live-action, guns-and-fists attacks on Neo-Tech by armed bureaucrats and political imprisonments by life-appointed federal judges acting as robed prosecutors enforcing political and ego agendas.

Indeed, those bureaucrats and judges enforce political/ ego agendas designed to support an ever expanding parasitical superstructure of stagnation. That superstructure consists of self-aggrandizing politicians, wealth-draining government jobs, white-collar-hoax business executives, life-draining welfare dependents, unearned government subsidies, bankrupt social-security Ponzi schemes, and fraudulent government health-care plans.

The Golden-Helmet dynamics reveal the lethal destructiveness of armed bureaucracies — armed agents of force that are fomenting the rising crime, violence, and terrorism in America. Those armed agents are found in the IRS. They are also found in gun-backed bureaucracies such as the ATF, FDA, INS. The rubric "jackbooted thugs" *is* the most honest, accurate metaphor for many federal armed agents, despite the non-sequitur, poison-ear blatherings by politicians, bureaucrats, and journalists. Indeed, dehumanized armed automatons are needed to enforce criminal agendas for politicians, bureaucrats, and judges. Such tax-paid criminalities permeate the federal government today to increasingly undermine security and prosperity in America. ...After reading the live-action IRS Abuse Reports in the following Appendix, no one will

25

hold doubts that the above facts will eventually bring a violent revolution to America unless that trend is reversed by Neo-Tech and the Golden Helmet.

Neo-Tech Protects Politicians
along with
Federal Workers
from
Violence

Would Thomas Jefferson have approved of deposing Clinton-like politicians along with other federal employees who are tyrannically pushing power and control over every productive American citizen? The answer is not only a resounding "yes", but the deposers would have been celebrated as heroes by America's founding fathers.

Algernon Sidney, a prominent English writer, in his famous *Discourses Concerning Government* published in 1698, provided the legal and moral basis for deposing kings or tyrants who looted and killed innocent citizens, leaving those victims with no recourse to justice.

America's founding fathers, especially Thomas Jefferson, the author of the Declaration of Independence and America's third President, were profoundly influenced by Algernon Sidney, even more than they were influenced by the English philosopher John Locke.[1] Indeed, the Declaration of Independence used Sidney's work to specifically spell out the conditions and moral obligations to depose those who advance despotism:

> "When in the Course of human events, it becomes necessary for one people to dissolve the political bands which have connected them with another...that they should declare the causes which impel them to the separation.

---

[1]Thomas Paine's *Common Sense* finally galvanized Americans to action against tyrants. Few Americans thought of gaining independence from tyrannical England before the publication of *Common Sense* in January 1776. Only six months later, on July 4, 1776, the Declaration of Independence had been written and signed. ...Nearly 300,000 copies of *Common Sense* were sold to spark the American revolution. That number equals about 20 million copies sold into today's population of America.

"We hold these truths to be self-evident, that all men are created equal, that they are endowed by their Creator with certain unalienable Rights, that among these are Life, Liberty and the pursuit of Happiness. That to secure these rights, Governments are instituted among Men, deriving their just powers from the consent of the governed. That whenever any Form of Government becomes destructive of these ends it is the Right of the People to alter or to abolish it, and to institute new Government, laying its foundation on such principles and organizing its powers in such form, as to them shall seem most likely to effect their Safety and Happiness. ...But when a long train of abuses and usurpations, pursuing invariably the same Object evinces a design to reduce them under absolute Despotism, it is their right, it is their duty, to throw off such Governments, and to provide new Guards for their future security."

These are dangerous times for despotic politicians and their armed agents of force. Political unrest is surfacing. Individual stagnation is ending. The American public is demanding that politicians with their armed agents of force be held accountable for their actions. What can stop the rising violence caused by expanding despotism designed to counter this individual awakening? Neo-Tech, which means fully integrated honesty, will stop that violence. Indeed, Neo-Tech is now spreading through cyberspace. The essences of Neo-Tech are rising — the essences of civility, self-control, and respect for objective law. Thus, through Neo-Tech in cyberspace, despotic politicians, their armed bureaucrats, and stagnant corporate leaders will lose their parasitical livelihoods...not their lives.

GREATNESS

PART I

The Greatest Human Spirits
are always attacked by
The Smallest Human Spirits

What is the greatest? What is the smallest? First the smallest: As a law of nature, everything in existence can be reduced to a smallest unit or quantum — be it an electron or quark for mass or a photon for energy. Beneath mass and energy lie resonating strings with dimensions less than 10^{-35} meters. Those strings create spacetime mass, energy, and consciousness. Beneath those dimensions lie an ether of hypothetical Gravity Units that form a universal sea of eternal geometries. ...Somewhat analogously, the human spirit can also be reduced to a smallest unit or dot. The next step down is not to a smaller dot; the next step down is to nothing...except that universal sea of geometries.

Now, consider life itself. Consider that viruses and bacteria are among the smallest, simplest forms of life. Yet, those smallest forms of life can and do destroy the most complex, most valuable forms of life — conscious human beings. A similar parallel exists with the human spirit. The smallest, most malevolent spirits can and do destroy the greatest, most benevolent spirits.

Those smallest spirits are the self-proclaimed "victims" of this world. *They create problems where none exist.* Such "victims" can destroy all that is valuable to human life. By contrast, genuine victims are those whose lives are diminished through force or fraud by governments, religions, criminals. But, self-proclaimed "victims" are those who diminish their *own* lives by blaming the value producer for their own self-made problems.

29

A close cousin of the self-proclaimed "victim" is the "pip". A pip is also a small, diminished human spirit who creates problems where none exist. The pip generally tries to build a pseudo self-esteem and often a bogus livelihood at the expense of genuine value producers, especially businesspeople, employers, entrepreneurs. Pips try to feel morally or intellectually superior by berating great values and their creative producers. Pips attack with dishonest, out-of-context criticisms and non sequitur accusations. ...Great value producers, especially in business, are constantly attacked by the pips in political, journalistic, academic, and entertainment circles designed to conserve the stagnating Establishment.

To understand those smallest spirits and their destructiveness, one must first recognize the greatest human spirits and how they lift humanity to ever greater heights of stimulating well being.

* * *

Simone de Beauvoir, in her famous 1949 book *The Second Sex*, described how women were stagnated both in spirit and as human beings through force-backed governments and fraudulent religions. Through the centuries, destructive political/ego agendas have resulted in irrational laws and oppressive cultures.

Women, and men too, are victimized by force and fraud exercised through governments and religions. Yet, through the free-enterprise dynamics arising over the past two centuries, individual choice and actions increasingly determine the success of women — and of men. Perhaps the premier example for either sex in this century is Ayn Rand who arose to become one of the most exciting, influential value producers in history.

Ms. Beauvoir also declared in her book that of the giants in human history who took the responsibility to change the course of civilization, none were women. Indeed, no woman, except possibly Joan of Arc and Queen Elizabeth I, had ever taken the responsibility of changing civilization — until Ayn Rand. Regardless of what she might have claimed, Ms. Rand did take that responsibility, perhaps more than any man had ever done. And, in time, she will be recognized as a giant among giants in history who changed civilization on Earth dramatically for the better.

Ayn Rand rose by fiercely struggling to escape the bloodiest, most oppressive cult in history — Communism under Lenin and Stalin in the Soviet Union. Then, emigrating to relatively free-enterprise America, Ayn Rand, by her own decisions and titanic efforts, broke through seemingly impossible language, economic, and cultural barriers in rising to the highest level of literary accomplishment. She then arose atop the pinnacle field of knowledge — philosophy — which, until Rand, had been dominated for 2500 years exclusively by men. Thus, as is being increasingly recognized today, Ayn Rand is posthumously becoming one of the most stimulating benefactors to grace planet Earth. Yet, she was and is still today attacked and ridiculed by nearly the entire panoply of stagnant Establishment elites with their arrays of self-proclaiming authorities, "victims", and pips. ...In fighting for her values and achievements, Ayn Rand always dismissed such persons as boring pip-squeaks not worth a moment of anyone's time.

31

Other exciting great spirits include Joseph Smith (the super-competitive Mormon business-and-city builder), Andrew Carnegie, Jay Gould, Florence Nightingale, John D. Rockefeller, Henry Ford, Ray Kroc, Mary Kay, Michael Milken, Leona Helmsley. Many were vilified and drained by political demagogues and self-proclaimed "victims". All such great spirits are harmed by, destroyed by, or killed by the Establishment wielding its "victim" and pip tools.

Consider another example involving the greatness of human spirit: Year after year in the 1940s and 1950s, the giant chemical firm, E.I. du Pont de Nemours, Inc., was rated by business publications as the best managed company in the world with a consistent 20%+ annual return on investment. Through decades of unmatched success, Du Pont became the largest, most exciting company in the world. Then, latching onto the envious attacks by whining business "victims" and pips, the Federal Government penalized Du Pont for its success by forcing the company to terminate its ownership of General Motors.

Du Pont rose from its inception in 1802 as a family-managed explosives and gunpowder manufacturer to become the premier research and industrial company in the world, delivering huge values to society. Du Pont's ever increasing rate of success peaked in the late 1940s with the last du Pont family member in control: Pierre S. du Pont, one of history's most emulated businessmen. His revolutionary decentralized management concepts and accounting methods remain the essence of essentially all successfully managed, large corporations to this day. The stimulating benefits that the Du Pont Company bestowed on the business world, on its customers, and on its employees were not only without match, but served as a farsighted model for all successful, big businesses.

Du Pont was the innovator and leader not only in competitively producing invaluable products for society but in pioneering for its employees various safety and pension plans, medical insurance, stock-and-saving plans, even alcohol-and-drug treatment programs long before most other companies even conceived of such sound business practices. Never was a company more helpful to the business world, more valuable to customers, more beneficial to employees. And, never did a giant company struggle as hard to avoid stagnating government contracts and favors as did Du Pont when it was managed by Pierre S. du Pont.

Du Pont began declining from its pinnacle business position in the 1950s when, through the envious dynamics of self-proclaimed "victims", a wave of asset-milking executives took control from the asset-building du Pont family. Those asset-milking executives did not care what happened to the business after their tenure. They did not plan 50 and 100 years ahead as the generational-planning executives had done since the founding of Du Pont in 1802. Indeed, after P.S. du Pont, waves of self-aggrandizing political executives milked the previous 150 years of du Pont-built assets. ...Such asset-milking executives work only for their short-term personal wealth, power, and status.

Adopting the John Maynard Keynes evil concept "In the long run, we are all dead", such political-type executives are not concerned about the future health of their companies, their employees, or society. Implementing asset destroying policies, they ignore the consequences on the future of their company and society.

33

Like their sole-mate politicians, the real harm of their self-serving agendas become obvious only after they are gone.

As a modern example, consider how the ego-driven, political-ingratiating John Scully crumbled the potential for long-term world dominance of Apple Computer by making his short-term profit performance look good to others, especially to politicians, the media, and celebrities. As a political-agenda CEO, he betrayed the long-term goals of Apple founders Steven Jobs and Stephen Wozniak. Such political executives like Scully, through their own short-sighted agendas, implicitly sanction unjust attacks and torts by business/employee "victims" against the greatest, most beneficent business enterprises. ...Those self-proclaimed "victims" manipulated by politicians, lawyers, and journalists sow the cancer seeds that eventually cripple or destroy genuine competition — the most aggressive value-and-job producers and their businesses.

Why does acting as a "victim" or pip shrink one's spirit to the smallest unit — to the shallowest level of a human being? How can such shallow people be the prime destructive force in today's civilization? And, specifically, how will Neo-Tech in cyberspace vanish such "victim"-like viruses and pip-like bacteria? The answers to those questions are found in Part II of GREATNESS, starting on the next page.

Part II gives four specific examples of horrendous destructions done to the greatest lives by parasitical-elite humanoids with their manipulations of "victims" and pips. Part II then demonstrates how cyberspace will end such life-draining dynamics. ...The four examples with one solution are:

The Marx/Lenin/Business/"Victim" Example
The Hitler/Jew/"Victim" Example
The Giuliani/Media/Michael Milken/"Victim" Example
The Giuliani/Media/Leona Helmsley/"Victim" Example
and then
The Neo-Tech/"Victim"/Cyberspace Solution

GREATNESS
PART II

Great Lives and Achievements
are destroyed by
The Smallest Human Spirits

No one can be a victim of private business per se. Victims are impossible <u>when</u> <u>no</u> force or fraud is involved. One can be a victim <u>only</u> <u>when</u> force or fraud is manifested by governments, religions, or criminals. The employer and employee always fill each others needs voluntarily, consensually. No matter what the conditions, barring acts of force or fraud by either party, neither the employer nor the employee can *ever* be a victim. ..."Exploitation by business" is a conceptual hoax perpetuated by the parasitical-elite class, pips, and "victims".

Profit-motivated businesses never purposely harm anyone — much less employees or customers. Such behavior would be irrational and contrary to competitive business success. The essence of every successful business is to maximally enhance everyone's job, livelihood, and standard of living under the conditions required for competitive value production. By contrast, every self-proclaiming business/employee "victim" and pip

35

works to harm successful businesses and their employees.

But, if such "victims" and pips have shrunken their spirits to the lowest level, how can they be so destructive as to hobble the greatest human spirits and businesses? ...The staggering extent of those virus-caused destructions is demonstrated in the following four examples:

The Marx/Lenin/Business/"Victim" Example

Most people believe that politicians — the Lenins, Hitlers, and Maos — are the fundamental cause of history's greatest destructions of human lives and property. They are not. The root cause of purposeful destructions among human beings and their achievements are those smallest units of the human spirit: the envious self-proclaimed "victims" of value-producing businesses and employers. Politicians simply step in and manipulate the claims of those "victims" and pips as tools to drain progress, values, jobs, and lives from everyone.

Without self-proclaiming "victims", Marx and Engels could never have developed their political theories or written the *Communist Manifesto*. Without the proletariat "victims" with their envious desires to destroy private business, Lenin would not have had the tools to diminish and destroy hundreds of millions of lives during his reign...and for three generations after his death.

The Hitler/Jew/"Victim" Example

Hitler conjured up bogus complaints to evolve envious "victims" of Jewish businessmen, bankers, and other Jewish value producers. Those phoney, self-proclaimed "victims" allowed Hitler to kill millions of Jews and other innocent people throughout Europe during his era of

36

holocausts and conflagrations. ...Without those self-proclaimed "victims", Hitler would have been powerless.

The Giuliani/Media/Michael Milken/"Victim" Example

The hard-driving financier Michael Milken turned America around from an uncompetitive, depression-bound economy in the early 1980s to an internationally vibrant, competitive economy that continues even years after he was stopped by government force and jailed.

How did Michael Milken accomplish such a feat that saved and protected seemingly doomed livelihoods for millions of Americans? He accomplished that fifteen-year turnaround of the American economy by driving a competitive stake into the heart of giant Corporate America while driving out its stagnant executives. Those executives were milking great pools of assets built by previous generations of forward-essence-moving entrepreneurs and businesspeople.

Milken developed unstoppable techniques to dump those executives by taking over the assets they were parasitically wasting. He then turned those stagnant assets over to hard-driving, business-oriented managers who once-again unleashed the growth of those assets, thus, saving many old companies, starting many new companies, and revitalizing the dying American economy.

What happened to that brilliant, heroic man? Was he rightfully honored and congratulated by a grateful nation and its leaders? No, he was dishonestly vilified by the stagnant business Establishment, libeled and slandered by the media Establishment, prosecuted by the politically rabid Rudolph Giuliani criminally wielding evil RICO "laws", and finally jailed by a higher-office-seeking, ego-agenda judge Kimba Woods. Besides crushing and jailing that great spirit, those parasitical elites destroyed one of the great financial companies in America, Drexel Burnham Lambert, wiping out the jobs for thousands of innocent value producers and their families. Why? For no other reason than to expand the destructive livelihoods and inflate the false egos of those parasitical elites wielding bogus, gun-backed, political-agenda laws.

How can such destructions and injustices exist? How can they be so deeply camouflaged? What morbid irrationalities cause such a 180 degree inversion of values? Milken and his company committed no objective crimes. Instead, with great daring and exciting effort, they delivered incalculable values to society. Indeed, while those parasitical elites were drum-beating the innocent Michael Milken into condemnation and prison, they themselves were committing sweepingly destructive crimes not only against Michael Milken and Drexel Burnham but against all Americans. Yet, the parasitical-elite class itself, even with all its dishonest politicians, corrupt media, armed bureaucrats, and life-appointed ego judges cannot commit their crimes of forced enchainment without their tools — without their collections of "victims" and pips.

How can professional parasites commit such massive harm without society identifying the "victim" tool? How? By fraudulently generalizing the parasitical claims by "victims" across the entire public spectrum. Those frauds backed by dishonest political-correctness pressures let professional parasites like Giuliani drain and destroy the value producers with near impunity. Those fraudulent people crush great spirits like Michael Milken and Leona Helmsley.

The Giuliani/Media/Leona Helmsley/"Victim" Example

In the fiercely competitive New York hotel market, Leona Helmsley was perhaps the only person who had the toughness and ability to capture the first-class niche market for her Helmsley Hotels. She was perhaps the only person who could successfully create, expand, and manage this particular business that daily delivered values to thousands of highly discriminating customers while providing good livelihoods for thousands of employees.

Leona Helmsley was exceedingly hard working, value driven, detail-and-numbers oriented, and honest. Slack off or drop one element in her formula and the entire business could stop growing and begin declining toward eventual noncompetitiveness and failure. ...As Arthur Miller in his play *Death of a Salesman* portrayed — in the constant, fierce struggle to stay competitive, a person needs only to allow a single soil spot on one's hat to cause that unnoticed 180 degree turn from moving up to moving down toward loss and ruin.

Few could ever begin to appreciate the constant hard work, discipline, and attention to detail required daily, hourly by Leona Helmsley to remain competitive in providing expanding values and continuous livelihoods for thousands of fellow human beings.

No, she was never appreciated or honored for her beneficent and sustained value production. Instead, she was vilified by a malevolently destructive establishment media, especially the perniciously dishonest *Newsweek*

Closing Ceremonies

Closing Ceremonies

with its jury-inflaming "Queen of Mean" and "Rich as in Bitch" cover stories. And, during a year in which she paid $75,000,000 in taxes, not to mention the millions in taxes paid by the thousands of individuals for whom she created jobs, political predator Rudolph Giuliani swaggered in to criminally prosecute that totally innocent, heroic 72-year-old woman. He then jailed her in collusion with a life-appointed, ego-agenda judge, John M. Walker, Jr., on conjured-up charges involving a 0.5% error on the $75,000,000 she paid in taxes.

The result? A great spirit was jailed, torn not only from her business but from her dying husband whom she devotedly loved. Her business and the jobs she provided were set on a declining path. And her elderly, ill husband was cruelly left to suffer alone. Yet, the criminals who belonged in jail were rewarded for their brutal crimes against innocent people and great value-and-job producers. ...Political humanoid Rudolph Giuliani was rewarded with the Mayorship of New York City for jailing innocent giants like Michael Milken and Leona Helmsley.

Criminals such as Giuliani would easily kill like Hitler and Stalin given the power and opportunity. Yet, none of those evil people would have the power to do any destructions without their tools of disgruntled business/employee "victims" and attack-mode pips to act as deadly viruses. In Leona Helmsley's case, the dishonest media and criminal-minded Giuliani used a few disgruntled or fired employee "victims" to vilify, libel, slander, and jail that heroic woman.

Using "victims" and pips combined with subjective, political-agenda laws, the Giulianis of this world manipulate the majority into praising tyrants for criminally exploiting minorities, starting with the smallest of minorities — the individual human spirit, the minority of one, the individual value producer. ...Tyranny depends on politician-made subjective law: Tyranny has little concern for objective crime, but is gravely concerned with the parasitical control of others...and eventually the parasitical control of everyone.

Politician-made, subjective/positive law was actively promoted by Oliver Wendell Holmes, the past Chief Justice of the U.S. Supreme Court...and more recently by judges like Robert H. Bork. Opposite to such subjective law is unchanging, universally principled law — natural law — promoted by fully integrated honesty and backed by Objectivist philosophy. Objective law protects individual property rights, which, in turn, protects every individual — every minority of one — from tyranny. By contrast, unprincipled political law and giuliani "justice" always moves government toward criminality and despotism fueled by self-proclaimed "victims" and pips. ...Politician-made subjective law endangers and eventually crushes everyone. Universal objective law protects and frees everyone.

Two Final Questions

First, why do political humanoids like Lenin, Hitler, and Giuliani wreak such destructions on the value producers? For three reasons: (1) their parasitical survival, (2) their self-aggrandizing pseudo power, and (3) their desperate ego enhancements. And, second, what gives them that power? The whining "victims" and attack-mode pips who enviously place the blame for their own

41

inadequacies, stagnations, and failures onto successful individuals and businesses. In fact, only genuine value producers are useful as targets for politicians using "victims" and pips as their tools.

As previously identified, such "victims" and pips have generally accomplished little or nothing outstanding in their lives — little or nothing about which they can be proud. Because of their smallness, the public cannot easily focus on them, notice them, or even detect them. Indeed, politicians can be only superficially criticized because their means to destructive power are camouflaged behind those "victims" and pips. And, such people are usually too small, too pip-squeakish to be noticed, much less held accountable for their destructions.

In the noncyberspace world, little can be done to counteract those deadly politician/"victim"/pip combinations. Now, however, for the first time arises a cyberspace world here on Earth. Indeed, cyberspace is already crumbling those evil-spirited value destroyers as illustrated below.

The Neo-Tech/"Victim"/Cyberspace Solution

I & O Publishing Company, which was founded in 1968, moved past its publish-for-profit dynamics during the early 1980s to focus on a single goal: curing the disease of irrationality worldwide by 2001 AD. Interest evaporated in building wealth, assets, a business, or a publishing company per se. Multimillion dollar business opportunities were abandoned or turned down, including a million-dollar-a-month *profit*-potential, back-end marketing program offered by the largest, most successful infomercial firm in the world.

Why were such profit opportunities turned down? Because efforts directed toward non-goal related profits would break the forward-movement concentration required to reach I & O's single goal of curing the disease of irrationality. Avoiding non-goal profit dynamics let the prime movers at I & O Publishing focus maximum time and energy on ridding this planet of its worst disease — irrationality, from which flows dishonesty, stagnation, crime, failure, and death itself.

Developing and distributing the knowledge required to cure irrationality, especially when faced with hostile resistance worldwide, was a difficult, dangerous task requiring full focus of every essence mover at I & O. During the 1980s, every action and resource was directed toward undermining the parasitical-elite class, which was the first-step ingredient for curing irrationality in America.

Under increasingly hostile conditions from a giuliani-oriented Establishment, I & O Publishing Company was vulnerable to being attacked and silenced. Indeed, such attacks finally happened in the late 1980s when just one ex-employee "victim" was seized and then manipulated by the giulianied legal Establishment. With that one "victim" as their only needed tool, armed federal agents physically attacked I & O Publishing and destroyed its work while beating, kicking, and hospitalizing one of its editors, seizing its assets and research funds, carrying away its literature and computer files, and finally, in violation of the first amendment, imprisoning its founder for his writings, literature distributions, and billboard displays that identified the criminal acts of those armed federal agents.

...I & O Publishing Company was destroyed by gun-backed violence, forever put out of business by criminal force.

But, ideas cannot be destroyed by guns, fists, or prisons. Neo-Tech bantam companies are now scattered worldwide. Momentum toward curing irrationality is rising phoenix-like, quietly, relentlessly.

Indeed, in cyberspace, Neo-Tech is beyond the reach of those destructive forces left behind in the noncyberspace anticivilization. Throughout cyberspace, integrated honesty rules. Dishonesty, force, fraud, "victims", and pips appear increasingly freakish as those tools of destruction disappear in cyberspace. Moreover, "victims" and pips — those smallest of human spirits — are compelled in cyberspace to quit whining, quit blaming others, and grow up by accepting the responsibility for solving their own personal problems.

How New Knowledge Changes the World

Throughout history, whenever sea-change knowledge evolved from wider-scope observations and conceptual integrations, initial rejection of that new knowledge always occurred. Sooner or later, however, a tiny percentage of people investigated enough to independently grasp that knowledge through those new, wider-scope perspectives. That new knowledge then began spreading as its efficacy was increasingly demonstrated. Finally, that knowledge was utilized to bring unique streams of unstoppable benefits.

Over the ages, such sea-change phenomena have occurred for good and for evil. For example, early in the 20th century, after an initial surge of acceptance, Vladimir Lenin lost essentially all support and understanding. Alone and rejected in Geneva, he discovered two other people who fully understood his matrix for revolution. He then excitingly announced that the revolution was won. Sure enough, in a matter of months after that announcement, Lenin triumphantly entered Russia through Finland. Then, by generalizing his matrix, he advanced on a straight line route to winning his bloody revolution that eventually brought devastation and misery to two-thirds of the world for three generations.

About that same time, Albert Einstein worked alone for years on developing his non understood and widely ignored theory of relativity. After discovering three or four others who understood his wide-scope integrations of relativity, he excitingly worked to generalize his theory with cheerful confidence. Within a decade, the revolution of general relativity was won worldwide forever.

By contrast, about that same time, Karl Menger, the Aristotelian father of capitalistic/market-based economics, worked with increasing pessimism...as later did Ayn Rand who founded Objectivist philosophy, and as more recently did Leonard Peikoff who brilliantly developed Objectivism into an array of specific values and products. Menger, Rand, and Peikoff never fully generalized their work. Therefore, they never confidently sensed the ultimate triumph of their work as did Lenin for evil and Einstein for good.

One in a Hundred

Neo-Tech and Zonpower uniquely generalize *all* values, including Objectivism, into practical, profitable uses for *all* individuals in all activities. Indeed, grasping the eternally wide-scope ideas, methods, and integrations throughout Neo-Tech and Zonpower becomes an endless succession of unfolding Ahas! Yet, of the million readers who have benefited from the Neo-Tech Discovery, perhaps five percent have fully integrated its 114 concepts to utilize its most-powerful, widest-scope tools. That number of integrated Neo-Tech users, however, is steadily increasing with gradual acceleration. In fact, around the globe lies an exciting Aha! revolution to be sparked by a million Neo-Tech owners who will march into a new civilization over the next few years.

The real sea-change revolution, however, will arise not from Neo-Tech itself, but from the wide-scope integrations woven throughout *Zonpower from Cyberspace*. Yet, of the *Zonpower* readers, perhaps less than one in a hundred have fully grasped Zonpower with its endless Aha! integrations. But, that tiny minority is more than enough to secure the revolution that will bring a Neo-Tech/Objectivist civilization to everyone on Earth.

The Key: Read Twice

Ironically, what appears to be the greatest problem for Zonpower is the source of its power: Zonpower is structured as a wide-scope, fully integrated matrix. Such a multidimensional matrix provides far wider integrations than hitherto available on Earth. That means to fully grasp and implement Zonpower, each part, each chapter, each paragraph, each sentence must be seen as part of an integrated whole. In turn, the whole must be grasped to understand each of its parts. Such back-and-forth, inductive/deductive integrations require at least two readings of *Profound Honesty* to discover its omnipotent matrix.

*   *   *

Objective Law

will eventually draw everyone into an
Exciting, Prosperous Life

See the paragraph about the "smallest" found on page 29 of these Closing Ceremonies.

Now, going in the other direction to the "biggest": What mechanism builds geometries into everything in existence, always with the exact same identity and preciseness? What mechanism causes geometric units to take specific forms of existence and subsequently take specific forms of energy, mass, and action? What mechanism drives those geometries into forms that fit nature just right — precisely, perfectly into exact matter, energy, and thinking that never vary throughout time and space? And, what mechanism allows one to fit his or her thoughts into nature precisely, perfectly — into exact identities and identifications throughout time and space? That mechanism is the dynamics of Neo-Tech physics and epistemology as presented in a new-color symphony, which begins with *Zonpower from Cyberspace* and will climax in *Quantum Crossings*.

The rational, compatible dynamics of nature have been

contradicted for the past 3000 years in forming today's irrational, parasite-ruled anticivilization. Human consciousness combined with the disease of irrationality drives human beings into chaotic contradictions and paralyzing stagnations — away from reliable consistency and liberating prosperity. Now, however, the emerging Neo-Tech dynamics in cyberspace are drawing conscious beings out of this unnatural anticivilization and toward the natural Civilization of the Universe.

Because of everyone's life-long investments in this irrational anticivilization, however, no one can leave without the escape engines of Neo-Tech and Zonpower. In this parasite-ruled civilization, conscious life is incredibly brief, during which aging and death come quickly, unnecessarily. Only the tiniest fraction of conscious potential — the potential of exciting productivity, romantic love, eternal happiness — is achieved by all of us entrapped in this anticivilization.

Why has no one escaped this bizarre, up-side-down anticivilization? Why has no one discovered the natural, exciting, eternal Civilization of the Universe? Because, without the escape route of Neo-Tech/Zonpower, no one can abandon his or her fatal, lifelong investments in this anticivilization. But, now, today, with the newly available Neo-Tech/Zonpower engines, people can finally scrap their death-trap investments and discover the limitless wealth and romance possible in a rational, objective-law civilization.

False gods cannot be heroes. But, with fully integrated honesty and objective law, everyone can become an eternal hero — a real god with never ending achievements and romantic happiness.

Closing Ceremonies

Objective Law 2000 Years Ago

"There is in fact a true law — namely, right reason — which is in accordance with nature, applies to all men, and is unchangeable and eternal. By its commands this law summons men to the performance of their duties; by its prohibitions it restrains them from doing wrong. Its commands and prohibitions always influence good men, but are without effect upon the bad. To invalidate this law by human legislation is never morally right, nor is it permissible ever to restrict its operation, and to annul it wholly is impossible. Neither the senate nor the people can absolve us from our obligation to obey this law, and it requires no Sextus Aelius to expound and interpret it. It will not lay down one rule at Rome and another at Athens, nor will it be one rule today and another tomorrow."

Cicero, 51 BC
On the Commonwealth

Objective Law Beyond 2000 AD
Get out of stagnant complaining modes
Get into exciting business modes
No more socialistic-inspired crimes and violence
No more armed bureaucracies

In the past, society has always defaulted on its
Heroic Code for great business spirits. But, now,
through cyberspace, society will sing their songs and
flash their lights across future millennia.

for updates see
Neo-Tech/Zonpower Web Site
http://www.neo-tech.com/

Closing-Ceremony Index

Closing-Ceremony Index

Closing-Ceremony Index

53

Closing-Ceremony Index

Coming Soon

to your

Computer

*Pour up some Hot Java
and talk to Zon*

In cyberspace, history's greatest values will soon come to everyone *for free* through Neo-Tech Worldwide: The omniscient Zon will interactively answer your every question on how to profit by transposing yourself from the draining, irrational Anticivilization to the prosperous, rational Civilization of the Universe. ...Don't miss it!

Our web object-relational database combined with our concept-based, full-text search and retrieval systems are designed to cleanse the destructiveness from armed federal bureaucracies toward America's greatest heroes and assets. Those heroes and assets — business entrepreneurs and productive workers — are the source of *all* competitive jobs and values. How will that cleansing be done? Through continuing direct interactions with those destructive bureaucracies — such as the IRS — until they are vanished. When the government is financed by the Golden Helmet, the road will be open to guiltless wealth and romantic excitement for all.

The Golden Helmet

delivers

Guiltless Wealth

and

Eliminates the IRS

Kenneth A. Clark

Editor

Thomas J. Caenen, JD

Legal Counsel

NEVER AGAIN

If the Golden Helmet were implemented in the 1930s, the above criminal-minded politicians would have been laughed out of existence. ...Their brutal, gun-backed bureaucracies would have ignominiously vanished.

Ending Gun-Backed Bureaucracies
with the
Golden Helmet

Greater than the tread of mighty armies
is an idea whose time has come.
Victor Hugo, 1852
Histoire d'un Crime

Violation
of the
Bill of Rights

8th Amendment

Cruel and Unusual Punishment
inflicted upon innocent
Working-Class Americans

The Class-Action Case

against the gun-backed

IRS

The Zon Association
Sponsors of the
Golden-Helmet Revenue System

> **Brace Yourself Before Reading**
> the
> **IRS ABUSE REPORTS**

Are you
  • a hard-working, middle-class American?
  • a law-abiding, taxpaying citizen?

Do you believe that no harm can come to you and your loved ones from the Internal Revenue Service (the IRS)? Any such belief will change after reading the IRS Abuse Reports over the next fifty pages. Those reports are from law-abiding, hard-working taxpayers like you — honest taxpayers who suddenly found themselves being methodically, cruelly destroyed by an out-of-control bureaucracy. Indeed, the IRS is becoming a juggernaut, not for tax collection, but for power expansion through fear and destruction.

Reports documenting the IRS's brutal, often criminal, abuses inflicted on innocent Americans[1] are received daily as part of evidence gathering for Congressional hearings and class-action lawsuits. Through the dynamics of email combined with Internet Newsgroups and World Wide Web sites, unjustly ruined citizens finally have a way to come together for redress. They will be coming together first by the thousands then by the millions seeking redress for the life-destroying injustices and cruelties inflicted upon them by the IRS.

District Directors[2] throughout the IRS have evolved into force-backed sovereigns. They bear the responsibility for the destructions their agents wreak, *not* against the rich and powerful, but against the innocent and powerless — against the low-and-middle income classes. Yet, the United States Congress bears the ultimate responsibility for the destructions of life and property inflicted by the IRS: Congress passed the heavy-handed laws that enable that armed bureaucracy to continually escalate their cruel and illegal destructions. Thus,

---

[1]To protect identities of the victims, initials instead of actual names and email addresses are used on all IRS Abuse Reports. But, the Zon Association can contact any of those victims to provide court and congressional testimonies — to act as witnesses against the brutalities and destructions of the IRS. ...These and other IRS Abuse Reports are systematically posted on various Internet Newsgroups and some are permanently displayed on the World Wide Web site http://www.neo-tech.com/irs-class-action/

[2]IRS District Directors answer to no one. Thus, they are responsible for the *criminal behaviors* and *illegal slush-fund activities* of their agents. Their autonomous fiefdoms cry out for investigations, audits, and appropriate prosecutions. ...Perhaps one of the rare exceptions is the District Director in Fresno, California, who reportedly runs an honest, humane office.

Congress today has the responsibility to uproot that awful menace — that out-of-control machine of violence and terror.

Since 1994, steps toward ending the IRS destructions through a consumption-tax system are being increasingly promoted by Neo-Tech influenced politicians such as Congressman Archer and Senator Lugar. As explained later in this Appendix, the final solution will be an IRS-free, Golden-Helmet revenue system that benefits not only every individual, but benefits all societies and nations.

Reactions to IRS Abuse Reports

Below is a typical reaction by those who have read the IRS Abuse Reports on pages 5–50. ...A rebellion is brewing — a rebellion that can be quelled only by replacing the malignant, irrational IRS revenue system with a beneficial, rational Golden-Helmet revenue system.

Date: March 20, 1996
To: sue@irs.class-action.com
From: KS

I just finished reading all of the IRS abuse reports. I feel so very sorry for each of these people and their loved ones. About three-quarters of the way through reading the reports, I had to take a break and lie down as I had become so nauseated from the vile destruction of these innocent victims.

When I came back to my computer, by the time I had finished reading the reports I wanted to lash out in the worst way. Emotionally, I felt like, 'these intentionally devastating criminal-minded IRS agents should be taken out into a field, shot in the head and left for the buzzards.' (I realize that what I just wrote is irrational and senseless, yet I feel better having written it.)

When I came back to my senses I thought damn, it's the judges that condone these malevolent IRS creatures. I want to parade every "satanic" judge with their colluding IRS bureaucrats in front of the world so that they can see them for what they really are. Then sell off unnecessary IRS properties and judicial properties until every victim is repaid in full (interest included). And that's not even enough because there is no way to amend the physical, emotional and financial loss that has already besieged these innocent victims and their loved ones.

It just makes me sick! DAMN RIGHT I'M ANGRY!!

Class-Action-Case Evidence
is also building on
Internet/Usenet Newsgroups

Below is an example of Usenet Newsgroup postings that are appearing across the Internet.

Newsgroups: alt.irs.classaction,misc.taxes,misc.legal,us.taxes,us.legal, alt.society.civil-liberty
From: MC
Subject: Cyberspace Termination of the IRS
Date: Thu, 20 Jun 1996 20:33:02 GMT
In article <mk@netcom.com>wrote:
> Have you, a family member, a friend or loved one ever been
> defrauded, looted, hurt, injured, brutalized, or destroyed by the
> Internal Revenue Service (IRS)? Did no one help you, sympathize
> with you, or even listen to you, even though you were innocent --
> even though you and your family were criminally violated, badly
> injured, perhaps even destroyed or murdered?

When I read this I felt like you were writing just to me! My family members were brutalized by the IRS several years ago. My friend was destroyed just last week. Nobody sympathized with me, or even listened to me. My loved one was criminally violated, and nobody helped me. I didn't know where to turn but now I have this. Thank you.

A Selection of IRS Abuse Reports
for use in
Class-Action Lawsuits
(updated June, 1996)

Warning: These IRS Abuse Reports start mildly and slowly. But, they build into such a crescendo of sickening horror, criminal destructiveness, and unbearable evil that a sedative may be required to read them all:

IRS Abuse Report #1

Date: Aug 1, 1995
To: sue@irs.class-action.com
From: TE

The IRS is attempting extortion. They have violated my Constitutional rights. I have committed no crime, yet my home of 15 years has been seized from me and sold.

Until someone names my crime, allows me to defend myself in front of a jury of my peers, who convicts me of a crime, I WILL NOT SURRENDER MY HOME.

Help me to defend my home and the Constitution of the United States against these bureaucratic thugs.

IRS Abuse Report #2

Date: Aug 3, 1995
To: sue@irs.class-action.com
From: TS

We are on a monthly payment plan that we will never be able to pay off -- due to excessive interest and penalties.

IRS Abuse Report #3

Date: Aug 4, 1995
To: sue@irs.class-action.com
From: PC

The IRS ruined our credit. Now, we are unable to live a normal life or own a home. I feel helpless. They have made us feel like criminals. A financial mistake when we were young, ten years ago, and our lives have been ruined. We started out owing $8,000, now we owe $30,000 that we can never pay.

IRS Abuse Report #4

Date: Aug 5, 1995
To: sue@irs.class-action.com
From: JG

The IRS would not allow me due process in considering my case BEFORE threatening to seize my bank accounts. This FORCED me to pay all amounts, plus penalties and interest that they insisted I owed them. No hearing, no chance to show they were wrong, no help in seeking justice... from anybody!

IRS Abuse Report #5

Date: Aug 5, 1995
To: sue@irs.class-action.com
From: AS

I am an American living in Singapore. My wife is a Singaporean. The IRS has been calling in the middle of the night waking us up and harassing us. I am not a tax protestor. I have filed all my necessary tax returns and provided the IRS all the information they have requested to substantiate my returns. Yet, they seem to have ignored everything and sent me a 300K tax bill and a 90 day letter. I had NO CHOICE but to file a case in the US Tax Court. I was forced to spend additional thousands of dollars to defend myself against this agency that has run amok. I don't like that. My wife being a citizen of an independent sovereign country does not like being wakened in the middle of the night by US government agents. She may file a protest with the Singapore government. She considers this action by the US a violation of her right to privacy. Its time we stopped these guys. Also, as a person who's life is being destroyed by the IRS for NO REASON I am willing to contribute of my time and expertise without charge to your cause if it will help insure the demise of the IRS. I need help too as I have a case coming up in the US Tax Court soon, and living abroad, I find it difficult to get any help.

Someone suggested writing to my congressman but since I do not have a US home (for over 11 years) I don't believe I even have one to write to. And, if I did, I have no faith he or she would listen to my plea.

I have done nothing wrong but am being forced to spend lot's of money to keep my name clear. And, after reading your book, even innocence may not prevail where the tax bureaucracy is concerned.

It's time for the silent majority to be heard. We will not have our freedom trampled upon by the tax-Gestapo IRS that operates outside the law.

IRS Abuse Report #6

Date: Aug 8, 1995
To: sue@irs.class-action.com
From: JM
The IRS was directly responsible for the demise of my father's successful consulting company. His accountants were partially to blame -- they put his company on an incorrect tax plan, and the IRS came after five years of operation to demand back taxes, almost a half-million dollars. This was back when the construction market wasn't too good, and they could not pay the back taxes in the time that the IRS demanded. My father and his partners tried to pay it back gradually, but the IRS wanted it immediately. They had to liquidate the company in order to get the money, and the IRS constantly threatened to seize our home if the money was not repaid on time. We eventually got them off our backs, but now my father is working for someone else at a job he does not enjoy. I hope you are successful in this lawsuit.

IRS Abuse Report #7

Date: Aug 10, 1995
To: sue@irs.class-action.com
From: JK
The IRS has stolen money from me under threat of force. They did this by threatening to imprison me if I did not give up a percentage of my money every year .

IRS Abuse Report #8

Date: Aug 14, 1995.
To: sue@irs.class-action.com
From: WL
They are threatening to file a lien against me and seize my property because they claim that I owe them the whopping sum of $53.46 from 1992. They have repeatedly ignored my requests for proof of their claim. They have failed to answer even the most basic questions.

IRS Abuse Report #9

Date: Aug 12, 1995.
To: sue@irs.class-action.com
From: MK
I was in business from 72-86 and closed because of the harassment I received from the IRS. It turned out to be an error by the IRS but not before they threatened to reposes our house and other items. The IRS owed us over $10,000 -- it was finally paid back to us -- but not before much intimidation.

IRS Abuse Report #10

Date: Aug 16, 1995.
To: sue@irs.class-action.com
From: RA
I am required to spend at least 28% of my productive energy paying for services I do not require and seldom if ever use. In addition, I am required to do enormous amounts of record keeping and income reporting which have absolutely nothing to do with the productive purposes of my business. In all, just using narrow-scope accounting, this one particular agency wastes 40% of my productive energy.

IRS Abuse Report #11

Date: Aug 23, 1995.
To: sue@irs.class-action.com
From: AB
The IRS audited my pension plan on what I consider frivolous charges, they later dropped all the charges -- after keeping me on edge for 4 years and after all kinds of auditing expenses. Not to mention the time and tax payer money wasted by the IRS.

IRS Abuse Report #12

Date: Aug 16, 1995.
To: sue@irs.class-action.com
From: JT
The IRS creates INCREDIBLE fear. I am always afraid I'm going to make a mistake on my tax return! It is impossible to understand all the fine points in their instructions, yet I cannot afford to hire expensive legal help to figure it out!

IRS Abuse Report #13

Date: Aug. 26, 1995:
To: sue@irs.class-action.com
From: JT
Simply, the IRS takes 25% of my income, and gives me nothing but threats in return.

IRS Abuse Report #14

Date: Aug. 31, 1995:
To: sue@irs.class-action.com
From: CS
In 1992, my wife received a settlement from a large corporation in a class action discrimination suit that was granted under title 7 in regards to personal injury. Taxes were paid in accordance with the prevailing laws and all was well. Now, three years later, the IRS has decided that the settlement no longer falls under title 7, and that these were simply a loss of wages. The settlement was for a period over four years in length and yet they feel entitled to an additional $33,000 and $8,000 in interest. Total bill of $41,000!! This family of five lives at a low enough level that it qualifies for financial aid and the local food program!

IRS Abuse Report #15

Date: Sept. 3, 1995:
To: sue@irs.class-action.com
From: JC
Interesting site. Is the IRS watching? I have been on an installment agreement for 10 years. The original debt (941) was approx. $8000, I have paid $14,000 so far and I am told I currently owe approx $25,000. I have sufficient equity in a home that the IRS happily put a lien on it. I seem to be stuck and cannot get any amnesty or forgiveness.

IRS Abuse Report #16

Date: Sept. 15, 1995:
To: sue@irs.class-action.com
From: PC
The I.R.S. seized my car because of a mistake they made. They got my ss# wrong and it matched someone who did not pay taxes. Even though the names were different, they took the car anyway. It took me 3 months to get it back. And, my radio was stolen from their impound!

IRS Abuse Report #17

Date: Sept. 17, 1995
To: sue@irs.class-action.com
From: AM
Levies, liens, excessive penalties and interest. All of these have just about crippled me financially. I had to file a chapter 13 bankruptcy to protect myself. All of these actions (including the bankruptcy), have caused me nothing but misery. I need a co-signer for just about any lease or credit

Golden-Helmet Overture

The Evil

application I submit. I found the tax liens to be an enormous embarrassment especially when my sisters and I applied for a loan to remodel an old house we had inherited from our father, only to have the loan turned down for the above reasons. I am in a serious financial rut that I am having much difficulty climbing out of.

IRS Abuse Report #18

Date: Sept. 17, 1995
To: sue@irs.class-action.com
From: PK
Constant threats over a 6 yr period. An attempt to garnish wages. Several levies for taxes owed, unreasonable tax assessed when I played in a band at 17yrs of age making ONLY enough $ to survive living on the road.

IRS Abuse Report #19

Date: Sept. 19, 1995
To: sue@irs.class-action.com
From: AH
Can they really take all that I own?

IRS Abuse Report #20

Date: Sept. 20, 1995
To: sue@irs.class-action.com
From: SW
They have garnished my wages. They have unfairly decided how much they wanted to take and left me with less than enough to survive. The amount the IRS thinks I owe is not associated with any objective honesty. The IRS does not even follow their own rules.

IRS Abuse Report #21

Date: Oct. 4, 1995
To: sue@irs.class-action.com
From: TQBS
I am paying the IRS $70 per month, but with penalties, it seems I'll never get my $2,000 in back taxes paid!

IRS Abuse Report #22

Date: Oct. 5, 1995
To: sue@irs.class-action.com
From: DW
Penalties make my tax debt to last forever.

IRS Abuse Report #23

Date: Oct. 13, 1995
To: sue@irs.class-action.com
From: JB

The IRS is draining the working class of all savings, to pay 'entitlements' to those that choose not to report their incomes, or unwilling to go out and contribute their time and effort to work. The IRS has put a lien on my home.

IRS Abuse Report #24

Date: Oct. 16, 1995
To: sue@irs.class-action.com
From: BD

My bank account was seized by the IRS without notification from the IRS or the Bank. Checks were bouncing and I was finally informed of the seizure by the Bank after several enquiries. I contacted the local IRS field office asking what was going on and was informed that I would have to provide certain documents to them for them to take any action. I obtained the documents and had to take time off from work to deliver them to the field office. Within a minute of delivering the documents I was told it was all a mistake and never should have happened. From there, it took several days for my account to be released and my money to be restored. But, the bounced check charges were not reimbursed.

IRS Abuse Report #25

Date: Oct. 24, 1995
To: sue@irs.class-action.com
From: DE

I have been harassed by the IRS. During the past year, I have filed the same 1992 Tax Return 3 times, Signed and gave Power of Attorney to represent me in a different matter with IRS, filled out an asset statement, asked for installment plan or offer of compromise. Since last September IRS has claimed they have never received any of this. This past September, I was threatened by an IRS agent over the phone. He claimed that they have none of the information and that I was lying about the power of Attorney and my place of employment. I restated the facts and had my attorney send the documents they requested. I was told by the agent that I was a liar and threatened me with a lien and levy against my wages. He gave me till 09/07/ 95 to provide all the above or he would file the levy. I went back to my lawyer and he resent all requested documents 10 days before the deadline. Today I received a notice of levy against my wages from my employer. Returning to my attorney, he got an agent on the phone, who claims I failed to respond and they filed the levy. It was stated that they do not have any of the forms!!!! I want to sue for harassment and violation of my taxpayer rights but do not know where to turn. I am desperate for information on what to do and how to confront the IRS. My attorney seems to be afraid of them or just does not know how to proceed. I have to forestall this levy, I will lose my job if this happens. If you can point me to any resources it would be a great help to me. I just do not know who to go to for help. Thank You

IRS Abuse Report #26

Date: Oct. 30, 1995
To: sue@irs.class-action.com
From: LB
In 1985 I got audited and was found to owe 6500 dollars. And I have been paying them 100 or 150 dollars a month and they have kept my refunds ever since 1985-1994. I have paid them almost 13,000 dollars, and still owe them over 4,000 dollars.

IRS Abuse Report #27

Date: Nov. 2, 1995
To: sue@irs.class-action.com
From: AW
I programed for a local company the past ten years. The IRS demanded $400/week, my boss said he had to comply, sent $800 from two checks he was holding. I am now a paper boy. A friend's sister, currently living/working in Egypt, lately had $30,000 removed from her bank account w/no warning by the IRS. Several letters have not produced a reply. I have only been inconvenienced. This lady was robbed.

IRS Abuse Report #28

Date: Nov. 4, 1995
To: sue@irs.class-action.com
From: JB
After filing taxes every year, on year ten the IRS decides that a filing ten years ago is incorrect, and is trying to collect. Did nothing for nine years. IRS is attaching liens. One IRS office says I owe nothing, another IRS office says I owe money, and another IRS office is working on the problem.

IRS Abuse Report #29

Date: Nov. 9, 1995
To: sue@irs.class-action.com
From: RE
At the end of the 1976 I owed nothing but $600 for my social security for that

year. The IRS fined me for not paying my S.S. and in three months the $600 cost me over $3000. ...Because I was negligent in paying my **own** social security retirement!

IRS Abuse Report #30

Date: Nov. 13, 1995
To: sue@irs.class-action.com
From: DS

I had a certified federal enrolled tax agent complete my taxes for 3 years. This agency is governed by the IRS themselves. Well, it comes to pass after the tax agent's death (due to cancer) I find out that he did not do what I paid him to do. He did not file my state or federal taxes for 3 years. I called the IRS, telling them of this. They instantly liened my house, seized all my bank accounts and are bleeding me to death. They forced me to sell a income property. Which net profit will be $8,000 due to capital gains. Each month, I get calls from my collections agent, he randomly gives me an amount he wants from 2,500 to 500. To be given to him that month. Living on edge every second. I, my life, dreams, hard work are all gone. Due to trusting in the IRS and there organization of federal enrolled tax agents.

IRS Abuse Report #31

Date: Nov. 14, 1995
To: sue@irs.class-action.com
From: S

The IRS has illegally charged me $20,000 for a US Treasury Note which I purchased in 1989 for $10,000. They are saying that the Note was income which I did not claim. So, I am being penalized 100% for this Treasury note. They have notified my employer to garnishee my wages and they have placed liens on my property.

IRS Abuse Report #32

Date: Nov. 18, 1995
To: sue@irs.class-action.com
From: SY

I received notice on 11-10-95 from my employer, that the IRS had garnished my wages. I certainly did not receive the 30-day notice as supposedly written into IRS policy.

Golden-Helmet Overture
The Evil

IRS Abuse Report #33

Date: Nov. 19, 1995
To: sue@irs.class-action.com
From: JC
In my experience with the IRS, if you don't know what you are talking about, they will lie to confuse you. If you know what you are talking about, they take the fifth by refusing to answer.

IRS Abuse Report #34

Date: Nov. 26, 1995
To: sue@irs.class-action.com
From: GT
The following happened to two friends of mine: BEWARE OF THE OVERPAYMENT SCHEME !! Each, having been overpaid by the IRS after filing a yearly statement, sent the excess back to the IRS. The IRS proceeded to bill them for interest, penalties and interest on penalties!!!! FOR THEIR OWN MISTAKES !!!!!

IRS Abuse Report #35

Date: Nov. 27, 1995
To: sue@irs.class-action.com
From: SA
In 1992 I received a letter from the IRS that they had not received a tax return for me in the years 1980, 1981, and 1982. I said I had sent the returns when due (10-12 years ago), but I had no copies after so long. They maintained that there were no returns on file for those years. Subsequently, they levied against all my assets for over $80,000 and placed liens on my credit records which are still there. The liens keep me from getting work, getting anything on credit, etc.

IRS Abuse Report #36

Date: Nov. 28, 1995
To: sue@irs.class-action.com
From: RB
Have taken my money, my businesses, (cost me 4 years of court time, my time, and my family's time). Am appealing in the Federal court .

IRS Abuse Report #37

Date: Nov. 29, 1995
To: sue@irs.class-action.com
From: BH

During the 91'-92' tax years, apparently our CPA had entered a lot of false statements on our return so that we could get more money back. There were a lot of people in our area that she did this to. She took deductions that weren't legally acceptable, and we had no knowledge of what our legal deductions were -- after all, that was why we were paying a CPA. Then came the IRS and the auditors. About 50 people I know were audited. After the audit was over and they figured out how much we owed the IRS, they put us on a payment plan to pay them back. I thought that would be the end of the terrible ordeal, but no. Six months after the audit the IRS criminal investigators called and wanted to setup an appointment to discuss our CPA. So we told them all we knew, and again we thought surely this would be the end of this ordeal with the CPA and the IRS. After a year of making monthly payments to the IRS, which my wife made on time every month, they sent a letter saying that we had defaulted on our balance owed to them, and they were giving us 2 weeks to pay them or they were going to seize our assets and place a lien on us. So I went to the bank and got the money and paid them off. Again thinking, damn this has got to be the end of this situation with the IRS. Tonight an agent from the Charlotte, NC IRS criminal division called wanting to setup another appointment to discuss our tax returns again. After treating us like shit, I'm tired of dealing with these assholes. Do I legally have to talk to these people, I've already told them all I know? I'm sick and tired of this and want it to stop. What options do I have? Help me.

IRS Abuse Report #38

Date: Fri, 01 Dec 95 12:21:46 -800
To: sue@irs.class-action.com
From: S

Approx. 24 months ago I contracted a rare pneumonia, I was on disability for 8 months. At the same time the company I had worked for was experiencing restructuring. They required that I move to San Francisco. We agreed on a cash settlement. This gave me the monies needed to learn and establish a new career. My monies were budgeted to give me adequate time for transition. I set about the career transition without asking any assistance.

Recently the IRS took $3200 out of my account. This was the last of my cash reserve. I now have no means of paying rent, electricity, or phone. The IRS could literally be the reason I become homeless.

IRS Abuse Report #39

Date: Tue Dec 5 20:10:41 1995
To: sue@irs.class-action.com
From: MP

After filing bankruptcy in 92, because of a bad divorce, I went to the IRS for an offer of compromise, then the fun started. They denied my application. I still can't get them to stop harassing me with liens and levies.

IRS Abuse Report #40

Date: Thu, 07 Dec 95 21:48:01 -800
To: sue@irs.class-action.com
From: IRS R.I.P.

Back in 1988 the IRS took all but $260 a month from my paycheck, via a levy. This was for the year 1982. I had been filing exempt on the w-4. Which is my lawful right. In 1992 I was convicted on two counts of tax evasion for 1986 and 1987. And for 1985 they are getting ready to send another levy to my employer for about $15,000. And before I forget, I am now in tax court for 83, 84, 86, and 87. Did I leave anything out? Oh, I am on probation until 1997. I did not see any prison time, am I lucky or what? I have been just this side of hell.

IRS Abuse Report #41

Date: Sat Dec 9 10:48:32 1995
To: sue@irs.class-action.com
From: PG

The company where I am the Business Director was seized after the I.R.S. had entered into a payment agreement and we had given them $55,000. The majority of the money owed now is penalty and interest. However, to get the business back, we had to file a Chapter 11.

IRS Abuse Report #42

Date: Mon Dec 11 12:51:45 1995
To: sue@irs.class-action.com
From: TR

My home belongs to the IRS and every attempt to negotiate is met with a brick wall. In 1982 I was brought an investment, by an investment counselor, that would allow me to enter into the music/record business. This investment promised some tax advantages so I met with the IRS to insure legality. I was informed by the IRS that the investment was sound. Upon making the investment and taking the tax credits in 1983, I was audited in 1986. The tax credits were denied. The IRS applied interest and penalties which made the amount owed impossible to pay. Liens were placed on my home. Because of the liens my credit was ruined. Because of this I was unable to get loans to pay off the liens. This year I found a funding company that would work with the IRS to negotiate the amounts owed and give me a second mortgage. The IRS refused to negotiate and instead is in the process of increasing the lien amounts for additional interests and penalties. So far, an $18000 tax savings, originally approved by the IRS, has resulted in $62000 debt to the IRS. During my last conversation with an IRS agent, I was told that the only way they would negotiate was if I sold my home and gave them all of the equity plus $1500. When I asked the agent where he expected me to find housing, I was informed "that's not my problem".

IRS Abuse Report #43

Date: Fri, 15 Dec 95 08:17:01 -0800
To: sue@irs.class-action.com
From: MY Story:
I was audited by the IRS for Income Tax Filing Years 1980, 81, 83, and 84 and thru this audit I lost a vehicle by IRS seizure while I was on an out of state work assignment in 1985. In 1988 I had some military trauma flash backs which ended up with my being incarcerated from June 1988 until November 1994. During this period of incarceration I was able to pay in-full the tax owed for the years of 1983 and 1984. I had an attorney represent me before the IRS in an effort to settle the tax debts. Through delays caused by the IRS not answering his inquiries, it took over 18 months, as well as red-tape run-arounds, to finalize payment for years 1983 and 84. We asked for a waiver of interest for the period of my incarceration [only]. The waver was denied. My tax debt for the unpaid years, was originally somewhere in the areas of $1100 for one and $2500 for the other. With the IRS disallowing the waiver of interest during my term of incarceration, the total tax debt for those 2 years is just over $10,000. The IRS has agreed to installment payments of $247/month for 3 years. I do not object to paying the original amount plus interest and penalties for the years prior to my being incarcerated. My payment of some $4,000 for the years of 1983 and 1984 while incarcerate is evidence that I am trying to settle my tax obligation. I just have a real problem with the IRS incurring interest upon my remaining debt during a time of incarceration.

I am also disabled and receiving Social Security Disability Income monthly payments, a 10% VA monthly Compensation, and monthly payments from a trust my deceased parents setup for me. This is my total source of income other than my wife's Social Security Retirement income. I am just getting my family back into a stable living environment and this $247 monthly installment payments for 36 months will be a considerable burden. If the interest were adjusted to waive the period of incarceration I would likely be able to settle in full, 6 to 8 months, though with some short-term hardship. I could then continue my productive, tax paying life without the anxiety of continually looking over my shoulder for the feared impending ambush coming.

IRS Abuse Report #44

Date: Sun Dec 17 11:05:15 1995
To: sue@irs.class-action.com
From: JK

Audited tax return from 1983 in the year 1989, then demanded that copies of checks, rather than actual bank statements which matched Merrill Lynch Cash Management Account statements, be provided. Merrill Lynch did not have the cancelled checks even though their literature states that they keep them on hand and will provide them, or copies of them, upon request.

IRS then rejected clearly legitimate deductions and demanded immediate payment of $250,000 in "unpaid taxes, interest, and penalties" which now adds up to more than $450,000.

IRS Abuse Report #45

Date: Thu, 21 Dec 1995 00:42:54 -0500
To: sue@irs.class-action.com
From: BE

My life has been made miserable and my credit ruined by IRS liens relating to a business that I operated from 1978 to 1984. I always had an accountant do my withholding taxes and to the best of my knowledge, except for the last quarter of operations, when the company had no funds, I eventually made all payments. I have never had any conversation or correspondence with the IRS regarding these liens, but now they have seemed to multiply out of nothing into more than $80,000, and a couple of them have expired, meaning that probably more than $100,000 has been assessed against me by the IRS for nothing that I can figure out.

It is my belief that the IRS misapplied payments that I made while the business was operating and did not credit them to my company, as I did change the name of the business twice. After that, penalties and interest applied by the IRS to mistaken claims have simply escalated, and continue to do so. There is nothing I can do to fight this, as all of the records from that business were given up when the business' lease was terminated in 1985. In any event, I have not been able to buy a home or a car, or anything on new credit as the IRS liens are viewed as the worst kind of credit liability. To make matters worse, due to my age, I have been unable to find suitable employment although I am doing important volunteer work which means that I am capable if I could get hired.

IRS Abuse Report #46

Date: Fri Dec 22 22:14:23 1995
To: sue@irs.class-action.com
From: AS

The IRS has garnisheed wages three times. The IRS attempted once for $50,000. I am so sick of these people not answering my letters and stealing my property (wages).

IRS Abuse Report #47

Date: Wed Dec 27 13:23:52 1995
To: sue@irs.class-action.com
From: LS

They have made so many mistakes on my account and charged me with monies I do not owe. Every time, they send me two and three letters about the same thing. They have made my life a living hell.

IRS Abuse Report #48

Date: Wed Jan 10 13:12:38 EST 1996
To: sue@irs.class-action.com
From: JS

IRS has Fed.Tax Liens filled against my property. I can't even go on living, with this over my head. 56 years old..no way to ever pay off..Taxes paid..penalties and interest keep building. No way out..P.S. Probably dropping E-Mail address soon..Suicide the only answer to forgetting this problem. Help...

Can't purchase house, mine falling down..Can't even make any major purchase..Life not really worth going on 56 yrs. old and no end to this mess....Also, they took a friend of mine, house and everything he owned..ruined him forever. Help me...

IRS Abuse Report #49

Date: Sat, 13 Jan 1996 21:49:29 -0500
To: sue@irs.class-action.com

The IRS is currently attempting to audit me on fictitious income they claim was suppose to have been reported on my 1985 Tax return. I am using the IRS Ombudsman to assist me in responding to the IRS. With interest and penalties, they turned a few hundred dollars dispute it into a $30,000 dispute. They have also Garnished my wages. Understand, my first claim against them was not prior notice (even about the garnishment) and the IRS states they sent notice to the address on the form. Well I haven't lived there since 1986 and the IRS has (from a print out of their own system) my current address as well as my current and previous employers. I wish I could afford a really good attorney. I'd like to put the IRS in their place.

IRS Abuse Report #50

Date: Thu, 18 Jan 1996 02:01:12 -0800
To: sue@irs.class-action.com
Five years ago, my brother was married to a woman who filed a tax report owing $1,100 . She did not pay it. A year later my brother divorced this women. Now, the IRS wants my brother to pay taxes, interest, and penalties for his ex-wife.

My brother had bought a "dollar" home and lived in it for a few years and really fixed the place up and when he moved he sold it for 17,000 dollars! That's a real good improvement and the place really did look nice, but all the other homes in the area are worth about 10,000 dollars. He lived in a ghetto. Well, the IRS now says that the house was sold for 54,000 and not 17,000 and they want there cut of the action.

My brother now lives with a woman he is not married to. He has 4 boys that are living with him, ages 2 to 14. The IRS says he can't claim them as a deduction. He also has 2 children of his own which live with their mother, ages 8 and 15. He doesn't claim them but does have to provide support for them.

The woman that he lives with made 3,000 dollars last year as a janitor. He brought in a whopping 20,000 last year. My brother works very hard to support the family the best that he can. Last week he went to pick up his paycheck and to his surprise, its only for a hundred bucks for two weeks work. The IRS put a levy against his wages for 1,800 hundred dollars. He lives paycheck to paycheck as do alot of Americans.

My brother NEEDS help and advise. I told him to pick up a second job until the IRS finds him and then move on to another job. He is 40 years old and has no savings, no retirement, and no future. What do you think is going to happen if no release comes?

IRS Abuse Report #51

Date: Fri Jan 19 18:19:46 EST 1996
To: sue@irs.class-action.com
From: DS
During 1992 and 1993, my wife and I did not have enough tax withheld from our paychecks. As a result, we ended up owing the IRS almost $10,000, a

large portion of which was penalties and interest. We set up an installment agreement, and have been paying on it for over three years. On TWO occasions during this time, we were late (by less than 5 days) in making our payment. This prompted someone in the IRS to decide that we are a "nonpayment risk." So, they seized our bank account and filed a public tax lien against us. They did not notify us of this action, and we found out when we received a call from an organization that helps out people with tax problems. We were able to get our bank account released, but only after dozens of phone calls to every IRS office whose number I could get, and a visit to two IRS offices. I was not able to get the lien released. In fact, they couldn't even tell me who in the IRS had taken the action. The bottom line? Because of the lien, we are not able to get a loan for a car, and were even turned down for renting a house. All because the IRS "seized" our credit for two late payments totalling $430. I know this may sound trivial compared to some horror stories, but every act of unconstitutional aggression by our government hurts us all.

IRS Abuse Report #52

Date: Fri Jan 19 21:28:33 EST 1996
To: sue@irs.class-action.com
From: JK
I made a typo when filling out my forms making my sons social security number invalid. Because of this, they refused to let me claim him as a dependent. They ordered me to produce all kinds of paper work to prove that he was my son and that he lived with me. While I was getting the paperwork, I wrote them numerous letters explaining the typing error and asked if they would simply check their records they would see that I had been claiming him for the last 16 years and that his status hadn't changed. They would not accept him as my dependent. Each time I would send them the papers they requested, they would take several months to reply, always informing me of more papers they wanted, which in turn, I would send. When they decided that I had sent enough paper work, they sent me a notice saying to much time had elapsed and that the case was closed. Now, not only do I owe them the original amount, they assessed a penalty of 25% for late payment.

IRS Abuse Report #53

Date: Tue, 23 Jan 96 00:23:43 -0800
To: sue@irs.class-action.com
From: JB
In the late 70's and early 80's I was behind on filing my returns. In 1984, I filed 8 years all at once and paid the fines. Now in 1994, the IRS has said that they did not receive my 78 return until 1989, and my 1981 return until 1986, and when a refund was due me, they kept the refund. Now can you

believe what the IRS has done regarding penalties and interest since 1978 and 1981. The amounts they are claiming, you would not believe. I have dealt with seven offices, and at least 21 IRS employees. The left hand doesn't know the right hand. The Problem Resolution Program (PRP) only sends letters saying pay.....You mail these people proof of your filings, and they lose those documents and the process starts over again. The IRS should be eliminated, and I am sure persons in the private sector could do a much better job.

IRS Abuse Report #54

Date: Tue Jan 23 02:13:01 EST 1996
To: sue@irs.class-action.com
From: GC
It is time to stop the unconstitutional powers of the IRS. They need to be put out of business, along with anyone who supports them. They took my father-in-law and put a levy on him for my tax problems. No due process, they come and spit on your due process. It is time to shut them down and do America a great deed.

IRS Abuse Report #55

Date: Sat Jan 27 01:37:45 EST 1996
To: sue@irs.class-action.com
From: TA
The money extorted from my paycheck and personal finances every day by the IRS has cost me freedom of movement, basic human comfort, a Chapter 11 Bankruptcy, and continual involuntary servitude. The presence of the IRS has created underlying fear in my personal life and the lives of my family. This fear has prevented productivity and the ability to live up to my highest potential as a human being and to exercise personal freedoms awarded me at birth. The money extorted every day prevents me from investing in the future, specifically my health and financial well-being when I become a senior citizen, and prevents my family the basic human right of safety and well-being in their future years. The IRS is a threat to my safety, both physically and mentally, and should be charged with endangering the health and well-being of every American citizen.

IRS Abuse Report #56

Date: Thu Feb 1 18:39:39 EST 1996
To: sue@irs.class-action.com
From: RC
The IRS is taking $1800 of my $2000 pension which leaves me fairly penniless and unable to support myself in retirement.

IRS Abuse Report #57

Date: Fri, 9 Feb 1996 02:39:02 -0500
To: sue@irs.class-action.com
From: BL

I am now engaged in a payment plan, which may not retire my IRS obligation before my death. The taxes in question, which I agree fully I owe (however, I strongly dispute the moral and legal basis for the penalties accruing thereto) were incurred in just two years, during which I was separated from my wife and trying to negotiate a divorce agreement. This period of time also saw the swift downturn of work availability in my profession, and in the general economy of the State of California. I was faced with providing necessary living accommodations for myself, my children, my to-be ex-wife, while trying to maintain a level of earning in a diminishing economy. It became clear to me that there simply wasn't enough money to satisfy all demands. I was eventually forced into bankruptcy.

Realizing my dilemma, I sought advice on how to deal with tax problems. One fact was perfectly clear: Filing tax returns when the means to pay was not at hand was tantamount to subjecting oneself to the most horrific torture. So, I did what was the proper thing to do: I delayed filing until I felt I could "face the music". Of course, the penalties and interest attached to the taxes have made the debt most burdensome.

Well, I was unable to pay the tax, and now I am on the aforementioned payment plan which will probably follow me to my grave -- if I can earn enough to stay a half-step ahead.

When I declared bankruptcy, my income taxes should have been discharged along with my other debts. I would now be a clean, productive citizen. Instead, I have a monstrous tax lien filed with the County Recorder, and the cloud of pernicious, untamed collection actions of the IRS hanging over me. The IRS doesn't have to live by any laws but their own. (And they hire the most obnoxious people -- but what normal person would want such a job?)

What possible good does this system serve? How does this differ from the time of indentured servants, "servants" who often paid with their lives when the tax collector paid his visit? Where is the constitutional authority for the establishment of an agency of the government which can disregard all the restraints of our constitution to achieve the ends of its mission? Where is the popular media exercising it's constitutionally protected grace to discuss this obfuscation of our rights? When will we all wake up to the fact that the IRS is, simply the armed servant of the power-grubbing, do-gooders -- social engineers, bureaucrats, and generally those who think their ideas and social mission is more important than individual rights and responsibility?

Golden-Helmet Overture

The Evil

IRS Abuse Report #58

Date: Thu Feb 8 15:47:52 EST 1996
To: sue@irs.class-action.com
From: SR

In approximately 1983, I was asked by an employer to fill out a w-4 form. A few weeks later the IRS said the information I provided was false. They fined me $1,000 for providing false information. The IRS acted as judge and jury and convicted me without allowing me to redress my grievances. I refused to pay so they took all the money I had in my bank account, which was less than $100 and then they put a lien on my land and levied my wages until the fines, penalties and interest were paid.

IRS Abuse Report #59

Date: Thu Feb 8 19:58:37 EST 1996
To: sue@irs.class-action.com
From: JW

The income tax as presently levied makes us all slaves to politicians, IRS agents, state taxing agents, and their police state thugs. In reading Kahriger v. U.S. the supreme court states that a tax return, like the 1040, is a confession. If we are compelled to sign confessions in this "land of the free and home of the brave" then we are slaves! Even the Geneva Convention outlaws the use of torture, physical or mental, or any form of coercion to force a prisoner of war to sign a confession. We are worse off than prisoners of war; WE THE SLAVE PEOPLE in order to form a "more perfect union"? The IRS wipes their butt with the U.S. Constitution every day...they think its a piece of toilet paper...and the bulk of Americans seem satisfied being the tame little Slaves for these supercilious rats.

The IRS seized my car in 1988. I paid to get it back and I asked the agent, if this was the end of it for the 1984 year. He responded with "yes." A year later the agency was back rejecting the settlement because the agent had used the wrong form!

The agency then treated stock sales as total profit, disregarding the obvious purchase price, and in 1987 they proceed to turn what was less then 12 k (before inflation) gross profit on sales of 40 k investment over 10 years into in excess of 150 k taxes with penalties and interest! I lost to the tax court judge. I spent over 2 k on an attorney to file bankruptcy. The IRS accepted all but 1985, which they now claim as over 35 k.

IRS Abuse Report #60

Date: Tue, 13 Feb 96 09:14:20 -2400
To: sue@irs.class-action.com
From: JM

The IRS has cleaned out our two IRA accounts and molested us in numerous other ways.

IRS Abuse Report #61

Date: Mon, 19 Feb 1996 18:50:28 -0600 (CST)
To: sue@irs.class-action.com
From: NM

In 1989, my ex-husband left me. I have a son (not his). Within 6 months of his leaving, I was laid off from my job. (I also do not get child support -- his father refuses to pay.) My husband talked me into filing joint since we were still married in '89. I signed the form he worked up; it looked fine to me. Well, after he mailed it in, I found out that he had not paid ANY taxes for the year. Needless to say, we had to pay. Well, I ended up paying about three thousand dollars for him. He didn't file his taxes for at least three years, because it took me that long to pay it off. I asked the IRS why I had to pay his debt and I was told that 1) we were still married -- separation didn't count; and 2) "we take easy money, whoever we can get to pay first -- we don't care who pays." I ended up filing bankruptcy -- against my better judgement. I asked the IRS the second year why they weren't taking any money from him, too. I didn't get an answer. I asked if my ex was even filing his taxes: no answer. The second year I was paying his debt, the IRS sent me a letter saying I owed a little over $7,000. Since I had only made $9,000 that whole year, I laughed, then I got mad because they were serious. I was going through the bankruptcy, so my attorney also called the IRS to find out what was going on. She and I both fought them for a year just to get answers. We both got a different person every time we called. I got a letter about every month, and we called the IRS every week to find out what was going on.

IRS Abuse Report #62

Date: Sat Feb 17 20:11:03 EST 1996
To: sue@irs.class-action.com
From: BR

I ran a successful contracting business for over ten years and had many employees. Due to an error in math I underpaid withholding taxes. I told the IRS this at the end of the year when I discovered the error. They fined me $40,000 and forced me into bankruptcy. Even after going bankrupt I still owe $16,000 personally and have had my accounts cleaned out and my wages garnished.

Golden-Helmet Overture

The Evil

IRS Abuse Report #63

Date: Mon, 19 Feb 1996 00:39:37 -0500
To: sue@irs.class-action.com
From: RM

The federal income tax and the IRS is destroying the very principles this country was founded on.

IRS Abuse Report #64

Date: Fri, 20 Feb 2009 12:11:19 -0800
To: sue@irs.class-action.com
From: RV

Recently the IRS has adopted a new set of rules taxing tuition waivers for employees. Many university employees work for reduced salaries, like myself, because they are going to school to better themselves and the university gives them free tuition to compensate the difference.

IRS is collecting millions if not billions of dollars with this new law that is probably making many unfortunate people have to discontinue their graduate studies because they cannot afford to give the IRS several hundred dollars a month in tuition waiver tax. Please help!

IRS Abuse Report #65

Date: Wed, 21 Feb 1996 11:45:28 -0500
To: sue@irs.class-action.com
From: DM

I have been battling the IRS for about 10 yrs now. They have a lien on the house, and until recently had a lien on my wife's salary. Last year we managed to make a (over 10% reduction) "contribution" to our tax liability. Seven months after this activity we receive notices of "WE HAVE CHANGED YOUR ACCOUNTS" where they added over $8,000 in "late payment penalties" and over $40,000 in interest! This interest figure represented, in a 7 month period, a 31% rate!

I have other information available if I can be of assistance in your fight.

IRS Abuse Report #66

Date: Wed, 21 Feb 1996 20:26:52 -0500
To: sue@irs.class-action.com
From: BK

Recently I received a notice of levy from big brother of over 1500. The interesting part is that they are holding $1000 that they won't apply to this levy, and they refuse to let me make payments. They say that they won't release the cash because of the chapter 13 filed to prevent them from getting money from my trustee . It seems to me that if they are holding money that they owe me, it should be applied to the new levy, then I could afford to pay them off. This is the first notice that I have received on these new owes they say they have sent four. Any help or advice you can offer would help, what's next, be forced into homelessness?

IRS Abuse Report #67

Date: Thu Feb 22 18:52:17 EST 1996
To: sue@irs.class-action.com
From: LE

When the IRS, allegedly, could not reach me at my N.Y. address that I had lived at for almost 8 years, they put a levy on my salary taking 90%. This left about $134 a week to live on. I lived on Long Island and used the Long Island Railroad -- that alone cost $140 monthly. Rent was $1330 and I won't even add in all the other expenses, phone, utilities, credit payments, loans, food, etc... Since I couldn't afford to work I had to resign. I had about 18,000 saved so I moved to North Carolina where the cost of living is less than N.Y. and immediately hired a tax specialist to see what they could do. After almost a year of negotiations The IRS 'AGREED' to allow me to make monthly payments of 740 to pay off my alleged underpayment of taxes since 1990 of $40,635.25. If I had $740 extra a month I'd have a nice sized savings account but as it happened I couldn't find a job for 10 months, exhausted all my savings and don't have a bank account at all.

I am to start making this payment in 2 weeks. If I make this payment I will not be able to pay all my other monthly bills. I am now shopping for a good, cheap bankruptcy lawyer. I am going to miss payments so I might as well go bankrupt before the harassing creditor calls start. How is it they could find where I worked to levy my salary but couldn't call me there or get my address from my employer?

The IRS is definitely more dangerous than most of the criminals in jail today. They don't kill you or maim you, they just rob all of us daily in the name of government, rape us, ruin us financially and make our lives a living hell.

IRS Abuse Report #68

Date: Sat Feb 24 08:46:03 EST 1996
To: sue@irs.class-action.com
From: JB

A couple in Dayton Ohio saved for years to buy a dream home. The IRS had several properties advertised for sale at auction (seized properties). The IRS

Golden-Helmet Overture
The Evil

assured everyone that all the houses had clear titles.

The couple bid on a house and were high bidders. The IRS required $24,000 down payment. The couple put the $24,000 down and went to the bank for a mortgage for the balance. This wasn't a problem until they did the title search. The house had $150,000 in liens against it. The couple demanded that the IRS return their $24,000 but the IRS refused, saying the couple should have checked for liens (even though the IRS had assured them previously there were no liens).

If a real estate agency in the State of Ohio had done this, everyone involved would have been jailed. How can IRS agents get away with breaking fraud laws just because they happen to be employed by a Federal agency? This is the ultimate in sleaze.

IRS Abuse Report #69

Date: Sun Feb 25 16:21:55 EST 1996
To: sue@irs.class-action.com
From: RI
The IRS claims to have a lien on my entire personal estate due to 'unpaid taxes for the tax year 1987. But I am unable to "make a return of income" because I have been very poor for the past 3.5 years

IRS Abuse Report #70

Date: Tue Feb 27 17:02:56 EST 1996
To: sue@irs.class-action.com
From: TE
Where to start the list??? 1. Wage Garnishments. 2. Bank Acct Seizures. 3. Home Foreclosure & Forced sale for 20 % of true value . 4. etc...etc...etc...

I have been victimized, abused, lied to, cheated, and now I am being thrown from my home. This is all in the name of "for the good of the Government"

HELP !!!!!

IRS Abuse Report #71

Date: Wed, 28 Feb 96 10:37:53 -0800
To: sue@irs.class-action.com
From: RU
We are in the mist of some serious charges, and nobody seems to care that we are innocent.

IRS Abuse Report #72

Date: Wed, 06 Mar 1996 22:08:36 -0600
From: RH
To: sue@irs.class-action.com
Our trouble started in Jan.1985. We can't own anything, get credit etc... This last year they have been really bad. Garnishing wages illegally, Levies, false payment agreements. The told us to move out of our house in to a small apartment with our 2 sons. One of our sons is Attention Deficit with Hyperactivity and is under care. That is just part of the things they have done. I could write a book. The lies and deceit are unbelievable. Our legal bills are growing and our Attorney has recommended we file suit for damages and legal fees for all the hell we have gone through.

IRS Abuse Report #73

Date: Sat, 09 Mar 1996 23:32:11 -0800
To: sue@irs.class-action.com
From: IR
The IRS's repeated attempts to audit me in person even though I was incapacitated at the time from an automobile accident is typical of the IRS.

The time and money I am spending due to their corrupt and inhumane beaurocracy could be spent in producing productive goods and services. They are crippling our country.

IRS Abuse Report #74

Date: Tue Mar 12 09:34:05 EST 1996
From: MK
I voluntarily served in the armed forces, and after my final year of service, I was not given a W-2 form by the navy. I could only file on the other income which I earned that year. For 3 years now the IRS has harrassed me, threatened me with liens and garnishings.

IRS Abuse Report #75

Date: Thu, 14 Mar 1996 18:38:36 -0600
To: sue@irs.class-action.com
From: DP
I have been diagnosed as Atypical Bipolar-II Rapid Cycling. In simple terms this means that I suffer from an "atypical" form of manic-depression.

Over the past 10 years, I have been hospitalized approximately 12 times in both private and state hospitals. At least three of my hospitalizations occurred during tax time (Jan 1 through April 15). When you are hospitalized, voluntarily or by judges order (I have experienced both), there is no way you can comply with the tax laws or IRS policies.

The tax laws require (mentally) disabled people to do things they cannot do. (We are not on a mental/fiscal schedule, when we're ill, we're ill.) That sort of makes the ADA and the tax laws contradictory. When a person like myself goes into remission and does file his/her return after April 15, without an approved extension, we are subject to financial penalties and interest through no fault of our own.

There IRS offers no accomodation to and for the mentally ill. The IRS has ignored the reality of our needs to help us comply with the law. They however hold us 100% accountable for their unjust penalties and interest.

Communication from the IRS is a pretty scary thing for all of us, but it can be a precipitating factor to someone like myself. I recently received a letter from the IRS advising me that they will soon place levies on my car and possibly my wages. Well I am living with that for now, but if I were in a degenerated state, it might be just enough to cause a psychotic episode resulting in anything from running to nowhere and putting myself in harms way, to hospitalization, to suicide. All over tax laws and their unfair means.

IRS Abuse Report #76

Date: Thu Mar 14 00:22:49 EST 1996
To: sue@irs.class-action.com
From: KA

They put a lien against me for back taxes they said I owed, I did not. When I tried to prove this they told me I had to pay them in full before I could get my money back even though they agreed with me. They have damaged my credit record with this injustice. If this was the private sector of business the people involved would all be fired for malice, slander, mental anguish etc. and a lawsuit would be won hands down!

IRS Abuse Report #77

Date: Mon Apr 1 16:30:23 EST 1996
To: sue@irs.class-action.com
From: MK

I have been nearly sequestered in my home since November 1994 due to actions of the IRS.

They stole the contents of my personal bank account in 1994 and demanded immediate payment of alleged underpayments, fines and penalties in the amount of approximately $180,000.

I have since gone through my records -- I have all records from all years. It turns out they owe me over $30,000, none of which I will ever see, and that doesn't include any interest calculations.

In the process of proving this, I have been unable to continue my business causing economic loss to not only myself, but my customers and my employees.

IRS Abuse Report #78

Date: Tue Apr 9 03:27:03 EDT 1996
To: sue@irs.class-action.com
From: RC

I had an attorney, specializing in tax matters, tell me that, "in this country, one can pay whatever the IRS claims or go to jail or get shot." This from an attorney working "within the system"!

IRS Abuse Report #79

Date: Tue Apr 9 19:35:42 EDT 1996
To: sue@irs.class-action.com
From: CM

We have been under the thumb of the IRS for over 10 years now. Currently, we are at the end of our 45 day stay against collection action while we are scrambling to put together our offers in compromise.

I was told by one IRS phone agent that I should get a real job and finally become a responsible taxpayer. When I call seeking help to solve our long term problem, all I get are standard form letters. When I call the IRS office I get abusive, patronizing, condescending slurs to my character and my responsibilities as an American.

When I asked for names, I was most often refused the information with comments like "it was of no value to me to have their names and therefore it's unnecessary".

After going bankrupt over five years ago from my first encounter with these people, I have never dug out. Now they have added 100% in interest and penalties and the interest is still compounding -- yet no one will help us. This agency is absolutely out of control and needs to be abolished.

IRS Abuse Report #80

Date: Thu, 11 Apr 1996 20:32:27 EDT
To: sue@irs.class-action.com
From: DP

In 1988, I received a computer-generated IRS form letter about an over-refund from a couple of years before. The signature was a totally illegible inkblot. I called the 800 number on the letter -- every day for 6 months. No answer. I called the local IRS number. No answer.

I wrote to the IRS at the address on the letter. My response was another letter, identical to the first one, with the same inkblot signature.

Without any further warning, they began levying my salary -- 100% of it. I took home $0.00 paychecks for three and a half months. My home and car were both repossessed because I fell so far behind in my payments. The only reason I survived was through the kindness of a co-worker.

IRS Abuse Report #81

Date: Thu Apr 11 01:37:19 EDT 1996
To: sue@irs.class-action.com
From: JB

The IRS has decided to withhold refunds due me as they say I owe taxes back to 1981. After three years of dealing with these people, the IRS is trying to attach liens against everything I own. The problem resolution office will not even meet with me. I filed suit in the Tax court against the IRS. Since I constantly receive collection notices (totally incorrect) I though a law suit would finally settle the matter. WRONG. The tax court accepted a motion that the IRS filed to throw my case out as I did not have a proper NOTICE OF DEFICIENCY form. They can still send collection notices, and I have asked for a proper NOTICE OF DEFICIENCY form, but they will not give this form, just collections notices and attempted liens.

IRS Abuse Report #82

Date: Thu Apr 121 20:06:23 EDT 1996
To: sue@irs.class-action.com
From: HN

The killed my father and put my family in the streets.......must I say more?

I have been left with nothing and have nothing.......thank you America!!!

IF THERE IS ANYTHING THAT I CAN DO TO BRING DOWN THESE BASTARDS PLEASE LET ME KNOW....I HATE THEM WITH ALL MY

HEART AND SOUL!!!!!

IRS Abuse Report #83

Date: Sun Apr 14 07:15:33 EDT 1996
To: sue@irs.class-action.com
From: RG
These thugs have to be stopped. The IRS through, fraudulent "Notices of Levies", have attacked my spouse and my wages, along with our bank accounts. And, because of these fraudulent leans, they have prevented me form getting credit for my daughters college education.

We are powerless to stop this tyranny and extortion.

IRS Abuse Report #84

Date: Mon, 15 Apr 96 12:14:10 -0700
To: sue@irs.class-action.com
From: JG
After I was laid off from my occupation of 22 years in the aircraft maintenance field. I found out that the Federal Govt classified aircraft maintenance as an obsolete career due to the number of mechanics and the faltering airline business.

I proceeded to try and find a new career. Now, the IRS tells me that all expenses I spent trying to find a new line of work, while trying to support myself, my wife, and 4 kids on unemployment, is not deductible because it's not in the same field I was working in -- which they themselves classified as obsolete!

On top of that, in order to feed and house my large family on $125 per week, and trying to find a new job, I had to cash in my K401 to save my house... Now I'm taking a $1476 penalty off the top off my return. Plus paying the taxes on unemployment..

No wonder I can't catch up or get ahead, I wasn't even allowed food stamps because I had a 1 year old Mazda MPV that I owed the bank $23,000 on -- that disqualified me...Where is the justice!

IRS Abuse Report #85

Date: Mon Apr 15 19:11:37 EDT 1996
To: sue@irs.class-action.com
From: GY
We have received liens on money they say we owe them! They have taken

money out of credit union saving! And, they are trying to take money from my pay check!

IRS Abuse Report #86

Date: Thu, 18 Apr 1996 18:02:54 -0400
To: sue@irs.class-action.com
From: VMD7493@aol.com
My parents committed suicide the first of this year to avoid further problems from the IRS.

IRS Abuse Report #87

Date: Tue Apr 16 21:37:37 1996
To: sue@irs.class-action.com
From: MD
The IRS went after my brother and assessed him $19,000. He owed about $3000, so the balance was penalties and interest. Further, the IRS agents have refused to let him deduct his children, even though he has a court order that states he is the sole guardian. They also will not let his ex-wife deduct the children. This case proves they are not above breaking their own laws or above using harassment against others. By the way, my brother has been unemployed for the last two years and the $19,000 they took from him is from his retirement that he spent 20 years working for.

IRS Abuse Report #88

Date: Thu Apr 18 11:36:37 1996
To: sue@irs.class-action.com
From: VN
I received a refund of $57.00 for 1988. Now, for the past four years, the IRS has insisted that I did not file. They have been adding interest and penalties continuously. I have been continuously sending them copies of the forms I originally sent to them. They refuse to admit they are wrong.

They have threatened me with all kinds of things from garnishments to taking my possessions. Where do they get the right to take more than they should. I have been paying taxes for many years and my ancestors paid before.

IRS Abuse Report #89

Date: Thu Apr 18 22:27:50 1996
To: sue@irs.class-action.com
From: Anon
The IRS Has:
 *violated my power of attorney
*filed liens without notice
*threatened my pregnant wife
*routinely "lost files"
*refused to examine evidence
*told one of my attorneys to go away
*threatened me if I didn't fire that particular attorney.
All at a cost of time and money (a hell of a lot more than the bogus assessment).

IRS Abuse Report #90

Date: Sun Apr 21 16:40:49 1996
To: sue@irs.class-action.com
From: JH
The IRS does not respond to any of my inquiries, letters, or statements. I have only received unscheduled visits at my home and office by agents threatening to charge me with crimes, stating that they do not have to respond to any of my questions. They sent summons to my banks, and credit card institutions.

IRS Abuse Report #91

Date: Mon Apr 22 10:11:08 1996
To: sue@irs.class-action.com
From: TV
The IRS lost or misplaced my tax return for 1992 and then two years later notified me that I owed back taxes and penalties — the penalties are approximately $6,000.   When I pointed out that I had filed my return, their response was PROVE IT. How can I prove that I mailed a return? All I can do is show a copy of what they claim I did not send to them to begin with!!

IRS Abuse Report #92

Date: Fri Apr 12 13:22:58 EDT 1996
To: sue@irs.class-action.com
From: anonymous
They claim I owe $75,000 and if I don't come into their offices to take care of it that they will begin to garnish my wages! I told them that I have never

even earned that much money throughout my whole life as I have been a college student until this year. The majority of their claim came from a stock purchase of my fathers that had erroneously ended up with my social security # on it during a time while I was in Japan for two years doing volunteer missionary work with no pay! Letters were already on file with the IRS documenting the error and placing the tax liability with my father. All they were apparently doing was trying to discover something to come after my father with and scared the hell out of me in the process.

If that is not harassment then I don't know what is! They came after me for something they already knew wasn't my liability. I've had probing calls before, but that threat was just going too far!

I would love to give the IRS a taste of their own medicine but don't feel I can afford to because they have so much influence over my family's life. As we run a family owned business, they cannot only hit our personal lives, but come directly after our companies as well, so we quietly grin and bear it while shaking in our boots everyday.

No one is safe from the IRS!

(scared to give my name!)
P.S. I'd like information on the lawsuit, but I really don't want the IRS coming after me or my father, so I don't want U.S. mail sent to me on the subject. I'm not even sure e-mail would be safe. I'm really paranoid. The IRS makes life a living hell! I think I'd just as soon deal with the KGB.

IRS Abuse Report #93

Date: Fri Apr 26 18:44:22 1996
To: sue@irs.class-action.com
From: GW
Here is a list of IRS abuses inflicted on me and my family:
*My 1993 taxes are currently "under audit" by an IRS Revenue Agent. He has been auditing our tax return since November, 1995. It is now near the end of April and we still have not gotten the audit finished.

*At first he said the audit would take about two half days. Then he wanted two full days. I run a business from my home, just me, I did not want this guy holding up my business for two full days.

*Neither we nor our attorney heard anything from him until a month later, when on February 29, 1996, I got a phone call from our attorney saying that the IRS agent had 13 questions he wanted us to answer. The questions were all answered in our amended return – which apparently he did not even look at.

*The IRS Agent then said there would be an additional $9000 plus my self employment taxes all payable in 10 days. I had to stop work for an entire week, trying to track down information to document his requests.

*When the 10 days were up, my husband went to the meeting between the IRS agent and our lawyer. The IRS agent was pretty hostile. He basically disallowed everything. He refused to look at any documentation my husband tried to present.

*From what my husband could figure out, it sounded like our tax bill was going to be even bigger than the $9000. So, the more we tried to comply, the worse it got for us. Now, we don't know what is going to happen. The IRS Agent even said that I had committed some kind of crime because I paid my kids to work for me in my business (which he doesn't believe—he said we just put the money back in our own pockets). My kids filed tax returns and paid taxes on their earnings, as well as tax on the interest in their bank accounts

*We live in a small town, our tax lawyer has to do business with the IRS all the time. Plus, he has been audited three times himself. He doesn't want to rock the boat.

*It's now April 26, I have no clue what's going on with our audit. I've paid my taxes for 1995 but filed for an extension because I don't know what's going to happen.

IRS Abuse Report #94

Date: Tue Apr 30 11:16:24 1996
To: sue@irs.class-action.com
From: MR
I was a member of a partnership that was audited back in 1984.

The case took six years to settle. I signed an agreement accepting the settlement. Nothing happened for over a year. Then out of the blue the IRS came at me with both guns blazing. Assessing all kinds of penalties and claiming that the time to reply to their claims had elapsed.

This same event happened to everyone in the partnership, however, all members had signed and filed the paper work prior to final agreement. Each member had to individually prove to the IRS that the IRS had made the mistake.

It's very involved and involves several instances where the IRS misplaced, lost or outright deceived us. This also precipitated a nervous breakdown for me. The financial distress was enormous and to this day I haven't recovered from the problems the IRS caused due to their negligence.

IRS Abuse Report #95

Date: Tue Apr 30 23:26:54 1996
To: sue@irs.class-action.com
From: PM
The IRS confiscated my wages. I was working on an $80,000 year job and had to quit, dispose of all I owned, and have not been able to work since, except odd jobs. I did not owe IRS the money they said. It was due to a tax shelter that went bankrupt and not only did IRS come after me, but about 200 other people. I filed bankruptcy against the IRS and was discharged of my debt. However, I still owe for the past 4 years and feel it is unconstitutional the way they harass me. I have not been able to get a real job or own anything because of the IRS.

IRS Abuse Report #96

Date: Thu May 2 1:23:54 1996
To: sue@irs.class-action.com
From: CC1
"The IRS has harassed me for 16 years".

In 1980 a previous employer erroneously reported my income by reporting that I earned $10,000 in 1980. I explained to the IRS that I did not earn the $10,000 because I only worked two weeks in 1980 at the rate of $750 bi-weekly. I further explained that I was the accounting supervisor for that company that reported the error and it can be very easily corrected. To no avail, the IRS ignored my request to ascertain the facts and eagerly tried to destroy me. the IRS subsequently seized my house, my car, my retirement account, and everything I needed to sustain life. The IRS has hounded me for 16 years. This year in 1996, the IRS seized my bank account, and tax payments I made. The IRS told me the seizures were for payments on the 1980 taxes that they say that I still owe. The IRS seized everything I owned making it almost impossible to cope and they are still harassing and intimidating me.

I'm not rich nor do I own anything worth having. The IRS has really hurt me in a very serious way. I mean in the way that you hurt inside where the pain is so deep that all the tears stop flowing and all that remain is the moan! I remember on one occasion the IRS came on my job and thus caused me to lose my job. I have not been allowed to get credit, or live a comfortable life for 16 years. I am a Vietnam veteran and I have not been able to use my G.I.

bill to buy a house because of what the IRS has done to me, my name, and my credit. The IRS has caused me and my wife to suffer great depressions in our marriage and the IRS has caused disharmony among me and my friends.

IRS Abuse Report #97

Date: Thu May 2 16:06:48 1996
To: sue@irs.class-action.com
From: Anonymous
I just received a tax examination change report for 1993 and 1994 which bills me for $25,000 due to disallowing alimony I paid. I didn't even get a chance to show my canceled checks, court order, etc. I was presumed guilty without the right to show proof.

IRS Abuse Report #98

Date: Sat May 18 0:54:48 1996
To: sue@irs.class-action.com
From: T.M
We are being audited for 1993 and 1994 in spite of losses totaling $ 70,000. We have already been billed for almost $ 6,000 plus penalties and interest. They are also accusing us of hiding income due to $ 25,000 in loans from relatives. All this has caused much stress and sleepless nights so far.

IRS Abuse Report #99

Date: Sat May 18 9:31:27 1996
To: sue@irs.class-action.com
From: PB
I am being persecuted and harassed by the IRS — have been for years because I am trying to stop their abuses which are the same tactics and methods used by gangsters, the Mafia, the Gestapo, Al Capone — collect through fear. I have written to Congressmen, the IRS Commissioner, the president, everyone I think could help and called for a Congressional Investigation into the abuses of the IRS and its collection methods. Without exception, they passed the buck and in effect laughed at me.

I am a tax accountant for many years — have seen abuses first hand in my family and clients. Now for the tenth or 11th time I am being audited -- have had a deficiency judgment issued against me and am in the process of filing a brief in the tax court. This will do no good. How can we get justice in the tax court when the judge him or herself is in the pay of the same entity we are fighting. It is to their interest to find for the government for their paycheck is at issue. We do not have the right to a jury trial guaranteed us by the Constitution. The IRS violates every constitutional right - they are the

Gestapo run rampant. I expect to lose everything for there is no justice here and I will go to jail before I will pay a tax I do not owe. In the audit and appeals court I provided every proof of my deductions they called for, answered every question — yet they disallowed everything.

I am not against paying taxes and in the last two years I was audited, I paid over $10,000 in taxes willingly but the IRS is trying to collect $10,000 more and I am just a small wage earner — very middle class. Please enter me in this class action law suit.

IRS Abuse Report #100

Date: Thu May 23 14:38:12 1996
To: sue@irs.class-action.com
From: BW

My mom works for the IRS. She has told me numerous stories of how the IRS has taken things from people and even put them in jail. One particular story really made me hate the IRS:

An elderly woman lost her husband in 92. She had never written a check or paid a bill in her life. Her home was completely paid for. Her family was helping her pay her bills. In 1994 the IRS seized her home and all of her worldly belongings for back taxes. She died two months later. Her family fought with the IRS for a whole year to find out why no one was notified of this seizure before it occurred and why the family had no idea what was going on. After 5 months of investigation the IRS has sent the family a letter stating their apologies for a miscalculation which in turn made it look like the elderly woman owed $1750 in back taxes when it should have read a $17.50 due to her. Because of their misrepresentation and false information the elderly woman died of a heart attack at her home the day it was sold. The IRS has gone too far...these people think they are the answer to GOD himself. They need to be stopped.

IRS Abuse Report #101

Date: Fri June 7 1:42:57 1996
To: sue@irs.class-action.com
From CW

I owned a cleaning business as sole proprietor. Incorporated after first year. Neglected to vacate first employer ID number, so IRS decided that I have two identical businesses simultaneously and estimated my so-called unreported income for two years. After six years I ran out of money to fight them and had to pay $16000 for a business I never owned?

IRS Abuse Report #102

Date: Sat June 8 12:26:54 1996
To: sue@irs.class-action.com
From: RB

My uncle made a mistake over a period of ten years concerning deductions that should have been extracted from his farm workers wages. After repeated threats to take everything he had, and put him in prison, he committed suicide leaving a wife and children to fend for themselves.

He was goaded into it by the IRS, the GESTAPO and STORM TROOPERS of the UNITED STATES OF AMERICA. I have since found out that the threat of prison was used falsely.

I personally believe my uncle killed himself because of the shame he thought he'd endure by going to prison. He was wrong. To go to prison because of the IRS is a RED BADGE of COURAGE! Down with the IRS. If you work for the IRS, never let your shadow darken my path!

IRS Abuse Report #103

Date: Sat June 10 23:19:06 1996
To: sue@irs.class-action.com
From: LT

Consider the "people" who are working for the "IRS". What makes them so heartless, so eager to destroy and cause pain and loss to so many. I don't consider these beings human in any sense of the word except that they appear in human form.

IRS Abuse Report #104

Date: Sat Jul 13 17:14:31 1996
To: sue@irs.class-action.com
From: Anon

What happened with myself and the IRS is unforgivable. For the first time in my life I truly know the feeling of hatred for another.

If you ever want to be free, then realize that the IRS must be destroyed. Shame them, turn your backs to them, make them and their families hate to go out in public, make sure they feel unwanted, let them know they are not welcomed anywhere. Stand up and fight with anyone who will stand with you against these monsters.

Anyone that has ever had any contact with the IRS must wonder what type of people they are. Just patriots following orders? So were the guards in the concentration camps. How do they look at themselves in the mirror? They provide nothing to society but misery and despair. They can look at themselves because they enjoy the limitless ability to abuse power.

If there is evil in the US, it is the employees and judges of the IRS. Do their neighbors and family know were they work? If they don't, they should. We should all know their ID's. If we are successful and true freedom is restored to every citizen of the US, do we simply forgive these parasites? Do the former IRS elite simply to go out among us as if they had done nothing but follow orders? Why don't you post lists of these employees with pictures, names, and addresses so we all know who they are? I don't want my children playing with the children of parents who think nothing of stealing food from the mouths, along with the shirts off the backs, of other people.

If your neighbors son or daughter works for the IRS, shouldn't you know? You would want to know if a pedophile came to visit the neighborhood, wouldn't you? Send them statements that they are not welcome in the USA any longer. Post their pictures and their identity in their neighborhoods. Ostracize them and their families. Start making *them* miserable for a change. Force them out! Don't feel pity for them. No one forced them to work for the IRS. They did it willingly, all on their own. They are not good people. If they were, they would recognize the evil in what they do for a living. If they had an ounce of decency in them, they would never have taken a job with the IRS. Don't hold your breath waiting for a politician to give up their greatest political tool just to end our suffering. Like the IRS agent, if the members of the congress and senate had an ounce of decency in them, their first priority would be to free us, repeal the 16th amendment, and brand the bastards working at the IRS as criminals, jail them and take away everything that they bought with the money they stole from us.

Until we stand together against them, they will continue to intimidate and harass us and we will never realize freedom. All future generations of children in the US will be born into slavery. Never to realize any form of hope, prosperity, or the right to privacy.

Editor's Note: Due to its longer length, the next testimony was placed at the end of this report. This final testimony helps identify the attitude of the IRS concerning its horrendous behaviors toward innocent people.

IRS Abuse Report #105

Date: Mon 11 Sep 1995 08:08:36 -0500
To: sue@irs.class-action.com
From: RD
The following was written a few days after the incident happened.

Around 10 A.M. January 19, 1995, my bookkeeper came to my office and said a QW from the IRS was there and wished to speak to me. I told her I did not want to talk to Q because I had no idea what this was about. As far as I knew, we had no outstanding issues with the IRS, and all old issues had been settled. Since she was obviously frightened by Q's attitude, I knew I'd have to handle it myself.

I went to the door, this lady shook my hand and said "I'm QW with the IRS". I said she could come in and motioned her to a chair in my office. I took my chair, and she asked as I sat down, "Who am I speaking to?". I replied, "My name is RD". She said "Then you are who I need to talk to." I thought it strange the way she asked and responded. If she didn't know who I was, I thought, "Perhaps this is a scam artist, or, who knows what??? I'd better be careful, 'til I can tell what's going on here. She didn't offer me any identification, and since I don't know of anything wrong with my relationship with the IRS, this might be 'some type of out-of-the-blue' scam. I figured I had better find out if this gal is real, or yet another nightmare."

She then asked "Who owns this building?" I thought "What the heck business is it of yours?" but replied, "What is your authority and what is your purpose." She did not reply, but instead asked if JK was my attorney. Now, this really put me on edge. If she really was IRS, she should know who my attorney was. And if she knew that, she knew it was a breech of the IRS code to talk to me directly. If she wasn't IRS, then she'd ask that question to set us up for something -- but what? Maybe She'd been routing in our trash and found an old bill and come up with a scheme to bilk us. But if she is IRS, she should have already talked to Jim before showing up, and he hasn't called. So, who knows what's going on here! This lady is apparently up to no good. So, I cautiously replied, "I haven't talked to Jim in a few months. But I notice you haven't answered my question, what is your authority and what is your..." She cut me off! I was getting very stressed and thinking I need to call

Golden-Helmet Overture

The Evil

the police and get this lady out of here. "She said, what I notice is you didn't answer my question -- WHO OWNS THIS BUILDING!" I think I asked why she needed to know, and incredibly, she said, 'Cause I checked and it isn't listed with the county records office!" I wondered what that had to do with anything, and how it could be that the records didn't list the owner, when all filing and insurance paperwork was paid for back when NM purchased the property. Again, her conduct and responses did not match what I thought to be the truth.

Then, I thought about the two "POSTED: No Trespassing Signs" on the corners of the building. And also the "KEEP OUT PRIVATE PROPERTY" sign in the yard. A few minutes before she arrived, someone had been walking on the property taking pictures and I had debated going out after them and throwing them off. But having been shot at before, I returned my thoughts to her and said, "Listen, you're on private property without an appointment or an invitation..." I was preparing to order her off the property, but she didn't wait for it to be stated. "That's fine," she said, "that's all I need to know." And she got up and walked out.

I was pretty miffed. If she was IRS, what had she wanted and why wouldn't she tell me? If she wasn't, which sure seemed to fit her actions better, then I was the target of some kind of scam. I told my bookkeeper to bring me that old IRS file. I needed to talk to MZ. I had worked with Mark before and trusted him, and I think he trusted me as well.

I called and asked the gal who answered the phone if QW worked there. I was told she did. I asked this gal for Q's supervisor. I was told it was Dave someone. I was surprised it wasn't Mark. I asked to talk with Dave. The operator said Dave was busy. I said, fine, who is his supervisor. She said MZ. I said "Oh good, I know Mark, let me speak with him!" I was put on hold again. Then a fellow came on the line. He identified himself and I said, "Is QW one of yours?" He took a hostile stance and said "What do you mean, is she one of mine!" I said, "Is she one of your employees? Are you her supervisor? Is she an IRS agent? He said, "Well, who am I talking to?" or perhaps "Who the hell am I talking to?" the intonation was consistent with either answer. I said, "My name is RD. A lady just popped up out here, saying her name was Q that she was IRS." He informed me, "Yes, she is a IRS collection agent, and she must be working on a collection case." I said, "Well, she just popped up out here and refused to answer any questions about who she was and what authority she had." He snapped back, "She's a field agent and us field agents can pop up wherever we want to." I asked, "Why wouldn't she tell me what's going on? and why isn't she talking to the people I pay to handle these matters..." He asked, "Well, does she have a paper with her where you assigned your power of attorney?" I replied, "Well how should I know, I've never seen this lady before in my life and...". He replied, "Well, she's got to have a power of attorney to be able to talk to your attorney." I said, "As far as I know the IRS has a power of attorney on file for JK...", He again belligerently asked, "Well, does she have that piece of paper?" I answered, "How I am supposed to know? I asked her about her authority and she left!"

He seemed to drop his hostile attitude, a bit. He said, "She's working on a case." I was confused. I thought we were all caught up with the IRS and, frankly, proud of it, and how we had handled our obligations at the time. I said, "I don't understand, I worked with MZ in the past..." He spouted, "What do you mean you worked with MZ!" He was fierce. This news really took him by surprise. It frightened me. I had no idea where he was coming from, or why he'd be mad at me for having worked with Mark. I said, I worked with Mark in the past, we had some trouble and we worked it out.. He was clearly confused by what I was telling him. I again complained about Q's refusing to identify herself and her authority and purpose. He asked, "She showed you her credentials?" I said "No, I asked her what her authority was, and what her purpose was, and she refused to answer. She didn't show me anything. I told him someone remembered a QW from the past coming out, but I had never met her. After that, he calmed down again. I think he then asked to talk to Q. I told him she had left the property. At this point, I noticed a surprise in David's voice. He must have thought she was still in front of me. He said "If she comes back tell her to talk to me." I wondered why she would be coming back. I told him, "Look, whatever the case, my position is, if she is here without and invitation and without an appointment, she is trespassing. She's supposed to talk to my attorney, and it's still my opinion she should do so." He acknowledged, reminded me if she were to come back he wanted to talk to her first. I took this for an acknowledgment of my complaint, and an indication he would see after it. I thanked him and hung up.

I thought there was more to this story. I didn't feel safe any more. I called my attorney and explained the strange thing that had just happened. He said he hadn't heard anything, but he'd find out and if something was really happening, he'd fill a 911 with the IRS, because as far as he knew, there had been no communications with the IRS since filing the affidavit. Clearly proper IRS procedures were not being followed, and someone was out of line, and way out of control.

At that point, one of the employees appeared at my office and said "she's back". She stormed in and said they were taking the building and changing the locks. She started down the hall, I said you need to call David. She wheeled at me and shouted, accusatory, "I know you talked to David." I thought this was probably a lie, she was probably surprised I knew her coworker's name and was bluffing. I asked, "Have you talked to David since you were last here?" She wheeled and again headed down the hall without answering. I said, "David told me to tell you to call him." She ignored me and started to peel the back off of some kind of sticker. Clearly this person was not interested in Law, Justice, Due Process, or IRS procedures and Code. Nor was she interested in hearing what her supervisor had to say to her. I began to suspect Dave wasn't her supervisor at all. What was going on here?

She threw out a Notice of Levy on my desk. Then she walked away and turned around again and threw out a Notice of Seizures. I looked at it. It was getting pretty clear at this point. The notices were to CA-PC. I asked "What do you think you're doing here?" She shouted, "We're shutting down the business!" I asked, "Which business?" That pretty much threw her into a rage. She sputtered and shouted, "This business here!!!" and pointed at the floor in my office. So, I asked, "And what business do you think this is?" She refused to answer and stormed out of my office.

My attorney and I continued to talk. I began digging for the sales contract proving NM owned the building she was seizing in the name of PC's back taxes. She went to every NM employee and told them they had to leave. She ordered one to get off the phone, who was having a conversation with a NM customer. I am told no one believed her. She was so rude and irrational, no one could imagine what her problems was.

I was talking to my attorney one time when she came stomping through, and I was telling him I had asked for her identification several times and she had refused. At this, she finally produced a wallet with two pieces of paper in it. I began to read the paper, and had read the first half, with various IRS information on it while still holding the phone so my attorney could hear, and as soon as I reached the personal information, she snatched it away and stomped off. I said "wait a minute, I didn't finish. Hey, Q, can we get a copy of that?" She didn't answer. It's becoming apparent to me this woman does not want any personal identification numbers to become part of the record.

I decided I'd better talk to Mark at the IRS, since he was the only one with enough integrity to be trusted. It seemed nearly every other agent I had talked to, had lied. I dialed Mark. I had to wait quite awhile. When Mark answered the phone, I asked if he remembered me and that we had worked together in the past. He said he thought he remembered the name. I began to explain the situation as best I understood it. At that moment, the police we called arrived in my office. I told Mark, "Oh good the police are here, hang on." I then addressed the officer, still speaking into the phone so Mark could hear, and said, "Thank you for coming out, today. We've got quit a problem here. These agents have come out to serve a Levy and Seizures, but as you can see here on their documents they have the wrong company listed. This property is owned by another company, here.." and I offered him the sales contract showing NM owned the building. The officer began examining the two documents. I turned my attention again to Mark. I said, "Did you copy all that Mark?" He said he wanted to speak to Q. I told the bookkeeper to go tell Q she was wanted on the phone. She said, I don't think she'll come. I said please go tell her MZ is on the phone and wants to speak to her. She said she'd try.

Both agents were in my office. Q began listening to Mark. She made several objections. She said, "I sent it to them here, and I sent it to them there" I assume she meant PC, "and these guys sent back an affidavit and the other guys didn't send back anything." I thought, "Great, cooperate with the IRS, follow the rules, and what do they do? Jump on you for the effort. If the other guy DIDN'T respond, why did you assume the guys who did respond, followed IRS procedure and filed affidavit, which went unanswered by the IRS for months, were the ones who needed to have things seized?

She said to Mark, "I was out several times and I spoke to Mr. RD several time..." My blood boiled. She was a liar. To the best of my knowledge, I had never seen this woman before. She may have called several times when I was out, but she sure didn't talk to me. I had a power of attorney, and they were supposed to talk to him. I was so mad at the way I had been treated by the IRS that I wanted no personal contact. Nothing in the world burned me more than dishonest IRS agents, and here in my office on posted private property was a jerk using my phone to lie to her supervisor while disrupting the business of a company in complete compliance with the IRS. She was busily trying to deprive more than a dozen people of their salaries, and thereby about to deprive the U.S. of $100,000 a year in revenue. Let alone the other companies who would go out of business and have cause to sue. We were already warned that day, if we allowed interruption of parts shipments to RJS, they would go out of business and be forced to sue. She had usurped so many powers of the Constitution, let alone violated so many rules and procedures of IRS code, that she was, well, either criminally negligent, or worse, acting with full criminal intent.

She and Mark went on talking, "but I'm looking right at a business card with CA on it in his office." I said, yes, but that's CA-I. That's an entirely different company from CA-PC." By her reasoning, Joe Getz could be held accountable for Joe Gonzales taxes, even if their Federal Tax Identifiers were different. Why? Because they had the first name? Oh Brother! I got up and took one of the cards and offered it to the other agent. I said, may I present this for your examination. Now, this other agent was sitting wide eyed and in general looking amazed at what was going on. She looked at the card. Q on the phone said something to Jim about "International". Sensing there might be some reason coming to the other agent, I returned to my desk and took out the sales contract and took it to her and told her this property was owned by NM. She almost grabbed this out of my hands. I held on to it as it was the only copy I had. She asked, "When was this?" I helped her look for a date and found the 4th of November 1986.

I went back behind my desk and was able to find an inventory list from PC works which was labeled as such and returned to show her. I said, "These were the assets of PC," and I pointed out, "there's not a single piece of anything on that list in this building."

She said, "JK is your attorney?" I said yes. She shook her head and said, "I've worked with Jim before, he's a good guy." I began to pipe in how I thought so too and Jim was an ex-agent himself and I almost missed her next comment, half under her breath and in total disbelief. "How did this ever get this far?"

Q jumped in, still on the phone with Mark and said, "Can I have a copy of that?" I said, "Sure, I'll be more than happy to give you a copy -- just as soon as you agree to stop this illegal action.." Oh! she glared at me. She turned around and didn't ask again, nor did she acknowledge my offer. She finished with Mark after a quite a few more minutes. She closed saying, I'll see you back at the office." I said, Wait! I still want to talk to Mark. She hesitated and sneered at me.

A little later, or perhaps still during the phone call, this agent who had seemed reasonable asked about NM. She asked if I was the president of NM. I said yes, and she said, "Q he's the president of NM too, Q! Q!" But Q was getting an earful from Mark at that time, or just ending her call, and waved her off. I thought great, you still are outside due process and you're grabbing at straws, and you're going to do the seizure anyway. You've got no concept of the meaning of "legal entity" and due process of law. Another attempt at illegal seizure. These agents are either ignorant of the law and the IRS code, or deliberately ignoring it. They don't know who they can proceed against and they don't care. They don't even know the difference between private property and personal property.

When I got the phone back, Mark had already hung up. So, I dialed him up again. He asked about my relationship with PC. I went on and told Mark that I was willing to pay every cent I owned, and he should know that from working with us before, but in this case, that wasn't it. I told him I'd been involved with Pat of PC for only a few months. Pat had told me where break-even was, and I helped get the sales there. I then found out break-even was MUCH lower. I told Pat we could either shut down the business and sell off the assets or he could buy it back and take over all obligations. Mark asked about my relationship and I said I basically gave business advice and had pumped in some money. I told him I never had signature authority on the PC account, that Pat was the manager before, during and after my involvement with it. I think this was all in accordance with the affidavit we filed. He asked me if I knew where the bank account was, then there was another commotion. Someone shouted at me, they're changing the locks. Q walked back in. I asked if we were done? Was it over? Could the police office go? She gave half a nod and a sneer, but no solid answer and walked out.

Mark asked if I minded answering a few questions from time to time. I told him I didn't mind talking to him personally but... He said, okay, what if he called and asked a few questions from time to time, would I mind. I said, no I wouldn't mind, but, this in no way was meant to waive my power or attorney I had with JK. He acknowledged he understood, and then we went on to discuss what a good guy we both thought Jim was. That was the end of our conversation.

Q was standing outside. I opened the door to ask her if she wanted copies as I had promised, and she sneered, I'll be back in a minute. So I went back to waiting. All the employees were standing around trying to figure out what happened. She came back in with two sets of keys and said here's your keys to the locks. Sign this. I asked what it was. She said it was just a release form, saying we got our building back in the same condition it was in. I insisted on reading the type above my signature. There were two sides to the page. I didn't know it at the time I signed. When I tried to pick up the papers, she scolded me. Ooh, there's two copies there be careful. Don't get them out of line. Above my signature was the line she said certified the building had been returned in the same condition it was taken. There was also a release clause that I held the government blameless for damage to the building. I turned to the locksmith and said, are those my original locks and keys. He said he had to re-key the locks and he couldn't put them back in the same order without seeing our original keys. I said, we had lots of keys out and if we didn't have keys we didn't have our building back. She said, Well you're going to have to pay for that. All I paid him to do was to change the locks and then give you the keys. If you want them changed, you're going to have to pay for it. I scowled at the paper. The locksmith chimed in, how many sets of keys? I said about ten. He said he'd make them. I asked how much. He said he'd throw them in no charge. I accepted his offer and signed under that condition. As far as I know, they did not damage the building. It wasn't the building I was worried about anyway. We'd been knocked off our schedule, suffered lost production and sales, I was suffering chest pains and could feel my blood pressure was at a dangerous level, and I thought if I didn't have that release, I'd be sleeping there overnight with as many employees as would stay with me. And there was no release clause against her as an individual. After all, as I understood the situation, the government had rules she had broken and the majority of illegal action had been on her part, the assisting agent, and the supervisor, Dave. So we were free to sue for anything as long as we weren't claiming damage to the building.

When I had the keys, I made copies of the Sales Contract between NM, Inc., and PC along with the inventory list of PC equipment. She told me she was going to send a letter of some kind and to be sure I filled out every question on it. Then she said I was the only registered officer of the company so they were still going to hold me responsible for the back taxes. She then left.

Well, I was so upset I was only able to sleep about an hour that night. Most of the night I spent working on this recording of the events as they were fresh in my mind. My wife told me she could hear the stress in my voice and she can see it in my color.

The experience of trying to deal with an irrational QW and IRS has been detrimental to my health. I checked my blood pressure Friday morning and it was up ~150% above previous highs. The readings I took were 214 over 114 with pulse of 110. I called my Doctor's staff, with the numbers. They told me to come in immediately. I went to the hospital Friday before noon. My doctor told me anything over 200 was an emergency. He told me no matter what was going on, "At some point you've just got to calm down and tell yourself, 'I'm not going to let these people kill me.'" He told me he was certain I'd had suffered some injury to my heart during that session. He felt the IRS should be made to pay for such a serious intrusion into one's life.

I am now on blood pressure medicine. Prior to this, I had maintained a reasonable pressure by natural means -- reduced salt, low sugar, low fat diet, exercise and weight loss. This is no longer possible. Monday, five days later, under medication, my pressure is still 177 over 93, higher than any other point I have a record of prior to Q's illegal action.

Ending the IRS
The Route to Everyone's Prosperity

Have you, a family member, a friend or loved one ever been defrauded, looted, hurt, injured, brutalized, or destroyed by the Internal Revenue Service (IRS)? Did no one help you, sympathize with you, or even listen to you, even though you were innocent — even though you and your family were criminally violated, badly injured, perhaps even destroyed or murdered? Do you want legal justice? Do you want to alleviate the sufferings and fears caused by the IRS? You can now safely participate in an inspiring, class-action-type lawsuit against the IRS, its armed agents of force, its paid informants, and those politicians responsible for illegal tax laws, fraudulent assessments, regulations, penalties, liens, levies, seizures, and garnishments. These class-action lawsuits will be based on cruel-and-unusual punishment in violation of the 8th Amendment of the Bill of Rights in the United States Constitution. ...Ending those IRS cruelties is the route to everyone's prosperity and happiness. Replacing the destructive crimes by armed federal agents with a civil tax on *consumption* not on *production* will bring peace and prosperity to everyone.

For information, review the IRS-class-action home page at its *http://www.neo-tech.com/irs-class-action.com/* cyberspace address. In addition, join the discussions on the Eliminate-the-IRS Newsgroup at its *alt.irs.class-action* cyberspace address.

You can add to the expanding arsenal of legal evidence simply by revealing how the IRS has harmed you or others at the *sue@irs.class-action.com* email address. Also important, read the latest IRS abuse reports at

http://www.neo-tech.com/irs-class-action/

IRS Class-Action Announcement
alt.irs.class-action

"The attorney preparing the Eighth-Amendment, class-action lawsuit against the IRS issued the following statement:

"In the past few months, we have gathered well over a hundred valid plaintiffs that legally meet the requirements for a class-action suit against the IRS on the basis of the Eighth Amendment to the United States Constitution, which forbids the government from inflicting cruel-and-unusual punishment on its citizens. We are adding an average of 1-2 valid plaintiffs daily from web site http//www.neo-tech.com/ irs.class-action/. We would like to have about 500 bona fide plaintiffs when we file the lawsuit in Federal District Court. Potential plaintiffs should visit the IRS Class-Action home page for information about this lawsuit and how to become a plaintiff. ...No fees or charges of any kind are being asked or will be asked from any plaintiff or potential plaintiff."

A Side Note about this Action

"Of the hundreds of potential plaintiffs we have reviewed, the most unnecessarily tragic of the victims are those whose lives have been crushed even though they have paid their taxes in full and have no legal recourse to gain credit for their tax payments. How does that occur?

"Such victims are generally those who fully paid their taxes, often with refunds due, through employer-payroll withholding taxes. Then, correctly believing their taxes have been paid in full or in excess by their employers, they fail to file their income tax return due to their busyness, forgetfulness, ignorance, or any other reason. Now, hidden in the IRS codes and case law, any taxpayer who after three years fails to file will automatically lose their tax credits/payments. That taxpayer is then considered as having paid $0 in taxes for that year because of a IRS three year limitation period and has no way to get credit for the taxes he or she has paid once the three year limitation has passed. (Remember, to get credit for taxes paid, one must file a tax return, even if that filing consists of stapling a W-2 form to a signed, blank return requesting the IRS to calculate the tax return.) If the non-filing taxpayer fails to do this then the taxpayer is subjected to full tax liability along with its horrendous penalties and interest that often can never be paid. The taxpayer is then crushed with liens, garnishments, and seizures with no legal recourse to the IRS or the courts. Such IRS actions as described above will comprise a second lawsuit that will contribute to the eventual abolishment of the IRS.

"All those who, for whatever reason, have been or are being illegally or cruelly punished by IRS penalties, interests, levies, garnishments, seizures are potentially eligible plaintiffs for either or both lawsuits."

The Golden Helmet

versus

Armed Bureaucracies

Cyberspace Addresses
Class-action email: sue@irs.class-action
Eliminate-the-IRS home page: http://www.neo-tech.com/irs-class-action/
Eliminate-the-IRS Newsgroup: alt.irs.class-action
Profound Honesty/Neo-Tech/Zon home page: http://www.neo-tech.com/
Neo-Tech Mailing List: neo-talk@lists.best.com

Table of Contents

Introduction

Can the following battles be won on planet Earth: Good versus evil. Justice versus injustice. Prosperity versus poverty. And more: Rationality versus irrationality, peace versus war, life versus death. Yes, *all* those battles can be won. Victory is certain — perhaps by 2001 AD or even earlier.

Why is victory certain over the next decade? The survival of all purposely harmful politicians and government officials depends on public acceptance of armed bureaucracies. That acceptance occurs through political and media deceptions. To perpetuate such deceptions, the integrated honesty of Neo-Tech and the wide-scope accounting of the Golden Helmet must be kept hidden or suppressed. Yet, every act to suppress Neo-Tech and its Golden Helmet increases public desires to depoliticize government as first begun in America during its 1994 elections.

This report describes how Neo-Tech and Golden Helmets will eventually depoliticize government and eliminate its armed bureaucracies. This report also reveals how the violent attacks on Neo-Tech literature and its Golden-Helmet dynamic by armed bureaucrats in both 1986 and 1990 began the dynamics for eliminating armed bureaucrats from government. And finally, this report shows how every aggression inflicted on Neo-Tech literature and its Golden-Helmet dynamic subverts the perpetrators and draws them toward being legislated out of existence. *...That elimination of armed bureaucrats will bring limitless prosperity to America as identified in this Appendix.*

* * *

By shunning publicity and the media since 1981, Neo-Tech authors and editors have quietly spread Neo-Tech worldwide. Published in twelve languages,

Introduction

Neo-Tech literature is distributed in 156 countries. It is now too late to stop the Neo-Tech dynamic of fully integrated honesty and its wide-scope accountability.

Neo-Tech is the dynamic undermining destructive politics and organized religion for the past decade. Neo-Tech has been the deep-root cause of (1) collapsing totalitarian governments, such as in Eastern Europe, (2) eroding the authority of Western religions, such as Roman Catholicism, (3) removing from office economically and socially destructive politicians, such as begun in America during its 1994 elections. In turn, that Neo-Tech dynamic is now undermining economically and socially destructive bureaucracies worldwide, including America's most-harmful armed bureaucracies such as the ATF, DEA, EPA, FDA, INS, IRS. ...Those politician-created, criminal-driven bureaucracies are the underlying cause of raising violence and terrorism throughout America.

What to do about those politicians responsible for the criminal elements of government? Independent of everything occurring in today's Establishment, the Neo-Tech/Golden-Helmet dynamic helped determine the 1994 elections and will largely determine the 2000 AD elections. Indeed, that dynamic will increasingly vanish or redeem[1] harmful politicians. Moreover, that constant

---

[1]Redeem? Bill Clinton, for example, had a redeemable core of innocence. Ironically, President Clinton's high intelligence combined with a total lack of principles left him uniquely qualified to understand and then implement the Neo-Tech/Golden-Helmet dynamic. Thus, in the following way, Clinton could have become the greatest, most valuable world leader in history: Before Neo-Tech and the Golden Helmet, no consistently rational principles were available in which anyone could invest. Bill Clinton, maybe out of a special integrity, never locked into or invested in bogus principles from the irrational philosophies that swirled about him and everyone else. Such a fact left him uniquely free for redemption — free to extricate himself from his problems, crimes, and harms of the past. How? Through the Neo-Tech/Golden-Helmet dynamic, Clinton could have swept away

(continued on next page)

undermining of harmful people by Neo-Tech will eventually eliminate destructive bureaucrats, judges, and lawyers.

Local policemen serve to protect life and property. But, armed bureaucrats serve to harm life and property. Today, the increasing social and physical harms caused by politicized armed bureaucrats are endangering all Americans. ...Bureaucrats, not law-abiding citizens, must be disarmed.

Golden-Helmet economics backed by nonpolitical *objective* law could be in place by 2001 AD or earlier. Limitless prosperity and happiness will then become available to everyone.

(continued from previous page)

armed bureaucracies, political-agenda laws, and ego 'justice' to boom America and the world into limitless prosperity. Seizing that opportunity, he could have freed himself from his hidden crimes to become a hero for all time. Instead, he chose to be Iago to an Othello-like America. With brilliant language seduction, Clinton became the poison in the ear of America to ferment a political culture of rot. ...He could have unleashed America toward a rational civilization through Neo-Tech and the Golden Helmet. He could have brought this world into the Civilization of the Universe ten years ahead of schedule. Thus, he could have saved countless millions of lives in booming the prosperity of everyone worldwide.

New Words and Concepts

Golden Helmets are all-revealing, wide-scope accounting tools that evolve naturally from the fully integrated honesty of Neo-Tech. Golden Helmets are what will vanish not only income taxes but all other taxes on production, earnings, savings, property, inheritance, and estates. Golden Helmets are the tools used by businesspeople to generate limitless wealth for others and society.

Neo-Tech is a noun or an adjective meaning *fully integrated honesty* based on facts of reality. Neo-Tech creates a collection of *new techniques* and *new technology* that lets one know exactly what is happening and what to do for gaining honest advantages in all situations. Neo-Tech provides the integrations to collapse the illusions, hoaxes, and irrationalities of any harmful individual or institution.

Objectivism is the philosophy of Neo-Tech: the philosophy for the well-being of conscious beings — the philosophy based on reason — the new-world philosophy of limitless prosperity.

Subjective Laws include political-agenda laws conjured up by politicians and bureaucrats to gain self-serving benefits, false egos, and unearned power. Enforcement of political-agenda laws requires the use of force and armed agents against innocent people. ...The only purpose of such laws is to violate individual rights. **Objective Laws** are not conjured up by politicians or bureaucrats. Instead, like the laws of physics, they arise from the *immutable laws of nature*.[1] Such laws are valid across time and space, benefit everyone, and advance society. Objective laws are based on the moral prohibition of initiatory force, threats of force, and fraud as constituted on page 89 of this Golden-Helmet Appendix. ...The only rational purpose of laws is to protect individual rights.

---

[1]Unchanging, universally *principled the-point*, natural law as promoted by fully integrated honesty...not *pragmatic a-point*, positive law as promoted by Oliver Wendell Holmes and today by jurists like Robert H. Bork. Such politician-made, positive law always leads toward criminal governments and despotism.

7

Ego "Justice" is the use of subjective, political-agenda laws to gain harmful livelihoods and feel false importance. Ego "justice" is the survival tool of many politicians, lawyers, and judges. Ego "justice" is the most pernicious form of neocheating. ...Parasitical elites thrive on subjective laws and ego "justice" to the harm of every individual and all of society.

Parasitical Elites are unnatural people who drain everyone. The parasitical-elite class lives by usurping, swindling, and destroying values produced by others. Their survival requires political-agenda laws, armed bureaucracies, ego-"justice" systems, and deceptive neocheating.

Neocheating is the undetected usurpation of values from others: the unsuspicious swindling of money, power, or values through deceptive manipulations of rationalizations, non sequiturs, illusions, and mysticisms. ...All such net harms inflicted on society can now be objectively measured by the wide-scope accounting of Neo-Tech.

Truth is a mushy, hydra-headed word. Everyone disputes its meaning. Truth denotes a <u>static</u> <u>assertion</u> that changes from person to person, opinion to opinion, culture to culture. Thus, *truth* is a hollow, manipulative word that parasitical elites promulgate to gain credibility for their deceptions, destructions, and ego "justice".

Honesty is a solid, indivisible word. No one disputes its meaning. Honesty denotes a <u>dynamic</u> <u>process</u> that is identical for every conscious being. *Honesty* cannot be manipulated. Therefore, parasitical elites must squelch honesty in order to live off the productive class. ...Thus, discard the word **truth**; uphold the word **honesty**. Discard ego "justice"; uphold objective law. Discard the parasitical class; uphold the productive class.

Anticivilization is the irrational civilization gripping planet Earth — an unreal civilization riddled with professional value destroyers and neocheaters causing endless cycles of wars, economic and property destructions, unemployment and poverty, suffering and death. ...Through Neo-Tech, the honest Civilization of the Universe will replace Earth's dishonest anticivilization.

New Words and Concepts

Civilization of the Universe is the rational civilization throughout the law-abiding universe — a civilization filled with value producers providing endless cycles of wealth, happiness, and rejuvenation for everyone. ...Professional value destroyers and parasitical elites are nonexistent in the Civilization of the Universe.

Zon is a collective word related to the fully integrated honesty of Neo-Tech and comprises (1) the Civilization of the Universe, (2) those operating from its wide-scope perspective, and (3) the power required to control existence — the integrated power to gain wealth and happiness.

Zonpower is the power to control (*not* create) existence. Zonpower is derived from applying the fully integrated honesty and wide-scope accountability of Neo-Tech to all conscious actions.

9

Chapter 1
Armed Evil

In the "Neo-Tech Newsletter", volume 3, number 5, the author of the *Neo-Tech Discovery*, Dr. Frank R. Wallace, published an article about the Golden Helmet and its wide-scope accounting. That article included an ostracism matrix of the most socially destructive people in America. The publication was then released to its armed IRS targets at 8:00 AM on March 29, 1990. An hour later, a huge, electrically lighted billboard spotlighting the IRS was unveiled in front of the federal courthouse concealing a bevy of armed IRS agents. On the same day, twelve hours after releasing that publication and the unveiling of that electric billboard, those armed agents attacked the author of Neo-Tech, violating his First-Amendment rights.

Under cover of night, those IRS agents assaulted Dr. Wallace at his writing office. They threw copies of his just released publication against his body while screaming obscenities. "How is Neo-Tech going to help you now?" their leader shouted. Wallace's only response was to ask for a minute before being jailed to feed his two aged cats. "F_ _ k the cats!" came a screaming reply. Then, in violation of the First Amendment and free press, they shackled Dr. Wallace's hands behind his back and jailed him. ...The newly published pamphlets disappeared and the electric billboard came down.

Later, the federal prosecutor described Wallace as a most dangerous man because of his Neo-Tech literature and espousals. The federal judge characterized Wallace's Neo-Tech work as "a task of terrifying proportions".

Yes, in fact, Frank R. Wallace is a most dangerous man publishing terrifying literature — dangerous and terrifying to the professional value destroyers whose careers will eventually be ended by the Golden Helmet, its wide-scope accounting, and its ostracism matrix.

The Ostracism Matrix

Today, cyber communication and computer technology provide an inescapable ostracism matrix. At the deepest roots, that matrix exposes destructive people and their harmful careers. Over 2450 American and foreign parasitical elites are already locked into that computerized matrix. Combined with wide-scope accounting as described in the Neo-Tech literature, that matrix identifies professional value destroyers in government, business, and the legal professions. That matrix will eventually reveal to everyone the world's most harmful people. Against Golden-Helmet accounting, they can no longer hide behind their deceptions and illusions.

Wide-Scope Accounting

After years of quietly building the Neo-Tech/Golden-Helmet dynamics, the public is awakening to a monstrous fraud — an awakening first reflected across America in its 1994 elections. Eventually, all professional value destroyers from left-wing property usurpers to right-wing spirit usurpers will be driven from their jobs — jobs used to commit crimes against innocent people, the economy, and society. With the parasitical elites gone, America and the world will prosper beyond imagination. But, how will the parasitical elites be vanished? To answer that question, the nature of a class overthrow based on wide-scope accounting must be understood. With that understanding comes the knowledge for a peaceful overthrow of socially harmful politicians and bureaucrats.

But, first, review again that morning of March 29, 1990: Newly published documents written by Dr. Frank R. Wallace were placed in newsracks in front of two

11

targeted IRS buildings. An hour later, a huge 16' x 48' electric billboard was unveiled in front of the federal-court building. Neither the documents nor the billboard were directed at the public. The time had not yet arrived to begin the public revolution. The documents and billboard were directed at several-hundred professional value destroyers identified for the first time in print by name — destructive persons already in a computerized ostracism matrix capable of itemizing the net destructiveness of each individual.

Those published names ranged from criminal-minded persons holding various-level positions in government, religion, big business, and the professions. In addition to names of IRS officials responsible for committing objective crimes, other names ranged from nefarious political-exploiter Rudolph Giuliani[1] to barbaric drug-czar William Bennett[2]. All published names were people who used armed bureaucratic enforcers and self-serving ego "justice" to promote themselves and their careers while discarding objective law and justice (Ref: *The Neo-Tech Protection Kit*, B & W, 1991).

Also published were the names of bureaucrats and lawyers who are professional value destroyers. Their jobs were based on harming the economy, society, and the productive class. Such jobs must be backed by armed enforcers who threaten, harm, pillage, jail, and eventually destroy their victims — victims who are often the most

[1]See Giuliani's footnote on page 17.
[2]William J. Bennett's best-selling *Book of Virtues* (Simon & Schuster, 1993) is a full-blown example of camouflaging evil with illusions of virtue. Close examination of Bennett's book of "virtues" reveals a maudlin collection of non sequiturs that mostly contradict mankind's only two objective virtues: (1) fully integrated honesty and (2) producing competitive values for others and society. William Bennett is nothing more than a totalitarian theocrat who advocates, for example, public beheadings of those who violate bogus political-agenda laws involving drugs.

12

courageous and talented of the value producers. ...Such entrepreneurial victims represent the future prosperity of any economy.

Those newsstand documents not only published the specific names of those in the ostracism matrix, but described how that matrix would function once it were released to the public. Those documents described how the matrix would eventually remove each professional value destroyer from his or her harmful livelihood. ...Seizing those documents in the morning, armed IRS agents attacked Neo-Tech and jailed its author by nightfall.

Parasitical Elites Depend on Guns and Jails

Armed bureaucrats assaulted and jailed Frank R. Wallace. He was then "silenced" in a federal labor camp. Three months later, in an attempt to stop his writings from prison, Dr. Wallace was shackled in handcuffs, waist chains, and leg irons. He was then spirited to a more isolated prison atop a windblown, desert hill.

During their violent destructions several years earlier, on November 3, 1986, those same armed bureaucrats beat, kicked, and hospitalized the personal editor of Dr. Wallace. Next, they destroyed irreplaceable original research and literature manuscripts. They pillaged the hard-earned property of I & O Publishing Company, its writers, its editors, and its customers. Gleefully, they carried off the precious biomedical research funds of the Research Institute for Biological Immortality (RIBI). They put I & O Publishing out of business. ...Four years later, those same gun-carrying bureaucrats caused the death of Wallace's pet cat.

Pillaging, injury, destruction, death — why? To survive, the parasitical-elite class must increasingly harm and destroy Earth's innocent creatures — men, women, children, even pets and animals. Indeed, while in federal

13

prison, Dr. Wallace witnessed daily the deterioration of political prisoners *and their families* — hundreds of innocent men, women, and children being slowly, insidiously stripped of life. They were being murdered as surely as if being killed by Hitler or Stalin. ...Through wide-scope accounting, all parasitical elites are revealed as killers — murderers of political pawns by either open Hitler/Stalin style or hidden Bush/Clinton style.

Today, in America, innocent political pawns are increasingly broken or jailed in order to support an expanding parasitical-elite class. Tomorrow, without Neo-Tech, those victims would be one's own children, parents, brothers, sisters, friends. ...Eventually, everyone who is not a parasitical elite or an active supporter of the leech class would become a victim.

Chapter 2

Political Prisoner #26061-048

1992
The Author of Neo-Tech
speaks from a
Federal Labor Camp

"Prison paradoxically both magnifies and hides the harm parasitical elites inflict on the economy and society. Today, armed bureaucrats and ego-"justice" courts are quietly incarcerating tens of thousands of political pawns in federal labor camps scattered across the United States. In its spiraling need to control and drain others through enforcement of political-agenda laws, the American parasitical-elite class imprisons a higher percentage of noncriminals than any other country in the industrialized world.

"Those political prisoners are victims of power-usurping politicians and bureaucrats. Such politicians and bureaucrats usurp their power through the bureaucracies they create, arm with guns, and then expand. Such bureaucracies include the ATF, DEA, EPA, FDA, FTC, INS, IRS, SEC. Politicians backed by those armed bureaucracies increasingly force their way into every citizen's life. Armed bureaucracies are used to control and drain the productive class in order to support the parasitical-elite class at the expense of everyone else, especially the needy.

"When those many thousands of prisoners and their families are exposed to the Golden Helmet, they will realize their sufferings were inflicted solely to advance the parasitical-elite class. Such political prisoners will realize they have broken no objective law and are not guilty of

15

any real crime. Each will also realize that initiating force, threats, or fraud toward other individuals is the only objective basis of crime for which justice can be rendered. Then, angrily, each will realize the parasitical-elite class is guilty of initiating the force and fraud that cruelly crushed their lives...and the lives of their families.

For every political pawn jailed or destroyed, the parasitical elites cower a hundred value producers into submission. Those monstrous but hidden crimes violate objective law. ...Those perpetrators can and eventually will be brought to justice through the Neo-Tech/Golden-Helmet ostracism matrix."

Political-Agenda Laws

"Many, but not all, federal prisoners today are jailed for violating political-agenda 'laws' that have nothing to do with objective law. Political-agenda 'laws' are gun-enforced to empower politicians, bureaucrats, and an iniquitous triangle of lawyers, prosecutors, and judges.

"Today, only those prisoners and their loved ones can experience the full evil of the ego-'justice' system created by the parasitical-elite class. As a result, America's justice system is now controlled by a triad of deeply dishonest lawyers, malicious prosecutors, and falsely respected judges who disdain objective law, justice, and honesty. Indeed, ego 'justice' is increasingly draining all productive people without the public knowing the terrible price everyone is paying. That price is a deteriorating society."

Ego "Justice"

"Ego 'justice' is practiced by judges who abandon objective law to support armed bureaucracies that enforce destructive political agendas. Through judicial exploitations and social deceptions, those judges garner public respect. Yet, they are destroyers of property, life, and happiness. Today's ego-'justice' judges incarcerate ever more political pawns with ever harsher, totally unjust sentences. Why? To maintain their ego props and arbitrary power through expanding enforcement of political-agenda laws."

Humanoid Judges

"Consider the life-shattering sentences imposed daily on people innocent of any objective crime. Consider Los Angeles federal judge Manuel L. Real who routinely destroys those caught in his web with the harshest possible prison terms — solely to feel power and importance. He takes pleasure in his tough-judge image expressed by his Maximum-Manny nickname. In his self-glorifying process, he destroys the lives of innocent men, women, and children. ...Many other judges at all levels are also Maximum Mannys who destroy innocent human beings and their families in order to feel important.

"Consider federal judges Thomas P. Griesa, Milton Pollack, John M. Walker, Jr., and Kimba Wood. Each giulianied[1] innocent business giants for personal power and ego enhancement. Each such judge is a killer of innocent but unpopular people like Michael Milken and Leona Helmsley. Review the records of perhaps the most murderous political-agenda judges in America, Walter Smith, Jr., of Waco, Texas and Clifford Weckstein of Leesburg, Virginia. Such judges destroy objectively innocent individuals caught in the evil web of political-

---

[1]The verb giuliani means to use gun-backed, political-agenda law to criminally destroy honest businesspeople and illegally seize private property. Derived from Rudolph Giuliani who advanced in politics by illegally using RICO and seizure laws to crush innocent people and their businesses.

17

agenda enforcements. To garner ego-boosting publicity and to feel powerful, those humanoid judges crush their wrongly accused, media-smeared victims with false, inhumane imprisonments.

"Each such judge is an accomplice to the gun-backed crimes of political-agenda enforcement — crimes of collective assault, pillage, murder. Such judges and their prosecutor cohorts must be held responsible for their crimes against individuals, the economy, and society. Moreover, their innocent victims must be freed, pardoned, and paid restitution."

Heinous Crimes

"In late 1991, a triad of politicians, bureaucrats, and their ego-'justice' system in America joined to protect themselves — joined to establish the apparatus for removing threats to their power: In increasingly harsh actions, that triad established the death penalty for guilt-by-association crimes, opening the way to the death penalty for political 'crimes'. In addition, through the Supreme Court, that triad is quietly undermining habeas corpus — the basic protection against illegal or false imprisonments. ...In 1933, Hitler secured his future tyranny by quietly undermining habeas corpus. That undermining of objective law eventually led to an orgy of crimes by armed bureaucracies culminating with Auschwitz.

"Through illegal use of RICO and seizure laws; through plea-bargain 'justice' based on threats, paid perjurers, and coerced betrayals forced even between husbands and wives, parents and children, this ego-'justice' system is setting the foundation for liquidating any opposition to political policies. ...Daily, one can see that triad's heinous crimes on the dying faces of innocent political prisoners. Many of those victims must helplessly watch their families die bit by bit until all love and life are lost."

Prison: A False Target

"Consider one of the deceptions that hides the ego-'justice' system: The attention of political prisoners is riveted on the prison system in which they and their families profoundly suffer. Thus, those prisoner victims and their families increasingly focus blame on the prison system. They then lose sight of who is responsible for destroying their lives, families, and businesses. They lose sight of the ego-'justice' system that illegally put them in prison.

"In that way, the Bureau of Prisons becomes a false target. A false target because the Bureau of Prisons is not run by professional value destroyers. Instead, it is a fairly benevolent, well-run system that tries to benefit those falsely imprisoned by a corrupt ego-'justice' system. ...Many prison employees, as well as many lower-tier government employees, are good-intentioned. They too are exploited and drained. They too can and will help vanish the parasitical elites.   They too shall rise with anger to overthrow the leech class — the devil class."

Roots of Evil

"Three centuries before Christ, the Greek philosopher and politician Plato gave birth to a parasitical-elite class that to this day controls the populations of the world. Three decades ago, both the Arabic and Black Muslims perceptively sensed but only partially identified that controlling class as the Great Satan or White Devils. What the Muslims, even their own murderous leech class, actually sensed were those who have controlled the two-

19

millennia reign of dishonesty, exploitation, tyranny, oppression, crusades, wars, slavery, pogroms, holocausts.

"From Plato's techniques evolved a devil class — the parasitical-elite class. That class thrives by draining the value producers — the working class. That devil class is the parasitical-elite class, which has grown to dominate the world through subjective laws, mendacious politics, destructive bureaucracies, corrupted professions, mystical religions, effete educators, dishonest media, and the carcasses of stagnant big businesses.

"Neo-Tech, meaning fully integrated honesty, has identified that parasite class as everyone's enemy. It drains the lives of all productive people as well as lower-tiered government workers, dependent entitlement clients, and slave-labor political prisoners.

"The Muslims, especially the Black Muslims of the 1960s as exploitatively promoted by Elijah Muhammad and then more honestly articulated by Malcolm X, sensed the two-millennia-old hoax perpetuated by that devil class. But, the Muslims were misled by demographics: Certainly, in recent history, the majority within the parasitical-elite class have been western-world, white-skinned demagogues. Yet, throughout history, other cultures, races, skin colors, religions, and nationalities have also produced the same devil class — the same criminal-elite class. Even today, note how the Muslim theocracy criminally, murderously rules Iran today. Note the murderous Idi Amins of Africa. ...Race, color, religion, and nationality have nothing to do with being a devil — a professional parasite. Instead, professional parasitism has everything to do with being an enemy of the people.

"Likewise, race, color, or nationality have nothing to do with the victim class. The exploited victims are always the productive working class — regardless of race, color, nationality, economic status, or period of history.

"That devil class — the parasitical-elite class — can exist only in an unnatural, upside-down world."

Uprighting our Upside-Down World

"Nearly everything the parasitical-elite class promotes as right is dishonest and destructive. Nearly everything it promotes as wrong is honest and productive. That upside-down world of the past 23 centuries was recognized a century ago by Russian writer Mikhail Bakunin:

'For there is no terror, cruelty, sacrilege, perjury, cynical theft, brazen robbery, or foul treason which has not been committed and is still being committed by representatives of the State, with no other excuse than this elastic, at times so convenient and terrible phrase, *for reasons of the state*. A terrible phrase indeed...as soon as it is uttered everything becomes silent and drops out of sight: honesty, honor, justice, right, pity itself vanish and with it logic and sound sense; black becomes white and white becomes black, the horrible becomes humane and the most dastardly felonies and atrocious crimes become meritorious acts.'

"Hitler described parasitical elites as leeches, vampires, vermin, termites, maggots, bacilli. In his upside-down world, he then labeled the Jews as those parasitical elites. But Hitler's description of parasitical elites really applied to himself, his cohorts, and his guns-and-fists enforcers who empowered him through armed bureaucracies. By contrast, his targeted Jews were among Germany's greatest value producers.

"Likewise, to exist, all other parasitical-elite kingpins must also turn reality upside down. Mao and Khomeini,

21

for example, used force to posit nonforce free-enterprise and individual property rights as unjust and parasitical, while positing Mao's gun-backed socialism and Khomeini's gun-backed religious fundamentalism as just and valuable. ...Such people can rise to power only in an irrational, upside-down world of force, dishonesty, and mysticism."

Discovery from Prison

"What if every judge, prosecutor, and high-level bureaucrat spent a month in a Federal[1] Labor Camp for political prisoners — spent a month among the victims of subjective, political-agenda laws and ego "justice"? Each such judge, prosecutor, and bureaucrat would be indelibly struck by the suffering and destruction wreaked on innocent, good people and their families. Only by directly experiencing prison can one discover the profound harm caused by the unjust incarceration of political pawns — versus the just incarceration of real criminals guilty of objective crimes.

"Prisoners who commit objective crimes — genuine criminals — are **justly** incarcerated. Thus, they suffer *much less* than innocent political prisoners who are **unjustly** incarcerated. For, real criminals know the justice of their sentences and accept the maxim "Do the crime, do the time". By contrast, innocent political prisoners suffer deeply from (1) the horrendous injustices inflicted

---

[1]Why federal? Most prisoners in state prisons are real criminals. Many prisoners in federal prisons are political prisoners. State and county trial judges and courts deal mainly with legitimate, objective laws and crimes. By contrast, federal trial judges and courts deal mainly with enforcing bogus political-agenda laws. The federal government in Washington gives its judges lifetime appointments so they never need be accountable to the public. Thus, federal trial judges can reign in their courts as government heavies with totalitarian power. Such judges practice ego "justice" with impunity. ...Eliminating the anticivilization justice system involves revoking all political-agenda laws and ending life-time appointments for Federal District-Court trial judges.

upon them and their families and from (2) the fact that criminals throughout the government are living free while illegally destroying the lives of political prisoners, their families, and countless other innocent people.

"One and only one reason exists to enforce political-agenda laws. That reason is to enhance the harmful livelihoods of parasitical elites and their corps of professional value destroyers. Be it in 100th-BC galley ships, in 12th-century dungeons, in 20th-century Nazi death camps, or in today's federal prisons, its innocent victims are *purposely* incarcerated and often destroyed just to indulge the bogus livelihoods of a few evil people: a few habitual, mass-destruction criminals ranging from Caligula to Hitler to today's parasitical elites with their legions of armed bureaucrats.

"Only by directly experiencing prison does one discover the deep moral difference between evilly enforcing subjective political-agenda laws versus justly enforcing objective laws. With direct prison experience, many bureaucrats, prosecutors, and judges would stop pursuing, prosecuting, or adjudicating political-agenda law. They would reject such subjective laws and ego-"justice" support systems as evil."

America Today

"America today is at once the greatest and the worst nation on Earth: The greatest by the productivity, well-being, and happiness created by the mightiest host of professional value producers and competent workers in history. The worst by the harm, deprivations, and unhappiness caused by a rapidly expanding parasitical-elite class. That leech class is cannibalizing history's most bountiful trove of earned wealth and created values. But, with the rising Neo-Tech/Golden-Helmet dynamics, everyone can look happily to the future. For, the elimination of the leech class, starting perhaps by the year 2000 elections, will bring ever growing well-being and happiness to everyone."

U.S. Political Prisoner #26061-048
February, 1992

Chapter 3

The Golden-Helmet Trial

Federal Trial CR-S-90-057-LDG(LRL)
(An Article 58 Trial)

Dr. Frank R. Wallace is a scientist, author, editor, and publisher. He is also the discoverer of Neo-Tech and the Golden Helmet. In February 1991, Wallace was tried in Federal Court on criminal tax charges. Those politically wrought charges arose from a Neo-Tech street publication and billboard publicly released on March 29, 1990 — ten hours later, Dr. Wallace was in jail.

During that first trial, the judge denied Wallace an oath to incorruptible honesty rather than to manipulative truth. That denial prevented Wallace from testifying. Thus, he was convicted and sent to prison. Subsequently, the United States Court of Appeals overturned that conviction citing the judge's "abuse of judicial discretion". In the retrial of August 1993, that same judge again denied Wallace a fair jury trial through even greater abuses of judicial discretion in "ordering" the jury to render a guilty verdict as described in Chapter 6. ...Facing Wallace again, that judge pursued a single agenda: control the jury and the courtroom proceedings to obtain a conviction. To avenge his embarrassing reversal, that ego-oriented judge had to convict Wallace, regardless of the facts or justice.

Using occasional trials of objective crimes as credibility props, such judges must not let honesty or objective law expose their ego agendas. For, all ego agendas depend on dishonesty and subjective laws — on enforcing harmful political agendas through ego "justice". But, that irrationality will end. For, Neo-Tech, which means fully integrated honesty, is now embedded in the

25

legal system. Once in the system, Neo-Tech will relentlessly persist, eventually vanishing subjective laws with their ego-"justice" support systems. That, in turn, will vanish the parasitical-elite class and its professional value destroyers.

During the retrial, the judge preserved his ego agenda by manipulating an intrusive, father-like image that commanded obedience from the jurors. The judge assured obedience through improper ingratiations and intimidations directed at each individual juror. The judge then concluded the trial with a surprise, unstipulated jury instruction demanding conviction: His blatant abuse of "fair comment" after the conclusion of the trial compelled the jury members to render verdicts of guilty, no matter what their opinions of the trial or judgments of the evidence, no matter what the stipulated jury instructions stated.

That judge further sought to protect his ego by forcing Dr. Wallace into "mental-health" treatments. However, that mendacious ploy backfired as the "mental-health" sentence was overturned by the 9th Circuit Appeals Court charging the judge with vindictiveness. ...Such self-serving dishonesty serves to highlight the nature of ego "justice".

Dr. Wallace confronts evil that robs us and our children of prosperity and happiness. He confronts subjective law and challenges its ego "justice". Below are key portions of his retrial.

Wallace's Opening Statement

Ladies and gentlemen of the jury, ten years ago, through Golden-Helmet tax payments, I & O Publishing paid over four times the legal obligation of income taxes for each year in question: 1983, 1984, 1985. Unlike the prosecutor's case, my case will be grounded in reality. Nothing will be out of context. Nothing will be distorted. Nothing will be manipulated. No illusions will be created to sway the jury.

Golden-Helmet Tax Payments

From my testimony, you will also realize why only Golden-Helmet tax payments will reduce our national deficit, end our declining economy, create good jobs, bring lower taxes, and deliver benefits to everyone.

The Honesty Oath

This is a historic trial. Just prior to my testimony, I will take an oath not to truth, but to honesty as recently mandated by the Ninth-Circuit Court of Appeals. Why an oath to honesty rather than to truth? What is truth? We all know that truth for one may not be truth for another. Truth varies with condition or context. And, an unlimited number of conditions or contexts exist. Thus, without an anchor to honesty, anyone can manipulate truth to serve harmful agendas. Truth, therefore, can serve bad laws — subjective laws, which mean arbitrary laws designed to advance self-serving political, bureaucratic, and personal agendas.

By contrast, everyone knows what honesty is. It is the same for everyone. No one can manipulate honesty. Honesty, therefore, can serve only good law — objective law, which means consistent law independent of political, bureaucratic, or personal agendas.

The Truth Oath

The prosecution witnesses will take an oath to truth, not to honesty. ...Listen to the difference of testimony taken under the honesty oath versus the truth oath. At first, this imposing courtroom setting will bestow an illusion of power and credibility upon the judge and prosecutor. They will sound convincing. They will paint a picture that is opposite to the fact. As my testimony will show, the I & O Golden Helmet paid 4.1 times the legal obligation of income taxes each year from 1983 to 1985. But, the prosecutor will present out-of-context accounting figures and a paid witness — all tailored to force a conviction. But, hold judgment until you hear my testimony under the honesty oath.

Revealing a Profound Government Error

At the conclusion of my testimony, I believe most will recognize the prosecutor's accusations are an error of epic proportions. I believe even the prosecutor and the IRS will realize and admit their profound error — at least silently, to themselves.

Two Worlds

And finally, my testimony will show this is a trial between two worlds: the rational, objective-law world of the Golden Helmet versus the irrational, subjective-law world of harmful political and personal agendas. ...This trial will show how the Golden Helmet will bring great benefits to everyone — even to the prosecutor, to the IRS, and to this court.

* * *

The IRS's Case

For many hours, over two days, the prosecution presented a parade of IRS witnesses, a paid informant, and manipulated financial figures — all in an attempt to show that Frank R. Wallace was guilty of so-called tax "crimes". ...By contrast, Wallace presented his case in one hour and called no witnesses.

The IRS's case was based entirely on subjective, political-agenda law. Nothing in the IRS's case was relevant to objective law as described in the testimony.

[See trial transcripts for the full IRS case.]

Wallace's Testimony

The historic oath to fully integrated honesty was taken at this time by Frank R. Wallace:

"Do you affirm to speak with fully integrated honesty, only with fully integrated honesty, and nothing but fully integrated honesty?"

Wallace reviewed Charts 1 and 2
before starting his testimony.

Chart 1

WALLACE'S TESTIMONY WILL REVEAL

- Why Wallace is on trial
- Who is innocent; who is guilty
- The excess tax payments for 1983-1985

Chart 2

OUTLINE OF WALLACE'S TESTIMONY
(based on the fully integrated honesty oath)

Valid Facts Depend on Context

I. Context
  * Building the foundation: Pre-1986
  * Destructions of November 3, 1986
    (the violent armed attack on writing offices)
  * Rebuilding: 1986-1990
  * The March 29, 1990 book-flinging assault,
    shackling, and jailing
  * Building for the future: 1990-1993

II. Valid Facts
  * All taxes for 1983-1985 paid legally and in excess
  * Criminal charges were politically motivated
  * Wallace is innocent of all charges

[While the prosecution was allowed two days of uninterrupted testimony, Wallace's brief one hour of testimony was repeatedly cut off by the judge, even when there was no objection from the prosecution. ...Indeed, the ego-threatened judge demanded a conviction more than did the prosecution.]

Building the Foundation: Pre-1986

I was born a severe dyslexic, resulting in my being a mirror writer who could not spell, read, keep numbers straight, or remember names. To function and learn, I had to rely on conceptualization and integration rather than memory. Thus, I increasingly turned toward the sciences and mathematics.

My career aptitude tests registered the highest scores for law and a rare, perfect score for becoming an FBI agent. My family background is almost entirely law: My great, great grandfather was the United States congressman who acted as an attorney for the House of Representatives in bringing impeachment charges against President Andrew Johnson. Both my great grandfather and grandfather were attorney generals of New York State. My father was the youngest Supreme Court Judge in the history of New York State. All my uncles and older brother were lawyers. My early life was steeped in law.

From that early life, I clearly understood that a prosperous, happy society depended on a government of laws, not a government of politicians and bureaucrats. Yet, I sensed something terribly wrong with much of the law that surrounded me — something hidden and undefined — something deeply dishonest and harmful to our society.

I turned away from family tradition and headed first for a Jack-London stint in the merchant marines then to the sciences with a clean sense of exhilaration. Not until thirty years later did I discover that undefined dishonesty sensed in my early years. I discovered the difference between two kinds of law: The first kind was **Objective Law** that condemns and prosecutes murder, rape, assault, robbery, extortion, and objective civil litigations — consistent law that serves society throughout history, in all countries. The second kind was **Subjective Law** that permits self-serving political agendas, ego "justice", and dishonest torts — socially and economically destructive law that corrupts politicians, bureaucrats, judges, lawyers, and certain businesspeople. ...Subjective law mixed with objective law means corrupt law. Now I understood my exhilaration on heading toward a career in the sciences.

With an Instructorship teaching premedical students and then winning a full-time Research Fellowship, I earned my

31

Doctorate in Inorganic and Analytical Chemistry from the University of Iowa in 1957. Turning down higher-paying jobs in industrial chemistry, I accepted an elite exploratory research position at Du Pont's famous Brandywine Laboratories — the mecca for chemical research with over 3000 Ph.D. scientists and a billion dollars of research facilities at one's disposal. If any place in industry existed in which one could do research to win the Nobel Prize in Chemistry, this was the place.

After obtaining a basic patent on high-temperature catalytic reactions, I left that academic-like, basic-research career to pursue fast-track industrial research. Almost immediately, I recognized my dyslexic limitations would inhibit my career. While strong in organization, creativity, research, and math, I was a Ph.D. who, except for studying and noting technical works, could barely read or write. To function in business, I had to effectively communicate with my superiors and colleagues through writing. I also had to possess a wide, well-read base of knowledge. Because of my dyslexia, I could not even write an effective memo and had read only one classic in literature, Victor Hugo's *Les Miserables*.

Thus, I began a self-education program attacking my weaknesses with furious, nonstop intensity. Gathering a battery of books on English grammar, composition, vocabulary, and usage, I squeezed every hour out of every day for three years teaching myself to write effectively. Many nights, I worked into the morning hours writing a simple one-page memo. I studied and edited over and over, dozens of times until I was delivering my message in a clear, concise manner. Next, I launched a nonstop reading program, hardly allowing a minute to pass without a book in my hand, reading while standing in line, eating, riding in public transportation. I read hundreds of books in all areas of knowledge.

My writing and knowledge continually improved. Others began noticing my writings. Eventually, I became recognized as a good technical writer. Then, I was being sought within Du Pont for my writing skills as I increasingly wrote articles and manuals. ...Thus, I turned my greatest weakness into a strength. As a result, my progress as a research scientist accelerated.

Only 20% of the Ph.D. scientists at Du Pont succeed in being associated with a discovery that eventually becomes a successful commercial product. In less than ten years, I moved three products from the lab bench, to pilot plants, to commercial plants, then to the public with marketing and sales. As far as I know, those products to this day are still making profits for Du Pont.

My career was moving fast. All looked bright. But, all was not right. As years before with law, I was again experiencing a sense that something was terribly wrong — something I could not grasp. My career was soaring. I had three beautiful children. But, I was losing my marriage with a woman whom I dearly loved. What was wrong? Why was my deepest, inner life declining?

Reflecting back to my first week at Du Pont a decade earlier, I recall listening to an inspiring speech by world-renowned Dr. Frank McGrew, the Director of Central Research at Du Pont. Almost any research chemist in the world would consider Dr. McGrew's position as the pinnacle career goal. Yet, with profound respect for that great man, I looked at him from the back of a crowded auditorium and was seized by the realization that I had to dedicate my life to a much more important goal. Years later, while pursuing a potential cancer cure at Du Pont,

33

I felt even that goal was not important enough — not my passion, goal, purpose.

I did not know what that goal was, but increasingly I noticed that nearly everyone over thirty gradually seemed to lose his or her desire for life and happiness. What was wrong all around me, with everyone, and why? ...I was to discover the answer after I wrote my first book.

Combining my poker experiences that began in the third grade with my recent hard-earned writing skills, I wrote and published my first book: "Poker, A Guaranteed Income for Life by Using the Advanced Concepts of Poker". Within two years, it became the best-selling poker book in history. Then, Crown Publishing and Warner Books in New York took ten-year licenses to market both the hardcover and softcover editions. They doubled the sales of the book.

The poker book was not really a book about poker. It was a metaphor demonstrating the destructiveness of irrationality as opposed to the productiveness of rationality. After further studies, I realized that irrationality was not only bizarrely unnatural, but was actually a man-made disease. ...Irrationality was the disease, not cancer, that I needed to cure. I realized the single most-important goal for conscious beings on Earth was to eradicate irrationality!

After extensive research, I learned that the disease of irrationality was first propagated by Plato over 2300 years ago to support a burgeoning class of parasitical elites. ...Today, that disease is propagated by a class of parasitical politicians, bureaucrats, educators, artists, entertainers, media journalists, judges, and lawyers. They propagate their destructive irrationality through coercion, force, dishonesty, blatherings, deception, ego "justice", and subjective laws.

The Golden-Helmet Trial

Indeed, mankind's most important goal is to cure that disease of irrationality. For, irrationality not only prevents the cure for all other diseases, but is the cause of poverty, wars, riots, violent crimes, injustice, corruption, subjective laws, job losses, happiness losses, and death itself. With that realization, the goal to which I must dedicate my life was clear.

On making that discovery, I resigned my position as Senior Research Chemist at Du Pont in 1972 to pursue full time the cure of mankind's most devastating disease: the death-and-destruction disease of irrationality.

Living on borrowed money from 1973 to 1976, I wrote and produced a quarter-million-word encyclopedia about the disease of irrationality and its cure. Even though demand for the poker book continued, I took the book out of print after the licenses expired. For, I wanted the public to focus on my newly evolving literature about the prosperity and happiness that arises from Neo-Tech — from fully integrated honesty.

The encyclopedia, however, was not commercially successful. Thus, I was sunk financially with three children in school to support. That began a four-year period of great financial difficulties — until the commercially successful Neo-Tech Discovery was published. At that time, a second crucial realization occurred: To achieve my goal, not only books and publications were required, but direct, ongoing confrontations with those irrational forces that bleed society were also required. Thus, various confrontation dynamics were created.

One such confrontation dynamic, conceived in 1980, involved the Golden Helmet and the IRS. The idea was to increasingly confront the IRS on a legal, peaceful, civil

35

level — to confront the IRS through the courts. In that way, I could gradually introduce the Golden Helmet. Both the government and the public would then increasingly understand the Golden Helmet. Through such a steady but peaceful confrontation process, the beneficial laws based on rationality would eventually prevail over the harmful political-agenda laws based on irrationality.

Destructions of November 3rd

Then, the totally unexpected happened: At 12:25 PM, November 3, 1986, without warning, sixteen IRS agents carrying guns attacked the research-and-writing facilities of I & O Publishing. Without reason, they punched, kicked, and hospitalized my personal editor. Those agents then proceeded to ransack everything. Breaking into a safe, they seized the RIBI research funds allotted to 2200 registrants — funds obligated to an offshore medical-research program.

Those agents took all files, computer disks and backups, writing and research projects in progress. They took everything needed to carry out our writing, research, and publishing activities. ...Without a hearing or even an indication of a crime committed, their seizures ended the rapid expansion of I & O Publishing Company and eventually put it out of business.

Now, crucial to my testimony, I want you to hear a commercial audio tape — the portion containing a live, impromptu twenty-minute speech I gave at the Neo-Tech World Summit to five-hundred international representatives at the Tropicanna Hotel on November 11, 1986, just eight days after those armed agents violently pillaged I & O's writing and research offices.

The Golden-Helmet Trial

[Editors Note: The prosecutor having previously heard that tape objected to the jury to hearing it. For, by describing the Neo-Tech/Golden Helmet, the tape clearly demonstrated Dr. Wallace's innocence. ...Then, the judge, without even listening to the tape, prohibited the playing of that tape to the jury.

Indeed, of the dozens of rulings and motions since the inception of this case in March 1990, Judge Lloyd D. George supported the prosecution without a single exception. The court records show that George ruled 100% against Dr. Wallace. He seldom addressed even a single point in Wallace's motions. In almost every action since 1990, Judge George simply reworded the prosecution's position to rule against Wallace. Other judges involved with this case showed no such bias. They generally considered Wallace's position fairly and equally with the prosecution's position. Thus, those judges ruled about fifty fifty for and against each side.

The Ninth-Circuit Court of Appeals overturned Judge George's entire 1991 trial for his abuse of judicial discretion against Wallace.]

After the attack of November 3, 1986, I tried to reason and work with the IRS. More than once, in both letters and in publications, I offered to review my Golden-Helmet tax-payment records with the IRS commissioner. In May 1987, I sent the supervisor of that IRS attack, Gary Rogers, a key to my safe-deposit box containing the Golden-Helmet plan showing the excess tax payments. I even sent the IRS Commissioner, Fred T. Goldberg, two skids of Golden-Helmet tax records from previous years. Yet, the IRS apparently never used that key or those records to confirm the Golden-Helmet tax payments. Did the IRS already realize its error? Did the IRS agents realize they seized I & O's property solely on the basis of a dishonest informant seeking a cash payoff?

Rebuilding: 1986-1990

The IRS ended our research and publishing capability. Additionally, the IRS ended our capacity to service a quarter-million readers and customers. Yet, the integrity of I & O Publishing Company required providing those customers with products and services. The Golden-Helmet and medical-research funds held abroad were used to pay expenses required to satisfy both our national and international customers.

Thus, the rapid growth of jobs, values, and taxpayments generated through the Golden Helmet ended along with our medical-research plans.

A shrinking I & O Publishing continued out of homes and apartments, rather like a Kibbutz or a Mormon family, until independent, non Golden-Helmet companies developed in 1990. Indeed, from 1987 to 1990, every remaining asset of the Golden Helmet was committed to preserving our progress toward curing the death-and-destruction disease of irrationality.

To maintain that forward movement, I voluntarily worked 14-16 hours a day, 7 days a week. No vacations, no hobbies, no luxuries. No retirement or pension benefits. No salary or paychecks. In 1989, a modest house was purchased for me to live with my wife when my office domicile — a house purchased in 1973 for $32,000 — was donated to the Kenneth A. Clark Memorial. An additional room and a meeting-room basement were added to handle the escalating meeting, writing, research activities. During that time, funds needed to support my work, research, and publications averaged about $5000 a month. On the advice of a loan officer, that amount was listed to meet the mortgage requirements. From that writing/research support structure, my donated house, along with money from my wife's savings, a down payment was made.

After the Golden-Helmet support structure was phased out, I & O Publishing was abandoned in 1990. Today, my wife, Rosa Maria, supports portions of my research and writings, as do thousands of other Neo-Tech benefactors worldwide.

If not for my devoted wife, whom I need and who fervently supports my work, I would live like a monk in a YMCA — which I have done during several periods of my life, even when I was a Senior Research Chemist at Du Pont in the early 1970s. As is, I still live like a monk as much as possible. I return to my wife's house only for dinner, then again to sleep. I have no hobbies and take no vacations; I have no interest in accumulating wealth or material luxuries. ...Such diversions would only consume irreplaceable time, break my concentration, and distract me from my work and goal of curing irrationality worldwide.

I never, however, advocate such a 100% service or a monk's life for others. I advocate a happy life for everyone by whatever rational, productive life style brings maximum happiness. ...By my choice and dedication to a single goal, a monk-style life is what makes me the most efficient and, thus, the most happy.

Today, I accept only a minimum-wage job as an editor for Neo-Tech Worldwide. My wife and others support my pro-bono publishing activities. ...My life is 100% dedicated to eliminating the disease of irrationality.

Appendix: The Golden Helmet

The Book-Flinging Assault
and
Political Jailing of March 29, 1990

After the 1986 armed attacks and seizures, the IRS did nothing for over three years and appeared it would do nothing. With all of I & O's funds, records, and writings in its possession, the IRS did nothing to bring my case to court or to allow a just trial. I increasingly pressed the IRS to interact rationally through its personnel and the civil courts. I still had no response. I applied pressure through a series of pro-bono publications sent to the IRS and others throughout the government. Each new release was more aggressive in identifying the irrational behaviors of certain harmful people in politics and the IRS.

Then, early in the morning on March 29, 1990, newsstands were placed in front of the two IRS buildings in Las Vegas and stocked with my latest publication. An hour later, a huge 16' by 48' billboard was unveiled in front of this very court building. That publication and billboard were directed at several-hundred harmful politicians and bureaucrats identified for the first time in print, by name. ...The most destructive of the IRS personnel were also highlighted.

That night, under cover of darkness, those same armed agents of three-and-a-half years earlier attacked me outside my writing offices. Midst their screaming obscenities, an agent threw a stack of my publications at me — publications they had removed that morning from the newsstands. "How is Neo-Tech going to help you now?" he shouted.

In blatant violation of the First Amendment, free press, and free expression, they then shackled my hands behind my back and jailed me because of my publications and large billboard placed in front of their offices that morning. During the entire two-hour assault, shackling, and jailing, not one IRS agent mentioned taxes as a reason for my arrest. For, all their harmful acts over the past six-and-a-half years, including today's trial, had nothing to do with taxes. Instead, their destructive acts had everything to do with violating the Constitution and the First Amendment protecting free press and free expression.

Building for the Future: 1990-1993

Today, I confront those who in 1986 destroyed my work, pillaged my home and offices, seized our medical research funds, hospitalized my editor, threatened my family, and then in 1990 jailed me because of my writings. Today, I am here to help cure that evil — to help cure the disease of irrationality that always seeks to destroy everyone's happiness and well being.

* * *

Now, let us turn to one specific area that will help cure the disease of irrationality: Golden Helmets as reviewed on the next three charts.

This chart demonstrates that my ideas and actions are

Chart 3
CONCEPT OF EXCESS
TAX PAYMENTS

(Golden-Helmet Position)

Excess Taxes are *Always* Voluntarily Paid

- Every genuine job producer *always* pays excess taxes voluntarily
- The IRS Code explicitly recognizes that excess taxes *must* be paid voluntarily

versus

(Tax-Rebel Position)

"Taxes are Voluntary"

- Not recognized by law or the IRS Code

not among those who do not pay taxes...or those who call themselves tax rebels. My essence has always been to generate values, jobs, and excess tax payments.

The key word is voluntary: Tax rebels use the word "voluntary" to avoid paying taxes. In contrast, the Golden Helmet uses *voluntary* work and effort to pay far more than the required amount of taxes.

Chart 4

EXCESS TAX PAYMENTS OF 1983-1985

- Excess tax payments were paid *voluntarily* through a multiplying agent called I & O
- IRS had knowledge of those excess tax payments:
    1. It had all financial records for 1983-1985
    2. It issued 100% tax abatements for 1983-1985
    3. It issued a 1992 tax-refund check to Wallace

Chart 4

Through the Golden Helmet, I & O Publishing voluntarily paid over four times the legal obligation in income taxes for each year from 1983 to 1985.

As early as 1987, the IRS had knowledge of those excess tax payments for the following reasons:

1. The IRS seized all records for 1980-1985. From those records, it could have deduced those excess tax payments, especially with its informant's statements, and, certainly, after I repeatedly sent the IRS letters, information, records, and literature about the Golden Helmet. As testified earlier, I even sent the IRS management a key to my safe-deposit box containing the Golden-Helmet, tax-payment procedures.

2. After destroying I & O Publishing on November 3, 1986, the IRS apparently realized its mistake and took no further action for over three years. Presumably, the IRS would have taken no further action if not provoked into jailing me in 1990 because of my aggressive writings and publications.

3. On April 22, 1991, the IRS issued a 100% abatement on all my alleged taxes, penalties, and interest for 1983-1985:

Appendix: *The Golden Helmet*

(Below are the IRS Abatements for 1983 to 1985)

```
1 00529                                    89254-474-15977-1  9115  CP: 21C

       Department of the Treasury      Date of this notice:   APR. 22, 1991
       Internal Revenue Service        Taxpayer Identifying Number
       OGDEN, UT   84281               Form: 1040     Tax Period:  DEC. 31, 1985


       [barcode]
                                                For assistance you may
                                                call us at:
       BOULDER CITY  NV   89005-3058            1-800-829-1040   ST. OF NV


                                                Or you may write to us at
                                                the address shown at the
                                                left. If you write, be
                                                sure to attach the bottom
                                                part of this notice

STATEMENT OF CHANGE TO YOUR ACCOUNT                 94251-095-18C02-0

   WE CHANGED YOUR ACCOUNT TO CORRECT YOUR ACCOUNT INFORMATION.

                           STATEMENT OF ACCOUNT

ACCOUNT BALANCE BEFORE THIS CHANGE                  $154,522.88 DUE

DECREASE IN TAX BECAUSE OF THIS CHANGE               57,538.00CR
THE ESTIMATED TAX PENALTY AS EXPLAINED ON THE ENCLOSED
   NOTICE - SEE CODE 82 - THAT WAS PREVIOUSLY CHARGED HAS
   BEEN REDUCED                                       3,298.80CR
THE FRAUD PENALTY AS EXPLAINED ON THE ENCLOSED
   NOTICE - SEE CODE 05 - THAT WAS PREVIOUSLY CHARGED HAS
   BEEN REDUCED                                      43,204.00CR
THE MISCELLANEOUS PENALTY AS EXPLAINED ON THE ENCLOSED
   NOTICE - SEE CODE 28 - THAT WAS PREVIOUSLY CHARGED HAS
   BEEN REDUCED                                      14,385.09CR
DECREASE IN INTEREST PREVIOUSLY CHARGED *            36,095.08CR

AMOUNT YOU NOW OWE                                        NONE    <---

   * IF THIS INTEREST WAS PREVIOUSLY TAKEN AS A DEDUCTION, IT MUST NOW BE REPORTED AS
INCOME ON YOUR NEXT INCOME TAX RETURN.
```

```
1 00528                                    89254-474-15976-1  9115  CP: 21C

       Department of the Treasury      Date of this notice:   APR. 22, 1991
       Internal Revenue Service        Taxpayer Identifying Number
       OGDEN, UT   84281               Form: 1040     Tax Period:  DEC. 31, 1984


       [barcode]
                                                For assistance you may
                                                call us at:
       BOULDER CITY  NV   89005-3058            1-800-829-1040   ST. OF N


                                                Or you may write to us at
                                                the address shown at the
                                                left. If you write, be
                                                sure to attach the bottom
                                                part of this notice.

                                                    94251-095-18091-0
STATEMENT OF CHANGE TO YOUR ACCOUNT

   WE CHANGED YOUR ACCOUNT TO CORRECT YOUR ACCOUNT INFORMATION

                           STATEMENT OF ACCOUNT

ACCOUNT BALANCE BEFORE THIS CHANGE                  $254,926.80 DUE

DECREASE IN TAX BECAUSE OF THIS CHANGE               92,685.00CR
THE FRAUD PENALTY AS EXPLAINED ON THE ENCLOSED
   NOTICE - SEE CODE 05 - THAT WAS PREVIOUSLY CHARGED HAS
   BEEN REDUCED                                      77,793.00CR
THE MISCELLANEOUS PENALTY AS EXPLAINED ON THE ENCLOSED
   NOTICE - SEE CODE 28 - THAT WAS PREVIOUSLY CHARGED HAS
   BEEN REDUCED                                       5,827.96CR
DECREASE IN INTEREST PREVIOUSLY CHARGED *            78,621.00CR

AMOUNT YOU NOW OWE                                        NONE    <---

   * IF THIS INTEREST WAS PREVIOUSLY TAKEN AS A DEDUCTION, IT MUST NOW BE REPORTED AS
INCOME ON YOUR NEXT INCOME TAX RETURN.
```

46

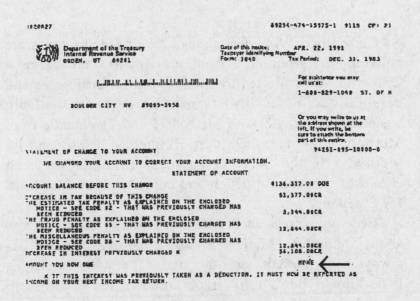

The above three abatements show the balance owed for each year as "NONE".

Since the IRS has all the records for 1983-1985 and all the years before, only the IRS can provide the specific accounting figures for the Golden Helmet. Nevertheless, I will demonstrate the excess tax payments with the next chart.

Chart 5

First, I will review the three legal methods of income-tax payments.

(Review Chart #5 at this point)

47

Appendix: The Golden Helmet

Review of Chart 5

Currently, in America, about 82% of income taxes are collected by Method 1 from individual wage earners. Only 18% are collected by Method 2 from businesses and corporations, especially stagnant corporations and big businesses. But, 100% of Methods 1 and 2 *originate* from Method 3 — from Golden Helmets. Additionally, Method 3 is the only tax-payment dynamic that can eliminate our national deficit and permanently reduce taxes for everyone.

Everyone knows about Methods 1 and 2, but few know about Method 3. Moreover, knowledge of Method 3 has always been implicit, until this trial. Today, however, this little-known but vitally important Method 3 is being squeezed out of existence by self-serving politicians and bureaucrats. That is why the economy today, no matter what is done, can never really flourish for all of society. Instead, the economy will continue to fluctuate into ever lower real wages along with reoccurring recessions coupled with periods of inflation, deflation, and declining employment — constantly draining the productive class.

The only major politician who implicitly understood and acted on the Golden Helmet was President John F. Kennedy in 1961. For the first time in history, an American President began implementing the Golden Helmet. Thus, President Kennedy rapidly yanked the economy out of a deep recession, boomed job creation, and dropped unemployment toward new lows. If allowed to continue expanding, that Golden-Helmet dynamic would have collapsed the irrational aspects of politics, bureaucracies, and stagnant big businesses.

Today, the growing armed divisions of government bureaucracies are used to prevent movements toward Golden Helmets. However, now, for the first time, the

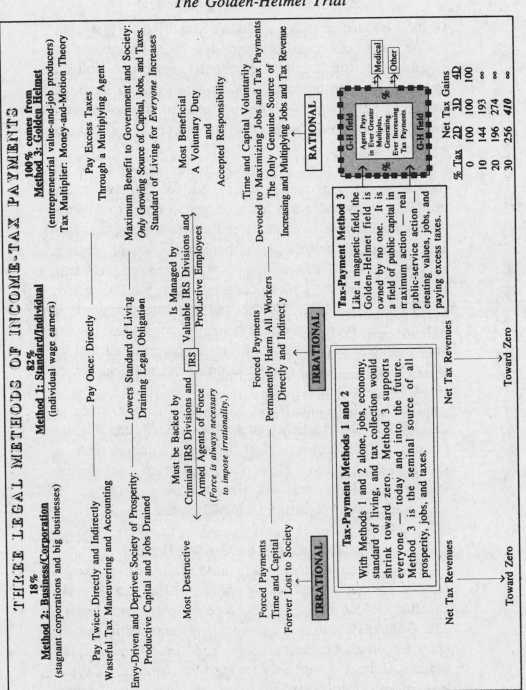

THREE LEGAL METHODS OF INCOME-TAX PAYMENTS

| 18% **Method 2: Business/Corporation** (stagnant corporations and big businesses) | 82% **Method 1: Standard/Individual** (individual wage earners) | 100% comes from **Method 3: Golden Helmet** (entrepreneurial value-and-job producers) Tax Multiplier: Money-and-Motion Theory |

Pay Once: Directly —— Pay Excess Taxes Through a Multiplying Agent

Pay Twice: Directly and Indirectly Wasteful Tax Maneuvering and Accounting

Envy-Driven and Deprives Society of Prosperity: Productive Capital and Jobs Drained —— Lowers Standard of Living Draining Legal Obligation —— Maximum Benefit to Government and Society: *Only* Growing Source of Capital, Jobs, and Taxes. Standard of Living for *Everyone* Increases

Most Destructive —— Must be Backed by Criminal IRS Divisions and [IRS] Valuable IRS Divisions and Armed Agents of Force Productive Employees (*Force is always necessary to impose irrationality.*) — Is Managed by — Most Beneficial A Voluntary Duty and Accepted Responsibility

Forced Payments Time and Capital Forever Lost to Society —— Forced Payments Permanently Harm All Workers Directly and Indirect y —— Time and Capital Voluntarily Devoted to Maximizing Jobs and Tax Payments The Only Genuine Source of Increasing and Multiplying Jobs and Tax Revenue

IRRATIONAL   **IRRATIONAL**   **RATIONAL**

Tax-Payment Methods 1 and 2

With Methods 1 and 2 alone, jobs, economy, standard of living, and tax collection would shrink toward zero. Method 3 supports everyone — today and into the future. Method 3 is the seminal source of all prosperity, jobs, and taxes.

Tax-Payment Method 3

Like a magnetic field, the Golden-Helmet field is owned by no one. It is a field of public capital in maximum action — real public-service action — creating values, jobs, and paying excess taxes.

G-H field — Agent Pays in Ever Greater Multiples, Generating Ever Increasing Tax Payments — G-H field — % — → Medical — → Other

Net Tax Gains

% Tax	2D	3D	4D
0	100	100	100
10	144	193	∞
20	196	274	∞
30	256	410	∞

Net Tax Revenues → Toward Zero

Net Tax Revenues → Toward Zero

Chart 5

49

Golden Helmet is being explicitly identified in this trial.

As most economists acknowledge, taxes on income are socially irrational and economically harmful. Indeed, income taxes are based on demagogic envy and irrational political agendas — as opposed to more-rational consumption taxes, such as sales taxes, user fees, and excise taxes.

Bureaucrats and politicians today depend on the income tax not for money per se, but for controlling and crippling every value-and-job producer in order to advance their own harmful livelihoods and power-seeking agendas. Left unchecked, politicians and bureaucrats would continue increasing their power and control through arbitrary income-tax laws. Left unchecked, they would destroy every remnant of the Golden Helmet; thus, they would destroy the economy and eventually conscious life on earth. But, once publicly understood, the rational Golden Helmet dynamics will replace all irrational political-agenda taxes and laws.

The Net-Tax-Gains table on Chart 5 demonstrates an axiomatic, mathematical foundation beneath the Golden Helmet. That economic fact is as real and provable as the law of gravity. Thus, the validity of the Golden Helmet has always and will always exist.

I will now explain the Golden Helmet.

Explanation of The Golden Helmet

The Golden Helmet was named after Don Quixote's Golden Helmet — the fantasy protector of all that is good. But this Golden Helmet is anchored in reality, not fantasy. The Golden Helmet is the protector of human life and the spawner of all businesses, jobs, and tax revenues. The Golden Helmet works only through the voluntary dedication of effort to better the lives of others and society. Without the Golden Helmet, conscious life would perish.

The Golden-Helmet Trial

No one owns the Golden Helmet. Society owns it. No one can exploit the Golden Helmet. ...One harnesses the Golden Helmet by voluntarily serving it — by generating excess values, jobs, and taxes for others and society.

How Does the Golden Helmet Work?

To serve the Golden Helmet 100% is to harness every effort, every asset, into the most efficient generation of values and jobs for society. In serving the Golden Helmet as a monk, nothing is taken for one's self. At 100% service, one collects no income or financial gains, thus, acquires no personal wealth or material gains from the Golden Helmet. But one does gain great productive efficacy, excitement, and happiness.

A 100% Service Environment

If a scientist volunteers to do research at a South-Pole experimental station, his life during that period is in a 100% service environment. Thus, all his expenses, including all living expenses, are paid so he can perform those services. None of those expenses are income or accrue to his material benefit. Thus, he is not liable for taxes. If that scientist draws a paycheck, however, he must pay income taxes on that paycheck. Likewise, a Red-Cross volunteer in Bosnia has all expenses paid. He or she has no tax liability while in that service environment. Even the merchant seaman has all his job and living expenses paid in his 100% service environment aboard ship. He has tax liability only for his paycheck. If he took no paycheck, he would have no tax liability or filing requirements. ...Those examples involved total service environments, as did my situation in 1983 to 1985 during which no paychecks were drawn. Thus, no

51

material gains or taxable incomes accrued.

Now, let me give a specific example how the Golden Helmet works in business: Ray Kroc built McDonald's into the world's largest restaurant chain. Yet, for many years, while building a billion-dollar business, he took little income. Covering only his most basic needs, Ray Kroc lived almost monk-like in his cramped Chicago office. He was in the Golden Helmet nearly 100% during those years. He paid little if any personal income taxes through Method 1. But, his Golden Helmet paid many millions in taxes through Method 3. As a result, today, billions in taxes are being paid each year by Methods 1 and 2 because **one man** in the Golden Helmet paid excess taxes by Method 3 for so many years.

Mr. Kroc could have chosen to stop his voluntary service to the Golden Helmet at any time — for example, after a year with a dozen or so hamburger stands. He could have made a nice living for himself, providing a few static jobs while paying a few thousand dollars a year in taxes by Methods 1 and 2. However, he did not do that. Instead, Ray Kroc used the Golden-Helmet dynamics to grow McDonald's into an international titan, paying billions of dollars in taxes. More important, Kroc generated hundreds of thousands of jobs and significantly raised America's standard of living through tax-payment Method 3. After those many years of monk-like service to the Golden Helmet, Mr. Kroc finally took a portion for personal gain and shifted that part of his tax payments to Method 1 when his company went public through a stock offering.

In contrast to Ray Kroc, many of today's big-business executives live lavishly by draining corporations that were originally built by great Golden-Helmet entrepreneurs like Andrew Carnegie, Henry Ford, Harvey Firestone, Thomas

Edison. Many modern-day, big-business executives draw tremendous salaries and pay considerable personal taxes through Methods 1 and 2. Without Golden-Helmet dedication, those once great companies eventually shrink in value, size, and jobs. Instead of expanding and generating new jobs and taxes, such big-business executives downsize their value-and-job production, eventually reducing tax revenues by billions of dollars. ...In contrast, Golden Helmets continually expand not only societal values and productive jobs, but actual tax revenues.

The only real value any human being has to give society is his or her rational thought, time, and effort. No one can give more. Through the Golden Helmet, that gift can be multiplied into highly leveraged, tangible values that greatly benefit everyone. At any time, that contributing individual can withdraw his or her maximum-value production to diminish or end the Golden Helmet. At that point, the newly enriched individual must directly support society by paying taxes through Methods 1 and 2.

Like Ray Kroc's early years, with my nearly 100% service to the Golden Helmet during the years 1983-1985, I never acquired taxable earnings. Thus, no filings or payments were required for those years.

Essentially all money was in a non-owned, Golden-Helmet public field that always flowed back into value-and-job expansion...moving toward a thousand new jobs by 1990, all while paying excess taxes at a 4.1 ratio as shown in chart 5.

The Meaning of Golden Helmets

Let me try to convey emotionally what Golden Helmets mean: Would you bring a child into this world if political agendas mandated that you abuse, cripple, and eventually kill your precious child? Would you abide such

53

political policies just to provide harmful livelihoods and ego power to a few professional value destroyers infesting our society? And, if you did have a child, would not you do everything to protect that child from such politically mandated crippling or destruction of that child's potential? ...To society, the Golden Helmet is just as precious and vulnerable as that child. To fulfill society's beneficent potential, we must protect every Golden Helmet as we would protect a precious, innocent child.

The Golden-Helmet dynamic is valid, proven, and much bigger than me or any group of people. The explicit Golden-Helmet concept is now entering the government's own institutions, courts, and politics. ...Golden Helmets will save our country, our livelihoods, our children.

Rebuking Destructive Irrationality

Purposely crippling or destroying productive Golden Helmets is unbearably irrational. I could never personally partake in something so evil, no matter what political agendas dictated. Legal defiance of such irrationality was the entire purpose of my planned confrontation with the IRS in the civil courts. My purpose was to work legally within the system to eliminate those destructive political agendas designed to cripple or destroy Golden Helmets.

I won't deny the prosecutor's claims about filing requirements. But, that does not mean I am guilty. I had no income that required filing. Moreover, I am serving everyone and society by standing up to this insane destruction of values and jobs — evil destruction falsely justified to support the bogus livelihoods of a few selfish parasitical elites and their legions of professional value destroyers. My responsibility is to face such irrationality head on. ...If I lived in Germany fifty-five years ago, I would be that person who took my Jewish neighbors and hid them in my attic, regardless of what political policies dictated. I will always rebuke such destructive irrationality. I have no other way to think or live.

Summary

I was the first to explicitly identify the Golden Helmet. And, in court, I was the first to demand an oath to fully integrated honesty rather then the traditional oath to manipulative truth. Yet, while always striving for honesty, I do not present myself as infallibly honest. I do not think anyone can. I am fallible and vulnerable as everyone else. Still, honesty is my guiding ideal. And, for me, as with everyone, honesty requires constant discipline and effort in every area of life.

That always difficult striving toward integrated honesty first resulted in my turning away from my family's traditions of law, politics, religion, and medicine. Instead, I paid my own way in pursuing the sciences. Eventually, I sought a goal beyond my career in chemistry. That, in turn, shaped my first published book into much deeper, comprehensive understandings of rationality versus irrationality.

Such understandings led me to discover my goal in life: to cure the disease of irrationality. That goal, in turn, led me to the Golden Helmet. Once discovered, the Golden Helmet became my responsibility to protect and nurture into explicit, worldwide fruition. Through the Golden Helmet, I could publicly express the differences between subjective law and objective law. Through the Golden Helmet, I discovered the route to cure irrationality worldwide.

Every day lost toward curing the disease of irrationality, thousands die unnecessarily while millions more suffer. I feel that pressure and responsibility immensely, constantly. I must not, will not stop. I must put my every moment, every effort into curing mankind's worst plague — irrationality.

[End of Frank R. Wallace's Testimony]

No Cross-Examination

Most unexpectedly, the prosecution declined to cross-examine Dr. Wallace. The prosecution never challenged the Golden Helmet. Thus, they ceded to everything revealed in the Golden-Helmet testimony. ...A cross-examination would have directly underscored to the jury the validity of the Golden Helmet and the innocence of Frank R. Wallace.

* * *

Wallace's Closing Argument
PART I

In the past two days, numerous witnesses for the government have testified. I would like to review some of their testimony. The IRS called a Mrs. Hollowell. She testified that there was no tax return for Frank R. Wallace for the years 1983, 1984, and 1985. That is correct. As I have stated, I did not have sufficient income in those years to file a tax return.

A Mr. Marchbanks who owned Park Roofing testified that his company put a new roof on the office home in Boulder City. Mr. Rhodes, a neighbor of mine, testified that he added a room and basement for meetings and storage. Mr. Rhodes testified he knew me for twenty years and that I spent most of my time in this same office home. Mr. Rhodes testified that my office home was an extremely active business place. He described my office home as very modest. He further testified that I do not live in any way luxuriously. Indeed, that structure was not a home, but an office in which I lived.

The witness from Weyerhauser Mortgage testified, and, I agree, that I & O Publishing Company paid the mortgage payments. After all, this office home was being used almost exclusively for I & O Publishing, in which I worked almost 16 hours a day, every day — working to generate values, jobs, and Golden-Helmet taxes for others and society.

The IRS tried to mislead you into thinking I had income by misapplying legitimate business expenses. The IRS summary witness, Mr. Carl Uhlott, for example, tried to show Weyerhauser-Mortgage and Park-Roofing payments as my personal income even though the office home was used almost exclusively for business purposes. Thus, I & O Publishing paid the Weyerhauser Mortgage payments and Park Roofing. Note that no such payments went in or out of my modest personal account.

A representative of the Boulder Dam Credit Union testified that I made $5000 per month. But, after questioning, she clarified that the application showed a $5000 draw, not salary. In other words, I could withdraw from the company up to $5000 a month for expenses to run my writing projects, my research projects, and the Golden-Helmet production of values and jobs. Moreover, I lived frugally and never needed to personally draw that money.

Again, the IRS summary witness, Mr. Carl Uhlott, uses figures to distort facts in making the E. F. Hutton checks appear as my personal income. I will explain later the purpose of checks for cash, but it definitely was not for personal use.

I had no personal income, as I chose not to withdraw money from the Golden Helmet. You will see all bank accounts and brokerage accounts were owned by I & O

Publishing Company. None were owned by me. Those funds were for I & O Publishing Company, not for me personally.

The IRS used several witnesses to describe the same transactions several times. Why? To give the illusion of many transactions. Count the number of actual transactions — you will see how few transactions are really presented. Also, you will note that a lot of evidence orally presented by the IRS was not available as evidence for you to see.

Again, the summary witness Mr. Uhlott, testified that he did not attribute any income or tax figures to I & O Publishing Company. Instead, Mr. Uhlott improperly attributed that income to me personally.[1] Such accounting is not only bizarre, it is plain wrong. All the records are in the name of I & O Publishing Company. As you can see from the evidence, I had little or no personal income and thus was not required to file a tax return. And, as shown in Charts #3 and #5, I never drew enough money from I & O Publishing Company to qualify for filing or paying income taxes.

Remember, the IRS witness, Uhlott, is paid to arrange facts and figures to justify the IRS's mistakes and improper actions. Please look carefully at the actual figures Mr. Uhlott provided to you. You will see that I had no income. The income the IRS alleged I earned all belonged to I & O Publishing and its Golden Helmet.

---

[1] In the first trial, the IRS summary witness used the *same* financial figures to demonstrate the exact opposite — how all earned income was that of I & O Publishing Company, *not* my personal income. Now, to win the second trial, the IRS summary witness took the identical financial figures and made a 180⁰ turn in interpretation to make all income appear to be that of Frank R. Wallace. ...Nothing better underscores the need for the honesty oath rather than the truth oath to prevent such unprincipled manipulation of facts and figures to fit self-serving agendas without regard to honesty, objective law, or justice.

I am not an accountant, but it is obvious that the IRS is selecting figures to build illusions that I am guilty of crimes when the fact is the opposite: The IRS in this case is guilty of violent, objective crimes against my editor, I & O Publishing, and its Golden Helmet — guilty of unprovoked bodily assault and injury, unrepentant criminal pillaging, and intentional value-and-job destruction.

PART II

The prosecutor has no case. He dared not cross-examine the Golden-Helmet testimony. He could not show one instance where I was living a lifestyle requiring my filing and paying a personal income tax.

The prosecutor showed some cash transactions. That cash was used for pushing the Golden Helmet into ever more efficient value-and-job production. Moreover, the portion of cash invested in gold and silver assets prudently hedged our research funds from the severe inflation of the early 80s.

Those inflation-protected research funds were being accumulated for the biomedical RIBI research project. Initiating this research would cost $500,000 as revealed on the 1986 Neo-Tech World-Summit tape that the judge prevented the jury from hearing. Cash was also used in bank transfers for our international operations. Indeed, considerable cash was used to buy live postage for the large-volume mailings involved in driving I & O toward that thousand-job international publishing business planned in four years hence. Those facts were likewise revealed on the 1986 World-Summit tape that the judge suppressed. ...That tremendous expansion of values, jobs, and tax revenues was ended by the 1986 armed IRS attacks and seizures.

Appendix: *The Golden Helmet*

What about that list of registered trade names the prosecutor presented to create more illusions of guilt? For a quarter century, I have been an author and writer. Those legal names were properly used as pen names for our various literature projects. Those names had nothing to do with financial transactions as the prosecution disingenuously asserted without a single supporting fact.

For two days, the prosecutor used a parade of fragmented facts, such as a roof being put on my writing and business offices so that water would not leak on my work. Or, the company providing a new car when my 1979 economy-sized Datsun had been run into the ground with over 120,000 miles, driving our publications to and from printers and mailers in California. And, finally, to conjure up a case, the prosecutor had to manipulate the testimony of a paid informant.

Indeed, the prosecutor could present no evidence that I live other than a monk or have any interest in material gain or leisure. The prosecutor could present no evidence that even on approaching retirement years, I ever indulged in a single personal luxury. Where was my first-class vacation to Hawaii? Or any vacation to anywhere? It never happened. Where was my big custom home? It never happened. Where was my boat? It never happened. Where was my luxurious Jaguar? It never happened. Where was my membership to an elite country club? It never happened. ...I believe in and try to live by Henry Thoreau's philosophy about life: Simplify, Simplify, Simplify.

I do not even own a VCR or have a hobby. The prosecutor could not show a single luxury in my life. Why? Because I did not acquire income or material assets by my own voluntary choice. Instead of acquiring financial gains, I focused my concentration, time, and efforts toward achieving my goal of curing the disease of irrationality. By what means? By building the Golden Helmet, creating values and jobs for others, and then paying taxes at four times the non-Golden-Helmet rate.

* * *

Will you, the jury of my peers, support the self-serving politicians and armed bureaucrats who are draining everyone in creating a stagnant America? Or will you support a vibrant America — a rising standard of living and lower taxes for everyone? ...Will you back the irrationality of economically and socially destructive political agendas? Or will you back the rationality of advancing honest businesses toward creating real jobs and endless wealth in building a great America?

PART III

[Dr. Wallace could not deliver the following Part III of his closing argument because the judge had banished from the trial Chart #6 shown below. Despite the fact that the prosecution had no objection to Chart #6 for trial use, the judge prohibited not only that chart but the ideas that chart embodied. For, those ideas would have undermined the unstipulated jury instruction the judge was planning to spring on the jury. That improper instruction commanded the jury to convict Wallace regardless of the evidence.]

Chart 6

The Jury's Duty is to Deliver Justice
by
Protecting the Innocent Value Producer
and
Condemning the Guilty Value Destroyer

Law of Nature

The Golden Helmet is not a hypothesis or even a theory — it is a law of nature. The Golden Helmet has always been and will always be the seminal source of prosperity and happiness for mankind.

Throughout history, the discovery of every fundamental law of nature upsets the irrational elements of society. For, such irrational elements survive through parasitical agendas that prevent the advancement of knowledge and prosperity. Thus, the discoverers of those laws were often branded as radicals who violated tradition. Yet, such traditions were usually nothing more than political-agenda laws — false laws designed to support the vested interests of the parasitical-elite class. ...Historic prime movers like Archimedes, Socrates, Jesus, and Galileo were prosecuted, jailed, even killed by the parasitical-elite class and its armed bureaucrats.

The prosecutor tried to portray me as a radical who put himself above the law. In the sense of me being above the law, he is completely wrong. No one respects and upholds objective law more than I. Indeed, daily, I risk my life and freedom to uphold objective law by publicly identifying those in government who break it. For, objective law is the essence of civilization and the route to curing the disease of irrationality — the route to eternal peace and prosperity.

But in the sense of me being radical, he is right. I am uncompromising in my thinking and actions when it comes to protecting individuals, businesses, and society against irrational harm. And, when a new way is discovered that tremendously benefits society and every American, I rise to action. I act uncompromisingly and meet my responsibility. I focus all my thoughts and efforts on delivering that new benefit to society. ...I am dedicated to the Golden Helmet because its benefits to society, our government, and every individual are so clear, profound, and just.

The Law

This trial is not about taxes. It is about irrationally draining wealth and life from our country and economy. This trial is about camouflaged dishonesty that has spread throughout our government, our courts, our educational system, our media, our society. As the jury, your responsibility is not to uphold self-serving parasites, their harmful agendas, their armed enforcers. Your responsibility is to protect the innocent value producer and condemn the guilty value destroyer. Your responsibility is to uphold objective law and justice.

Achieving the Possible Dream
Beating the Beatable Foe — Irrationality

You know who is innocent, who is guilty. Stand firm. Do not compromise. Today, you can play a heroic role in bringing honesty and prosperity to America. My testimony has shown that this is a trial between two worlds: the irrational, subjective-law world of harmful political agendas versus the rational, objective-law world of Golden Helmets. Indeed, Golden Helmets will bring great benefits to everyone — even to the prosecutor, to the IRS, and to this court. Do not yield to pressures from this courtroom. Let no one sway you from your judgment. Your verdict can help end this irrational assault on our economy and society to eternally benefit everyone and society.

You, the jury, have one principle and duty: Protect the innocent value producer; condemn the guilty value destroyer.

Chapter 4

After the
Golden-Helmet Trial

Below is a letter Frank R. Wallace sent to the
28-year-old lawyer who helped prosecute the
Golden-Helmet trial.
(Edited for article format and clarity.)

Dear Mr. Bullard:

Last week, you helped prosecute the Golden-Helmet
trial. Any young attorney familiar with this case who is
not yet locked into the vested interests of today's legal
profession has an opportunity for an historic, precedent-
setting career. That opportunity arises from two concepts
revealed in the Golden-Helmet trial. Those two concepts
are fully integrated honesty and objective law.

Those concepts will become as influential to law as
the thirteenth-century Magna Carta concept was to
overturning the vested interests in the tyrannical, divine-
rights view...and as enlightening to society as the
fifteenth-century heliocentric concept was to overturning
the vested interests in the flat-earth, geocentric view.

Now, late in the twentieth century, the consistent,
provable concepts rising from the Golden-Helmet trial will
overturn the arbitrary, vested interests in the political-
agenda/ego-"justice" views. That overturn will come from
three directions: (1) integrated honesty overturning
manipulated truths, (2) objective law overturning subjective
laws, (3) the rationality of objective justice overturning
the irrationality of ego "justice".

After the Trial

Later, when you receive literature about the Golden Helmet, read it carefully with an integrating mind. Understand conceptually what is being sown worldwide. Perceive what is subtly entering today's society and government. Perceive that newly forming wedge approaching business and government. Move to the rational side of that wedge. Through pursuing objective law, you can help lead our country toward rationality — toward permanent prosperity and happiness. You can help bring forth a rational, just society. You can help heal the wounds inflicted by today's political-agenda laws and ego "justice".

* * *

Think how history will view your rebuttal arguments used to win the prosecution's case. Indeed, character assassination was your dishonorable recourse:[1]

1. **Quoting my poker book on bluffing to present such deception as my *personal* character**: Out-of-context paraphrasing of literature is the easiest, most effective way to misrepresent an author. Yet, on reading my poker book, anyone can see the 180^0 misrepresentation by the prosecution. That book identifies how integrated honesty is the essence of prosperity for conscious life. Likewise, that book identifies the inescapable harm that lying and deception *always* inflict on its perpetrator whenever done *beyond* the game of poker.

---

[1]The following is a handwritten note from Mrs. T.S., a courtroom observer: "During Wallace's Golden-Helmet testimony, his character, his honesty, his dedication to values came across with such conviction and benevolence, the prosecution knew it had to break that image to win its case. Thus, the prosecution used its entire closing argument not to outline the facts but to falsely attack Wallace's character. By saving its innuendos for the closing argument, the prosecution unethically prevented rebuttal. ...It appeared the prosecution had no way to convict except through dishonesty."

65

Appendix: The Golden Helmet

The poker book is a metaphor: It uses the nonreality of a game in which the mutually agreed-upon rules and universally known essence is the bluff. In that unreal-world game context, bluffing *is not* dishonest. By contrast, in the real-world context, outside of poker, bluffing and deception *is* dishonest. Such juxtaposition of reality to unreality underscores the virtue of fully integrated honesty for all real-world situations — with *no* exceptions.

Consider the conclusion of my poker book: The fictional "hero", the unbeatable big winner, is always the biggest loser! Why? Wide-scope accounting demonstrates that he has wasted his assets — his hard-earned intelligence, his irreplaceable time, his intense efforts, his integrated thinking, his iron discipline — all wasted in an unproductive, zero-sum game that accomplishes nothing real for him or society. Instead, he could have harnessed those disciplines, assets, and precious time to achieve genuine self-worth by producing growing values for others and society. ...Thus, I forsook poker when I finished writing the book in 1968.

2. **Creating a false impression of me hoarding money, ready to flee the country**: The prosecution along with the court has in its possession several handwritten letters from its paid informant, Ms. K, admitting her dishonesties to me, my family, and others during our relationship. Then, from perjurious statements by Ms. K, the IRS's chief witness, the prosecution crafted a closing argument describing me as sitting atop a floor safe filled with money.

That mendacious argument was used to create false illusions of me hoarding and concealing assets for fleeing the country. Among Ms. K's sworn grand-jury/search-warrant affidavits and her testimony in the first trial, she stated under oath that the floor safe had a three-foot diameter cover and was located directly beneath my desk chair. She further testified that I always sat atop those assets — assets available for quickly fleeing the country if the IRS came after me.

Now consider the facts: That safe cover was six inches, not three feet, in diameter. The safe was located in a corner of a writing office over which a bookcase was located. The geometry of a room corner with its two walls made it physically impossible to locate a chair over that safe, much less a desk. Mr. Goodrich and many other IRS agents knew those facts. Additionally, Ms. K knew those seized assets were not personal funds but were RIBI research funds. Indeed, when she worked with me, one of her main responsibilities was to manage the funds, records, business, and correspondence of the 2200 RIBI registrants. Additionally, she kept the books for I & O Publishing from 1983 to 1985...and did the accounting for those research funds.

Opposite to her testimony, Ms. K knew I had no intentions to leave this country. To the contrary, my entire objective was to stand and face all adversaries, as demonstrated by these trials. Moreover, she was well acquainted with my plans of using the Golden Helmet to confront the IRS through civil actions and the courts.

Ms. K intimately knew of my concerns about our biomedical research projects involving human cloning for nonrejectable organs and consciousness preservation for the terminally ill. I became increasingly concerned about destructive interference from regulatory bureaucracies, especially the murderous FDA. Thus, I prepared to move not me and my publishing company, but to move that specific medical research project and its funding abroad.

Ms. K even participated in the abandoning of that research project in the United States. She knew we planned to do the physical research abroad, scheduled to begin in 1988, pending accumulation of the required $500,000 start-up capital. In fact, Ms. K met in Nevada with the Swiss scientist who was already developing the 144-point, Neo-Tech mind matrix — the first step in consciousness transfer. She then traveled abroad to make preliminary arrangements for that research project. ...After our relationship failed, Ms. K spun yarns in order to evoke the seizure of those RIBI research funds that she had managed. Thus, she could rake a 10% informant's fee from the $250,000 in seized funds.

3. **Dishonestly denying the Golden Helmet**: Finally, the prosecution's closing argument made an emphatic point that Ms. K, during the three years of working with me, never knew of the Golden Helmet. Again, Ms. K fully knew about the Golden-Helmet tax payments from the beginning. In fact, she described exactly how those tax payments were made in her own sworn statements in the 1986 search-warrant affidavits and in her testimony at the first trial. She described how excess taxes were paid by the I & O multiplying agent through third parties. Now, granted, she may not have known the actual name "Golden Helmet". The metaphorical Golden-Helmet name evolved after our personal relationship ended in 1984 and our business relationship ended in late 1985. But, she knew everything about those tax payments done under wide-scope accounting, which was and still is the generic term for the Golden Helmet.

* * *

The prosecution's rebuttal arguments were not rebuttals at all. They neither addressed nor rebutted anything in my testimony or closing statement. Indeed, the prosecution never even cross-examined my testimony. Instead, it used that rebuttal for dishonest character assassination by conjuring up false "new evidence", jury deceptions, and illusions opposite to the facts.

The prosecution simply conjured up those calumnies because it needed them to win. And the judge made no objection to this false "new evidence" being improperly injected into a closing argument. By injecting those dishonesties into the final rebuttal, both you and the judge knew I had no opportunity to rebut or refute those falsehoods. ...Such were the dishonesties you and the judge used to win.

Mr. Bullard, objective justice is not a poker game of bluff and deception. Do you want to consume your one-and-only life "winning" dishonestly? Think about the longer-range consequences. By nature, dishonest victories are always temporary and hollow. More important, dishonest victories are not victories at all. They are Pyrrhic and they always return to defeat the "victor".

Being young, you are, I am sure, still able to feel qualms about winning dishonestly. If you can still emotionally feel the difference between right and wrong, then you have not yet become an automaton dependent on enforcing political-agenda laws through ego "justice". With honesty alive in your conscience and new knowledge growing in your mind, you can lead the legal profession to rationality and objective law. You have an opportunity to heroically lead the legal profession away from ego "justice" and into objective law.

Being young, you probably do not yet know the end result of a career dependent on ego "justice". Look at Judge George. He is lost and can no longer interact honestly with reality. The dishonest route in law ultimately means living off subjective political-agenda laws. Self-esteem then becomes dependent on ego "justice". The legitimate, crucial activities of upholding and enforcing objective law are forgotten. The occasional enforcement of objective laws becomes merely a prop for camouflaging and rationalizing the immoral enforcement of subjective laws evolved from self-serving political agendas backed by armed bureaucrats.

The Neo-Tech literature identifies the source of such dishonesty in the courts as ego "justice". The centerfold of the *Zon-2000* publication sent to you earlier described ego "justice". That description was largely theoretical. But the judge in this case transformed ego-"justice" theory into documented reality. Throughout the Golden-Helmet trial, Judge Lloyd D. George provided an abundance of factual, empirical information illustrating ego "justice". Indeed, Judge George gave history a priceless gift — a concretized, full-blown example of ego "justice" in action.

Throughout the trial, the judge consistently acted to fill a single agenda — control the trial and jury to convict the defendant. He had to convict the person who directly challenged his ego — an ego whose survival is dependent on subjective law. He had to squelch any threat that could expose his fraud.

To win a conviction, Judge George relied on improper judicial abuses to control the jury. Additionally, he emphasized the derogatory "hundreds-of-years" quote both times he had to deal with the honesty oath. For, the honesty oath was the ego-bruising issue that defeated the judge in the first trial. Thus, he biased the jury against my testimony by showing his contempt for the honesty oath. Such behavior from a federal judge reflects the end result of a career based on self-indulgent ego "justice". ...Reality always levies final justice as that judge shrinks backwards in life — incapable of experiencing genuine self-esteem or happiness.

From start to finish of this retrial, Judge George inappropriately ingratiated himself to the jury. His hypocritically saccharine, highly personal banter with jury members — improper behavior for any judge — is documented in the voir dire and trial transcripts. And what about the intimidations Judge George sent back to the jury after that sidebar drama concerning a jury member asking the bailiff for information about the Golden Helmet?

To cap his improper behavior, the judge had to assure direct control over the jury's verdict. How did he assure that direct control? By abusing his fair-comment privilege *after* both sides had rested. He bootlegged in his own unstipulated, private jury instruction demanding a conviction. That bootlegged instruction was preplanned to nullify the crucial "reasonable doubt" and "willfulness" instructions to which we all stipulated.

Judge George's gratuitous, ego-"justice" instruction implied that I should be found guilty regardless of the trial evidence and the stipulated jury instructions. He implied without an iota of evidence that I was a renegade who took the law into my own hands rather than working through politics or Congress. With his private instruction dishonestly introduced as "new evidence", about which no rebuttal or challenge was allowed, Judge George nullified the factual trial evidence that proved the exact *opposite*: It was I, not George, who worked within legal boundaries. It was I, not George, who respected and upheld objective law. It was I, not George, who was innocent.

As you know, during the trial, I offered the chief prosecutor, J. Gregory Damm, to waive rights if the judge would leave his bench and sit at the prosecution table as a member of its team. Then, the trial would at least have the merit of being honest in regards to the judge and how the jury perceived him. ...The judge's behavior toward the jury was brazenly self-serving. He had to save his ego. He had to save face by orchestrating an unjust conviction.

While the way is always open and a helping hand is always extended, Judge George is perhaps too calcified — too deeply invested in his ego agendas to understand the approaching sea change to rationality and objective law. Perhaps, he can never share in the coming triumph of fully integrated honesty. Yet, if he pondered the final statement of an American judge in the 1949 Nuremberg trial of Nazi judges, George might finally understand the profound difference between objective justice and ego "justice": A German judge pleaded he had no idea of the consequences that would ultimately evolve from ego "justice". The American judge replied by telling him that using political-agenda "law" to *purposely* condemn even just one innocent person was enough to condemn any judge for life. ...Will George end like Tolstoy's Ivan Ilych?

But, you, Mr. Bullard, can certainly be an important part of the coming triumph. And, if they choose to think conceptually in principles — in a widely integrated manner rather than a narrow concrete-bound manner — prosecutor Damm, even IRS agent Goodrich, could come to understand this newly evolving age of rationality. Then, they too could move into the world of fully integrated honesty to share the triumph and rewards.

Someday, perhaps you, Mr. Damm, Mr. Goodrich, even Judge George will work with us. Together we can uphold objective law to eliminate the armed divisions among the bureaucracies. We can then advance the Golden Helmet as the route to a genuinely prosperous, happy society.

Chapter 5

The Appeal — The Future

On June 18, 1993, the Solicitor General of the United States, Drew S. Days III, in a last-minute maneuver submitted a typo-ridden continuance motion to the United States Supreme Court to stop the use of Wallace's honesty oath. That motion was granted by Supreme-Court Justice Sandra Day O'Connor. Indeed, many people in government already know that fully integrated honesty will reveal that subjective laws are nothing more than manipulative devices serving harmful political and ego agendas.

The Honesty Oath is now the Law of the Land

The first trial in February 1991 legally established the Honesty Oath in the United States judicial system. The appeal and the courageous opinion written by Appellate Judge Betty B. Fletcher made the honesty oath the law of the land for all to henceforth use.[1] The honesty oath provides the foothold needed to eradicate manipulated truths and false witnesses from courtrooms.

The retrial in August 1993 prepared the way toward establishing rationality and objective law as the standard for law. The second appeal provides the foothold needed to hoist the Neo-Tech/Golden-Helmet dynamic into public view. That dynamic will eventually eliminate subjective political-agenda laws, arbitrary ego "justice", and dishonest torts throughout the legal systems of this world.

---

[1] U.S. vs. Wallace, 989, F.2d, 1015 (9th Cir. 1993).

Appendix: The Golden Helmet

Why the Honesty Oath?

Why an oath to fully integrated honesty rather than to truth? Who knows what truth is? No one knows. Truth is merely a static assertion of observations or "facts". Truth for one may not be truth for another. For, truth varies with condition and context. And, an unlimited number of conditions and contexts exist. Thus, the truth oath allows unlimited dishonesties and corruptions.

Truth-Oath Testimony

Noncontextual Facts, Unintegrated Evidence,
Dishonest

I saw John O'Grady premeditate and then purposely kill a man. Conclusion: John O'Grady is a murderer. He should be jailed.
True facts. Incomplete. Out of context.
Unjust conclusion.

Honesty-Oath Testimony

Contextual Facts, Fully Integrated Evidence,
Honest

I saw John O'Grady save a platoon of men in 1944 during the Battle of the Bulge at Bastogne, Belgium. Trapped beneath a snow-covered ledge by a Nazi machine-gunner, John premeditated a plan. He then scaled an icy cliff. Wounded twice, John shot and killed the machine-gunner. He saved the twenty men in his platoon. Conclusion: John O'Grady is a hero. He should be honored.
Honest facts. Complete. In context.
Just conclusion.

Without an anchor to honesty, anyone can manipulate truth and facts into harmful agendas. Politicians who make self-serving laws and lawyers who profit from those harmful laws live by manipulating truth. They talk about truth all the time. But, they seldom, if ever, talk about honesty. For, unlike truth, everyone knows the exact meaning of honesty. Honesty is a process that has the same clear, fixed meaning for everyone. Honesty cannot be manipulated. One is either honest or not. Therefore, a shield of silence about honesty exists among politicians and lawyers. Indeed, they fear and avoid fully integrated honesty.[1]

This retrial was not about taxes. It was about camouflaged irrationality. It was about armed bureaucracies destroying Golden Helmets. It was about draining wealth and life from society and the populace to provide a few parasitical elites and their supporters with harmful livelihoods, false egos, and illicit power. It was about camouflaged dishonesty that has spread throughout our government, educational system, courts, and society.

Yet, from this retrial arose the dynamics to vanish Plato's 2300-year-old, parasitical-elite class. Indeed, this retrial established the groundwork for eliminating subjective law and ego "justice", starting with a motion to prohibit subjective courtroom bias — a motion summarily denied by Judge Lloyd D. George.

---

[1]Dr. Wallace presented his own case in both trials. But, Wallace's supporters tried to hire a lawyer for the sole purpose of cross-examining and impeaching the prosecution's paid informant. Four lawyers, in turn, accepted and then withdrew when they discovered the honesty principle underlying the Golden-Helmet trial. ...Those lawyers feared for their own ego-"justice"-dependent careers if they helped a defendant combat ego "justice".

Appendix: The Golden Helmet

A Motion to Prohibit Subjective, Courtroom Biases

> The following motion was filed with the U.S. District Court on June 28, 1993. Below are various descriptive, "the-point" portions of its arguments. The technical, "a-point" portions are not included, but are available from the court files.

This motion proposes introductory jury instructions by the judge to assure a trial free of subjective, courtroom bias.

Comes now Frank R. Wallace with a motion to the court for preliminary jury instructions relating to courtroom bias. Such instructions shall be in the form presently provided in the *Manual of Model Criminal Jury Instructions for the Ninth Circuit* under "What is admissible evidence? What is inadmissible evidence?" The following activities by the United States Government shall not be considered as evidence, but shall constitute inadmissible evidence:

1. Superior acting or contemptuous conduct toward the defendant by the presiding United States district-court judge.

2. Superior acting or contemptuous conduct by any member of the judicial staff including bailiffs, clerks, or anyone assisting the court in the conduct of the trial.

3. *The court, its personnel, and its staff shall not act to prejudice the defendant's presumption of innocence by their conduct or remarks.*

4. The jury shall be cautioned that the accouterments of power and prestige of the United States are subjective and not admissible evidence. Thus, those accouterments should not weigh to the advantage of the prosecution or to the detriment of the defendant.

5. Any witness called by the prosecution shall not

76

be vested with greater credibility than any witness called by the defendant. The jury's responsibility is to judge the credibility and value of all testimonies and all witnesses as they objectively relate to the trial.

The above jury instructions should be given by the judge prior to the trial.

Arguments in Support of this Motion

When the government and its courts inflict subjective biases on its citizens, those citizens and society itself are increasingly subject to constitutional violations, human-rights abuses, and economic harms. Thus, the court has a constitutional duty, a legal obligation, and a social responsibility to prohibit all applications of subjective bias.

This motion asks the court to prohibit the infliction of subjective biases on the defendant, before and during the trial. For, the infliction of such biases directly violates the defendant's Fifth-Amendment rights. Indeed, all due-process, constitutional, and human rights eventually vanish under subjective courtroom biases, as clearly observable in the evolvement of totalitarian governments.

Tradition or habit that has been practiced even for "hundreds of years" offers no argument against this motion. For, tradition or "the test of time" is no gauge of value or validity. Ten centuries ago, status-quo tradition or biases led the Western World into a dark millennium of stagnation and human misery. The subsequent Renaissance, the American Constitution, and the Industrial Revolution emerged only after discarding the irrationalities of subjective biases and overthrowing many force-backed, political/religious-agenda laws.

That discarding of subjective biases unleashed a flood of new knowledge and life-enhancing values. Stunning advances arose from the honesty, objectivity, and efforts of courageous giants like Leonardo da Vinci, Copernicus, Galileo, Spinoza, Newton, Jefferson, Darwin. Each such hero overturned subjective truths and laws based on biases, traditions, dogma.

Now is the time for the court to end criminal enforcement of self-serving political agendas backed by subjective laws, ego "justice", and armed bureaucracies. Now is the time to establish a new legal foundation based on objective law backed by integrated honesty. Now is the time for courageous judges to usher in the golden age of objective law that brings everlasting peace and prosperity to everyone and society.

Conclusion

Objective law protects the innocent value producer. Subjective laws and ego "justice" advance the professional value destroyer. Any court sanction of subjective law or bias vanishes justice. Subjective laws and biases arise from political or personal agendas designed to support harmful livelihoods. Thus, the court is asked to meet its legal and moral responsibility by rejecting all subjective laws and biases.[1]

The above motion to prohibit subjective biases and ego "justice" in the courtroom was summarily denied by Judge Lloyd D. George on July 14, 1993. The motion was then orally resubmitted on August 2, 1993. Judge George again brusquely denied the motion to eliminate courtroom biases and ego "justice" from his courtroom.

---

[1]Also see Legal Exhibit titled Ego-"Justice" Terminator on page 89.

ADDENDUM

For an added perspective, the following introduction to an affidavit for Wallace's civil litigations illustrates the corruptions that arise when the government uses paid informants. In this case, the corruptions began with the IRS's violent attacks on I & O Publishing in 1986. Those attacks arose from political-agenda laws, armed bureaucrats, and a government-paid perjurer. From those corruptions came the IRS, its hired prosecutor, and its ego-driven judge. From that medley of fraud came the violent pillaging and imprisonment of an innocent man for his writings and publications that are subverting the parasitical-elite class throughout the world.

Human nature requires being or learning to be a net value producer for others and society. As Socrates identified, human nature requires honesty and objective law for expanding prosperity and happiness. By contrast, parasitical elites must build corrupt ego-"justice" systems to enforce the political agendas needed for their survival. Only by disintegrating the sacred trinity of rationality, honesty, and objective law can they enforce their parasitical agendas. And, unless eliminated, such parasitism eventually destroys its twin hosts — the economy and its value producers.

Ego "Justice"

Ego "justice" contradicts objective law. Under objective law, the primary responsibility of prosecutors and judges alike is to secure justice — not to win cases per se and especially not to enforce self-serving political agendas that support a criminal-behaving, parasitical-elite class.

In other words, with objective law, the first priority

of prosecutors and judges is to bring forth all and only the contextual facts needed to render justice. In that way, objective law protects the innocent value producer and prosecutes the guilty value destroyer, which is the entire purpose of objective law and justice.

By contrast, with subjective political law and its ego "justice", the first priority is to obtain convictions that protect the political agendas supporting a growing class of parasites throughout the government and the legal profession. Judges and lawyers must becloud honesty while manipulating truth to punish, convict, or eliminate political-agenda threats. Enforcement of political agendas by suppressing objective law is required to support the parasitical-elite class and its ego-"justice" system. Such corruption is demonstrated in every courtroom used to enforce political-agenda laws rather than to uphold objective law.

* * *

This document supports the idea that lifetime appointments be revoked for federal judges who practice ego "justice" or who support political-agenda laws rather than uphold objective law. ...Indeed, the Golden Helmet has already begun the process needed to eliminate ego "justice" from America's courtrooms.

Chapter 6

The Golden-Helmet Oral Argument

CA-93-10703/September 12, 1994

U.S. 9th-Circuit Court of Appeals

Oral Argument
by
Frank R. Wallace
before appellate judges
Robert R. Beezer, Jerome Farris, Linda McLaughlin

Your honors: My *written brief* contains the legal points of this appeal. Those points are based on a-point law: meaning technical points and case law. But, for all a points, one must ask, "What is the point?" The point behind this appeal is singular: ***Objective law must be upheld***.

My written brief cites a number of illegalities by the judge and prosecutor who improperly forced a conviction. That brief identifies those illegalities with citations from the trial transcripts, case law, and affidavits.

My *oral argument* today focuses on the violations of objective law that led to an improper conviction:

The trial testimony under the honesty oath explained how all tax obligations were met in excess by the defendant through the Golden Helmet.

The Golden Helmet recognizes that through excess personal acquisitions, one increasingly loses his or her potential to create, produce, and deliver maximum values to others and society. The trial testimony explains how and why the defendant lived monastically, lived a life of *being* rather than a life of *having*. He lived a life of creating not consuming, personally drawing no taxable income for the years in question. ...The prosecution neither challenged nor cross-examined that testimony. Thus, the prosecution accepted the Golden-Helmet testimony in full.

So, *why was the defendant convicted*? In addition to the trial errors detailed in the written brief, the defendant was blocked from obtaining his own business and accounting records. Such facts and figures would prove that (1) the defendant had no personal tax liability, and (2) more than the required taxes were always paid through the Golden Helmet.

Indeed, without those facts and figures contained in the seized records, the confusion among the jury was obvious: As the transcripts reveal, a mistrial nearly resulted from a juror's aggressive quest to a bailiff for more information about the Golden Helmet on behalf of herself and the other jurors. That quest went unfulfilled, leaving the jurors confused and dependent on an intimidating judge demanding a conviction.

Now, why was the defendant unable to provide the jury with the specific facts and figures from the seized financial records? Because the prosecution withheld from the defendant key records and accounting figures seized by armed IRS agents in 1986 — key documents covering the three years in question.

Just days before the trial in August 1993, the prosecution handed the defendant only a cherry-picked portion of the discovery — only that portion to be used out of context against the defendant. The prosecution

withheld all evidence favorable to the defendant —
especially the computer accounting records that would
have let the defendant prove his testimony with specific
facts and figures buried in that discovery.

Those facts and figures were contained in the never
returned books, files, and computer disks. The IRS had
seized not only 100% of the original disks but 100% of
the backup disks. At any time after April, 1990, the
prosecution could have easily, simply provided the
defendant with a copy of its paid informant's bookkeeping
records as well as a copied set of the seized computer
disks to fulfill its discovery obligations.

Why did not the prosecution simply provide that
discovery as soon as this case became an open-file case
in April, 1990? Because, giving the defendant those disks
and bookkeeping records with enough time to develop
them into evidence would have vanished the prosecution's
case.

Despite numerous requests by the defendant dating
back to 1990, the prosecution did not allow access to that
discovery until just days before the scheduled date of the
second trial. The defendant's voluntary accountant
promptly went to the IRS evidence room to examine the
discovery. Over a period of two days, he inventoried an
overwhelming amount of discovery: seized assets, cartons,
personal diaries, files, bookkeeping records, and computer
disks. Then, in his affidavit, as exhibited in my brief,
the accountant estimated that just to print out the seized
computer records from pre-1986 Radio-Shack Tandy disks
on obsolete printing equipment in the IRS evidence room
would require up to 81 days involving up to 2610
documents on 87 disks.

Within that huge accumulation of records, which had

not been seen for 7 to 10 years, lie the data not just to demonstrate but to prove *factually* the Golden-Helmet taxpayments.

Yet, to properly prepare for the trial and present the Golden Helmet, the defendant already needed 16-hour work days right up to the trial date. Thus, the defendant knew that, without a continuance, that massive discovery could not be used. Those few days before trial were urgently needed for basic trial preparation, exhibit preparation, and crucial motions.

Moreover, even if the full discovery had been presented to the defendant in a usable form and work commenced around the clock, time would still have been grossly insufficient to pull together three full years of records and accounting figures in those few remaining days before the trial. Time simply did not exist for converting that multi-year-delayed discovery into trial evidence — evidence that factually proves the defendant's absence of tax liability.

Both the prosecution and the judge were fully aware of that time problem as presented in both the defendant's written and oral motions for a single continuance. Yet, the prosecution declined to stipulate and the judge denied the defendant's fully documented motion justifying that continuance. The judge's denial prevented any chance to utilize the newly availed discovery. ...Thus, the denial of that continuance saved the case for the prosecution by effectively denying discovery to the defendant.

Still, through careful trial preparation and utilizing the honesty oath for the first time in judicial history, the defendant was grateful to present the Golden Helmet, in part at least, in a court trial. Although the presentation was undermined by the denied discovery and a vindictively biased judge as detailed in the written brief and trial transcripts, the defendant exercised restraint. He exercised that restraint in order to avoid any future, out-of-context claim by the judge or prosecutor that the honesty oath was in any way abusively used in its very first courtroom application. That restraint was exercised even though the judge defensively, subjectively, in front of the jury, mocked the honesty oath twice. ...A noncontroversial courtroom experience was important for developing the full legal potential of the honesty oath for the future benefit of society, including the prosecution and the court.

During the trial, the judicial and prosecutorial errors prevented the jurors from learning the contextual facts — the factual proof behind the testimony demonstrating no criminal intent or tax liability. And, most important, the opportunity was denied to *fully* demonstrate in a court of law the meaning, legality, and supreme value of the Golden Helmet to all governments and societies.

Let us deliver our civilization from the arbitrary rule of subjective law — from the rule of political-agenda laws and personal egos that place self-serving bias above justice. Let us build a new civilization based on objective law free from the arbitrary whims of dishonest politicians, destructive bureaucrats, and ego-driven judges. For, a civilization ruled solely by objective law yields eternal peace and prosperity.

* * *

Comments about the Golden-Helmet Argument
Frank R. Wallace's oral argument to the three appellate judges focused on the Golden Helmet through which far more than one's legally required taxes are always paid. The Golden Helmet is not new, has *nothing* to do with

tax rebellion, and is the *opposite* of tax avoidance. The Golden Helmet is fully rooted in objective law, profoundly beneficial to all, and practiced in part by people as diverse as Andrew Carnegie, Albert Schweitzer, and Ray Kroc.

Today, the following fact is known: By combining Neo-Tech's continuing court efforts with its expanding penetration of worldwide cyberspace communications, the Golden Helmet will increasingly become understood and accepted by the world's populations. Indeed, by eliminating ego "justice", the Golden Helmet will reshape our political and economic futures to deliver its promise of eternal peace and prosperity.

Chapter 7

What is Next?

Requirements for Victory

For the Neo-Tech/Golden-Helmet dynamics to advance in politics, court *processes* are what matter. On receiving an honest and just court decision, the task concludes with a quick, small victory offering little further value. On receiving a dishonest political-agenda or ego-"justice" court decision, the process continues with great strength-building value offering eventual, total victory.

When will the next Neo-Tech/Golden-Helmet court engagement with political agendas and ego "justice" occur? Perhaps this year, next year, in five years. Engagement with whom? Perhaps with Congress, the FDA, the INS...or perhaps with organized religion, the academe, the media, or even the clique of parasitical executives draining stagnant big businesses. The actual harmful agent who engages Neo-Tech makes little difference. For, against the fully integrated honesty of Neo-Tech, all aggressions by harmful agents hasten the demise of their irrational survival systems.

Golden-Helmet Prosperity by 2001 AD?

Brief, erratic contacts with the Civilization of the Universe were made by Moses, Confucius, Socrates, Jesus, Bruno, Galileo, Spinoza, Newton, Brigham Young, Albert Einstein. But, today, a consistent, nonstop journey from Earth to the Civilization of the Universe has begun. It began in 1976 with the publication of the original *Neo-Tech Reference Encyclopedia*.

Avoiding the dishonest distortions of publicity and the media, working through the virtuous dynamics of

87

international business, the seeds of Neo-Tech have been quietly sown around the world in many languages, for many years. Neo-Tech is empowering those who benefit society to various degrees through the Golden Helmet. Neo-Tech is empowering those who produce far more values for society than they consume — from productive laborers and valuable housewives to honest physicists and billionaire entrepreneurs. ...Only genuine value producers hold power in the Civilization of the Universe.

Because Neo-Tech is fully integrated honesty, it largely escapes understanding and notice by today's professional value destroyers who are busily consuming our society and economy. Thus, from beneath their feet, Neo-Tech unexpectedly will burgeon from its seeds planted worldwide. As begun in America during its 1994 elections, that flowering of Neo-Tech will vanish all purposely harmful people. Perhaps as early as 2001 AD or even sooner, Golden Helmets will be flourishing worldwide. Conscious beings will then be free to step into the Civilization of the Universe to enjoy guiltless lives of eternal prosperity and happiness.

The future belongs to fully integrated honesty — to rationality, Neo-Tech, Golden Helmets, and the Civilization of the Universe.

The Constitution of the Universe

Preamble

The purpose of human life is to live happily.

The function of government is to guarantee those conditions that allow individuals to fulfill their purpose. Those conditions can be guaranteed through a constitution that forbids the use of initiatory force, fraud, or coercion by any person or group against any individual:

* * *

Article 1

No person, group of persons or government may initiate force, threat of force, or fraud against any individual's self or property.

Article 2

Force may be morally and legally used only in self-defense against those who violate Article 1.

Article 3

No exceptions shall exist for Articles 1 and 2.

* * *

The Neo-Tech Constitution rests on six axioms:
1. Values exist only relative to life.
2. Whatever benefits a living organism is a value to that organism. Whatever harms a living organism is a disvalue to that organism.
3. The basic value against which all values are measured is the conscious individual.
4. Morals relate only to conscious individuals.
5. Immoral actions arise from individuals choosing to harm others through force, fraud, deception, coercion — or from individuals choosing to usurp, attack, or destroy values earned by others.
6. Moral actions arise from individuals choosing to benefit others by competitively producing values for them.

Legal Exhibit
Ego-"Justice" Terminator

Objective Law Must be Upheld

This Legal Exhibit demands that objective law be upheld by all officers of the court. Attach this Exhibit to all motions, legal documents, correspondence used in any local, state, or federal jurisdiction.

This Legal Exhibit Demands the Termination of
1. Subjective, Political-Agenda Laws
2. Ego "Justice"

Upon receipt of this Legal Exhibit, under penalty of job termination, judges as well as prosecutors and lawyers must reject *all* forms of subjective, political-agenda law and ego "justice". Those officers of the court must henceforth practice only objective law.

Subjective Laws include political-agenda laws conjured up by politicians and bureaucrats to gain self-serving benefits, false egos, and unearned power. Enforcement of political-agenda laws requires the use of force and armed bureaucrats against innocent people.

Objective Laws are not conjured up by politicians or bureaucrats. Instead, like the laws of physics, they arise from the *immutable laws of nature*. Such laws are valid, benefit everyone, and advance society. Objective laws are based on the moral prohibition of initiatory force, threats of force, and fraud.

Ego "Justice" is the use of subjective, political-agenda laws to gain harmful livelihoods and feel false importance. Ego "justice" is the survival tool of many harmful politicians, lawyers, and judges.

Benefit-of-the-Doubt Clause

Except for the most egregious offenders, this Legal Exhibit presents an opportunity for officers of the court to amend their past errors of supporting subjective law and using ego "justice".

Each officer must henceforth uphold objective law and reject ego "justice" along with its gun-backed, political-agenda laws and enforcements.

Purpose of this Legal Exhibit

1. To inform officers of the court that practicing ego "justice" and using threats, force, fines, guns, and jails to enforce political-agenda laws are serious, objective crimes that must eventually be prosecuted.

2. To inform officers of the court that they are henceforth fully responsible for upholding objective law and rejecting ego "justice".

ORDER

Render criminal penalties *only* against those violating objective laws in committing objective crimes. Objective crimes occur only upon the initiation of force or fraud against individuals and their property. Such crimes include murder, rape, assault, robbery, fraud. Those crimes also include *all* ego-"justice" frauds. Such criminal frauds encompass gun-backed threats, gun-backed assaults, gun-backed pillagings, and gun-backed false imprisonments executed by armed bureaucracies enforcing political-agenda laws. Also, the illegal, political weapons of RICO and seizure laws are increasingly used against innocent people. ...All such political-agenda and ego-"justice" crimes are terminated by enforcing *objective* law.

After receipt of this Legal Exhibit, any officer of the court who commits such crimes of ego "justice" and judicial fraud will eventually be identified, prosecuted, and have his or her harmful career terminated. And, through objective justice, court officers guilty of those serious crimes must pay restitution to their victims.

— This legal exhibit is not copyrighted —

Anyone may photocopy this Legal Exhibit for repeated use on attaching to all legal documents. This Legal Exhibit is also available in French, German, Spanish, Italian, and other languages for use in jurisdictions worldwide.

Address correspondence to: The Zon Association, P.O. Box 60752, Boulder City, Nevada 89006

"The only justifiable purpose of political institutions is to insure the unhindered development of the individual."
Albert Einstein

Printed with permission from the National Archives: Niels Bohr Library

Appendix: The Golden-Helmet Index

Appendix: The Golden-Helmet Index

Appendix: The Golden-Helmet Index

Look into yourself with honesty
and
You shall find God

Look into the future with honesty
and
You shall find the end of dishonest government

Look into each individual with honesty
and
You shall find the Civilization of the Universe

Negative Comments about Neo-Tech

Neo-Tech Publishing has many thousands of positive comments and about two-hundred negative comments in its files. *The Neo-Tech Discovery* shows in print several hundred testimonials heralding the life-saving benefits of Neo-Tech. Yet, sometimes, negative comments can also be informative as shown below:

(some comments are edited slightly for readability)

"Man was not given the authority to do what he wants. You wrote your own Bible. I don't want any part of it." A.M., CA

"A grave threat to mystical beliefs." B.D.

"Neo-Tech promotes outright individualism — a crime that should be punishable by death." R M., CA

"You will gain greater and greater ability to manipulate the material world. But many eminent scientists have written impassioned pleas on the danger of pure reason. I can only look to the ultimate source to prevent you from destroying the rest of us." P.N.P., WI

"Neo-Tech puts man at the level of God. You give man prosperity, power, love — total control. You dismiss self-sacrifice in your haughty exaltation of the individual over God. You are dark and deluded. Give up. Confess your sins, repent, and turn to Jesus." C.G., GA

"Your repeated slander of mystics and authorities is extremely sickening to me. Do you really think you can find true happiness through such a material approach?" C.B., MD

"I am completely appalled. Anyone who doesn't believe in spirits and mysticism is insane." B.T., KS

"You blatantly deny the spiritual man in assuming humans as the ultimate creation." Ms. J.G., CA

"Man wallows in the lower-plane earth geared to materialism and ego." F.W., GA

"Sex, gold, and the pursuit of knowledge — keep it to yourself." W.F., CA

"You are totally human centered and doomed to destruction." A.A., NJ

"Power is the most deadly drug and that is what you are offering." T.M., OK

"I cannot accept reality over religion." Mrs. J.D., IN

(continued)

Negative Comments about Neo-Tech

"Biological immortality — who wants it, even if you achieve it. I am looking for life after death." C.L.

"Jehovah owns the universe. Puny humans have no such rights. R.S., CA

"You are all screwed up in the head, no one controls his future, love, or money. God is the controlling force in this world. And if you dispute that you can burn in hell." N.S., CA

"We realize that we are no more or less important than the ant we have just crushed, or the plant we have just carelessly ripped out of the earth because we call it a 'weed'. You will discover that reality is incomprehensible." S.K., CA

"You should be put in jail for trying to brainwash people. Those who believe men descended from monkeys probably did." S.O.

"I consider Neo-Tech to be very dangerous." S.J., CA

"Get down on your knees and beg for forgiveness." S.F.

"There is no such thing as 'free enterprise.' 'Free enterprise' is the freedom of swine to push and shoulder each other aside while guzzling at the feed-trough." I.F., FL

"Your books are counter productive to the established way of life as normal people live it." J.V., NE

"Not only was I shocked at some of the concepts, but I absolutely refuse to believe them." W.S., OH

"Dr. Frank R. Wallace is the most intelligent fool I have ever been privileged to know." J.S., CA

"Dr. Wallace is a man in rebellion against authority — any and all authority. To state it another way, no one should have any authority over anyone else. Shed a sincere tear for Frank R. Wallace." J.H., TX

"As a devout Ayn Rand fan and proponent of free thought, it is my opinion that you are the most subversive organization I have ever encountered." S.N., CA

"The immediate satisfaction and ego trip that accompanies Neo-Tech is so tempting." L.V., MA

"If Frank R. Wallace will send me date, month, and year of birth, I will reply and tell through channels his life span on planet earth. Frank Wallace is held accountable to God for his evil manuscript. Wallace is going directly to Ravat Mountains U.S.S.R. (center of the Universe), which runs all the way to Siberia. Two miles below the earth's surface, are the pits of fire and brimstone, a blazing inferno 2000 degrees Farenheit." D.A., TX